THE NEWLIGHT BAPTIST JOURNALS
OF
JAMES MANNING AND JAMES INNIS

BAPTIST HERITAGE IN ATLANTIC CANADA

Documents and Studies

A Series Sponsored by

Acadia Divinity College
(Wolfville, Nova Scotia)

and

The Baptist Historical Committee
(United Baptist Convention of the Atlantic Provinces)

EDITORIAL COMMITTEE

Jarold K. Zeman, Chairman
(Acadia Divinity College, Wolfville, N.S.)

Phyllis R. Blakeley
(Public Archives of Nova Scotia, Halifax, N.S.)

Barry M. Moody
(Acadia University, Wolfville, N.S.)

George A. Rawlyk
(Queen's University, Kingston, Ontario)

Robert Wilson
(Atlantic Baptist College, Moncton, N.B.)

PUBLISHED VOLUMES

1. *The Diary and Related Writings of the Reverend Joseph Dimock (1768-1846).* Ed. George E. Levy. 1979.

2. *Repent and Believe: The Baptist Experience in Maritime Canada.* Ed. Barry M. Moody. 1980.

3. *The Journal of the Reverend John Payzant (1749-1834).* Ed. Brian C. Cuthbertson. 1981.

4. *The Life and Journal of the Rev. Mr. Henry Alline.* Ed. James Beverley and Barry M. Moody. 1982.

5. *The New Light Letters and Spiritual Songs.* Ed. George Rawlyk. 1983.

6. *The Newlight Baptist Journals of James Manning and James Innis.* Ed. D.G. Bell. 1984.

The Newlight Baptist Journals

of

James Manning and James Innis

Edited by

D.G. Bell

Acadia Divinity College and
the Baptist Historical Committee of the
United Baptist Convention of the Atlantic Provinces
Saint John
1984

Printed and distributed by
Lancelot Press Limited,
P.O. Box 425,
Hantsport, N.S., B0P 1P0
Canada

This volume appears with generous assistance from the New Brunswick Department of Historical and Cultural Resources, the New Brunswick Bicentennial Commission and the Jackman Foundation, Toronto.

Canadian Cataloguing in Publication Data

Manning, James, c.1764-1818.
  The Newlight Baptist journals of James Manning and James Innis.

(Baptist heritage in Atlantic Canada; v. 6)
Bibliography: p.
Includes index.
ISBN 0-88999-251-7

1. Manning, James, c1764-1818. 2. Innis, James, c1744-1817. 3. Baptists — New Brunswick — Biography. 4. Baptists — New Brunswick — History — Sources. 5. Dissenters, Religious — New Brunswick — History — Sources. 6. New Brunswick — Church history. I. Innis, James, c1744-1817. II. Bell, David Graham, 1953-   III. United Baptist Convention of the Atlantic Provinces. Baptist Historical Committee. IV. Title. V. Series.

BX6252.N48M3 1984   286'.1715   C84-099356-0

CONTENTS

Maps

PREFACE

Happy are they that gather manna every morning.

Alline

On 27 August 1783 the small vessel carrying Henry Alline slipped unheralded into a St. John harbour crowded with thousands of exiled American Loyalists. In his brief preaching career the charismatic Falmouth Newlight had set Yankee Nova Scotia ablaze with a religious excitement that contemporaries could liken only to the Great Awakening of the 1740s. Now Alline had turned his dying gaze on New England, anxious to spend his remaining energies redeeming the land of his ancestors. As fleet after fleet carried the bitter losers of the American Revolution northward to King George's remaining provinces, the lone Alline embarked to reconquer New England for "King Jesus". Yet the accident of a sprung mast had presented the "Apostle of Nova Scotia" with his only recorded opportunity of ministering to Loyalists. The attempt proved remarkably unsuccessful. In the course of a ten day wait among the multitudes at St. John harbour Alline found an opening to preach only once. He condemned his auditory as "hardened" and "careless".

A few days later Alline saw the Maritimes for the final time as he sailed down to New England. Within five months he was dead. Back in New Brunswick-Nova Scotia the Allinite awakening did not end with the 1783 departure of its leader. Even during Alline's lifetime nearly a dozen young Newlights had followed him on the preaching circuit. In the two decades after his death literally scores of young imitators asserted their claim to fill the vacuum created by his loss. Reaction against the religious anarchy they triggered in large sections of the Maritimes was the primary stimulus to the rise of a distinctive Baptist religious party.

Two of the men deeply stirred by the charismatic Alline and drawn into the religious vortex of the 1780s and 1790s were James Manning and James Innis. Both are now relatively obscure. Manning (c1764-1818) is remembered chiefly as a figure in the background of his distinguished brother Edward. Innis (c1744-1817) is footnoted by Baptist denominational historians only because he became a martyr for contravening New Brunswick's *Marriage Act*. Neither man is among those preachers Baptists have chosen to place in the first rank of the mythical "Patriarchs" and "Fathers" of their cause in the Maritimes.

The journals of James Manning (1801) and, especially, of James Innis (1805-11) do, however, repay careful study. They highlight the religious character of a decade when most ordained Allinites were moving towards a close communion Calvinist Baptist fellowship. Their journals capture Manning and Innis at a point when they had so far departed from Alline's teaching as to preach the external discipline of immersion, but while their religious impulses remained in great measure those of a Newlight. Of all the documentation on the rise of the Maritime Baptists, these two journals offer the most extended view of this critical decade of transition.

The Manning and Innis journals are also of unique value because they focus interest on the religious contours of the Loyalist St. John valley of New Brunswick. Henry Alline's spectacular preaching success had been among pre-Loyalist Yankees, whose heritage of New England Congregationalism attuned them to the Newlight message of inward conversion. Alline's single attempt to win a hearing among the Loyalists swarming St. John harbour was a notable failure. It was one of the most important accomplishments of Alline's successors that they were able — as the Manning and Innis journals testify — to draw into the Newlight and Baptist fold Loyalists from the religiously heterogeneous Middle Colonies, who had become spiritually "hardened" and "careless" in the upheavals of the American Revolution.

Henry Alline stands unrivalled as the greatest "Canadian" of the eighteenth century, the greatest Maritimer of any age and the most significant religious figure this country has yet produced. With Alline began a distinctive, self-confident religious culture that remained a major vehicle of Protestant expression in large sections of the Maritimes and northern Maine until well into the twentieth century. In the New Brunswick context, where the tradition flourished longest, there was a perceptible cultural transmission from Allinite to Newlight Baptist to the Free Christian Baptist conference (1832) with its two purist schisms (the Primitive Baptists and the Reformed Baptists) and its remnant of Free Baptists who refused to follow the Free Christian Baptists into the United Baptist reunion of 1906. That religious tradition is now all but extinct. It finally succumbed to the gimmicky Americanization of much of Maritime evangelical Protestantism. With the recent absorption of the Reformed Baptists into the American "Wesleyans" and of the Primitive Baptists into the American Free Will Baptists, the last major expressions of indigenous Maritime Protestant culture have vanished. The Allinite tradition survives only in a few Free Baptist congregations in the upper St. John River valley and in southwestern Nova Scotia.

This edition of documents focuses on the relationship between Allinism and the rise of a distinctly Baptist religious party in New Brunswick. The documents themselves are prefaced by an introduction surveying the period from the 1784 death of Henry Alline to the separation of the Maritime Baptist movement into a Boston-inspired close communion Calvinist Baptist stream and an Alline-inspired open communion Free Baptist stream about 1809. Only when the pace of the Baptist documentary revolution has slowed will it be possible to give this chaotic transitional generation the careful second view it deserves. By charting the basic contours of the period I hope to prepare the way for future studies of a less internal, more analytical approach.

As with its predecessors in the Baptist Heritage series, the mandate of this volume was to approach the past from a critical and scholarly rather than a pious, denominational perspective. A "pious" historian would account for the sudden resort to immersion by the Allinite leadership in the late 1790s in teɪ ɪns of an enhanced understanding of the New Testament. That is how the Baptist "Patriarchs" themselves explained it. A "critical" historian, on the other hand, simply takes it for granted that men clothe their actions with such internal rationales and presses for some further and broader reason why so many Allinites experienced Baptist enlightenment at about the same time. Both approaches can lead to "truth", but the former can be largely assumed while the latter is the very essence of the historian's challenge. The book's broader aim is to help rescue evangelical Protestantism from the condescension and disdain that has denied it a place in the writing of general Maritime history.

* * * * *

The journals of James Manning and James Innis are published with the permission of Acadia University and under the sponsorship of the Historical Committee of the United Baptist Convention of the Atlantic Provinces, chaired by Dr. Barry Moody. Publication was financed in part by generous grants from the Jackman Foundation, and from the government of New Brunswick in honour of the province's bicentenary. The actual content of the colume is, of course, the author's responsibility alone.

The writing of Maritime religious history is necessarily a co-operative enterprise. Among those who kindly contributed documents or expertise to this volume were Karl W. Beyea, Frederick C. Burnett, Ernest Clarke, John V. Duncanson, David Facey-Crowther, Robert Gardner, Ernest G.C. Graham, Philip G.A. Griffin-Allwood, Josephine Innis McCready, Elinor Mawson, Barry M. Moody, Roger Nason, George A. Rawlyk, Catherine Somerville, Patricia Townsend and Julia Walker. Ernest Clarke also generously contributed two fine maps. Leona Black and Catherine Gould produced a typescript which, in its documentary portions, would have tried the patience of a Baptist "patriarch". The major costs of manuscript preparation were cheerfully borne by my family.

No one moves far in Maritime Baptist historiography without incurring deep obligations to Patricia Townsend, archivist of the Baptist Historical Collection at Acadia University. When the story of the current renaissance in

Baptist historical scholarship comes to be told she will have a central and honoured place.

Finally, I am pleased to thank Frederick C. Burnett, Philip G.A. Griffin-Allwood, Barry M. Moody and George A. Rawlyk for their detailed scrutiny of the manuscript. They confirmed that in many respects I see as through a glass, very darkly. To Fred Burnett and George Rawlyk in particular I owe a debt of scholarly fellowship and inspiration that cannot adequately be expressed.

ANNOTATION AND TERMINOLOGY

The Manning and Innis journals are prefaced by individual notes explaining editorial policy. In other quotations from original sources I have endeavoured to retain authentic spelling and capitalization while sometimes standardizing punctuation. Most of the primary material quoted is held in the Atlantic Baptist Historical Collection in the Acadia University Archives. In citing it I have reduced this cumbrous formula simply to "Acadia".

Until 18 June 1784 the territory that is now New Brunswick was part of what may be called *Old Nova Scotia.* In reference to this early period it is often convenient to label Nova Scotia in its present boundaries as *peninsular Nova Scotia.* Historically the term *Cumberland* and the even older term *Tantramar* refer to the whole Sackville-Amherst region which in 1784 was divided by the intercolonial boundary. *Horton* refers to the vicinity of the present Wolfville. The old term *Shepody* remained in common usage long after the area was erected into the township of *Hopewell* (approximately the present parishes of Hopewell and Harvey in the present county of Albert). In 1785 the township of *Maugerville* (which the New Englanders often called *Maugerfield*) was divided into the parishes of Maugerville and Sheffield. What had formerly been known as the Maugerville Congregational church soon became known as the *Sheffield Congregational* church.

In Congregational and Baptist usage a *church* is a particular group of Christians who have set themselves apart from the world by entering into a covenential relationship with each other and with God. In Maritime usage the term *society* was used almost synonymously with the modern word "congregation"; *ie,* to refer to the whole company of those who attended religious exercises, both members of the "church" and others. The term society also refers to a group regularly meeting for religious exercises where there is no church; *eg,* the Allinite societies at Lower Millstream and Upper Sussex. The building set apart by Congregationalists or Baptists for the holding of religious exercises was called a *meeting-house* (not a "church"). The word *Church* (with the capital "C") usually refers to the Church of England.

In common usage a *Calvinist* was one who held to Jean Calvin's view of the New Testament concept of "election"; *ie,* that we are predestined (elected) by God to salvation or perdition, without ability to influence that result. The contrary view — the notion that men have the free ability to accept or reject the offer of electing salvation — is known as *Arminianism* or *free will.* In the nineteenth-century Maritimes one of the two major Baptist factions was denominated *Calvinist* (or "Regular") *Baptist* and the other as *Free Baptist* (really, *Free Will Baptist* and *Free Christian Baptist*). This difference between predestinarian and free will views of the doctrine of election usually corresponded to an important practical distinction concerning who was allowed to participate in the communion sacrament. Calvinist Baptists generally practised *close communion; ie,* they would commune only with other close communion Baptists. Free Baptists, on the other hand, would allow all reputable evangelical Christians to sit at their communion table, a practice called *open* (or *mixed*) *communion.*

Even the term *Baptist* is a slippery one. It can refer to any immersed person or can be restricted to those only who were members of a Baptist church (a church composed *exclusively* of Baptists). Except where the context indicates otherwise, I use the term "Baptist" in the latter sense. Thus, when I write of the decline of the Baptist cause in New Brunswick after (say) 1805, I do not mean that there were fewer immersed Christians in the province but that there were fewer who were prepared to associate with an exclusively Baptist church.

In the eighteenth-century Maritime (if not the New England) context the term *Newlight* can be used to describe anyone who believed in the necessity of a perceptible, dramatic conversion experience, whether Allinite, Wesleyan, Huntingdonian or Baptist. At the beginning of the nineteenth century the Newlight consensus shattered and the word became virtually synonymous with *Allinite; ie,* one directly in the anti-formal religious tradition of Henry Alline.

Although this edition of documents is intended to map the major features of New Brunswick Baptist history only until 1810, it has frequently been necessary to remind readers that the tensions perceptible within the Baptist movement as early as the first decade of the nineteenth century remained of fundamental importance until the general Baptist reunion of 1906. In referring to that stream of the Baptist movement that was more closely in the tradition of Henry Alline (as being anti-Calvinist in doctrine and open communionist in practice) I use the convenient term *Free Baptist,* even though I readily acknowledge that it has almost no correct usage until the twentieth century. I also more than once refer to the transformation of Allinite societies into the New Brunswick *Free Christian Baptist* conference in 1832 even though that name was not adopted until 1847. It was really the *New Brunswick Christian Conference* that was formed in 1832 and it was not, strictly speaking, "Baptist". These are important and little understood distinctions, but they need not be refined in the present context.

Chapter One
THE PARTING OF FRIENDS:
AN OVERVIEW, 1775-1810

THE PARTING OF FRIENDS: AN OVERVIEW, 1775-1810

*We have in this country almost as many religions as there were
living creatures in Noah's ark.*

Jacob Bailey, 1785

SEPARATIONS, WARS, DISORDERS

The rise of the Baptist cause in New Brunswick and
Nova Scotia was part of the general intellectual and political
upheaval of the last quarter of the eighteenth century. To those
inspired by the French and American Revolutions the 1780s
and 1790s were the best of times; but to those of a more sober
disposition or connected with political and religious
establishments, the subversive contagion of liberty, equality
and agnosticism was propelling North Atlantic civilization
towards an apocalyptic climax. To Britons, especially, the
obvious parallel with the events of their own time was that
lately highlighted in Gibbon's bleak and fascinating *Decline
and Fall of the Roman Empire* (1776-88).

Even in the obscure, lilliputian world of New
Brunswick and Nova Scotia, where most people had known
the hardships of the rebellion in America, the social and
religious revolution in France "excited an alarm that was never
known before".[1] Nova Scotia's attorney-general, Richard
Uniacke, offered perhaps the most eloquent warning against
the political and spiritual errors of the day. "It has been our
misfortune", he wrote in 1805, "to live at a period, during
which every art has been used to destroy the principles of true
religion, and to subvert the rules of civil government".

> It has been our lot to see those venerable principles,
> which our forefathers considered fixed as firmly as the
> pillars of the earth, shaken to their basis, and the
> fundamental rules of human happiness scoffed at .... To
> give the name of a revolution to the events which have
> sprung from those novel doctrines, would be applying a
> term too feeble to comprehend the horrid and
> sanguinary actions of the apostles of liberty and

equality. [T]hose diabolical principles, during the short period I avert to, have produced to the world more human wickedness, distress, and misery, than any equal space of time has exhibited in the previous history of man.[2]

This jeremiad was directed not at the revolutionary French but at an audience in New Brunswick and Nova Scotia. Its purpose was to ensure that the spirit of radical innovation in civil and religious institutions would not gain a following in what remained of Britain's empire in America. By the mid 1790s there was reason for those in the colonies' political and religious establishment to think their fears justified.

The two colonies were geographically fractured and institutionally weak. Their population was newly arrived: principally a wave of New Englanders in the 1760s and an influx of Loyalists in the 1780s. Most of the pre-Loyalist Yankees had initially sympathized with the colonies in the American revolutionary crisis. But with the advent of tens of thousands of Loyalists in 1782-84 — populating the newly-separated colony of New Brunswick and counterbalancing the Yankees of peninsular Nova Scotia — it was assumed that an era of loyal harmony had begun. Instead, the arrival of the Loyalists inaugurated a generation of intense political unrest. It was a time of "analyzing all the principles of Government, fixing the political Longitudes and Latitudes, and establishing the boundary line between prerogative and privilege".[3] Embattled elites in both colonies did not hesitate to brand their public critics as democrats, Jacobins and rebels.

Although the Maritime political crisis at the close of the eighteenth century was acute, it was not a root and branch attack on the constitutional system of the colonies. The concurrent religious upheaval was more powerful and more lastingly successful. Proportionate to their population New Brunswick and Nova Scotia in the 1780s and 1790s presented one of the more remarkable religious spectacles in the North Atlantic world. For the most part the religious innovations of the period were embraced by Dissenters. In surveying the complex and shifting pattern of religious dissent in the two colonies it is useful to distinguish among those sects and sentiments transplanted into the region by movement of

3

population, those imported as intellectual novelties, and those which had a local genesis.[4]

Several of the varieties of religious dissent found in New Brunswick and Nova Scotia in the latter part of the eighteenth century were simply the product of one of the great movements of population into the colonies. As one Nova Scotia religious leader reported, "A colony settled by emigrants from so many nations and upon such a variety of different occasions, must exhibit a multitude of sects and afford great confusion both in principles of Speculation and in the exercises of devotion".[5] Thus, Standing Order (Old Light) Congregationalism came as the intellectual baggage of the pre-Loyalist Yankees, the Wesleyan variety of Methodism arrived with the Yorkshire-Cumberland immigrants to Cumberland, and Presbyterianism, with the Truro planters, Alexander McNutt's colonists and the Pictou Scots. Similarly Lutheranism, Quakerism, Sandemanianism and the Baptists (until the 1790s) gained their small presence in the colonies largely through immigration rather than proselytism.

There were also a few in the two colonies who flirted with Swedenborgianism,[6] anti-Trinitarianism,[7] Deism[8] and even atheism.[9] This is not so much a witness to the speculative genius of late eighteenth-century Maritimers as a reflection of the fact that Halifax, Saint John and other ports were not immune to the intellectual fashions sweeping the rest of the North Atlantic world.

This much said, the dominant feature of religious dissent in the Maritime colonies, earning intense hostility and suspicion from political and religious establishments, was the prolonged Newlight awakening that began late in the 1770s and lasted for thirty years. The term "Newlight", like the movement itself, is an ill-defined one, embracing in its broader sense not only the radical stream of Congregationalism but also Wesleyans, Baptists and any number of unclassifiable enthusiasts. All shared an emphasis on the need for a perceptible conversion experience. Imposition of doctrinal labels on streams within the movement is at times difficult and suggests a degree of definition that is often anachronistic. In 1783, for example, the Anglican rector of Annapolis attempted a taxonomy of Newlight sects in his neighbourhood.

He found "anabaptists, pansonites, Allinites, Chipmanites, Kinsmanites, blackites, welchites and a number of other[s] ... [denominated] according to the names of their leaders". Two years later he said, with revealing exaggeration, "We have in this county almost as many religions, as there were living creatures in Noah's ark".[10] The same was true in New Brunswick's central St. John valley. From Maugerville a leading Anglican reported "Hammonites", "Palmerites", "Brookites" and the "Pearlyites or Burpeites".[11] While this intense Newlight activity must certainly be viewed against the background of the political and intellectual "Separations, Wars and disorders" that characterized the age,[12] it was more directly the consequence of an indigenous Maritime phenomenon — the preaching career of Henry Alline.

THE APOSTLE OF NOVA SCOTIA

Two centuries after his death Henry Alline remains an elusive but alluring figure. His public career was brief. It began with a Fast Day observance in Falmouth Nova Scotia on 18 April 1776. It ended with his death at North Hampton New Hampshire on 2 February 1784 at the age of 35. In the eight intervening years the relentless, consumptive Alline sparked the greatest religious "reformation" any extensive part of Canada has ever seen.[13] Simeon Perkins, the sober Liverpool merchant and magistrate, probably typified the general pre-Loyalist response to Alline when he equated his work with that of George Whitefield: "Never did I behold Such an Appearance of the Spirit of God moving upon the people Since the time of the Great Religious Stir in New England many years ago".[14]

The younger son of Rhode Island immigrants to newly-vacated Acadian lands in Falmouth, Alline spent adolescence in a township where public worship was rare and private religion was "sunk into death and formality". Yet in March 1775, after a prolonged internal struggle (carefully kept secret) in the classic Congregational mould, Alline surrendered to conversion. The year following he began to exhort and then to preach. Almost at once he was instrumental in gathering the Falmouth-Newport Newlight church. As in all the churches Alline was to foster, membership was open to both Baptists and Congregationalists on giving a satisfactory account of conversion. Thereafter, from 1777 to 1783 Alline itinerated on an ever-expanding circuit of Yankee Nova Scotia, even venturing to what is now Prince Edward Island. In addition to the Falmouth-Newport Newlight church, he organized (or stimulated organization of) seven others: Horton-Cornwallis, Maugerville, Annapolis-Granville-Wilmot, Sackville-Amherst, Argyle, (probably) Barrington, Liverpool.[15]

In 1778 Alline had also given friendly assistance to some Baptists in Horton-Cornwallis in the formal gathering of their church. Presaging the coming tensions in the Newlight movement, this Baptist church promptly denied fellowship to Alline (as a Congregationalist) and his Newlight church, some of the members of which were themselves Baptists. Thereafter, on his Falmouth-Annapolis circuit much of Alline's energy was spent in softening disputes among his followers over the mode and subjects of baptism. The only true baptism, he wrote, was that "of the spirit of Christ". Water baptism was a "small circumstantial," a "small external observation".[16] In one of his earliest hymns, composed about 1780, "Against any separations or warm debates among true Christians, with respect to different sentiments in the externals of Religion," Alline taught:

> 'Tis not a zeal for modes and forms
> That spreads the gospel-truths abroad;
> But he whose inward man reforms,
> And loves the saints, and loves the Lord.[17]

Thus, although Alline certainly did not oppose immersion (occasionally baptizing in that manner),[18] and although he would administer the ordinance indifferently to adults and infants,[19] he held that the whole subject was a matter of private conscience. The churches Alline gathered opened their membership to all who gave credible evidence of conversion, whether sprinkled or dipped (or neither[20]), and the ordinance of the Lord's Supper was open to all reputable Christians, whether church members or not.

By the spring of 1783 Alline was "apparently on the confines of the grave," exhausted by tuberculosis and by his ceaseless travels. Yet the nearness of death presented the

6

charismatic Alline with an opportunity to preach all the more affectingly, and he had it in mind to expend his remaining energy on a journey to New England, "as long as I could ride or stand".[21] There is a paradoxical aptness in the fact that this rebel against the New England Congregational tradition, raised in the despised colony that had refused to join the Revolution, should embark as a missionary to the newly-independent land of his Puritan ancestors. It was "Anti-Traditionist's" ultimate declaration of independence from accepted religious norms.

After some months in Maine, where he made a profound impression on the nascent Freewill Baptist sect, Alline died in New Hampshire early in 1784. Although the end came among strangers, in what he regarded as a land of spiritual declension, Alline's exit was a triumphant one. In 1839 one of his nurses, then in her 96th year, could still recall the "prayerfulness & heavenly frame of mind" with which this unknown Nova Scotian approached his death. In words that have resonated across two centuries the Revd David McClure, in whose house the stranger died, likened him to John the Baptist ("a burning and shining light"), and his North Hampton gravestone affirms that he was "justly esteemed the apostle of Nova-Scotia".[22]

Contemporary reaction to Henry Alline amply attests to the profound religious stir his preaching triggered. To Simeon Perkins Alline was like a second Whitefield; but even those who were indifferent or hostile to Alline stand witness to his impact. To the Revd Jacob Bailey, the cynical Anglican "missionary" at Cornwallis and Annapolis, Alline was "our famous preacher".[23] To the Revd Aaron Bancroft, sent fresh from Harvard to shore up what remained of Nova Scotia's orthodox Congregationalism, Alline was a man who "by his popular talents made many converts".[24] Bancroft was so impressed with a sense of Alline's importance that he prompted Hannah Adams to give the Nova Scotian greater prominence in her 1784 *Alphabetical Compendium* of religions than any other North American. At Truro, where he was known only by reputation, the Presbyterians gazed at him "as I passed their doors, with as much strangeness, as if I was one [of] the antediluvians".[25] To the Revd Jonathan Scott,

Alline's most trenchant critic, he was the "Ravager of the Churches".[26] The Allinite stir is not, therefore, simply an illusion created by the foreshortened perspective of the preacher's *Journal*. Even his detractors recognized his contemporary stature. This magnetic force of personality overcame many potential objections to Alline's views on baptism and election. For this reason he could gather eight churches of mixed Baptists and Congregationalists, and persuade both the Wesleyans in Cumberland and the Calvinists at Chebogue that he and they should unite in the work of reformation. The charismatic power of Alline's character also explains why literally scores of young imitators were inspired to come out as preachers in his wake and why the fragile Newlight consensus spun apart once his dominant presence was removed.

THE NEWLIGHT HOST

In Henry Alline's time almost all Newlights were "Allinites". There were Congregationalists at Chebogue (followers of Jonathan Scott) and Baptists at Horton-Cornwallis (followers of Nicholas Pierson) who were Newlights although not admirers of Alline; but their number was comparatively small. Yet after Alline's departure for New England — and especially from 1785 — the broad Newlight· movement was effectively divided into two distinct tendencies — Allinites and Wesleyan Methodists. At the leadership level the Wesleyan separation was pronounced; at the congregational level it was much less so.

Maritime Wesleyans are usually said to have taken their impetus from the labours of William Black, but the importance of the Methodist party within the Newlight spectrum before the mid-1780s has probably been exaggerated. William Black, who had emigrated with his parents from Yorkshire to the Amherst area in 1774, was converted in 1779 in a spontaneous local revival. The following summer he and a number of other pious young men began a modest itineracy of the region. In 1781 Henry Alline arrived on his triumphant inaugural tour. Among the "sincere christians" he reported finding was William Black, who joined in when Alline gathered a Newlight church.[27] This point must be emphasized, because Black and the early Methodist historians left the impression that he was never in fellowship with Alline. To be sure, Black was, from the first, a Wesleyan, but this did not preclude him from taking inspiration from the Falmouth Newlight.

Black began major itineracy as an unordained Wesleyan preacher early in 1782. He soon became known — both personally and by reputation — to the acerbic Jacob Bailey. Bailey mentioned him twice in the summer of 1782 — once at considerable length — and again at the end of 1783.[28] All three references link his name with that of other Newlights. In no case was he called a Methodist. According to John Payzant, it was at first said (at Liverpool?), "that Mr. Black preached the Same Gospel that Mr. A[lline] preached". To Simeon Perkins of Liverpool, writing in mid-1783, Black was simply "a Methodist or Newlight preacher". The followers of Alline, Perkins noted, "Seem very fond of him". It was not for another year that Perkins would see a distinction between Black "the methodist preacher" and Joseph Bailey "a NewLight Exhorter".[29] In fact, many of the Wesleyans around Amherst, including Black, had declared their independence from Allinism towards the end of 1782; but it was still a couple of years before the Wesleyans would attempt a Nova Scotia-wide division of Newlights into Allinites and Wesleyans. That aggressive and successful separatist policy was led by the American Freeborn Garrettson.

Garrettson arrived in peninsular Nova Scotia early in 1785 and remained only two years. According to a recent study, it was Garrettson who precipitated the province-wide reformation of the mid-1780s.[30] At a time when the Allinite stream of the Newlights was apparently stagnant, the Methodists were organizing classes and churches all over the peninsula and going to great lengths to distance themselves from "Allen's small party".[31] Although the chief source of information for the period is the writings of the Wesleyans themselves, George Rawlyk is probably right in suggesting that Garrettson gave Nova Scotia its first effective evangelical leader since Alline himself. That leadership was consciously anti-Allinite. When Garrettson quit the province in 1787 he left the Wesleyan movement in the hands of Loyalists and a succession of Englishmen and Americans, who (apart from

Theodore Harding and William Black) had never met Alline and were determined that the future course of the Newlight movement would be predominantly Wesleyan. More socially respectable and better organized than the Allinites, they appeared towards the end of the 1780s as though they would succeed.

The Allinites spent most of the 1780s in disarray. Their extreme congregational orientation made some confusion inevitable, both before Alline's death and after it; but the confusion of the 1780s coincided with the determined challenge (a "wonderful Stab," Garrettson called it)[32] from the Wesleyans. As a result, the Allinite tendency within the Newlight movement went into relative decline. This stagnation was not, however, the result of a shortage of preaching talent. The Church of England's Jacob Bailey — who knew both New England Congregationalism and the peculiar effects frontier life could have on the religious imagination — was nevertheless startled on his arrival in Cornwallis at the end of 1779 by the sheer number of Newlight preachers he encountered. "Two of my nearest neighbors," he soon reported, "who are able with a little spelling to read Bunyans Pilgrims progress a[n]d a chapter in the bible without hard names have lately commenced [as] preachers, and are regarded as powerful, gifted a[n]d godly learned dispensers of the word."[33] In New England, he cynically observed, such young men would have formed a Patriot committee; in Nova Scotia, where Rebel activity had become futile, they became "preacher[s] and founders of churches".[34] Even during Alline's lifetime at least nine young Maritimers were inspired to come out as preachers or exhorters.[35] His published *Journal* names only two of them (Thomas Chipman and John Payzant) and refers to two others — unnamed exhorters in Maugerville and Shepody (Hopewell). But other sources add several to the list. One of these preachers — William Black — is well known but the others — Benjamin Kinsman Jr.,[36] Joseph S. Bailey,[37] Daniel Welsh,[38] Ebenezer Hobbs[39] — are obscure. These young Allinites, all active in Alline's time, were soon joined — in peninsular Nova Scotia alone — by several other preachers (Isaac Dexter, John Waggoner, Harris Harding, John Sargent); so that the Allinite preachers in Nova Scotia within a few years of Alline's death could scarcely be numbered. In this sense, Alline's removal did not leave his followers without leadership. There is also a sense in which he gave his churches (at least those gathered in the latter part of his ministry) a joint "Constitution".[40]

Yet the Allinite movement stopped expanding in the 1780s and probably contracted. The evidence (admittedly fragmentary) suggests that only the Allinite churches in Liverpool, Horton-Cornwallis and Annapolis-Granville retained much life. Only these last two had pastors (John Payzant and Thomas Chipman), and only one Allinite is known to have been ordained in the 1780s (Payzant, 1786). The key to the apparent failure of the Allinites is lack of unifying leadership. They had many preachers and exhorters, but no strong leader — no one to play Joshua to Alline's Moses. Payzant and Chipman simply did not have the fallen leader's charisma. Unlike Wesleyan preachers they had no claim to hierarchically-appointed authority over the movement. They could not organize circuits for preaching or summon their fellow preachers into an association. The whole Allinite message was against such anti-congregational forms. Labouring under these handicaps and competing in the Newlight constituency against fairly numerous, better organized and rather more respectable Wesleyans, the Allinite impulse seemed towards the end of the 1780s to have spun itself out.

The Newlight movement of the 1780s was divided between Allinites and Wesleyans. In the 1790s not less than four sectarian tendencies are discernable within the broad Newlight spectrum. It must be stressed, however, that these classifications are useful chiefly in labelling preachers rather than hearers. Only at the leadership level can one confidently arrange these tendencies along a spectrum suggesting degrees of formalism. At the radical, anti-formalistic end of the Newlight spectrum are the antinomian *New Dispensationalists*. Next come what may be called, paradoxically, "orthodox" *Allinites*, uniting Alline's insistence on daily transcendence to the divine with his rigid morality. Thirdly, at the end of the 1790s it becomes for the first time meaningful to speak of a distinct *Baptist* party among

Newlights. Finally, at the comparatively formalistic end of the Newlight spectrum come the *Wesleyan Methodists*.

These four tendencies amount to something more than just so many movements of the same Newlight spirit but a good deal less than rival schemes of salvation. Evidence suggests that the rank and file of Newlights would attend meetings staged by almost any Newlight preacher.[41] Newlights were attracted to religious exercises by the titillation of hearing a preacher whose father had been hanged for murder (the Mannings) or who had been kidnapped by Indians and educated by Jesuits (John Payzant) or who made "Extravagant Jestures & wild motions of his Body & hands" (Harris Harding and Joseph Dimock)[42] and by the spectacle and sensation they associated with manifestations of the Spirit. "[T]he world [*ie*, the people of Cornwallis] say the New-lights are Right," recorded John Payzant, "for their preaching is attend[ed] with power and brings a since of Devine thing[s] on our minds . . .".[43] As there was seldom more than one Newlight preacher visiting a neighbourhood, most Newlights attended whatever Newlight preaching was available. Even admirers of the notorious Harris Harding would go to hear the Methodists.[44] People attended Newlight preaching simply because "they ha[d] the best meetings there."[45]

ORTHODOX ALLINISM At the very end of the 1780s Allinism broke out of years of drift with a reformation in the Minas townships. Among the conversions it triggered were those of James and Edward Manning. In 1790 one or both of the Mannings, Joseph Dimock and, probably, Daniel Shaw and Thomas Bennett came out as preachers; Gilbert Harris and Peter Martin followed in 1793. All were firmly in the Allinite rather than the Wesleyan camp (probably all had heard Alline himself preach). Joining with Payzant, Chipman, Harding, Bailey and the other established preachers, they commenced a vigorous itinerancy of all the old preaching stations, including Sackville and Maugerville. They also took the Allinite gospel to the upper settled parishes on the River St. John and brought the Newlights at Machias and Eastport (Maine) firmly into the Allinite fold.

For all the undeniable vigor of the Allinite resurgence of the early 1780s, it soon brought about a profound cleavage between "orthodox" and antinomian strains within Allinism, and proved more an end than a new beginning. The forces of what may be called orthodox Allinism were led by the two preachers who had stood beside Alline himself — Payzant and Chipman. The Allinism they preached combined primary emphasis on the soul-ravishing new birth with a firm injunction to a life of strict morality. So far as we know, Payzant and Chipman were the only Allinite preachers not seduced into antinomianism, and it seems that their New Dispensationalist opponents would have little to do with them. Chipman was in favour of cutting them off, root and branch, but Payzant took a more patient, reasoning approach, delaying confrontation until he was sure of his position. His own careful account of the arguments by which he convinced his erring brethren of the absurdity of their principles bears an ironic resemblance to Jonathan Scott's weary labours at Chebogue a decade earlier. By the mid-1790s the worst of the New Dispensationalist crisis was past, as the Mannings, Dimock and, at last, Harris Harding recoiled from the destructive consequences of their journey into antinomianism. Strangely, however, in their scramble to distance themselves from New Dispensationalism the young Turks did not retreat to the orthodox Allinism of the Payzant variety. Rather, they formed an increasingly distinct Baptist party within the Newlight spectrum. The ultimate result was that orthodox Allinism — which had opened the 1790s seemingly stronger than ever — entered the nineteenth century increasingly reduced to a fringe of the Newlight movement. Apart from John Payzant's continued labours at Liverpool, Allinism led a localized existence almost unnoticed in the surviving historical documentation until it re-emerged in the 1830's as a major strain in the anti-Calvinist "Free Baptist" movement. In this form a distinct Allinite impulse survived in Nova Scotia and, especially, in New Brunswick until well into the twentieth century.

WESLEYAN METHODISM After a dynamic decade of Garrettson-triggered growth the Wesleyans lost their momentum in the 1790s. They were remarkably unsuccessful

13

in taking advantage of the civil war raging within Allinism, and seem to have done no better than hold their own in peninsular Nova Scotia. In 1796, for example, the rector of Annapolis reported with satisfaction that the Methodists were "now much on the decline". He himself had married three of their preachers (one of whom — unfortunately unnamed — characterized as a "wild goose" and a "spiritual quixote"), all of whom had left spiritual for secular labours.[46] Two of these are probably those mentioned by Bishop Inglis in his journal:

> Of the Methodists, [John] Cooper, their principal preacher, has left off preaching, & has taken a pew in the Church of Annapolis, where he married & resides — & the other Methodist preacher, [Thomas] Whitehead, had turned merchant — these circumstances have checked the Methodists.[47]

The "check" to the Methodists was even more severe across the Bay of Fundy. In 1804 William Black reflected that twelve years of Wesleyan activity in the St. John Valley had been an almost total failure.[48] The fields had been white, but other labourers had been more assiduous in the harvest.

The most likely cause of this relative failure after so promising a beginning was the very institutional structure that· had served so well when Wesleyanism was a novelty in the Maritimes. Upwards of twenty Wesleyans preached in New Brunswick and Nova Scotia in the 1790s, but most of these were English or American and most stayed only a short time. As a result Wesleyan preachers probably could not relate to Maritimers in the way Allinites could. Even for those gathered into Methodist churches, the constant appearance of newly-arrived preachers must have been disheartening. Another reason the Wesleyans stalled in the 1790s was the pull of New Dispensationalism. Surviving correspondence among the Methodist leadership indicates a deep concern that they were losing both hearers and preachers to the likes of Harris Harding.

NEW DISPENSATIONALISM The force that shook Allinism to its foundations and ultimately destroyed its credibility while simultaneously luring even Wesleyans was an outburst of antinomianism early in the 1790s that came to be known as "New Dispensationalism". The label itself has no particular content, although it was given prominence in the first (1813) edition of David Benedict's *General History of the Baptist Denomination*.[49]   It was Edward Manning who described for Benedict the chance origin of the phrase:

> At a certain time when their extravagancies began to appear a Number of Ladies were in company of an afternoon when some remarks were made upon the Novelty of the Doctrine, when a young Lady rather partial to the new way Said, O Madam! this is a new Dispensation.   From this circumstance those that neglected the ordinances were called new Dispensationers, whose distinguishing Tenets are to neglect all christian duties except when they feel the Spirrit . . . .[50]

Manning — whose obsessive historical ruminations were a way of exorcising the spectre of his own career as an antinomian — put the blame for the outrages squarely on Henry Alline. Alline himself had been irreproachably correct in his morals; but his "lax observance of Divine institutions fostered in the minds of his followers the Idea of all such being only circumstantials, outward matters and mere non-essentials, that the Scriptures are not the only Rule of Faith and Practice, And that no Person is under any obligation to perform any external duty untill God immediately impressed the mind so to do. . . ". The subversive implications of Alline's teaching were apparent to some Newlights even during his lifetime. In 1780 William West, a founder of the Horton-Cornwallis Newlight church, charged that Alline's radical emphasis on the conversion experience alone reduced all the externals of religion — the Bible, the church, the sacraments — to mere matters of opinion, with one convert's opinion being as valid as another's. This, argued West, amounted to being "guilty of Quakerism" and opening the door "to receive the Papis[t]s with their Beads, & Crucifix, or any others that deny prayer".[51]

15

There are more than twenty accounts of antinomianism in New Brunswick and Nova Scotia between the 1780s and the 1820s. The earliest reference is in the Sackville area in 1782. "I rode over to *Tantramar*," wrote William Black in November of that year, "where I was sorely grieved to find *Mysticism* and the foulest *Antinomianism*, spreading like fire; and its deadly fruits already growing up on every side".[52] Perhaps the very last reference to a party of "New Dispensationers" in the Maritimes comes in 1847 in New Brunswick.[53] The term New Dispensationalism itself was not coined until the early 1790s, in connection with the most virulent episode of Allinite antinomianism. For decades Baptist historians felt obliged to portray their antinomian ancestors in the blandest of terms, on the faith of which even so discerning a student as Maurice Armstrong could conclude in 1948 that, "Actual evidence of immorality among the Newlights . . . is entirely wanting".[54] In fact the evidence is abundant. Edward Manning, once himself a New Dispensationalist, confessed that, "at this time a great flood of Immorallity crept in among professors". John Payzant recalled that, "Many of them gave away to carnal desire . . .".[55] Duncan McColl on New Brunswick's southwest frontier observed that, "It was dreadful to see the end of the new-light work: whoredom, adultery and the abolishment of all law, both divine and human. . .".[56] The worst examples of practical antinomianism all occurred in New Brunswick: in 1793 at Waterborough the preachers John Lunt and Archelaus Hammond introduced their converts to sexual liberation;[57] in 1802 Peter Clark assaulted several Anglicans in the Woodstock area "under pretense of receiving orders from heaven";[58] finally and most soberingly, in 1805 Amos Babcock of Shediac "ordered himself to be worshipped and thereafter divided his sister or cut her [in] twain," for which he was hanged.[59]

Quite apart from the constant threat that antinomians would act out their belief that conversion had freed them from obedience to the rules of moral and religious conduct, the New Dispensationalist movement of the 1790s placed a profound strain on Newlight church structure. In 1786 John Payzant called together the warring factions of Henry Alline's Falmouth-Newport Newlight church to see whether they would walk together after four years of separation. The effort came to nothing when his brother-in-law William Alline Jr. (one of the church's ruling elders, and the brother of Henry Alline) and "many Other[s] declared that Church rules were but outward Forms, and that they would have not[h]ing to do with them."[60]

An even more serious eruption occurred six years later in Payzant's Horton-Cornwallis Newlight church. In a move that is considered the opening event in the New Dispensationalist craze *per se*, Lydia Randall rose in church on the May sacrament day and denounced "all orders of the Church" as "but outward forms and Contrary to the Spirit of God". Her party was soon numerous and so zealous in propagating their "great discoveries beyond what ever was known before" that they threatened dissolution of the Horton-Cornwallis church. The situation was the same in Chipman's Annapolis-Granville Newlight church and at Liverpool. (It was even graver in Waterborough on the River St. John, where a number of extremists separated into a cult.) Among those who soon fell in with Horton's Lydia Randall and her sympathizers were the preachers Harris Harding, James Manning, Edward Manning, Thomas Bennett, Daniel Shaw and Joseph Dimock. Indeed, there are only two Allinite preachers who were definitely not New Dispensationalists (Payzant and Chipman). Although most of the preaching antinomians confined their views to the realm of church order and government, at least two fell into personal immorality. Daniel Shaw was excommunicated from the Horton-Cornwallis Newlight church for lying about his adultery. Still more notorious was the fact (as one Wesleyan minister gossiped to another in 1796) that, "one if not more young Women here [Liverpool] prove to be with child by Harris Harding".[61]

By 1797 New Dispensationalism was perceptibly on the wane, although the Newlight church of Horton-Cornwallis continued to be troubled by "erroneous principles" into the nineteenth century. Edward Manning later wrote that the development that triggered his own retreat from antinomianism was the Lunt-Hammond affair at Waterborough:

17

> [V]isiting New Brunswick [1793] where there was a great Reformation and many Irregularities among professors . . . was the cause of my searching the Scriptures more critically, And found that the Scriptures were the only Rule of Faith and Practice.[62]

In 1795 Manning was forced publicly to recant his errors in order to clear the way for ordination, although some still "Scrupled his Sincearity".[63] In the middle of the following year came word of Harris Harding's escapades at Liverpool. This proved a turning point. It put a temporary stop to Harding's preaching and prompted a conference between Payzant and Edward Manning. Payzant "thought it was best for us to asstablish an association among us to unite us togather and Shuch as would join us Should be Sound, as Relating to their doctrine and practice".[64] Accordingly, on 19 July 1797 Payzant, Chipman and the two Mannings met and agreed that Harris Harding be put on church trial for his beliefs. At their 1798 meeting the four preachers of this "Nova Scotia Association, Congregational and Baptist" and Harding

> discoursed largely on the necessity of order and discipline in the churches, and continued until midnight in observing the dangerous tendency of erroneous principles and practices, and lamenting the unhappy˙ consequences in our churches.[65]

Harding was then forced to a humiliating public acknowledgment of his errors. Although he soon showed characteristic signs of rebellion, he was clearly cowed by the displeasure of his preaching brethren. With the end of Harding's grosser extravagances the last major New Dispensationalist preacher[66] had been brought back into the orthodox fold.

But what was orthodoxy now? The trauma of the New Dispensationalist years had turned orthodox Allinites perceptibly towards formalism. Formation of their ministerial association represented a giant stride away from Alline's congregationalism; its first resolution was that standard church articles (a "Constitution," as Payzant called it) be put in print. The Association had also forced Harris Harding to repent his "treating the ordinances[s] of God['s] House with contempt"; but Harding's view differed only in tone from Alline's teaching that ordinances were mere circumstantials and non-essentials. The New Dispensationalist episode had convinced even John Payzant that Allinism could be saved from self-destruction only by a retreat to forms, orders and externals. The recoil of other preaching Allinites (most of whom had themselves been New Dispensationalists) was even more extreme. All submitted to be immersed and, at the end of the 1790s, coalesced into a distinct and aggressive Baptist party. Through its instrumentality the greatest casualty of New Dispensationalism became Allinism itself.

BAPTISTS Historical writing on the period between Alline's death and formation of the Nova Scotia Baptist Association in 1800 is dominated by a "Newlight to Baptist" paradigm. It has, therefore, to be emphasized that a distinct Baptist party did not occupy a numerically significant place in the Newlight spectrum until the close of the 1790s. Alline himself had reported considerable tensions within the Newlight movement over the mode of Baptism (tensions probably generated — but also kept under control — by formation of Nicholas Pierson's Horton-Cornwallis Baptist church) but he was evidently successful in reconciling the contending forces; and there is no evidence that the Allinite compromise collapsed until the end of the century. As late as 1797 there were only two or three Baptist churches in the Maritimes — the Horton church and predominantly Black ones in Halifax and, perhaps, Shelburne. Most Newlights who had been immersed were members of an Allinite church. Although these can in a certain sense be called Baptists, they did not feel that immersion was an issue sufficiently important to render themselves into a distinct group.

The figure of Thomas Chipman perfectly represents the ambiguity of the label "Baptist" before the end of the 1790s. Chipman was immersed in 1778 and ordained in 1782. He did not, however, thereby become a "Baptist" minister. Chipman was, rather, an Allinite minister who happened to have been immersed; he did not *preach* immersion. John Payzant makes

19

plain what one would otherwise infer from the absence of baptismal controversy in the 1780s and 1790s — that Chipman regarded immersion as a personal choice, not a party line. He both dipped and sprinkled.[67] He was not, therefore, a Baptist minister in any ordinary sense of the term. After Chipman in 1778, the next of the "Patriarchs" to be immersed was Joseph Dimock in 1787. Dimock did not, however, come out as a preacher until about 1790, and it seems most unlikely that he then went forth as a "Baptist". The fact that he immediately fell in with the New Dispensationalists strongly suggests that he put little emphasis on the externals of religion. Of seventeen letters to or from Dimock in the published version of Thomas Bennett's New Dispensationalist letterbook, none mentions water baptism, although one gives an especially graphic account of a 1791 reformation at Granville.[68] Furthermore, as Payzant pointed out, Dimock severed his connection with the exclusivist Horton-Cornwallis Baptist church and "thought [it] to be his duty to . . . join with more free Christeans, as Mr. Chipman had done".[69] To be sure, Dimock began immersing those who desired it immediately following his 1793 ordination, [70] but that is what any Allinite or Wesleyan and some Anglicans would have done. What must be emphasized is that Dimock was probably not assertive on the immersion issue until several years into his ministry. That is part of why it is unnecessary to distinguish between Allinites who were Congregationalists and Allinites who were Baptists until well into the 1790s.

The series of ministerial immersions that laid the basis for a distinct Baptist party began in 1795 with Joseph Crandall. Almost at once Crandall began to preach, although not at first as a "Baptist".[71] In 1797 James Manning was immersed. In 1798 his brother Edward followed and, in 1799, even Harris Harding. Apart from Crandall, all were men who as New Dispensationalists had treated baptism and the Lord's Supper with disdain. Now, by publicly submitting to this external order, they were undergoing a psychological ritual of cleansing. Immersion put symbolic distance between them and their tainted New Dispensationalist past. By implication it was also a repudiation of Allinism in a sense that Chipman's 1778 immersion had not been, and in a manner of which the consistently orthodox Payzant felt no need.

Coincident with these ministerial immersions, the years 1798-1800 were marked by a major reformation in the Annapolis Valley. Apart from events in early Sackville, this was the first distinctly "Baptist" reformation in Maritime history — the first broad series of religious exercises where success was counted in terms of the number of immersions. The immersions began under Thomas Chipman in the spring of 1798. In the thirteen months that followed Chipman dipped 173 persons.[72] Joseph Dimock also described the reformation in Annapolis and Kings in distinctly Baptist terms.[73] The suddenness with which a Baptist party emerged among the Newlights is confirmed by the comments of the much-maligned Bishop Charles Inglis. Not until 1800 did Inglis make his first significant reference to peculiarly Baptist activity.

> Formerly they [Newlights] were Pedobaptists [ie, child baptizers], but by a recent illumination, they have adopted the Anabaptist scheme, by which their number has been much increased and their zeal inflamed.[74]

Inglis thought the outburst worst in Annapolis, Granville, Wilmot and Aylesford, just the areas in which Chipman was active.

If one explains the otherwise unaccountable resort to immersion among the Allinite preachers as a "rite of passage" out of the nightmare of New Dispensationalism and into a semi-respectability, what does one say of the scores of their Nova Scotia followers who suddenly went into the water at the close of the century? In part, there was likely the same impulse to a symbolic break with the past that Harding and the Manning brothers felt. Further, it is only to be expected that when almost all major Allinite preachers had been immersed, they would start to push the unique "Baptist" message with an urgency; and the circumstances of the 1798-1800 reformation gave them a strategic opportunity to do so. Finally, there is the most obvious factor: baptism by immersion was just the latest phase of a whole generation of religious novelties that had begun with Alline himself. Bishop Inglis' characterization of the sudden resort to immersion as a "rage" for dipping is an apt one. New Dispensationalism had claimed its "thousands".

Dipping — the antidote to New Dispensationalism — would claim its "tens of thousands".[75] Each seemed plausible enough at the time.

THE PARTING OF FRIENDS

The Allinite preachers immersed late in the 1790s were attempting to distance themselves from their New Dispensationalist past. Yet that need not have led them to a radical repudiation of Allinism, and certainly not at once. Belief that Christians should witness to their conversion by immersion was at least congruent with the Allinite preoccupation with experience. The very fact of formation of the Congregational and Baptist Association in 1798 evidenced the Baptists' determination to continue to walk together in the Allinite mould. Yet immersion did indeed become the pretext on which most Allinite ministers rejected their heritage, and the process of rejection began at the astonishingly early (from the perspective of 1798) date of 1800. Of course not all Baptist preachers would come to reject Allinism as fully or as rapidly as Edward Manning. Harris Harding always identified himself with Alline, and the James Manning and James Innis of the journals printed here are still in great measure Newlights. But however much or little individual Baptist ministers journied. away from Allinism, the process began when they seized the ministerial association and made it purely Baptist in 1800.

The Baptist coup of June 1800 was stage-managed by the senior Baptist minister, Thomas Chipman. Chipman had visited Boston in 1797 and formed a friendship with one of the city's leading Baptists (probably Dr. Samuel Stillman) with whom he subsequently maintained a correspondence.[76] Late in 1799 or early in 1800 he again visited Stillman at Boston and got "certificates" to the effect that the Nova Scotia ministerial association was in fellowship with the Baptist Danbury Association. The certificates were, however, to have effect only when the Nova Scotia association became fully Baptist; ie, when it ousted its only unimmersed member, John Payzant.[77] Chipman had "given his word of honer to Mr. Stilman and Some others" that it should come to pass. When he met the June 1800 Association Chipman supported his plan by arguing that, as a purely Baptist body allied with the well-

22

established Baptist associations of New England, they would be better able to defend Enoch Towner, a Baptist minister then under prosecution for illegally solemnizing a marriage. According to Payzant, Chipman

> told me that Mr. Towner had been sued for Marrying and in order to defand the Suit he had adopted that plan, that they might be called by Some names for they were looked upon as nobody ....[78]

James Manning "Rose up" and denounced the whole business as an unworthy deception. Edward Manning "took it hard, and he oposed Mr. Chipman, and there was So much hard talk between them which took the most part of the time, on account of Mr. C[hipman] ... trying to blind my ey[e]s, and than turn me out". Joseph Dimock, also, "had never heard of it before". Yet when all the sputtering was over it is clear that what the other ministers resented was Chipman's duplicity towards Payzant and not the substance of his scheme. Having thus assuaged their consciences, they joined Chipman in changing their name to that of a Baptist association, thereby effectively excluding Payzant.

Unpredictably early although the 1800 change was, there are two factors which disposed the other Baptist ministers, when faced with the exclusivist proposal, to fall in with it despite its negation of the Allinite principle that externals of religion ought not to separate those who were "New-lights indeed". One is the reformation of 1798-1800. The fact that so many of the new converts and already-converted Newlights sought immersion must have made it plain to the Baptist preachers that the tendency toward immersion would create tensions within the Allinite movement. Yet the very fact that momentum was on their side would dispose them to preach more boldly on the subject. Perhaps, then, this first Baptist reformation gave the preachers a sense that they would leave the Allinite fellowship sooner or later; and through Chipman's deft manoeuvering the moment of choice came sooner.

A second factor subtly disposing the Baptist ministers to fall in with Chipman's plan was the growing desire for respectability that was part of the retreat from New

Dispensationalism.[79] Chipman, it will be recalled, had proposed fellowship with the Boston Baptists "that they might be called by Some names, for they were looked upon as nobody ...". The Calvinist Baptists of New England, as epitomized by Samuel Stillman, had attained that status in the eyes of the world to which their northern brethren now aspired. Their chief ministers were called "doctor"; they dressed in black and wore bands; they had attended college. Chipman himself was a friend and correspondent of Dr. Stillman. So was Joseph Dimock. In 1797 and again in 1798 Dimock had been "verry agreeably entertained" by the doctor. (Significantly, perhaps, this was the time the former New Dispensationalist "lost my prejudice against reading of sermons in some measure".[80]) The Baptist minister Theodore Harding would also boast of an encounter with the great Dr. Stillman.[81] Chipman's proposal of June 1800 was easier to accept because it explicitly promised alliance with the august Boston Baptists. Then, Chipman assured them, they would no longer be "nobodies".

The revolution of 1800 had the effect of constituting a Baptist association at the ministerial level only. Most of the churches attending, either by ministers or by lay delegates, were of mixed Baptist and Congregational membership, notably Edward Manning's Cornwallis church. Two points of Baptist contention in the years following 1800 were to move the associated churches towards ever greater exclusivity, and finally shatter the Allinite ideal of Christian fellowship. The first was whether the mixed membership (Congregational and Baptist) churches should transform themselves into "open communion" Baptist churches; ie, composed of only immersed persons but with fellowship and the communion service open to all reputable Christians. In time, most of the churches would reach this open communion Baptist stage. Compromise though it was, the move was deeply offensive to true Allinites and, in the case of Cornwallis (which we know best), caused great turmoil, bitterness and lamentation in the first decade of the nineteenth century. Edward Manning's attempts to make this old Allinite church Baptist provoked many separations, but finally it was Manning himself who was obliged to separate and gather a small Baptist church proper.

The second stage of transition through which some of the Baptist churches passed was even more bitter and divisive:

24

the move from an open communion Baptist standing to "close communion" (*ie,* where the church would admit to the communion only its own immersed members and those of other "close communion" churches). Close communion represented an entire negation of the spirit of Henry Alline. It was the kind of divisive formalism he despised. It resonated theologically with Calvinism's exclusivist concept of the "elect", something those who understood Alline's emphasis on free will would have utterly rejected. Yet the evidence suggests that in this critical first decade of the nineteenth century, the issue was not generally perceived or debated in terms of Calvinism versus Arminianism. Rather, the issue that parted friends and created wounds within the Maritime Baptist movement that would take a century to heal was whether Baptists would bar other reputable Christians from the communion table. Those of the Baptist ministers who drew inspiration from the meridian of Boston favoured a move to close communion as rapidly as possible. At the Association of 1800, for example, Thomas Chipman urged Edward Manning to have Cornwallis "made into an open Communion [church], than to give them an other turn and make them close communion Baptist".[82] Cornwallis proved to have too many admirers of Henry Alline for Manning to succeed; but in general this did become the policy of the Baptist ministers. In a limited sense it was successful. At the Association meeting of 1808 there was an equal division in voting whether a policy of close communion should be adopted. A year later the Association finally resolved — with only Harris Harding in dissent — to transform itself into a "Regular close communion Baptist Association" and to "Withdraw fellowship from all churches who admit unbaptized [*ie,* unimmersed] Persons to what is call[e]d occasional [*ie,* open] communion".[83]

After the watershed of June 1800, eventual adoption of close communion was entirely forseeable. Like immersion, close communion would put symbolic distance between the Associated Baptists and their Allinite past. The ritual of excluding all but church members from the bench around the Lord's Table would evidence a resolve to seal out all taint of residual New Dispensationalist heterodoxy. In place of the high Allinite ideal of Newlight fellowship it offered the high (and highly orthodox) Calvinist ideal of communion among only those certified as visible saints. Yet one must ask why close communion was adopted in the Association as early as 1809, given its immediate, predictable and acutely disruptive consequences. Probably one factor disposing the Baptist leadership to act as boldly as it did was the exhilarating impact of the Nova Scotia reformation of 1806-08, the most intensive since Henry Alline's time. "Multitudes are turned to God", exulted Chipman at the close of 1806. "I cannot with ink and pen ... describe the one half God has done."[84] Apart from Payzant's Liverpool, the excitements had a predominately Baptist character. In Yarmouth Harris Harding reported "upwards of two hundred persons have been savingly united to Christ", with 140 immersions in less than four months.[85] At neighbouring Argyle Enoch Towner reported 120 immersed and a further 24 waiting on the weather.[86] From Newport and Rawdon on Minas Basin came a report of 61 immersions.[87] These spectacular statistics and the evident pride with which they were reported to Boston suggest that the Baptist ministers may have timed their move to close communion to take advantage of the momentum of reformation.

The chief purpose of adopting close communion was to bring the Nova Scotia Association into harmony with the New England Baptist associations, and this factor, too, may have been involved in the timing of the move. In the wake of the events of 1800 the Maritime Baptist leaders were drawn deeply into the American orbit. They visited New England with some frequency. They made themselves heard in the pages of the *Massachusetts Baptist Missionary Magazine.* They welcomed "missionaries" from the Baptists of New England. For a few years the Americans visited only remote Charlotte County in southwest New Brunswick, but at the end of 1807 two emissaries of the New England Baptists — Isaac Case and Henry Hale — penetrated Nova Scotia. In a tour of three months they met all of the key Baptist leaders and counselled the re-ordination of Edward Manning over his new Cornwallis Baptist church.[88] It was at the Association meeting held just after their visit that close communion was for the first time debated (1808). Hale and Amos Allen were back in Nova Scotia in August 1808 for a long tour. In the spring of 1809

Hale returned to participate in the session of the Baptist Association that finally broke fellowship with all churches not practising close communion. The "whole season", he wrote with satisfaction in his journal, was "pleasant and profitable".[89] There is no positive evidence on the point, but it seems likely that the presence of Hale and his fellow missionaries, preaching the gospel of close communion and manifesting Boston's solicitousness for its poor Nova Scotia cousins, encouraged the Baptist preachers to take the weighty step of close communion earlier than they otherwise would have. Only by moving towards formalism and denominationalism and away from the volatile spirit of Henry Alline could they come into full fellowship with the sober, respectable Baptists of New England.

The 1809 victory for close communion proved a short-term disaster for the Associated Baptists. Its immediate effect was to disfellowship over one-third of the Association's membership. At the 1809 annual meeting membership in the Associated churches totalled 1430. In 1810 it was down to 924.[90] Ten years later it still numbered only 1785, with most of the twenty-eight Associated churches reporting a membership of less than fifty. There were, of course, hundreds of other Baptists in the Maritimes (in both churches and societies) with whom the close communionists had broken fellowship. Indeed, it would be difficult to name more than two or three churches in which the move was accomplished without bitterness and separation, as the close communionists expelled those whom hitherto they had looked on as brothers and sisters in Christ. One case in point is Chester. Joseph Dimock, Chester's roughhewn pastor, travelled with his fellow ministers far towards formalism. It is not without irony that in 1806 this former New Dispensationalist should have written the Baptist Association's circular letter cautioning churches against receiving self-appointed preachers ("unsteady unstable watchmen").[91] Dimock was among the supporters of close communion at the Association of 1809 but, as his own church refused to part company with its unimmersed and open communion Baptist members, was among those disfellowshipped by the result. Dimock continued, however, to press the issue, which by his own admission introduced the serpent of discord into a theretofor completely harmonious church. By 1811 he had succeeded in refashioning the Chester church on close communion lines. Church statistics suggest that the open communion party either separated or were effectively ousted by a determined combination of the pastor and his close communion party. In 1809 the Chester open communion church had 122 members. In 1811, when it was readmitted to the Association as a close communion Baptist church, it had only 43 members.[92] Close communion had cost the Chester church nearly two-thirds of its strength and, by Dimock's own reckoning, most of the departed brethren were Baptists.

The impact of close communion on the church at Onslow is also instructive. Gathered in 1791 by John Payzant on pure Allinite lines, the church underwent predictable strains in the 1790s owing to differing opinions over the propriety of hearing preaching from Harris Harding and Edward Manning. Immersions began in 1799 and in 1804 the church put itself on an open communion Baptist footing, but with existing unimmersed members continuing in fellowship (the standard compromise in turning an Allinite church into an open communion Baptist church). Not until the spring of 1808 was the issue of close communion raised in the church, and at once passions were roused and feelings hurt. The discord was occasioned by the visit of William Delaney, the Baptist pastor at Newport.[93]

> [Saturday] March 12 [1808] ... The Members of the Church such [as] ware previously Baptized [*ie,* immersed] renewed their Covenant. The Rev'd W. Delany attended who only admits of communion with those who have been Baptised, on which account those who were not Baptised stay'd back by his signifying to them in the opening s'd Meeting that he wish[ed] those who ware baptised only & in regular standing in the Church to renew their Covenant & go forward. This is the first time a Discrimination took place with Members with regards to Church Prevaledge.

* * * * *

[Sunday] 13th March 1808 Nathaniel Marsters [church clerk] asked Deacons Thomas & John Lynds Previous to the Sacrament of the Lord's Supper being dispensed whether any of the Members who were in covenant together with the Church who were not Baptized would be allowed to partake with them in the Sacrament of the Lord's Supper that day & they said none of them. S'd Nathaniel observed that they were in Solemn Covenant and wished them to be cautious how they conducted [themselves] as he must make [a] record of their conduct in this respect. S'd Deacons replied that they thought of it all & so provided & Several Members who were not Baptized did not partake on s'd account. After the Sacrament was over said Nathaniel reproved the s'd Deacons for s'd conduct in presence of the Rev'd M'r Delany and told them that they had done wrong & broke their Covenant, But M'r Delany Advocated for them & said they had Done right.

Thus, in a high-handed and tactless manner the close communion party suddenly barred its covenant brethren from sitting at the benches surrounding the communion table — a ritual of exclusion more dramatic and bitterly wounding than any dispute over Calvinism and free will, and directly contrary to the Allinite constitution on which the church had been gathered. On 26 April 1809 matters reached a crisis. The church voted 19 to 8 in favour of close communion.

At [the] same time in a Clamorous manner [the majority] declared themselves a Baptist (in close communion) Church not having taken any regular steps of Organization to make them so, the Rev'd M'r Cleavland being by appearence their leader and very active for the purpose of having the members which are not Baptized to be separated from the Church.

It is not clear precisely when the separation took place, but by 1814 there were two churches in Onslow: a close communion Baptist church under Nathan Cleveland, consisting of nineteen members, and a slightly larger Allinite church under William Delaney (whose sentiments had altered since 1808). The close communion church did not prosper. There is no information on the open communionists except that their relationship with Delaney (a drunkard) was unprofitable. In general, then, the issue of close communion had all but destroyed the Baptist cause in Onslow.

The Allinite ideal of Christian fellowship was the major casualty of close communion, but even some of the most familiar of the Baptist leaders did not at first prosper under their new system. The case of Harris Harding is special. He had been the only opposition to close communion at the Association of 1809 and was disfellowshipped by the result. More than any other ordained Baptist (except perhaps James Innis), Harding remained true to the catholic spirit of Henry Alline. In 1813 a Scotch Baptist (Alexander Crawford) in Yarmouth wrote a fascinating description of Harding's loyalty to the Falmouth evangelist — now thirty years dead — whom Harding had never actually seen.[94]

> I thought ... when we [Harding and Crawford] should get acquainted with each other's manner of expressing ourselves, we should agree better. I read several of Henry Alline's writings, and also Jonathan Scot's review of them [the *Brief View*]: and I could not help, in general, approving of the lat[t]er; for when I saw the. manner in which M'r Alline ridiculed the atonement and intercession of Jesus Christ, I saw that no one could be saved by believing the doctrines which his books contain .... I found that M'r Harding was heartily resolved fully to deffend M'r Aline as a servant of God, and one who, if he was not infalible, had an uncommon measure of the Spirit, and his writings as being the mind of God, while he condemned M'r Scott as an opposer of the work of God, and his book as an engine of the devil.

This ironic vindication of Jonathan Scott and critique of Alline and his disciple Harding was written for a man who would have found it very acceptable — Edward Manning. Manning was the polar opposite of Harris Harding. Probably none of the first generation of Baptist ministers travelled faster or farther from his Allinite roots. He made an effort to acquire book learning. He started preparing his sermons in advance.[95]

He began to reject and despise the name of Newlight and use it as an epithet: "Brother" Samuel Freeman was criticized as "mystically New lightish".[96] Instead Manning preferred to label himself as "evangelical," a term as catholic as Newlight but (at least in Manning's time and place) perceptibly more bland and respectable.[97] As early as 1806 James Innis found Manning one "who thought that evrey Sheaf Should Bow to his Sheaf," who "thought himself Sumbod[y]" and who now spoke "against the life of God in the Soul of man".[98]

By 1820 Manning had become so conservative that he viewed the religious exercises in Payzant's Liverpool meeting with total revulsion;[99] yet he seems never to have been completely sure his own course had been correct. He continued to serve his new Cornwallis close communion church for most of the rest of his long life. The place had been the scene of some of his early religious extravagances in opposition to the orthodox Payzant, and Manning must often have wondered whether God had set him over the Baptists of Cornwallis in punishment for his sins. His career there was often deeply unhappy. The large Allinite party — soon augmented by Christ-ians, Freewill and Free Christian Baptists — haunted Manning as long as he lived, all taking a stand vociferously opposed to close communion. "How gladly I [would] go to heathen Asia, or Burmah, to spread the light of the gospel among them," he assured himself in 1818; "but this is not for me. No, no, no, I must drag the poor remains of life along the tiresome road in Cornwallis".[100]

Although Manning never directly allowed himself to doubt the propriety of his move to close communion, it is clear that he was obsessed with the question in the 1810s. In 1812 he admitted that he and his brother James (of Granville) received little financial support from the people, and then volunteered, "but if we were almost any thing but that odious thing called close communion Baptists we might do better ...". Elsewhere he spoke of his religious party as "despised" and "persecuted".[101] In 1814-15 the sensitive, insecure Manning suffered a prolonged breakdown in health, as much mental as physical. Wondering whether he were dying (he lingered another thirty-six years) he ensured the world would find the following in his journal.

My becoming a Baptist, adopting what's called close communion, and the doctrines I have indeavoured to inculcate for these many years, and uniformly [*sic*] bearing testimony against the errors that have been propagated in this country, I glory in now. I expect to die soon.[102]

Manning's affected confidence that he had been quite right in the direction of his spiritual travel masks a deep and persistent anxiety that he had been quite wrong. A reader examining Manning's mass of fragmentary reminiscences, covering the same general ground again and again, and his large collection of letters — obsessively re-read, with the addition of little prayers, editorial asides and plenty of "Amens" — would justifiably conclude that this was a man haunted by his past, deeply uncertain whether he had acted correctly as regards Henry Alline, New Dispensationalism and close communion.

Edward Manning's brother James derived even less satisfaction from the course of events after the watershed of 1809. He, too, suffered a mental breakdown, temporarily losing his faith. He died in 1818. We know too little about James Manning to link his crisis specifically to developments put in motion by adoption of close communion, but at least two other Baptist ministers certainly did repent their support for the new plan. One was Horton's Theodore Harding. Harding had begun his preaching career as a Wesleyan, then turned Baptist and had become a supporter of close communion. By 1812, however, he was ready to throw over both close communion and the Baptists in general. Reports that Harding was turning "Presbyterian" (he freely admitted it) prompted the revealing admission from Edward Manning that he had always thought Harding an "imposter" anyway. On a later occasion Manning "found him confused, apparently passive, and not settled in open, or closed communion, and in his present standing calculating to do much hurt".[103] Not until late in 1816, after four years of uncertainty, could Harding reaffirm his Baptist orthodoxy.[104] Others evidently could not. In 1809 Harding's Horton church had boasted 270 members. In 1818 membership stood at a mere 45.

Even more unhappy was the case of William Delaney. Ordained over a Baptist church in Newport on 2 December

1807 he had spectacular success in the ongoing reformation.[105] Within a few months, however, there were difficulties in the church "respecting Br. Delaney".[106] Presumably the difficulty was drunkenness. Delaney attended the 1809 close communion Association at Cornwallis but, significantly, was not mentioned in Edward Manning's minutes.[107] Three months later his church excommunicated him for drunkenness.[108] Five years later he turned up in Onslow as pastor of an Allinite church. Here he resumed his intemperate ways and was probably expelled within a couple of years. Eventually he completed his recoil from Calvinism and close communion with a grand flourish by gathering (at Pugwash) eastern Canada's first Universalist society.[109]

In the longer term the revolution of 1809 produced an organic rift in the Maritime Baptist movement that was not healed until the reunion of 1906. The peremptory, physical, dramatic exclusion of a large part of the Allinite and Baptist movement from a seat at the Lord's Table; the procrustean alteration of church articles to suit new revelations from Boston; the breaking of covenant fellowship with those who theretofore had been tenderly embraced as brothers and sisters in Christ; the repudiation of the catholic tradition of the saintly Alline: all these engendered an acutely personal bitterness that amply sustained the following nine decades of often bitter warfare between the two Baptist parties. Although the division began in terms of close and open communion, the two factions had by 1820 come to articulate their fundamental difference in terms of Calvinism (a theology of predestination) versus Arminianism (a theology of free will). It would be natural to assume that the open communion party adopted the rhetoric of free will as part of the legacy of Henry Alline. It appears, however, that the Maritime open communists were in great measure taught to voice the theological dimension of their quarrel with the close communists in terms of free will by visiting Christ-ian and Freewill Baptist preachers from the United States.[110]

The forces which would not submit to the close communion regime of 1809 were both open communion Congregationalists and open communion Baptists. Within a generation, however, almost all the open communionists had become Baptists. John Payzant's Liverpool was soon the only vigorous Congregational church, although John Pineo and Payzant's son William served a considerable congregation at Habitant.[111] Because the open communionists themselves primarily became Baptists it is fair to say that they, too, judged pure Allinism too high an ideal to survive long in this world. There is a sense, therefore, in which Allinism was extinct in the Maritimes within forty years of Alline's death. Yet the purist *spirit* of Henry Alline — anti-formal, unsacramental and mystical — continued to be the vital impulse of the open communion Baptists throughout the nineteenth century. To be sure, these Free Baptists, too, became more formal over time. Like the Calvinists, they formed ministerial associations (in the 1830s), published minutes, a newspaper and a treatise on faith, delimited the role of women and fostered Sabbath schools, missions and, at length, an educational institution: but in every case the move towards formalism and denominationalism took place at least a generation later than the parallel development among the Calvinist (close communion) Baptists. Thus, of the two large Baptist alignments, the Free Baptists always seemed distinctly the less formal. Indeed, until the 1850s they were repeatedly subjected to the same criticisms formerly levelled at the Allinites: that their religious exercises were noisy and confused, that they put too much value in the appearance of zeal, that they gave too large a role to the sisters of the church, and that they paid too little attention to the sacraments. Significantly, when the open communion Baptists did reach a settled denominationalism in the 1870s they were subject to a major anti-formalist schism. It was led by a preacher with the resonant name of George Whitefield Orser, whose mother's obituary boasted that as a child she had been "awakened to a sense of her situation under the preaching of the late Rev. Henry Allen".[112]

Unpredictably, the Allinite impulse was in time to exert the greater pull in New Brunswick than in Nova Scotia. In both absolute and relative terms the New Brunswick open communion Baptists became much more numerous than their Nova Scotia counterparts. At the 1881 religious census, for example, there were 32,000 Free Baptists in New Brunswick (and 49,000 Calvinist Baptists), while in more populous Nova

Scotia there were only 11,000 Free Baptists (and 73,000 Calvinist Baptists).[113] Some of the reasons for this surprising differential are obvious. After a vigorous beginning in the first years of the nineteenth century, Calvinist Baptist growth in New Brunswick was fitful. For many years the leadership of the close communists was concentrated in Nova Scotia, with New Brunswick a relative hinterland. Accordingly, when the open communionists staged their great reformation in the St. John Valley in the early 1830s there was little to stand against them. In Nova Scotia, on the other hand, the open communion Baptists faced a more potent opposition from close communionists. Further, in Nova Scotia the open communion faction was acrimoniously divided into Free Will and Free Christian Baptist parties, in each of which Americans had a prominent role. In New Brunswick there were only Free Christian Baptists, and these had home-grown leaders who were lineal as well as spiritual heirs of the Allinites. That the anti-formalist, purist impulse derived from Henry Alline exerted the stronger pull in New Brunswick is reflected in not only the Free Baptist/Calvinist Baptist dichotomy but also within the Calvinist Baptists themselves[114] and indeed, within the contemporary United Baptists.[115]

* * * * *

This edition of documents highlights the beginning of Baptist activity in New Brunswick's St. John Valley. It focuses on two Baptist leaders at a fascinating stage in their development. Both had been Newlights, both submitted to go into the water, and for both this marked a partial retreat from Allinite Newlightism. Yet the James Manning we see in the journal of 1801 is still in great degree a Newlight, though also a Baptist: he is still anti-formal, spirit-oriented, endeavouring to "gather manna every morning". Had his home been New Brunswick, far from Edward Manning, he might never have fallen in with the close communion party. That, it appears, was the experience of James Innis. Like Manning, the Innis of the journal printed here is remarkably true to the Newlight spirit. He deeply resented the growing formalism — the mere "evangelicalism" — of the Baptist leadership across the Bay in Nova Scotia, and he opposed the move to close communion. I

35

class both men — at the period of these journals — as "Newlight Baptists" because the term aptly suggests an intermediate state between Allinite Congregationalists on one side and (merely) evangelical Baptists on the other.[116] To most of those who became Calvinist Baptists this "Newlight Baptist" stage was also a transitional phase, which by the 1810s had led them far from their Newlight roots. But for many of those in the Free Baptist stream the term remains applicable for nearly a century. The James Manning and James Innis of these journals preached a purist, Newlight Baptist approach to Christianity that would, after the revolution of 1809, lead an almost underground life in New Brunswick until it emerged transformed as an open communion Free Baptist conference in 1832.

NOTES TO CHAPTER ONE

1   Jonathan Odell, "Reflexions on the importance of Religion, as a Support to the Civil Authority, and of national virtue as a means of national defense" (June 1795): Odell Papers, pkt 15, New Brunswick Museum (hereafter "NBM").

2   R.J. Uniacke, *Statutes at Large, Passed in the Several General Assemblies Held in His Majesty's Province of Nova-Scotia* (Halifax, 1805), p.*v*.

3   Winslow to Sewell, 14 January 1797, in W.O. Raymond (ed), *Winslow Papers* (1901), p. 710.

4   The only Protestant dissenting group which seems not to fit this classification is Huntingdonian Methodism. It had no immigrant clientele, was intellectually unfashionable, depended on an imported ministry, and yet through proselytism attracted a perceptible following in both colonies by the end of the 1780s.

5   Jacob Bailey, "Journal of a Journey through Nova Scotia" (1784): Bailey Papers, vol 100 (Letter 53, p. 413), Public Archives of Nova Scotia (hereafter "PANS").

6   T.W. Smith, *History of the Methodist Church ... of Eastern British America,* I, (1877), p. 173; Peters to Peters, 1 May 1785; 25 November 1785: Peters Papers, American Church Historical Society. This latter letter

indicates that even Lt-Gov Edmund Fanning had taken up the works of Swedenborg.

7   James Beverley & Barry Moody (eds), *Life and Journal of the Rev. Mr. Henry Alline* (1982), p.99; W.S. Bartlet, *Frontier Missionary* (1853), pp. 206-07; Bailey to Reynolds, 4 February 1783: Bailey Papers, vol 94, PANS.

8   Bailey to Reynolds, *ibid;* Bartlet, *Frontier Missionary,* p. 207.

9   Inglis to Bailey, 3 April 1799: Bailey Papers, vol 93a, PANS; Byles to SPG, 24 December 1801: Reel A-184, Public Archives of Canada (hereafter "PAC"); Horton-Cornwallis Baptist Churchbook, 1 May 1802: Acadia.

10 Bailey to Peters, 7 November 1783: Bailey Papers, vol 94, PANS (by "pansonites" Bailey presumably refers to the followers of John Payzant rather than Nicholas Pierson); Bailey to [Breynton], [23 January 1785]: *ibid.*

11 Hubbard to Winslow, 29 May 1792, in Raymond, *Winslow Papers,* p. 392.

12 Henry Alline, *Court for the Trial of Anti-Traditionist* [Halifax, 1783], p. 24.

13 Students of the period follow Maurice Armstrong in labelling the response to Alline's preaching as an "awakening". The term is a convenient one, but eighteenth-century Maritimers always used the term "reformation".

14 D.C. Harvey & C.B. Fergusson (eds), *Diary of Simeon Perkins, 1780-1789* (1958), II, p. 177.

15 Beverley & Moody, *Alline's Journal,* p. 46. The best introduction to Alline's life is J.M. Bumsted, *Henry Alline, 1748-1784* (1971). More sophisticated is Gordon Stewart & G.A. Rawlyk, *People Highly Favoured of God: The Nova Scotia Yankees and the American Revolution* (1972). The earlier part of this volume (pp.3-

76) gives a superb account of the context of Alline's life and work. The latter part (on Alline himself) can usefully be compared with the less demanding work of Maurice Armstrong, *Great Awakening in Nova Scotia, 1776-1809* (1948), pp. 61-138.

16   Beverley & Moody, *Alline's Journal,* pp. 115-16; [Henry Alline], "[To the]   followers of Christ scattered [abroad]," nd: Manning Collection, Acadia.

17   Henry Alline, *Hymns and Spiritual Songs on a Variety of Pleasing and Important Subjects* (Windsor, VT, 1796), p. 15. This is probably the "small piece of my writings" Alline delivered to a Halifax printer in December 1780 (*Journal,* p. 131), rather than the massive *Two Mites.* No copy of the Halifax imprint survives. We owe discovery of the Vermont edition to T.B. Vincent of the Royal Military College.

18   Alline is known to have immersed thirteen-year-old Elizabeth Garrison of Sheffield on the River St. John: Edward Manning, "Mistakes in Benedict's History of the Baptists," *c*1814: Manning Collection, Acadia.

19   As to infants, on 25 July 1779 Alline baptized two infant sons of Thaddeus Harris: Horton-Cornwallis Newlight Churchbook, Acadia.

20   This last point is not clear. On one hand the Articles of Alline's Horton-Cornwallis Newlight church, composed (probably by Alline) in 1778, describe baptism (by whatever means) as a "Door into the Visible Church," thereby suggesting that some external form was a prerequisite to church membership. Under date 22 July 1780 an entry in the same churchbook (which entry is, as F.C. Burnett has pointed out, in Alline's own handwriting) characterizes his view of the subject as follows:

    Viz, that is was not a positive command of God, but the practice of the apostles which example he thinks ought to be followed by Christians as the answer of their own conscience as they may be conscience Bound ....

On the other hand, it certainly follows from the general tenor of Alline's teaching that church membership should be open to all Christians whether baptized or not. When in 1783 he penned his "Articles & Covenant of a Gospel Church" it was "Christ" who was described as the "door" to the church, and baptism is unmentioned: see F.C. Burnett, "Henry Alline's 'Articles & Covenant of a Gospel Church' ", in (1984) 4 *Nova Scotia Historical Review* (#2). Furthermore, there is at least a possibility that the article in the Cornwallis Churchbook requiring some form of water baptism was inserted in 1799 or 1800, rather than in 1778: see William Alline's (the preacher's brother) comments in the Churchbook for 10 May 1800. As late as 1834, fifty years after his death, Alline's New Brunswick successors were still debating the question, "Should persons be recognized as members of our churches without baptism?": W.W. Eaton, "Origin of the Christian Connection in N.B.," in *The Christian* (Saint John, December 1840), p. 161.

21 Beverley & Moody, *Alline's Journal,* pp. 211, 213.

22 See D.G. Bell, "The Death of Henry Alline: Some Contemporary Reactions," in (1984) 4 *Nova Scotia Historical Review* (#2), 7-12.

23 Bailey to Brown, 15 April 1781: Bailey Papers, vol 94, PANS.

24 Quoted in Hannah Adams, *Alphabetical Compendium of the Various Sects which have Appeared in the World* (Boston, 1784), p.*lxiv.*

25 Beverley & Moody, *Alline's Journal,* p. 201.

26 "Records of the Church of Jebogue in Yarmouth," in Gordon Stewart (ed), *Documents Relating to the Great Awakening in Nova Scotia, 1760-1791* (1982), p. 135.

27 Beverley & Moody, *Alline's Journal*, p. 172; Brian Cuthbertson (ed), *Journal of the Reverend John Payzant (1749-1834)* (1981), p. 28.

28 Bailey to Brown, 22 June 1782; Bailey to Breynton, 13 June 1782; Bailey to Peters, 7 November 1783: Bailey Papers, vol 94, PANS. In the first of these letters Black is described in the following terms:

> The last mention'd holder forth has lately emigrated from cumberland and tho only a boy of nineteen [*sic*] is admired and caressed as an Angel from heaven. These preachers instead of following the example of Noah that ancient preacher of righteousness, endeavour to extirpate all righteousness and moral virtue and when to heven they make oration they scorn to use premeditation least is should give the Lord offense who[se] sense is better pleas'd with nonsense. This Black lately paid me a visit and I never conversed with such an ignorant, vain, conceited and impertinent fellow — and tho I carefully avoided entering into any altercation with him, he by a spirit of descerning instantly declared me a stranger to the power of divine grace and repeatedly charged me not to bolster up people in their self righteousness.

29 Cuthbertson, *Payzant's Journal*, p. 31; Harvey & Fergusson, *Perkins' Diary*, II, pp. 188, 228.

30 George Rawlyk (ed), *New Light Letters and Spiritual Songs, 1778-1793* (1983), pp. 4, 30-37.

31 Garrettson to Wesley, 25 April 1786, quoted in Nathan Bangs, *Life of the Rev. Freeborn Garrettson* (1845), p. 152. On his arrival in Nova Scotia Garrettson had found the Allinites "as deluded a people as I ever saw": *ibid,* p. 144.

32 Quoted in Rawlyk, *New Light Letters,* p. 33.

33 Bailey to Brown, 1 April 1780: Bailey Papers, vol 91, PANS.

34 Bailey to Wenman, 21 February 1780: *ibid.*

35 A *preacher* gave religious instruction from a text. An *exhorter* was a member of the congregation who, at the close of preaching, urged his listeners to conversion through prayer, direct appeal, *etc.* Exhortation was far more important than its nearest modern equivalent, "testifying". Newlight preachers generally began their public careers as exhorters. To the nine preacher/exhorters referred to in the text the name of Elisha Freeman might be added, but he removed to New England in 1784: W.G. McLoughlin (ed), *Diary of Isaac Backus* (1979), III, p. 1131.

36 Benjamin Kinsman Jr. (1743-179?), a Cornwallis Newlight Baptist, was an exhorter by 1779. He is said to have caused a separation in either his own (Baptist) or the local Newlight church, or both, and to have given up preaching on that account. He remained deacon of the Horton-Cornwallis Baptist church, but at the end of 1783 there is still mention of a religious party called "Kinsmanites": *Payzant's Journal,* pp. 26-27; Bailey to Peters, 7 November 1783: Bailey Papers, vol 94, PANS.

37 Joseph Sanford Bailey (1759-1791), a Newport Newlight Baptist, was a first cousin of Henry Alline (and uncle of the future Newlight preacher Joseph Dimock). He came out as an exhorter about 1780 and subsequently became an itinerant. John Payzant thought him a gifted exhorter, but neither he nor Simeon Perkins was favourably impressed by his preaching. Dr. T.O. Geddes of Barrington recalled that Bailey "stirred up the people more than Alline" had. In 1785-86 Bailey was preaching in Rhode Island: Cuthbertson, *Payzant's Journal,* pp. 28, 31; George Levy (ed), *Diary of Joseph Dimock* (1979), pp. 144-45; Rawlyk, *New Light Letters,* pp. 101, 111, 134, & perhaps 288-89; Edwin Crowell, *History of Barrington* (1923), p. 243; Harvey & Fergusson, *Perkins' Diary,* II, pp. 228, 235-37, 239-40, 257-58, 289; Ruth Sherman (ed), *Peleg Burroughs' Journal, 1778-1798* (1981). (I am

grateful to Philip Griffin-Allwood for this last reference.)

38 Daniel Welsh, a member of the Horton-Cornwallis Newlight church, is mentioned as a preacher in mid-1782: Bailey to Brown, 22 July 1782: Bailey Papers, vol 94, PANS; Rawlyk, *New Light Letters,* p. 134. This is presumably the Welsh with whom James Innis travelled in 1805-06.

39 Ebenezer Hobbs (d1790), an Argyle Newlight, was an itinerant exhorter by 1782. On 21 July of that year Simeon Perkins of Liverpool noted that, "One Ebenezer Hobbs of Argyle, a Lad of about 17 years, made prayers & Exhortation at an Evening meeting". Perkins thought Hobbs "too young for a Teacher," but the following year the great Alline told the Newlight church at Argyle that Hobbs might be "of growing benefit if he follows the Pillar of Clowd". Hobbs, otherwise entirely obscure, is a prime example of a young man impelled onto the Newlight circuit by the ravishing example of the saintly, consumptive Alline: Harvey & Fergusson, *Perkins' Diary,* II, p. 146; Alline to Spinney, 20 January 1783: Acadia. Hobbs was brother-in-law to the Newlight poet Mary Fletcher, eight of whose compositions appear anonymously in Levy, *Dimock's Diary,* pp. 73-82.

40 See F.C. Burnett, "Henry Alline's 'Articles & Covenant of a Gospel Church' ", in (1984) 4 *Nova Scotia Historical Review* (#2). The term "Constitution" occurs several times in Cuthbertson, *Payzant's Journal (eg,* pp.39, 66).

41 But there were many exceptions, most often involving Methodists: for example, Harvey & Fergusson, *Perkins' Diary,* II, pp. 235, 241.

42 C.B. Fergusson (ed), *Diary of Simeon Perkins, 1790-1796* (1961), III, pp. 177, 185.

43 Cuthbertson, *Payzant's Journal,* p. 42. Admittedly, Payzant was using the term Newlight to mean what I term Allinite (*ie,* as excluding Wesleyans).

44 Doane to Fidler, 4 March 1797, in Goldwin French (ed), "Papers of Daniel Fidler," (1960) 13 *Bulletin: Records and Proceedings of the Committee on Archives of the United Church of Canada* 28, p. 36.

45 Cuthbertson, *Payzant's Journal,* p. 88.

46 Bailey to Peters, 10 March 1796: Bailey Papers, vol 94, PANS.

47 Inglis Journal, 30 August 1793: PANS. The John Cooper mentioned subsequently resumed preaching for the Wesleyans but fell into adultery. Summoned to account for his conduct, he announced his conversion to the Baptists and ran off to the United States, becoming a Baptist pastor in the New York City area: Black to WMS, 17 September 1804: Wesleyan Missionary Society Reel A-258, PAC.

48 Smith, *History of the Methodist Church,* I, p. 342.

49 Vol 1, pp. 299-30. Interestingly, Benedict's account of New Dispensationalism came not from the material with which Edward Manning supplied him but was drawn from his conversations with Edmund Reis.

50 Edward Manning, Notes on Baptist Ministers [*c*1812]: Manning Collection, Acadia.

51 "T[o] ·M'r W[illiam] W[est]", 26 August 1780: Manning Collection, Acadia. This draught letter is signed with the initials of Abner Hall, clerk of the Horton-Cornwallis Newlight church, but may prove to be the work of Henry Alline himself.

52 Quoted in Rawlyk, *New Light Letters,* p. 46. In the passage which follows Black come closer than anyone else to alleging that Alline himself preached in a way that would suggest practical antinomianism. It will, however, be noted that Black was not reporting what he himself heard from Alline, only what rumour said.

       Mr. Alline himself told several persons one day that *a believer is like a nut, thrown into the mud, which may dirty the shell, but not the kernel.* That is, we may get drunk, or commit adultery, without the smallest defilement, etc, etc.

53   Abraham Gesner, *New Brunswick: With Notes for Emigrants* (1847), p. 321. I do not take Gesner very seriously although as a native of Kings County, NS, he ought to have known what he was talking about.

54   *Great Awakening,* p. 124. Armstrong produced his admirable study without ever having done research in Nova Scotia. He was, therefore, largely dependent on what Baptist denominational historians had put in print.

55   Cuthbertson, *Payzant's Journal,* p. 47.

56   "Memoir of Duncan M'Coll," in *British North American Wesleyan Methodist Magazine* (September 1841), p. 492.

57   Discussed in detail in Chapter Two.

58   Dibblee to the SPG, 23 June 1802, summarized in SPG Journal, 19 November 1802: PAC Reel A-58; Peters to Winslow, 26 June 1802, in Raymond, *Winslow Papers,* pp. 467-68.

59   Robert Scott to the General Assembly, 1805; uncatalogued petition misclassified under 1804: Provincial Archives of New Brunswick (hereafter "PANB"); *Royal Gazette,* 24 June 1805; *New Brunswick Magazine* (1899), pp. 214-22. See the discussion below in Chapter Three and in Appendix X.

60   Cuthbertson, *Payzant's Journal,* p. 39.

61   Cuthbertson, *Payzant's Journal,* pp. 44-45; Newton to Fidler, 25 August 1796, in French, "Fidler Papers", p. 30. Apparently Harding was in similar difficulties three years earlier in Annapolis: Rawlyk *New Light Letters,* pp. 177-78.

62 Most of Manning's historical recollections are in the great mass of miscellaneous Manning papers at Acadia. This quotation is from Manning's draught letter to the editor of a US religious magazine, *c*1810. Possibly it is Manning's initial letter to David Benedict.

63 Cuthbertson, *Payzant's Journal*, p. 72.

64 *Ibid.*, pp. 75-76. The founding date of the Nova Scotia Congregational and Baptist Association is always put at 1798 even though the first meeting was in 1797.

65 Saunders, *History of the Baptists*, p. 85.

66 The surviving primary sources are heavily slanted towards the doings of those Allinite preachers who subsequently became Baptist "Patriarchs". Accordingly, it is with diffidence that one calls Harding the last *major* Allinite preacher to come out of New Dispensationalism. Daniel Shaw was still a New Dispensationalist, Peter Martin may have been one, and one or more of the Waterborough sectaries might be so classified; and it may simply be the bias of the sources that we do not regard them as "major" preachers.

67 Cuthbertson, *Payzant's Journal*, p. 30.

68 Rawlyk, *New Light Letters*, p. 129. Significantly, in another letter Dimock exults at "bapti[sm] with the Holy Ghost," rather than with water: Dimock to Bennett, 9 December 1793, in John Davis, *Life of Harris Harding* (1866), p. 285. Rawlyk appends to *New Light Letters* two pages of what is labelled the "Joseph Dimock Journal 1791" (pp. 284-85), a more accurate version of which appears in Levy, *Dimock's Diary*, pp. 138-40. The tour of Digby therein described may indeed have occurred in 1791, but the account is not taken from Dimock's "journal" for the period (there is none). It is, rather, a recollection written in old age (Dimock says, "Those days were among the pleasantest of my life"). It is only from such a perspective that Dimock's well-known statement — "I suppose this was the first Baptist

preaching in Digby" — can be understood for what it is. Dimock was deliberately letting the reader believe that he preached the Baptist line as early as 1791, when in fact he was just an Allinite preacher who happened to have been immersed. The historical reminiscences of the Baptist "Patriarchs" — a considerable genre — are replete with what one suspects are deliberately coloured statements on sensitive issues like New Dispensationalism, pre-destination, immersion and Henry Alline.

69   Cuthbertson, *Payzant's Journal*, p. 59.

70   Levy, *Dimock's Diary*, p. 147.

71   Crandall began to preach under guidance from Harris Harding, and so can hardly have taken a "Baptist" line: J.M. Bumsted (ed), "Autobiography of Joseph Crandall," in (1973) 3 *Acadiensis* (#1) 79, p. 84.

72   *Brief Account of the Late Revivals of Religion Among the Congregationalists and Baptists, in . . . the New-England States, and also in Nova-Scotia* (Halifax, England, 1800) p. 20, printing Chipman's letter of 15 July 1799, probably to Samuel Stillman. The letter was reprinted in *Increase of Piety, or the Revival of Religion in the United States of America* (Philadelphia, 1802), p. 22.

73   Letter of Joseph Dimock, probably to Samuel Stillman, 25 May 1799, in *ibid.*, p. 19 (and *ibid.*, p. 21).

74   Quoted in Saunders, *History of the Baptists*, pp. 114-15.

75   Paraphrasing 1 Samuel 18:7.

76   See the references in *supra*, note 72. Chipman's second wife was a member of Stillman's congregation.

77   The only narrative account of the 1800 proceedings is that of John Payzant in Cuthbertson, pp. 78-81. Payzant regarded the events of 1800 as a calamity and his reminiscence must be read in that light. The other

major source is that printed in Saunders, *History of the Baptists*, pp. 86-87. The Baptist ministers — otherwise so garrulous on points of history and reminiscence — are remarkably silent on this landmark event. Were they ashamed of their conduct towards Payzant?

78 It should also be noted that Payzant's account is somewhat garbled in implying (at least to the ordinary reader) that the anger the Manning brothers directed against Chipman was a result of their initial dislike of his Baptist plan. They neither disliked the plan nor was its presentation at the Association a surprise (to them): it had already been discussed in the Horton-Cornwallis Newlight church (Churchbook, 7 June 1800). Rather, what the Mannings resented was Chipman's pretense (to Payzant) that the plan was prompted solely as a measure for the defence of Towner.

79 Attribution of such a motive to the Associated Baptist preachers is, of course, just a more or less well-informed judgment call. It may, therefore, be of some interest to note that it was a conclusion to which both G.A. Rawlyk and myself came independently: Bell, "From Newlight to Arminian Baptist in New Brunswick, 1776-1832" (Harvard Divinity School paper: 1981), pp. 29-30 (deposited at Acadia); Rawlyk, "New Lights, Baptists and Religious Awakenings in Nova Scotia, 1776-1843: A Preliminary Probe," in (1983) 25 *Journal of the Canadian Church Historical Society* (#2), p. 61; Rawlyk, *Ravished by the Spirit: Religious Revivals, Baptists and Henry Alline* (1984), p. 91.

80 Levy, *Dimock's Diary*, pp. 28, 68, 41.

81 I.E. Bill, *Fifty Years with the Baptist Ministers and Churches of the Maritime Provinces of Canada* (1880), p. 143. The account is undated but must have been fairly early as Stillman died in 1807.

82 Cuthbertson, *Payzant's Journal*, p. 81.

83 "Minutes of the Nova Scotia Baptist Association held at Cornwallis, June the 26th, 27th, 28th 1809": Acadia.

84 Chipman, 5 December 1806, in *Mass. Bapt. Miss. Mag.* (May 1807), p. 303.

85 Harding, 30 January 1807, in *ibid.*, p. 306.

86 Towner, 13 April 1807, in *ibid.*, p. 309.

87 Delaney, 4 April 1808, in *ibid.* (September 1808) p. 207.

88 Charles Tupper, "History of the Baptist Churches in Nova-Scotia" (1828) in (1829) 1 *Bapt. Miss. Mag.* (#10), p. 316. Case was the moderator and Hale the clerk at the re-ordination. The proceedings are described in Hale's Journal for 27-28 January 1808: Maine Historical Society, Portland.

89 Hale Journal, 28 June 1809: Maine Historical Society, Portland.

90 Various writers give various statistics. Those used here come directly from the manuscript Association minutes for 1809 and the printed minutes for 1810.

91 "Joseph Dimock of Chester to the Several Churches of Jesus Christ united to the Nova Scotia Baptist Association Residing in Nova Scotia & New Brunswick" [1806]: Manning Papers, Acadia.

92 Statistics are from the 1809 manuscript Association minutes and the 1811 published minutes. Dimock's own account of events is in Levy, *Dimock's Diary*, pp. 84-85, 147-49.

93 Onslow Churchbook, Acadia. See also Edward Manning Journal, 19 November 1814: Acadia.

94 Crawford to Manning, 2 October 1813: Manning Papers, Acadia. For other instances of Harding's identification with Alline see G.A. Rawlyk, "From New Light to Baptist: Harris Harding and the Second Great Awakening in Nova Scotia," in Barry Moody (ed.), *Repent and Believe: The Baptist Experience in Maritime Canada* (1980), pp. 12-13.

Enoch Towner's Argyle church was also among those effectively excluded from the Association by the close communion resolution of 1809. Perhaps Towner's case was closer to that of Harris Harding than that of Joseph Dimock, for Crawford writes Manning in the following terms: "[Y]ou have voted from your association, men who conscientously differed from you, and who, as it would appear in that instance, trembled at the word of God, so as to obey God rather than men". "I refer to Messrs. Harding and Towner."

95 Edward Manning Journal, 10 August 1821: Acadia.

96 Loose fragment of Manning's Journal, dated only 28 September and probably from the 1820s: Acadia.

97 Edward Manning Journal, 8 November 1812; 4 April 1813; 2 September 1821; 24 September 1822: Acadia.

98 *Infra*, Chapter Three.

99 Edward Manning Journal, 2 September 1821, printed in Cuthbertson, *Payzant's Journal*, pp. 101-02.

100 Edward Manning Journal, 7 April 1818. Manning was also much troubled by the local success of the Campbellites (Disciples of Christ). The Campbellites were anti-Calvinistic, but perhaps not open communionist.

101 Manning's draught of a letter to [David Benedict], [1812]: Manning Collection, Acadia; Edward Manning Journal, 25 September 1822: Acadia.

102 Edward Manning Journal, 15 January 1815: Acadia.

103 *Ibid.*, 26 & 28 December 1812; 12 & 17 February 1815; 25 July 1815; 6 & 16 July 1816.

104 Horton Baptist Churchbook, Acadia. In 1816 the Horton church was excluded from the Association, apparently for non-reporting — although Harding himself had attended — and not re-admitted until 1818.

The church's early history is discussed in P.G.A. Griffin-Allwood, "The Baptists of Horton Township, 1765-1819" (Southern Baptist Theological Seminary: 1983).

105   Delaney, 4 April 1808, in *Mass. Bapt. Miss. Mag.* (September 1808), p. 207.

106   Henry Hale Journal, 7 April 1808: Maine Historical Society, Portland.

107   Delaney to Manning, 16 November 1810: Manning Collection, Acadia.

108   Charles Tupper, "History of the Baptist Churches in Nova-Scotia" (1828), in (1829) 1 *Baptist Missionary Magazine* (#10), p. 316.

109   Delaney, 21 April 1834, in *The Trumpet*, 24 May 1834, quoted in *New York Christian Messenger and Philadelphia Universalist*, 31 May 1834; Russell Miller, *The Larger Hope: The First Century of the Universalist Church in America, 1770-1870* (1979), pp. 667-68.

110   At least this seems to have been the case in Nova Scotia. In New Brunswick — where the open communion forces were much stronger — there is, paradoxically, little direct evidence on the point.
      It has, of course, been suggested that the free will theology the New England Arminians brought with them to the Maritimes had been learnt from the publications of Henry Alline. See Stephen Marini, *Radical Sects of Revolutionary New England* (1982); especially pp. 139-43; D.G. Bell, "The Death of Henry Alline: Some Contemporary Reactions," (1984) 4 *Nova Scotia Historical Review* (#2), note 4; G.A. Rawlyk, *Ravished by the Spirit: Religious Revivals, Baptists and Henry Alline* (1984), ch. 2, especially pp. 68-69.

111   Post-Allinite Congregationalism has attracted no scholarly interest. There is, however, an excellent *History of the Congregational Church of Cornwallis, N.S.* (1900) by Jacob Cox.

112   [Woodstock] *Carleton Sentinel*, 10 May 1856 (Mary Orser).

113   Census figures in Saunders, *History of the Baptists*, p. 468.

114   The only major split among the Nova Scotia Calvinist Baptists was over race, but in New Brunswick there was a significant separation over doctrine early in the 1860s. The separating party accused the Calvinist Baptists of being insufficiently Calvinistic and, in 1859 or 1860, formed the "Particular Dependent Close-Communion Baptist" association, led by Joshua Bunting. Its sympathizers (the "Buntingites") were characterized by their detractors as "Hyper-calvinist and antinomian". By 1861 they had eight churches, all in what are now Westmorland and Albert Counties. See David Freeman Journal, 30 August 1860: Acadia; *Minutes of the Particular Dependent Close-Communion Baptists* [1861] (Sackville, 1862).

115   G.A. Rawlyk, "New Lights, Baptists and Religious Awakenings in Nova Scotia, 1776-1843: A Preliminary Probe," in (1983) 25 *Journal of the Canadian Church Historical Society* (#2) 43, pp. 45-49.

116   The term "Newlight Baptist" and near variants are found fairly often in the sources. In 1804, for example, a Presbyterian itinerant reported that Joseph Crandall styled himself "a new-light Baptist": John Mitchell Journal, 10 August 1804: PANS. That same year a Wesleyan found "Newlight Baptists" in Cumberland: Bennett to WMS, 16 November 1804: Wesleyan Missionary Society Reel A-258, PAC. Ten years later the Scotch Baptist Alexander Crawford labelled Isaac Bradshaw of Prince Edward Island a "newlight baptist": Crawford to Edward Manning, 28 December 1814: Manning Collection, Acadia. The historian of Annapolis County recalled that, as late as the 1840s, "I have sometimes . . . heard the terms 'Baptist New Lights,' and 'Methodist New Lights' used to distinguish evangelists of the two denominations": W.A. Calnek,

History of the County of Annapolis (1897), p. 301. Yet another example is found in the Chebogue Congregational Churchbook (typescript), p. 211: PANS.

Chapter Two
THE JOURNAL OF JAMES MANNING, 1801

THE JOURNAL OF JAMES MANNING, 1801

Oh I Can assure you
it had a resemblance of Heaven.

James Manning, 1801

THE RISE OF THE BAPTISTS IN NEW BRUNSWICK, 1760-1801

Although claimed by Great Britain since at least the Treaty of Utrecht (1713), there was no English-speaking settlement in the part of Nova Scotia that would become New Brunswick until early in the 1760s. Most of the arrivals were from land-hungry New England. As part of their intellectual baggage they brought well-developed religious sensibilities. The most important of the new settlements was that in Maugerfield (Maugerville) in the central St. John valley. In one of their first communal acts the planters of Maugerville, largely from Essex County Massachusetts, gathered a small Congregational church, reciting in their covenant that they had been "for that end orderly dismissed from the churches to which we heretofore belonged".[1] The church was stridently Calvinistic (abjuring "Pelagian arminian principles vulgarily so called"). Its expressed hope was to "sirname ourselves by the name of Israel" and "through grace . . . become Israelites indeed".

Another of the settlements planted in the wake of the defeat of the French and expulsion of the Acadians was in the area generally referred to as Cumberland, the Sackville-Amherst region (at the border of New Brunswick and Nova Scotia). As North America's most extensive marshland, already well-dyked by Acadians, the region was a magnet for aggressive New Englanders. Many of the 1763 arrivals were from Rehoboth and Providence, the border region of Rhode Island and Massachusetts. Before their departure for Sackville a few of the emigrants were set apart as a General Six-Principle Baptist church and Nathan Mason ordained pastor over them. In the 1760s Baptists were still not very numerous in North America, and the group that formed this church before removing to Sackville was in a minority even among Baptists.

As "General" Baptists they held to free will and open communion, the doctrine so abhorred at Maugerville. They were called "Six-Principle" Baptists because they added to standard Baptist usage the practice of laying hands on converts in receiving them into the church. Once at Sackville this Six-Principle group grew to about sixty members. Although many would accompany their pastor back to New England in 1771, the church's residual presence helped shape the distinctive religious character of the region.[2]

The Sackville Six-Principle Baptist church was probably Newlight in its tendency, but the first reformation in the region seems to have begun in the summer of 1766 among New England settlers who were not members of the church. The result was formation in 1767 of another Sackville Baptist church, consisting of thirty-seven members. Unlike the rival Six-Principle church this new group was Calvinistic in theology. From 1768 until about the mid-1770s it had pastoral care from Nathaniel Round. After Round's departure the church probably continued with a low visibility until the arrival of Henry Alline set the region ablaze.

Flanking the Baptist churches in Sackville were two other important communities of pre-Loyalists. One was the large Yorkshire-Cumberland immigration which set down in the Amherst area early in the 1770s. Although they settled primarily in what is now Nova Scotia, several families soon moved towards Sackville and crossed the Petitcodiac into Hillsborough and Hopewell. More importantly, these intensely Methodistical Anglicans soon fostered a reformation which William Black was to carry to Sackville and all the neighbouring townships along the Petitcodiac. On another flank of the Sackville Baptists were several families of Germanic settlers imported from Pennsylvania in the mid-1760s, notably the Steeves. Some settled first in Moncton township and on the bend of the Petitcodiac, but by 1770 most were clustered in Hillsborough. Their religious background is unknown; but in eighteenth and early nineteenth-century New Brunswick the Christians in Hillsborough and neighbouring Hopewell townships were one of the most consistently fertile preaching grounds.[3] Like the neighbouring Baptists and Wesleyans and like the Congregationalists in

Maugerville, the Germanic Protestants of Hillsborough were to exert an influence on New Brunswick religious development out of all proportion to their number.[4]

* * * * *

For a decade after its founding the Maugerville church received no regular preaching. In 1773, however, a local reformation was triggered by the death-bed exhortations of Francis Peabody. As a result, the settlement sent to New England for a minister. In 1774 they secured the services of Seth Noble, a 31-year old Massachusetts schoolteacher beginning his ministerial career.[5] The little that is known of Noble's early history suggests he was conventional rather than Newlight in his religious sympathies, but under his early labours the church in Maugerville built a meeting-house and experienced "a considerable shaking of the dry bones". As Noble reported with satisfaction early in 1776:

> Simeon Towns is daily rejoicing in the rock of his salvation. Asa Kimbill and wife are brought out into marvellous light. John Wasson . . . is now almost incessantly praising and adoring the lowly Jesus. Andrew Tibbets and wife, Mr. Gellison's wife [Lydia?], Thomas Saunders, Sarah Coy, and Alice Potter [Porter?] seem under the preparatory work of the Spirit.[6]

By themselves these are the accents of a Newlight, but the rest of Noble's letter was more concerned with gossip than "the lowly Jesus".

It was already clear that there was more than one "preparatory work of the Spirit" at work in the New England townships on the St. John. As early as 20 June 1775 Jonathan Hartt had publicly called the King "a damd snooty whelp", adding "by God if I was near him I would stab him for he is nothing but a damd Roman [Catholic] Bastard". Ironically, the first one learns of generalized pro-American sympathy is in the same letter in which Parson Noble had exulted in the work of God. In a postscript he added, "We have unanimously signed a paper, to join New England in the national struggle, and are making all possible preparations for war". The tone of this comment supports the general supposition that the recently-arrived Noble was a principal inspiration to active Patriot activity on the St. John.[7] On 24 May 1776 yet another "paper" was being handed around for signature, this one expressing "our minds and desire to submit ourselves to the government of Massachusetts Bay, and . . . we are ready with our lives and fortunes to share with them the event of the present struggle for Liberty however God in His Providence may order it". The Patriot committee — including several prominent members of the church — claimed to have gathered 125 signatures in support of rebellion, with only a dozen opposers.

When Jonathan Eddy's invasion force came to the River that autumn (1776) on its way to besiege Fort Cumberland (between Sackville and Amherst) upwards of two dozen Maugerville-area men joined the ill-fated adventure. The state of rebellion on the River St. John formally ended in the spring of 1777 when Col. Arthur Goold arrived with a small force from Halifax. Goold seized Israel Perley, secretary of the Patriot committee, and took him off to stand trial for treason. He searched diligently for Noble, but the preacher had escaped to Machias. The other inhabitants were allowed to make a grovelling submission and take the oath of allegiance.[8] Within a few weeks Noble was back on the St. John with an American force led by John Allan, formerly of Cumberland. Confounded by a pursuing British force in their attempt to win over the powerful Malecites, Allan and Noble made an arduous escape to their refuge at Machias.[9]

The flight of their pastor, the humiliation and disillusion of the whole community and the spirit of recrimination that would naturally follow such a catastrophe put great strain on the fellowship of the church. Nothing, however, is known of its travel until the arrival in April 1779 of Henry Alline. Alline's labours triggered a whole generation of reformations and separations of fundamental significance to the development of New Brunswick Protestantism. Much new documentation has lately come to light, but the resulting picture is still, as Edward Winslow once observed, "confusion worse confounded".[10] What follows is a brief summary of the general course of events.[11]

59

Alline reported that on his arrival in Maugerville he found that "there had been a church there, but [it] had separated on account of the greatest part holding the minister [Noble] to be an unconverted man, who afterwards went away, but the division still subsisted". Alline would, therefore, have it believed that he found the Maugerville Congregational church already divided. Then, portraying himself as peacemaker, he reports that he advised the church to "renew the covenant, and to come again into church order". He also writes that his preaching was much blessed, so that his initial visit to the St. John townships produced great good.[12] Independent documentation confirms that on 17 June 1779, towards the end of Alline's visit, fifteen males and nine females of the Maugerville Congregational church met to renew their covenant, just as Alline says he had advised. But, contrary to what Alline implies, this group — including several leading ex-Patriots and Seth Noble's wife — were not his sympathizers or in any great degree under his influence. On the very day of the covenant renewal four of the principal men of the church wrote the Revd Jonathan Scott of Chebogue to press him for a visit. The letter was brief and not explicitly anti-Alline, but the writers described themselves as "at Present destitute of the preached Gospel" while in fact they were in the midst of Alline's labours.

Alline departed the River St. John at the end of June 1779. Unless his *Journal* account is to be dismissed as a tissue of deliberate half-truths, then it was in his absence that a separate church was established by his sympathizers in Maugerville. The only explicit acknowledgment of the separation comes in a 29 July letter from eleven of the male members of the Maugerville Congregational church (all of whom had participated in the covenant renewal) to Jonathan Scott. In this, their second appeal for urgent help, they made their concerns explicit.

> We are sorry to acquaint you that, after a Manifestation of God's Goodness, by a visible Out-pouring of his Spirit in this Place, there hath Division and Contention arisen among us, issuing to an open Separation and setting up an independent Church on the different System.

To suggest that this "setting up an independent Church on a different System" occurred only after Alline's departure certainly strains plausibility, but there is no other way to maintain the credibility of his *Journal* account; and in its support it will be noted that the letter to Scott of 17 June (written late in Alline's visit) had not complained of formal separation.

Alline returned to Maugerville and the adjacent townships late in August or early September. "I was rejoiced," he wrote, "to find many souls born to Christ since I was last there; and what was something . . . uncommon, 3 or 4 were upwards of 50 years of age".

> The church met as soon as possible after I came there, and made choice of two elders and two deacons. One of the elders came since out in public, and appears likely to be a useful man. The power of religion was reviving, but the enemies raging . . . .

This can only have reference to the separate Allinite church, although Alline never expressly acknowledged that a separation had taken place. The "enemies raging" were the orthodox Congregationalists. Late in October, at the end of this visit to the River, Alline declined the Newlight church's invitation to settle as its pastor.[13] On the same day Alline penned this refusal, the orthodox Congregationalists were issuing their third appeal to Jonathan Scott. Pointedly they lamented the "Divisions and Separations being encouraged and strengthened by one who ought to labour to preserve the Unity of the Spirit . . . , and not from any specious Pretence labour to sow Error and Disssension among the People of God ...".

Apart from brief references in Alline's *Journal*, there is no further direct evidence regarding this church. Nothing is known of its leadership, membership or history. It does, however, appear that by the late 1780s (a decade after these events) an Allinite society was flourishing in the Waterborough-Sheffield area (*ie,* on the southern edge of the old township of Maugerville), the core of which had removed there in 1784 or 1785 from Gagetown. Accordingly it is natural to wonder whether the centre of gravity of Alline's Newlight church was below Maugerville, across the River in Gagetown. It was there that the young Elijah Estabrooks lived. His obituary says that Estabrooks joined Alline's organization (the obituary calls it both a "church" and a "society") in September of the year it was formed (1779).[14] The weight of circumstantial evidence is, however, against the proposition that the centre of the Allinite church was Gagetown. A careful reading of his *Journal* suggests that Alline did, indeed, do some preaching in Gagetown, but it equally indicates that he spent most of his time in Maugerville. Further, the Allinite organization in which he laboured most is clearly styled a "church" (the "church of Christ in Maugerfield"), while the Gagetown-Waterborough group of which the first firm knowledge comes ten years later was only a "society" (*ie,* not organized into a church).[15] Accordingly, one must conclude that the Allinite church gathered in 1779 was centred in Maugerville township, which means that nothing further is known of it except that Alline visited a third time in May-June 1780, again in November 1780 and, for the final time. in April 1782. In October 1782 he sent Thomas Chipman to the St. John.

* * * * *

The following spring the first of six great flotillas arrived at the mouth of the River St. John with a human cargo of exiled American Loyalists. Within two years upwards of 11,000 settled the St. John valley as far north as Woodstock, outnumbering the pre-Loyalists by tenfold. Passamaquoddy also attracted a large Loyalist settlement, and a small number set down in the Sackville area. In the St. John valley the land above Maugerville was allotted to military Loyalists ("Provincials") and the land below Maugerville to civilians ("Refugees"). Heavily-settled Maugerville itself was in the main left to its pre-Loyalist inhabitants. Pre-Loyalist township organization was, however, replaced by a structure of counties and parishes. Accordingly, in 1785 the old township of Maugerville was divided into two parishes: the upper part called Maugerville, the lower Sheffield. The strength of the old Maugerville Congregational church was in what had now become Sheffield; and, in 1789, when

62

Maugerville Anglicans seized the lot on which their meeting-house stood, the church moved the structure on the ice five miles down into Sheffield.[16] In consequence the Maugerville Congregational church became known as the Sheffield Congregational church. Another change in the contours of religious dissent wrought by the Loyalists was expulsion of many of the pre-Loyalists from Gagetown. The nucleus of the pre-Loyalist community removed across the St. John River and took up land in the less desirable parish of Waterborough (in that part of the old parish of Waterborough that is now the parish of Canning). There they adjoined the lower boundary of Sheffield and would soon make the Waterborough-Sheffield neighbourhood notorious for religious extravagance.

In the larger perspective the coming of the Loyalists triggered establishment of New Brunswick as a separate colony in 1784. As by far the largest proportion of New Brunswick Loyalists was from New York, the old notion that most of the arrivals were Anglicans is implausible. Yet it is true that the new colony's governing elite were deeply committed to making the Church of England the dominant vehicle of religious expression. Their concern with religion was (as we would now judge) primarily political. Governor Thomas Carleton's circle of advisers was dominated by New Englanders, whose background gave them ample reason to equate dissent in religion with disaffection in politics; and the example of recent events in Maugerville would only have confirmed their prejudices. Accordingly, the Church of England — although not formally "established" in New Brunswick — was given government sanction through land grants ("glebes"), large subsidies for erecting churches and a near monopoly in solemnization of marriages. The remainder of the church's financial support came primarily from the England-based Society for the Propagation of the Gospel. Popular financial support for the Anglican ministry was negligible.

Eighteenth-century missions were established at the three towns (Saint John, St. Andrews, Fredericton) and in Kingston, Gagetown, Maugerville, St. Marys-Nashwaak, Woodstock, Sussex and, for a time, in the Sackville and Norton-Springfield areas and on the Miramichi. It was the missionaries settled in these rural districts who bore the burden of planting Anglican civilization in the wilderness. Given every advantage they failed remarkably. Almost to a man they seem to have regarded their appointment as a sinecure in reward for loyalty. With sights fixed firmly on financial security in this world their larger hope was to pass their place to a son, at which they had conspicuous success. Their vocation was essentially political — preaching a gospel of loyalty and deference. Frederick Dibblee, rector of the vast mission of Woodstock, may have been one of the better specimens of the breed. Yet his extensive journal chronicles farming, trading and the weather; the deity and affairs of religion are scarcely mentioned. An English visitor to his mission provides a conscientious but ultimately damning assessment of Dibblee's outlook.

> [H]e preached from the first Epistle of John ... — Love not the world &c &c. [H]e first warned us against too great a love for the riches and pleasures of this world, but at the same time giving us very great lattitude, by showing that it was consider[ing] them as our chief good which made them sinfull ... . He said that the more we strove against the world &c the greater our merrit, and the greater our reward would [be]. [H]e made it appear that Heaven was to be obtained entirely by our own works. [A]s such he said nothing about Christ, repentence or faith, and not one word said to awaiken sinners &c. I consider M'r Dibble a very pleasant Gentlemanly man in company, but a very poor preacher of the Gospel ... .[17]

Dibblee and his fellow missionaries preached a gentlemanly message, just as they aspired to live in a gentlemanly manner. As such they did not fall below the Anglican standard of the time; and, as supervisors of the Society for the Propagation of the Gospel's local educational programme, they made a real contribution to New Brunswick development. But, preaching a lukewarm gospel, one day in seven, and on only a small circuit,[18] they failed the challenge of their environment. They were temperamentally unwilling to travel from neighbourhood to neighbourhood day after day offering the consolations of religion to those who experienced the "desolation of the spirit" that was soon the lot of New Brunswick's profoundly-disillusioned Loyalists.[19] A survey of the several parish registers indicates that in the early days of the province settlers made earnest efforts to have their children sprinkled and their dead interred with the service of the Church. Although not primarily Anglicans, the Loyalists initially showed every willingness to become Anglicans. But after 1800 the geographical and demographic scope of the Anglican parish registers shrank dramatically, a development coinciding exactly with the rise of religious dissent — especially the Baptist form of dissent.

SOUTHEASTERN NEW BRUNSWICK Before Alline's first visit to Sackville-Amherst in the summer of 1781 the region had already experienced a Baptist reformation in the 1760s and a Wesleyan stir in the 1770s. Accordingly, Alline found many in the Cumberland townships closely attuned to the Newlight gospel, such that this first tour was an unqualified success.[20] He was able to gather a church and even make a powerful impact on the Germans in Hillsborough. The second visit, a year later, met with opposition, the Wesleyans having already divided off. (Payzant attributed this to Chipman having preached the Calvinistic doctrine of "perseverance," but his chronology may be mistaken.) Alline also now met with disappointment among the Germans across the Petitcodiac, who were "chained down to the form of religion . . . without the power". He did, however, find one young Allinite convert "who laboured very much with this people", presumably either Henry or Christian Steeves.[21]

Following his departure Alline sent John Payzant to preach in Cumberland. Although he found the region "full of disputes" Payzant settled as pastor of the Allinite church for nearly two years, working in opposition to an unnamed close communion Baptist from the United States and to William Black. It was in the midst of Payzant's labours that Black found in Sackville the "foulest *Antinomianism* spreading like fire".

Payzant removed from Cumberland in 1784 and William Black in 1786. Methodist societies continued alive in the region despite only intermittent preaching, and in 1790 a meeting-house was erected in Sackville. The immediate fortunes of the Allinites are less clear. Payzant reported that the Cumberland church declined to send delegates to his 1786 ordination at Cornwallis because it was "So much broking to peaces," suggesting that it still existed but with a low visibility. Harris Harding, Thomas Bennett and Joseph Dimock all preached in Cumberland in 1790. One of Harding's letters makes specific reference to the "Church of Sackville," which — unless a loose expression — indicates that the Allinite organization still existed.

Too little is known of the further progress of either the Allinites or the Wesleyans to give a connected history, but it does seem that the Sackville-Amherst region was particularly subject to religious extravagance. William Black had been disgusted by it in 1782; and the presence of Harding, Bennett and Dimock in 1790 suggests that Cumberland, too, had a New Dispensationalist phase. This is confirmed by Joseph Dimock. He later recalled that the Christians at Sackville had been "formerly a very flighty people in their sentiments. Most of them carried away with what was called [the] New-Dispensation Scheme holding the Doctrine of predestination in such a light as to render all striveing against sin resisting temptation [and] praying without feeling the Spirit of God as useless Hypocrisy ...".[22] (Dimock did not add that he had once abetted those who held such views.) Other reports of residual New Dispensationalism were made in 1801, 1803, 1804, 1811 and 1828.[23]

A succession of Wesleyans visited the region in the 1790s, without spectacular success. In 1798 there were 120 souls on the Cumberland circuit. For the Allinites, Christian Steeves — one of the Hillsborough Germans — is thought to have started holding meetings in the mid 1790s. His brother Henry also preached.[24] Into the neighbouring township of Hopewell came Nicholas Pierson, formerly the Baptist pastor in Horton, about 1791. He had probably quit preaching but, twenty years later, he was still routinely opening his house for preaching by others. Following Pierson from Horton to Hopewell in the 1790s came Bennetts, Newcombs, Fitches, Sanfords, Bishops, Wickwires and others, all accustomed to experimental religion.[25] At least one of the Newcombs would turn preacher.

About 1797 the Chester Baptist Joseph Crandall visited the region as a preacher. On this first visit he found that the Steeves brothers already "held meetings in the different settlements and exhorted the people".[26] On his second visit, the same year, Crandall married and located in Salisbury, far up the Petitcodiac. For eighteen months he did no preaching. Then at a (presumably) 1799 religious exercise he was moved to speak, and as a result "the meetings continued for several days". "Oh it was wonderful," he recalled, "to see groups of people at the midnight hour, returning home from the meetings with their torchlights, and making the wilderness echo with the praises of God." Crandall was already preaching the distinctive Baptist message and he gathered a few like-minded converts both near his Salisbury home and in Sackville, a remote seventy kilometres away. Some of the Sackville group were probably survivals of the two Baptist churches gathered thirty years earlier, many of whom would also have fallen in with Alline. It was Crandall's friends in Sackville who in 1799 summoned Joseph Dimock, Edward Manning and Theodore Harding to gather them into an (open communion) Baptist church and ordain Crandall as their pastor. The latter event took place on 8 October 1799, the church itself having been organized a few days earlier.[27]

The presence of the four Baptist ministers in southeastern New Brunswick at the end of 1799 triggered a major reformation, paralleling that in Nova Scotia. For Joseph Dimock the "power & grace that was then Desplayed" was "beyond description".[28] After accompanying Theodore Harding on a three-week tour up the Petitcodiac, Peter Wickwire reported that "44 persons was Baptized ... and a number more made a declaration of the dealings of God with their Imortal Souls, which did not as yet see their way Clear to [go forward in] the Ordinance".[29] Perhaps the most important effect of the events of 1799 is that it inspired the newly-ordained Crandall to spread the Baptist gospel to the River St. John. Here Crandall — the first White Baptist to preach on the River — had extraordinary success, setting in motion a series of reformations that would within the space of a year establish the Baptist cause in New Brunswick's heartland.

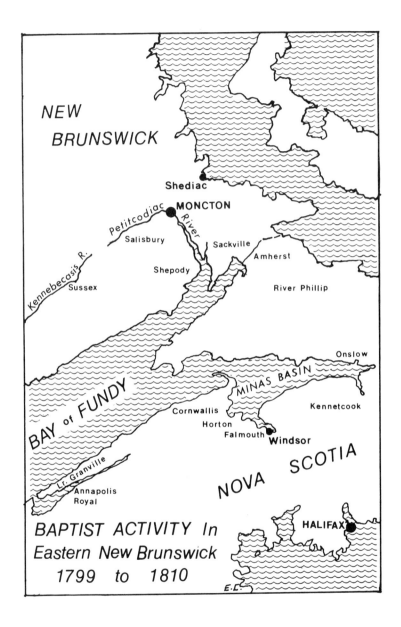

NEW
BRUNSWICK

Shediac

Petitcodiac   MONCTON   River

Salisbury

Sackville

Amherst

Kennebecasis R.

Shepody

River Phillip

Sussex

Onslow

MINAS BASIN

BAY of FUNDY

Cornwallis

Kennetcook

Horton

Falmouth   Windsor

NOVA SCOTIA

Lr. Granville

Annapolis
Royal

HALIFAX

BAPTIST ACTIVITY In
Eastern New Brunswick
1799   to   1810

E.C.

BAPTIST CHURCHES IN EASTERN NEW BRUNSWICK 1799-1810

Sackville area:
Church gathered in 1799 and Joseph Crandall ordained pastor. Meeting-house by 1803. Reverted to Allinism. Baptist character re-asserted in 1808.

Salisbury area:
Church gathered in 1800 with Joseph Crandall as pastor. Described for many years as a "branch" of the Sackville church. Meeting-house by 1811.

Sussex area:
Church gathered in 1800. Gilbert Harris ordained pastor about 1801. Divided by conflict between Harris and Ansley. Soon dissolved. Allinite meetings (including some former members of the church) established in Upper Sussex and Lower Millstream.

ST. JOHN VALLEY With the flight of Seth Noble in 1777 and the arrival of Henry Alline in 1779 the orthodox Congregational church in Sheffield entered a decline from which it would never recover. The church made the diplomatic gesture of opening its meeting-house to the Church of England in 1783-84, but was rewarded with ingratitude when the Anglicans claimed as a glebe the lot on which the building stood and, subsequently, the parsonage lot as well. Although the meeting-house would be successfully moved and the parsonage retained, the church had less success in attracting acceptable preaching. Significantly, in view of its tainted past, it sent to England (rather than New England) in 1783 or 1784 for a minister, and a certain Dr. Collins may actually have come out.[30] If so his stay was brief.

The next preacher to figure in the church's unhappy travel was John James, a Calvinist Methodist (Countess of Huntingdon's Connexion). The scheming James had already taken advantage of the death of the rector of Saint John to form a party among local Anglicans with a view to succeeding to this most desirable parish. Bishop Inglis, however, refused him ordination and would not, in any event, have been able or willing to give him Saint John. James' campaign seriously divided Saint John Anglicans and gave rise to a libel concerning Bishop Inglis and a soon famous prostitute.[31] Simultaneous to the unfolding of this rumour in Saint John, Halifax and London, James turned his attention to the Congregationalists in Sheffield, who agreed at the end of 1788 to settle him as their pastor. His labours here did not meet with particular success. In 1789, when the church renewed its covenant, it numbered twenty-five (plus the pastor), only one more than at the covenant renewal ten years earlier. Apart from Mary Coy, "All the Members ... was far advanced in year[s]; there was no young people belonging to it".[32] Three years later James' "scandalous Indecencies" became the subject of church inquiry; but before he could be excommunicated for his misconduct James threw himself into the arms of the Church of England, "the most indulgent and least censorious church in the world". He read the Church service in the Congregational parsonage for some time —
70

prompting local Anglicans to form a vestry in Sheffield for the very purpose of securing the parsonage lot — before fleeing to New York.

Having been imposed upon by a Calvinist Methodist the Congregational Dissenters at Sheffield were next beset by the Wesleyans. Wesleyan Methodism had arrived in the St. John Valley with the Loyalists, but no society was formed until Abraham Bishop gathered one at Saint John in 1791. Of its fifty-four members the majority was Black.[33] Bishop was also the first to preach the Wesleyan message up the St. John River, as far as the Nashwaak. At Sheffield he made a deep and favourable impression; he was even allowed to use the Congregational meeting-house. Years later Mary Coy would recall that until Bishop's labours she had never heard a young person tell a religious experience, had never heard of a prayer meeting and had never heard a female pray in public. Bishop remained on the River for about six months in 1791-92 and was the catalyst of a reformation that would eventually do the cause of vital religion much harm. Bishop himself would not see it, for in the spring of 1792 he was replaced on the River by William Black and the Saint John layman Stephen Humbert. They found the Sheffield region on fire with religious excitement and formed a Wesleyan class in the neighbourhood. The Congregational deacons, not surprisingly, were "very Jellous" and "did not like to see the young people go to the Methodist Meeting".[34]

Thereafter Saint John, Long Reach, Fredericton, the Naskwaak and particularly Sheffield received a rapid succession of Wesleyan preachers. Apart from Saint John the most determined effort was made at Sheffield where, it was thought, the pastorless Congregationalists might be won over and fashioned into a rich and powerful organization. Duncan McColl of St. Stephen spent the whole winter of 1792-93 in Sheffield, where he formed the Methodist society anew (the first society had probably fallen victim to the Allinite excitements, to be noticed below). In 1794 Benjamin Wilson, an unordained Wesleyan from Virginia, was stationed there as was James Boyd. By early 1795 the American Daniel Fidler was serving alternately in Sheffield, Fredericton and Nashwaak, with visits from both William Black and James

Mann. From this point Wesleyan preaching in Sheffield seems to have been rather sporadic. One of the reasons the cause declined for a time in the latter 1790s was the fact that by 1795 the Congregational church was enjoying the services of the lapsed Wesleyan James Boyd.[35] Boyd, at Sheffield in 1794 as a Wesleyan, was serving the Congregationalists at least by the fall of 1795; and on the 31 March following they voted "to envite Mr. Boyd to tarry with us at least one year longer or for life if the congregation [*ie,* the 'society'] shall approve of it". When the Wesleyans speculated that Boyd was "getting a separate Church" on the St. John River, they presumably meant this preaching for the Congregationalists at Sheffield.[36] His labours, probably reclaiming some Methodists for the Congregationalists, following on the Hammondite frenzy and the Newlight preaching of James and Edward Manning, gave the Wesleyans a great scare. Boyd did not, however, remain long with the Sheffield church, returning to the United States about 1798. Thereafter the Congregationalists flirted with Presbyterianism,[37] appealed to the (Congregationalist) London Missionary Society and, in the first decade of the nineteenth century, were reduced to a marginal influence on the contours of religious dissent in the St. John valley.

The spiritual travels and travails of the neighbouring Allinites in the 1790s were altogether more spectacular. Henry Alline's Maugerville Newlight church, gathered in 1779, is never heard from again; but the Allinite society formed about the same time and centred first in Gage and then — from the mid 1780s — across the St. John in Waterborough probably retained a constant visibility. The earliest evidence of its post-Alline activity indicates that religious exercises were being held about the year 1790 in the homes of Archelaus Hammond, Elijah Estabrooks and others in that part of Waterborough now called Canning.[38] For nearly a decade after Thomas Chipman's 1782 visit to the River this society met for prayer and praise (Alline's hymns were commonly sung) without preaching. Then in the summer of 1791 the Shelburne Black David George became the first Baptist to preach and immerse on the River St. John. George twice travelled as far as Fredericton but is not actually known to have stopped in Waterborough.[39] On his return to Shelburne George sent one of his Black disciples, Sampson Colbart (one source gives "Tolbert") to the River St. John. Colbart did labour briefly among the Allinites at Waterborough and was received with joy. Then in the fall of 1791 the frail, Alline-like Wesleyan Abraham Bishop arrived in the St. John valley. The epicentre of Bishop's reformation was among the Congregationalists and the Wesleyans of Sheffield and Maugerville and the Allinites of Waterborough. Like the parallel development in Nova Scotia, the Allinites would soon themselves divide into an "orthodox" faction and a New Dispensationalist fringe.[40]

The best account of the commencement of the reformation is provided by the Wesleyan Duncan McColl. "During the winter of 1791[-92]," he recalled,

> while brother Bishop was preaching on the east and west sides of the Saint John river, a precious work broke out among the people. But these were a people who professed to be awakened to a true sense of religion, under the ministry of Mr. Henry Allen, a number of years past. Some of these were a well informed people; their morals also were good. They were esteemed highly by other Christians. The generality of them fell in with Mr. Bishop, and the work, and proved faithful.

When he says that the "generality" fell in with Bishop, McColl means that they sympathized with the reformation — not necessarily with the Wesleyans — for Bishop formed no class in Maugerville, Sheffield or Waterborough.

By March 1792 Bishop was gone. When William Black visited the River a few months later he found "much wildfire and many wrong opinions" in the Sheffield-Waterborough area,[41] but this may indicate no more than that a number of Allinite exhorters had become active, who declined to be channelled into Wesleyanism. The first extended eye-witness account of the work of reformation is that of John James, the Anglican Calvinist Methodist turned Congregationalist (and then returned into Anglicanism). In a letter dated in Sheffield on 18 October 1792 and addressed to his Calvinist Methodist sponsors in England James reported that:

73

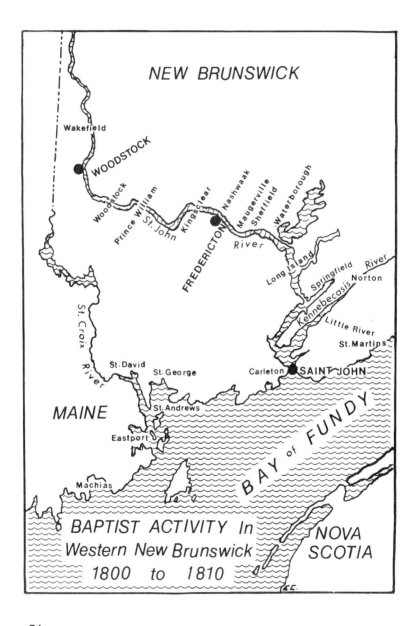

NEW BRUNSWICK

Wakefield

WOODSTOCK

Woodstock

Prince William

St. John

Kingsclear

FREDERICTON

Nashwaak

Maugerville

Sheffield

Waterborough

River

Long Island

Springfield River

Norton

Kennebecasis River

Little River

St. Martins

St. Croix River

St. David

St. George

Carleton ● SAINT JOHN

MAINE

St. Andrews

Eastport

BAY of FUNDY

Machias

BAPTIST ACTIVITY In
Western New Brunswick
1800 to 1810

NOVA
SCOTIA

BAPTIST CHURCHES IN WESTERN NEW BRUNSWICK 1800-1810

Wakefield area:
Church gathered in 1804. Joined Association in 1805. Divided by Allinism and close communion. Allinite meeting set up in opposition in or after 1810.

Woodstock area:
Church gathered in 1800 or 1801. Located in what is now northern York County. Divided over Allinism and close communion. Dissolved about 1810.

Prince William area:
Church gathered in 1800. Joined Association in 1804. Lathrop Hammond pastor in 1810. Probably divided over Allinism and close communion.

Kingsclear area:
Church gathered in 1801. Joined Association by 1808.

Keswick area:
Church existed by mid-1811, so possibly gathered in or before 1810. Close communion by 1812.

Nashwaak-St. Mary's area:
Church gathered in 1804. Meeting-house by 1805.

Waterborough area:
Church gathered in 1800 and Elijah Estabrooks ordained pastor. Joined Association in 1804. Succeeded to the 1793 meeting-house of the "Brooksites." Some of these Brooksites (Allinites) continued to preach against the Baptists after 1800.

Long Island area:
Church gathered in 1801. Charles Lewis ordained pastor in 1802. Dissolved by 1810. Allinite meeting set up.

Springfield area:
Church gathered before 1803. Benjamin Fairweather elected

pastor in 1803 and again in 1811 but not ordained. Reorganized as a close communion church in 1809.

Hampton area:
Church gathered before 1803. Centred in French Village-Smithtown and Gondola Point (not at the present Hampton). Benjamin Fairweather elected pastor in 1803 but not ordained. Soon dissolved.

Norton area:
Church gathered in 1800 and James Innis ordained pastor. Probably reverted to Allinism. Close communion in 1811. Meeting-houses in 1802? and 1814.

Carleton:
Church gathered 1810. Never heard from again.

Saint John:
Church gathered 1810.

St. Martins area:
Church gathered · by 1808, probably by 1805. Joined Association by 1808.

St. Andrews area:
Church gathered in 1806. Soon dissolved.

St. George area:
Church gathered in 1806. Soon dissolved.

St. David area:
Church gathered in 1806. Soon dissolved.

This poor wicked Place will afford little worth transmitting: but that last spring [1792] Mr. Wesley's Preachers have made an Incursion into this Parish and the country has ever since been overrun with them. Disputes, Quarrels and Divisions has been the unhappy Consequence — preachers by the meer Impulse of a heated Imagination have been Multiplied. I have been present at a meeting where about 25 or thirty have been bawling as loud as they could at the same Instant of Time consisting of Male & Female, old & young, and many of them Persons of infamous Character . . . .

Although these aspersions against the Wesleyans must be understood as coming from a Calvinist Methodist, it will be noted that James did not purport to be describing a Wesleyan meeting. Rather, he reported the kind of religious exercise the fervor of reformation had inspired.

By remarkable coincidence there is a second major account of such religious exercises, written about the same time as James' letter and in highly similar terms.[42] Its author, the Scottish traveller Patrick Campbell, located his encounter with the Allinites at Maugerville, but the term was (and is) loosely applied to the whole pre-Loyalist belt of Maugerville-Sheffield-Waterborough.

As we were conversing along, I heard a great noise in a house at some distance, on which I stopped to listen, and told the gentleman that there were some people fighting in that house; at which he smiled and answered, "That he knew the place well; that it was a house of worship, where a number of religious fanatics assembled at all hours of the night and day; that no body preached, every one prayed for himself, and the louder they roared, the more sincere and devout they were supposed to be; so that the one vied with the other who should bawl out loudest." When we had come nearer, I was struck with amazement at the hideous noise they made . . . ; I asked him if he supposed they would permit me to go in to see them; he said I might, provided I behaved properly, and did not laugh, or offer to ridicule them in any shape; that they would not prevent me, or give me the least trouble; thus encouraged, I went in, and found they consisted of about three score persons, of both sexes, all on their knees, and in tears, every one praying for himself, as already said, and bawling out, O Lord! O Lord! which were the only expressions I understood of what they said. After standing for a few minutes in the house, my hair almost standing on end at the horror of the scene these miserable people exhibited, I returned, and just as I was passing the window of their apartment, some one called out, that the devil was among them; upon which they all gave a yell, louder and more horrible than any Indian war hoop I had ever heard; and if the devil himself was to show his physiognomy in all the frightful grimaces ascribed to him in the middle of them, every door bolted, so that none possibly could escape his clutches, their screaming could not have been louder or more horrible. I returned to the road with deep impressions of the deplorable effects of fanaticism on the human mind . . . .

Again one must be aware of the observer's bias. Campbell was writing what he hoped would be an anecdote interesting to a British reader. One suspects that he pitched his tone and embroidered the truth with that end in view. Thus one might well discount everything that follows Campbell's description of the language he heard. The prefatory remarks by the "gentleman" may also be a stage-managed fiction. These non-essentials aside, Campbell's account is in close agreement with that of James. Both emphasized that which they found novel: the noise and "confusion" of a Newlight meeting, the posture of prayer (on the knees) and the equal role assumed by women. Both imply that the meetings described were led by local preacher-exhorters. This accords with what is known of Allinite religious exercises. The meeting described could well have been in Waterborough.

Religious ferment reached a new intensity beginning in the fall of 1792. In Waterborough the Allinite society led by Archelaus Hammond — a former member of the Horton-Cornwallis Baptist church — Elijah Estabrooks, Zebulon

Estey, Samuel Hartt and others experienced thirty to forty conversions between September 1792 and March 1793, all without aid of an ordained preacher. One young member of the society later recalled that meetings were held day and night, with much singing, confrontational exhortation and tears. Secular business, except for tending animals, was largely suspended. Early in 1793 there was also a considerable reformation on adjacent Long Island, promoted by the unordained Nova Scotia Allinite Edward Manning. At the same time the St. Stephen Wesleyan Duncan McColl was at Long Island, on his way to Sheffield where he would remain for the winter. McColl was disappointed to find that "an Antinomian preacher was in the house, very lively and full of animation," probably a reference to Manning. By the spring of 1793 Manning had spread the reformation to Kingsclear and the other parishes above Fredericton. Thereby Manning became the first Allinite to win an extensive hearing in a region populated almost entirely by Loyalists.[43] On 20 May he wrote ecstatically from Kingsclear:

> If ever I knew what GOD could do its since I came to St. Johns [River]. . . . I could not tell you all in a Week — Near 70 Souls (if not more) has found GOD to be all and in all and truly lives in green pastures, and grows as the Calves in the Stall.

It was probably after this that Manning did his most extensive preaching in Waterborough. Presumably he also sent for help from his brother James, who remained on the St. John River when Edward left. The only information on this point comes from the second of Edward Manning's widely-quoted letters on the subject, dated 10 October 1793.[44]

> I've much to tell you about St. John's but must omit at present. Certainly there has been the greatest reformation there I ever saw in my Life, And they thirst gloriously thirst for the Liberty of the Gospel. When I left them many were longing for the appearing of the Son of Man. James Preaches and it seems as if nothing stands before him.

79

Joseph Dimock supplies one last fragment of evidence. On 9 December he told Thomas Bennett that, "James Manning writes from St. John, that numbers of souls are baptized with the Holy Ghost."[45]   Nothing further is known of James Manning in the St. John valley.   Concerning Edward, one source relates that he preached with sensitive moderation in Waterborough, aware that his hearers were becoming skeptical of vital religion owing to the excesses of the Hammondites.

The Mannings' labours are the last evidence of the general course of reformation on the River St. John. All further reports focus on the irregular conduct of one particular group. About the end of 1792 five families separated from the main Allinite society in Waterborough because the latter had come to seem too restrained and "pharisaical". All five families (those of Archelaus Hammond, John Lunt, Thomas Perley, Aaron Cross and the late Joseph Garrison) were pre-Loyalists who had heard Alline himself preach; but in this they did not differ from their neighbours.   Commonly called "Hammondites" (or "Hammonites") after their senior exhorter, their effective leader was John Lunt, a man whom Walter Bates aptly characterized as "an abandonate profligate character, a sort of necromanser and fortune teller" who claimed prophesies and promised miracles, apparently with a semblance of success.   While the group's extravagances are documented in considerable detail, it is sufficient to note that they far exceed anything known of New Dispensationalism in contemporary Nova Scotia. The Wesleyan Duncan McColl, who lived in neighbouring Sheffield during the early stage of their career, provides a highly restrained summary of their conduct.

> [U]nhappily, five and twenty of them [the Allinites in Waterborough] fell under the influence of pride, [and] began to pretend to pre-eminence in the spirit's power and experience. They separated from the rest, and became extravagant indeed. They soon undertook to prophecy, and to speak with new tongues, and to work miracles. They called multitudes together to hear their new language, and to see the miracles about to be

wrought by a Mr. [Archelaus] H[ammond], and John L[unt]. By the time I got up they were fully engaged. They sometimes broke into other public meetings, and scattered the congregations . . . .

Neither McColl nor the memoirist Jarvis Ring (who attended some of the Hammondite meetings) could bring himself to name the ultimate cause of their downfall. Walter Bates, the aggressively Anglican sheriff of neighbouring Kings County, was less discreet.

[M]en and women, espetially young women, became so infatuated by him [Lunt] as to believe that what the Spirit dictated him to do he might do by himself or by a crew — no matter who. When once converted it was no sin for lambs of God to play all together. At one of his popular meetings held late of night a young lady having more modesty or not being suffitiently converted as to comply with his spirit — one of his pure converts by the name of [Archelaus] Hammon attempted to assist him in his design. On application to proper authorities they were both arrested and brought to trial before Chief Justice Ludlow in a Supreme Court at Gagetown, Q[ueens] Co.

It is natural to wonder whether Bates was led by malice to portray an isolated incident as if it were a whole course of religious conduct in which "lambs" were encouraged to "play all together". Yet surviving court records suggest that Bates may have been correct. Lunt probably did preach the notion of perfectionist love without sin, and with the preaching eventually came the practical experimentation that brought him and many others to grief. The legal proceedings opened in Queens County circuit court on 25 June 1793. Lunt was first charged with "a rape commited on the body of Sarah Garrison" (probably either his sister-in-law or his niece). Ten witnesses were called for the Crown and six for the defence. So great a number of witnesses suggests that the incident did indeed take place in a public (presumably religious) gathering and that most of the witnesses would themselves have been Hammondites: (for the Crown) Sarah Garrison (the alleged victim), Lathrop Hammond (Archelaus' son), Archelaus Hammond Jr., Jerusha Hammond (either Archelaus' wife or daughter), Sarah Hammond (Archelaus' daughter), Abijah Garrison (Sarah's brother), Joseph Garrison (Sarah's brother), Mary Angus (Sarah's mother), Gervas Yeaman, Zebulon Estey (not a Hammondite); (for the defence) Israel Perley, Elizabeth Hammond (relationship uncertain), Moses Perley (a known Hammondite), Daniel Perley, Nathan Palmer, George Fox. In the result Lunt was pronounced "not guilty".

John Lunt then stood trial for the rape of Sarah Hammond (Archelaus' daughter), and Archelaus himself was co-charged with "being present aiding and assisting the said John Lunt in the Commission of the rape". Only three witnesses were called for the Crown (Sarah Garrison, Archelaus Hammond Jr., and Sarah Hammond) and none for the defence. This may indicate that the incident was less public than the encounter with Sarah Garrison; but it may also mean the Crown's case had collapsed with the acquittal on the Garrison charge. This is rather suggested by the Supreme Court minute disclosing that the jury "without going from the bar f[ou]nd the Prisoners severally not guilty of the Felony wherewith they st[oo]d charged," Chief Justice Ludlow having presumably instructed them to that effect.[46] This turn of events was so unexpected and the public authorities so unwilling to allow Lunt to escape unscathed that they now for the first time charged him with the crime of blasphemy. Owing to the impossibility of proceeding immediately against him in this irregular and peremptory manner, Lunt was required simply to find sureties for his good behaviour for twelve months and appear at the next sitting of the court. In fact, however, there is no record of subsequent proceedings against him. Sheriff Bates recalled that he fled to the United States.

While the fact of these charges, resulting in acquittals, casts a rather uncertain light on the proceedings of the Hammondites, and while Walter Bates is hardly the most trustworthy of witnesses to the character of the religious exercises,[47] the two prosecutions do tend to support rather than contradict Bates' suggestion that sexual encounters among the "lambs" had become part of the Hammondites' divine discoveries. So many witnesses could not have been mistaken on this point; the charges must have arisen from real incidents. If this inference is correct — that physical contact of an intimate nature did take place — then the real question for the jury was whether the contact occurred in circumstances amounting to rape (*ie*, whether the girls did or did not consent). The jury was evidently persuaded that they did consent, which indirectly confirms the "religious" character of the proceedings. While Bates is the only source explicitly to portray the downfall of the Hammondites in these terms, Jarvis Ring hinted at much the same when he wrote that "a Grate deal of thair Exercises was don By dancing Before the Arck; the Most of thair Conduct and word was so Indesant and low I Shall not Record them".

This aspect of the Hammondite proceedings comes as no great surprise. Sexual innovation tied to religious speculation was one of the giddy novelties that flourished at the end of the eighteenth century. One extreme is represented by Lydia Randall of the Horton-Cornwallis New Dispensationalists, who proclaimed with Shakeristic fervor that all sexual relations were equally sinful. Simultaneously Waterborough's John Lunt was evidently preaching that sexual relations among converts was a divine privilege, without spot of sin. Similar notions had sprung up in northeastern Rhode Island forty years earlier in the wake of the Great Awakening, and southern Maine would generate a remarkably similar cult ("Cochranism") in the 1810s. In the longer term something of the same nature was one of the alluring miscellany of fringe beliefs that Joseph Smith bundled together in Mormonism.[48] However intense and remarkable the Maritime religious kaleidoscope sometimes appears, there is little that does not have its anticipation and parallel in New England.

Periods of intense religious activity were generally followed by a pulling back from vital religion. Among the Hammondites of Waterborough the reaction was complete. According to McColl they soon "denied the truth of all religion, and became a very gay and dressy people". About 1797 some of them — notably the Hammonds — removed above Fredericton to Kingsclear and Prince William. Here

83

they would eventually recover their interest in religion, but as Calvinist Baptists.

Unlike the Hammondites, the majority of the Allinite society in Waterborough (the "Brooksites" and the "Hartites" of Sheriff Bates' account) did not turn away from religion; indeed, in 1794 they finished a meeting-house (which was located, rather confusingly, in lower Sheffield). They did, however, become consciously more formalistic, permitting only one person in the meeting to speak at a time. Perhaps this moderation was what encouraged the Wesleyan leadership to try to win them over as a whole by examining one of their central figures — Elijah Estabrooks Jr. — with a view to ordination. As might have been forseen, Estabrooks' lengthly public examination foundered over the issue of perseverance.[49] Thereafter Wesleyan activity on the St. John fell off. In 1800 a lay leader among the Sheffield Wesleyans reported that there had not been a preacher stationed on the circuit for two years and that the society was on the decline.[50] Similarly, nothing is known of the further history of the Allinite societies in Waterborough and elsewhere[51] until January 1800 and the arrival of Joseph Crandall.

Until October 1799 there was not a single Baptist church in New Brunswick, no active ordained preachers[52] and very few Baptists.[53] Until 1800 the only ordained Baptist ever to have preached on the River St. John was David George in 1791, and his labour had been among Blacks. Yet between the close of 1799 and the close of 1801, open communion Baptist churches were gathered in Sackville, Waterborough, Norton, Prince William, Sussex, Woodstock, Kingsclear, Long Island and Salisbury. By the same date there were four ordained Baptist preachers in the province: Joseph Crandall in Salisbury, Elijah Estabrooks in Waterborough, James Innis in Norton and Gilbert Harris in Sussex. All four were pre-Loyalists and all had been deeply-shaped by Allinism. Likewise the churches in Waterborough and Sackville (and perhaps that in Salisbury) were almost wholly of pre-Loyalist membership, and there was an important leaven of pre-Loyalist ex-Allinites in all the others. This much being allowed, one of the most remarkable features of the rise of the Baptist cause in New Brunswick is the fact that most of these churches were composed primarily of Loyalists. In one sense this was a tribute to the zeal of the Baptist preachers, especially as compared with the Wesleyans. But it was also a reflection of the loosening of the original Loyalist consensus at the end of two decades in the wilderness. In the early days of the province, when the governing elite consciously set out to make their uniquely "Loyalist" experiment an hierarchical, erastian, genteel model for a British colony in America, they sent an unmistakable signal to the general populace that political dissent would not be tolerated and religious dissent would be severely discouraged.[54] Within a generation this elite-imposed consensus was in manifest disarray. Economically and demographically the colony was stagnant. Politically it was bitterly factionalized. Far from becoming the boasted "envy of the American states" New Brunswick was reduced to the status of a remote backwater in the empire's struggle against the revolutionary French. One symptom of this loss of hierarchical consensus is the fact that some Loyalists felt free to demonstrate that they had no more regard for the elite's Church of England than the Church had shown for them. The Loyalist frontier needed the social organization religion could provide, and Baptist preachers arrived at a time when many no longer feared taking a stand with religious dissent.

The man whose preaching planted the Baptist cause in the St. John valley was the newly-ordained Joseph Crandall. He arrived in Waterborough (evidently his destination) uninvited and unknown towards the middle of March 1800, having already stopped briefly with James Innis and the Allinite society in Norton.[55] Crandall was youthful (28), fresh from the exhilarating reformation in Sackville and along the Petitcodiac and sickly, all combining to make him a deeply affecting preacher.[56] Apparently a total stranger, Crandall soon brought on tears, groans and shouts of praise in a neighbourhood that had long been without preaching. He then moved on to the parishes above Fredericton, where he reawakened the Hammonds to the pull of vital religion. This was the very area where Edward Manning had had his most spectacular success in 1793 and where the Wesleyan Fidler had preached in 1796. In Kingsclear the wife of Albus Cole sought immersion. The spectacle of a dipping routinely attracted many sightseers, both pious and profane, and the novelty of this proceeding — the first immersion above Fredericton — brought out 400. Enthusiasm at the water side was contagious and, before he had done, Crandall baptized fourteen. "It was wonderful," he romanticized in old age,

> to see the young converts going around among the people as they came out of the cold water, praising the Lord and exhorting others to come and embrace the Saviour. Surely this was the beginning of good days; the work of the Lord spread in every direction. As they returned from the meeting they said the bible was altogether a new book to them.

Crandall then took the Baptist revelation to Bear Island, Woodstock (below the present Woodstock parish) and Keswick Ridge and village. He does not mention further immersions, but when he returned to Waterborough the people had already "heard about such numbers being immersed," suggestive of a tally greater than the fourteen in Kingsclear.

It was on this second visit with the "Brooksites" of Waterborough that Crandall's preaching on believer's baptism had the desired effect. After a ten-hour conference meeting a number of the society — including Elijah Estabrooks — signified willingness to submit to immersion. The following day a vast concourse, with many mockers, assembled by the water to see Crandall baptize ten, the very first of whom was Zebulon Estey, hitherto the leading opponent of immersion. The next day there were a further twenty-one immersions, including Samuel Hartt (of the "Hartites," so called) and the future preacher Jarvis Ring. Although no source mentions actual formation of a Baptist church, this is the most likely time. Thereby an Allinite society that had travelled together for upwards of twenty years became the first Baptist church in the St. John valley.[57] In July of that year the church elected Elijah Estabrooks as teaching elder, Zebulon Estey as church clerk, and Joseph Estabrooks (Elijah's brother) and Edward Coy (Mary Bradley's brother) as deacons.

Crandall departed Waterborough late in May or early in June 1800. On his descent he preached a few days on Long

Island (often used as a general term to include the adjacent shore of Hampstead and Wickham parishes). Here he "immersed quite a number, some of whom had experienced a change some years before," a reference to Duncan McColl's short-lived Wesleyan society and to Edward Manning's labours in 1793. Crandall then apparently crossed the Bay to attend his first meeting of what became the Baptist Association. But while he was still in Waterborough a letter had arrived for the society from Edward Manning, soliciting an invitation to come over and join in the work.[58] The society (perhaps now a church) responded by sending to both Manning and Horton's Theodore Harding to request visits. Crandall carried these letters to the Association, which resolved at the end of June to "give Edward Manning and Joseph Dimock a certificate on their leaving for St. John [River], to assist a people to come into gospel order and to ordain their minister".[59]

In the event it was Manning and Harding (rather than Dimock) who were sent. Together with Crandall they arrived in Waterborough via the Petitcodiac in September 1800. Several more were immersed and, on 15 September, Elijah Estabrooks was ordained. By this time the church had thirty-five members. All but a handful were closely related to Estabrooks.[60] Crandall and Harding remained less than a week. Seven days after Estabrooks' ordination they were ordaining James Innis over a Baptist body in the parish of Norton. This, western New Brunswick's second Baptist church, was initially composed of eighteen members. Shortly thereafter Harding and Innis gathered a Baptist church of about forty members in Sussex.[61]

Edward Manning did not return to the east with Crandall and Harding but journeyed instead to the parishes above Fredericton to revisit his converts of 1793. On 27 November 1800 he gathered a church in Prince William with forty-seven members.[62] One of its deacons, John Barker, was a pre-Loyalist but its other deacon (John Manzer) and its clerk (William West) were Loyalists, as was the great majority of its members. It may have been at this time also that the Baptist church in Woodstock was gathered.[63]

The year 1800 was the *annus mirabilis* of the Baptist cause in New Brunswick, but 1801 was scarcely less so. Elijah Estabrooks was now active on the St. John River, three times visiting as far north as Prince William in 1801. By year's end that infant church would boast "one Hundred members and the gates of Zion still throng'd with converts". In August James Manning arrived on the River to join in the work. Travelling as far as the Woodstock church (lately visited by the young Waterborough Baptist Jarvis Ring) Manning experienced that "resemblance of Heaven" for which Alline had taught his followers to strive here on earth. Under his preaching the young people in Woodstock came "alive like a be[e] hive jest ready to swarm". On his descent Manning gathered a church of about thirty in Kingsclear.[64] On Long Island (below Waterborough) he encountered Theodore Harding making his second visit to the region. On 12 Octoer 1801 the two formed a church there, no doubt embracing the adjacent shores as well. It was on Long Island that they first heard Charles Lewis preach and, in Manning's words, "I Could Say I was pleased to heare [the] engenity and Simplosity of the dear man".[65] James Manning continued on his return to Nova Scotia but Harding passed the whole winter of 1801-02 on the St. John. Here he was joined by Gilbert Harris, newly-ordained pastor of the Baptist church in Sussex.[66]

JAMES MANNING

James Manning's initial visits to the River St. John, in 1793 and 1801, followed closely on those of his younger brother Edward, as if it were Edward who had directed him there. This circumstance reinforces the historiographical impression that James Manning lived in Edward's shadow. The fact that he was Edward Manning's brother was itself sufficient to ensure that the early Baptist historians would canonize James as one of the denomination's "Patriarchs"; but of all the saints he is distinctly portrayed as the least. Bill's *Fifty Years* dismisses him after only two pages. In the seven-page "Memoir of the Rev. James Manning" published by the denomination in 1835 Manning himself is scarcely mentioned.[67]

Certainly one reason James Manning had to be handled with care was his unhappy end. But perhaps even more important was the fact that he died in 1818, decades earlier than the other Baptist saints. Unlike them he did not live long enough to become a mythical figure in his own lifetime; and,

88

unlike the other Patriarchs, he did not live to complete the transition from Newlight to respectability. Dying in 1818 Manning would not see his converts enter the Baptist ministry, get his name among the founders of Acadia or become merely "evangelical". By the time of the 1835 "Memoir" he already seemed the kind of preacher that Baptist leaders — exhilarated with recent inroads into Halifax's Anglican elite — wanted to forget. Manning may have been, as his brother defensively wrote, "a plain, honest Country Preacher, verry inelegant ... [though] acceptable to God," but he was not the stuff of Baptist hagiography.[68]

Concerning the first thirty years of Manning's life little is known. He is thought to have been born in Ireland between 1763 and 1765, the son of Peter and Ann (Carroll) Manning.[69] By 1770 the family resided in the Nova Scotia township of Falmouth, having perhaps spent a few years in Pennsylvania. In the census listing for that year Peter Manning's name appears adjacent to those of William Alline (father of Henry) and Malachy Cagen (step-father of John Payzant). Although the family was Protestant it had little access to vital religion until the Allinite reformation began in 1776. James and his brother Edward (three or four years his junior) are said to have heard Alline preach in their father's house; if so, this must have occurred in the summer or fall of 1776 as Peter Manning was executed later that year for the murder of John Payzant's step-father.[70] This, rather than conversion, was the searing event of James Manning's adolescence. Ironically, conversion — when it finally came in the reformation of 1789 — was under the labour of John Payzant. It was presumably at this time that he joined the Horton-Cornwallis Newlight church. In the list of church members his name appears just ahead of those of his sister Nancy and brother Edward.[71]

Whether James, like Edward, entered on an itineracy as early as 1790 is uncertain. What is known is that by 1792 both Mannings were prominent among the New Dispensationers disrupting order and discipline in Payzant's Newlight church. Recalling this time Payzant distinctly characterized the Mannings as "Preachers".[72] The next year James followed Edward on a tour of the St. John valley, where they were the first (White) Allinites to preach in eleven years. Of his

89

brother's labours here Edward Manning wrote that, "it seems as if nothing stands before him".[73] Despite the sweeping enthusiasm of such a comment and the fact that James was in Waterborough at the very height of the Hammondite extravagance, he was not remembered as having added to the local troubles.[74]

In 1795 Manning made the first known of his many visits to the Passamaquoddy region of Washington County Maine (principally Eastport and Machias) and adjacent Charlotte County New Brunswick. Little is known of his labours among the Loyalists of Charlotte[75] but a good deal about some of his encounters on the Maine side of the water.[76] Like the Yankee communities of pre-Loyalist Nova Scotia, this frontier region of New England was settled in the 1760s, at the end of the French wars. From the time of settlement to the mid-1790s there was only one religious organization east of the Penobscot. Given such an opening, a succession of Newlight preachers, spearheaded by the Mannings, brought the region into first the Allinite and then the Maritime Baptist fold.

Although the first Allinite to visit the American shore of Passamaquoddy may have been James Murphy in 1794,[77] the earliest positive evidence of Maritime penetration is James Manning's tour of 1795. On 9 July of that year Manning reported that he had been at Moose Island (Eastport) two Sabbaths "and the Lord has been preasent at every meaton". There was "a glowrous work in these parts". James Murphy, also, was present (lately returned from Nova Scotia, it seems); his labours had been "bless'd in a wonderful manner". Manning contemplated going next to Machias and then deeper into Maine. He concluded his letter by urging Edward Manning to come over on his own preaching tour. Perhaps that is what occurred, for one of the American sources reports that in January 1796 Edward gathered an Allinite church ("part Baptists and part Pedo-baptists") on Moose Island.

To this point James Manning may well have continued to live in Falmouth, but as his brother aptly observed, "Falmouth was a nursary for Preachers till they began to Preach and then a Poor place to instruct and support them".[78] In 1796, at the age of thirty-two, James took a wife — Francis

(Fanny) Farnsworth of Annapolis County — and it was likely on this occasion that he removed there and associated himself with a religious society in Lower Granville.[79]

In the summer of 1796 Manning again crossed the Bay into eastern Maine. By 10 June he had been in Machias some time and was about to welcome his brother. Together with James Murphy the two Mannings invested Machias steadily for several months. Unlike Eastport, Machias had a long history of regular preaching. James Lyon had removed there via Boston from Nova Scotia in 1771 and acted as the town's settled Congregational minister until his 1794 death. A hymnwriter of note and a man of minor literary attainment, Lyon was the very antithesis of a Newlight. The discipline of his church expressly provided that admission would not require a public relation of experience. Edward Manning later heard that Lyon had admitted that in twenty years of preaching in Machias he did not know whether he had been instrumental in a single conversion.

Towards the end of 1795 Lyon's place was filled by the young Clark Brown. Brown may have been less formal than Lyon but never really had his chance for, by mid-1796, there was a Newlight separation, the first in the town's history. One product of the separation controversy was an exchange of three long and remarkable letters between Stephen Jones, one of Machias' leading Congregationalists, and Edward Manning. Jones' letters are as apt a catalogue of the objectionable features of the Newlight style as one could find anywhere. Among his points were the following:

> [M]y objections against you, your brother [James] & M'r [James] Murphy are a firm belief, that you, and they, have usurped the office of a minister of Jesus Christ, neither of you being regularly called thereunto, according to the order of the New England Churches; neither have you, in my oppinion, the necessary prerequsites of a Gospel minister.
>
> I believe, that you, & the other two persons, I have mentioned are men of warm immaginations — That your minds have been wrought upon, and that a Spirit of Enthusiasm has seized you, and that you have

91

worked your selves up into a religous frenzy.

Does it not discover great vanity in you, to declare that you, are absolutely sure of heaven ... .

Does it not discover Great vanity in you, to intrude your self into another mans vineyard, and to suppose yourself the only instrument, the wise, and Holy God, can make use of, to convince, & convert sinners, & edify the saints.

Did not M'r Murphy discover a great deal of vanity ... when he declared that no minister, ever went to heaven, who penned his sermons, & preached by notes; or that had received a liberal Education.

Did not you discover a great want of charity when you declared, that you believed, M'r [Clark] Brown learn[ed] the prayers by heart out of some book ... And was it not a piece of ill manners, (to say the least) in you, to ask him, if he could not repeat it. Was it not a breach of Christian charity, in you, publickly to mention him, in your prayers, as an unconverted person.

[Their prayers are] a jumble of words, not half articulated, & bellowed out with all the violence of a mad man, & which cannot be understood by the audience ... .

[I]t appears as if you thought you might treat the Divine being in the same manner [as a familiar spirit], and that he was bound to assist you when called upon.

Jones further charged that Edward Manning sought to drive Parson Brown out of the town so that he could obtain a settlement for himself. Half of this prediction came true when Brown resigned his pastorate in 1797. The Congregational church and society were so divided by the Newlight incursion that they could not settle another orthodox minister until 1801. The fate of the Allinite church is unknown.

In 1797 James Manning moved to put some of the extravagance that had characterized the Machias campaign behind him by submitting to baptism by immersion. On 10 September 1798 he was ordained over a (presumably) Allinite church in Lower Granville.[80] In 1797-98 Manning joined with

92

several of the other preachers in bringing Harris Harding to heel by forming a ministerial association. Yet, perhaps significantly, it was James Manning who was called to Yarmouth to dip Harding on 28 August 1799.

> [I]n the time the ordanance of Baptism was admin[i]ster'd the people look'd as Solm as the grave. It seem'd like Christ Comeing to Jordin M'r Hardings Comeing to the water. After he came from the water He pray'd with the people in the Street. It seam'd as tho he Rec'd a doble portion of the spirrit. Some of the dear Christian[s] broke forth in prayses of God and the Lamb.[81]

The year following Manning joined in the bitter step of excluding Payzant from the Association, just as he would later fall in with the move to close communion.

The surviving minutes of the Baptist Association disclose that Manning was a frequent attendant at annual meetings. Yet he seems to have played no role in the wider affairs of the Baptist cause. More significantly, Manning was evidently unable to show much leadership at the local level. In February 1808 the American Baptist Isaac Case spent a week preaching at Lower Granville. He found the people "kind and attentive" but

> They complained of being low in religion. I did not wonder that they were, for I found that family worship was greatly neglicted. Brother James Manning is their minister; he is a good honest man.[82]

The earliest statistical view of the church, in the Association minutes for 1809, shows seventy members. By 1814 it was down to forty, where it remained until Manning's 1818 death. Thereafter the church could not attract another pastor for four years.[83] In 1812 Edward Manning wrote that his brother had only a small farm and received little help from his people, a situation which worsened towards the end of his life.[84]

Perhaps it is an illusion created by the chance survival of source material, but Manning's greatest sphere of activity and importance seems to have been in eastern Maine and the

St. John valley of New Brunswick. He is known to have been in Machias or Eastport in 1795, 1796, 1815 and 1816-17 (twice). He visited the St. John valley six times (1793, 1801, 1808-09, 1813, 1814, 1817), perhaps more often. In contrast, his tours within Nova Scotia seem to have been largely confined to visiting the site of the annual Association meeting. Like his brother, he preferred to preach far from home, where people did not know him. .So far as the evidence suggests, the only churches Manning gathered were those at Kingsclear and (with Theodore Harding) Long Island in 1801.

Baptist historians, hard-pressed to find something special about James Manning, mentioned his effectiveness in public prayer. This is given credibility by the memoir of Jarvis Ring, who recalled him as having a

> lively farmileer turn of mind, Easely muved. When the love of God was Burning in his sole, all would see and feal it. His adress to the unconvarted was Solemn. The Sinner would trembel under its Power. His prayars was of a powerful Charricter. But few ever drew Nearrer to the Marcey Seet.

Ring, who first met Manning in the charged atmosphere of Waterborough in 1793 when he was thirteen, also remembered him as a "chearful lively happy man," in contrast to his sober brother. Edward would spend his time among the elders of the house but James would go into the kitchen and talk to the women and children.[85] Perhaps James noticed wives and children in particular because he was so deeply attached to his own domestic circle. Half of his surviving letters are to his wife Fanny, and they are deeply affectionate. When she was carrying their first child he wrote her that he too felt the "little burden" and that it "sweetin[ed]" his trials.[86] (At the same time he urged her not to be backward in asking the neighbours for whatever she might want). Readers of his 1801 journal will notice the several occasions when Manning feels his mind "stole away to my little famaly". Altogether, James Manning seems to have been engagingly earnest, modest and without guile.

Manning's journal reflects fluctuating mental and bodily health. Physically he may possibly have died of a

94

"lingering consumption".[87] Mentally his distress began (as in 1801) with a true Allinite sense of his daily unworthiness; that (as he explained to Fanny) "nature is in oposion [opposition] to Grace". Another time he referred to "my Self who am allways Complaining".[88] One suspects that, as he grew older, much of the cause of his depression was his inability to stir up his own moribund church in Lower Granville, and, beyond this, that he missed the potent reformations of his Newlight days, before he settled into a pastorate. By the standards of his Allinite youth he was a failure.

Late in 1816 Manning began a three-month winter visit to Eastport and Saint John. In both places he found the Baptists distressingly divided.[89] On his return he suffered a mental breakdown. On 21 May 1817 he disappeared from his home. He was "3 days and nights lost in the woods being deranged during the time and come to his recollection the 4th morning, and returned himself to the settlement without any human aid". Wrote Manning's nearest neighbour:

> He eats but little & wishes to talk less. Stupidity or a painful anxiety of mind are his constant companions. He still declares himself unfit company for either Saint or Sinner, the one is a burthen, the other a grief to him.

His trouble, as his brother Edward admitted, was "mental altogether".[90] Yet by the middle of July 1817 James was

> able to go among the dear people, and visit, is more cheerful, takes more food, reads, hath taken up the delightful, and much neglected duty of prayer in his family; and the prospect is that he will be restored to his bodily and mental health ... .

Late in 1817 Manning again sought to prove that he still had what it took to excite a reformation, and again his impulse was to do so at the scene of his Newlight success in Eastport. To Fanny he reported, "Thare seames a grate attention; Some has profest to be Converted".[91] Success may have renewed his spirit, but on his return to Granville he weakened in body. On 27 May 1818 James Manning died at the age of about fifty-four. His brother Edward comforted himself with the thought that James had "sure and certain hope of a glorious immortality".[92] Meeting four weeks after the death the Baptist Association also carefully emphasized that, in the end, he had "departed in the full assurance of the heavenly rest".[93]

* * * * *

Unlike the published memoirs of Henry Alline, John Payzant, Joseph Crandall and, to a great extent, Joseph Dimock, and unlike the James Innis manuscript, the James Manning document printed below is a true "journal". It is a daily narrative of events composed primarily for a semi-public purpose, although in Manning's case it also resembles what would now be called a "diary". Keeping a journal was a practice Maritime preachers inherited from their New England spiritual ancestors and, more directly, was part of the imitation of Henry Alline. Its principal use was to allow an itinerant to give an account of his successes on his return home. At one point (17 October) Manning noted that he wrote the journal for "the Satisfaction of my dear partner at home". More generally, Manning was prompted to keep his "minets" (as he called them) simply becuase that was one of the things ministers were supposed to do.[94] Apart from Dimock's, Manning's is the earliest journal surviving for any Maritime Baptist. The volume in which it is found deals entirely with the New Brunswick visit. Whether he kept earlier or later journals is not known.

The portion of Manning's New Brunswick journal to survive runs from 2 August to 28 October 1801. Two leaves (four sides) are missing from the front of the journal, suggesting that Manning had been at Saint John since about mid-July. The final entry in the journal as printed here is its actual termination. In editing I have supplied paragraphing and a few sub-headings and endeavoured to suggest sentence structure through use of an oblique stroke. Where the end of one sentence and the beginning of another is unclear I have let sentences run together. Otherwise, this edition attempts to be faithful to Manning's spelling, capitalization and what little punctuation he supplies. Two letters Manning wrote during the currency of the Journal (although not part of it) survive and are given below. Then follows the Journal proper.

96

[Manning's letter to his wife, dated 20 August 1801 at Saint John]

Dere Fanney   These are to let you know that I am well in health more so than I have Been Sence I Came from home and knowing That you will be uneasy to heare how I do I take pen to let you no/ I pray the [this] may find you Enjoying the Same blessing and our poor little Son [James Edward]/ I did not know how much I loved him/ I hope he gets better for I no if he does not that your life must be very un happy and of Corce I must Share in Some of the feelling/

Since I Came to this place I have found real frinds/ the Lord be prazed for his Goodness/ The people Comes more and more to here and I feal my mind very much lead to reason with them of the Rightness and of Judgment to Come and I have ever remarked when eve[r] my mind is lead in Such a manner that Good was dun/ oh that GOD might lay me down in the dust for I See that I am awful prowd and prown to follow my very desearful which all ways brings [me] into darkness but oh the morning Stare stil[l] leads my way/

next Sabouth I Exspect to administ[er] the ordanance of baptizem/ how long I Shall [stay] in this place I Cannot assertain but hope I sh[all] not Stay any longer than the Lord Calls me to be Sarvasable/ I have Invations every day to go to one part or other but I Cant find it [my] duty to leav[e] this place/

I feal very empatiant to heare from you/ I have wrote before to you and Exspected to have a letter by the packet/ I have like ways wrote to Mr [James] Delap [Deacon of the Lower Granville church] and told him to Call and See you/ Mr [Elijah] [Esta]Brooks Came last week from passmaquda [Passamaquoddy, *ie*, Eastport, *etc*] and told us of the work of GOD in that place and likeways of Mr [James] Mu[rphy] Comeing home [to Granville] with Mr [Daniel] Shaw which eased my mind on the acount of the people being destitute of preaching but I feal quite [quiet] as to that/ I hope you will not make your self uneasy but wate with patiance/

I have a grate deal to write but have not time/ therefore must Conclude/ you must Give my love to Mr & Mrs Hall and and [*sic*] all the famaly and all the neighbours/ you must tell

97

Mr Murphey to write to me for I long to heare from him/ till
him that he must Go over all the ———— and preach every day
and not fear none but God/ tell Mr Hall to see that the[y]
Contribute for Mr Murphy and you must till him to Come and
Stay as much as he Can with you for mee and I will pay him
some time or other/ I am your loving

Husband James Manning

PS   Mrs [Daniel] lovit sends you a fan as a
Complyment and a grate deal of love and longs to see
you in this place/ you mus write nead [Ned, *ie*, Edward
Manning] and tell him that I Say that he must Com [to
Granville] next month and stay 2 Saboths for I am on
his masters Busnes/

[Manning's letter to his wife, dated
10 September 1801 at Woodstock (parish)]

My Deare Fanney   Thes[e] are to let you no that I [am]
well both in Body and mind for which blessing I desire to bless
GOD/ I hope these may find my dere wife with Such a sence of
God that you may pray for your absent Husband/ I hope my
dere son [James Edward] gets better/ I hope to find him
Walking when I Come which I exspect will be in the Corce of
five or six weeks/

if I had time I have a Grate deal to write but I must Cut
short onely tell you that I feal devine preasence/ I have meatin
all most Every day/ Esq'r [Zebulon] Easty has Rode with me
as my Companian 75 miles up the Rive[r] and found me a
horce bridle and Sadle and Stays with me till I Return/ last
Saboth I Baptized 8 persons and admini[s]terd the Supper to
nigh 100 Communicants and oh I Can assure you it had a
resemblance of Heaven and I Exspect to have a Conference
meatin to morrow in this place and the Sacrement on Saboth
for the first time/

you must give my love to all frinds and till them I oft
think of them for the[y] are a people that lays near my heart
more so than any other people under Heaven/ I dont no how
well I love them till I am a way but Emportant [work] Calls me

in these parts for the[y] are with oute healh like sheep with out a sheapard/ dere Child dont siffer for any thing that you want for the LORD will provide/ I feal as tho we never should want for any thing that is neadful for the jurney/ I Exspect to get you a few notions when I Come to St Johns/ I am now one hundred and forty od miles up the River and the people is Calling for me evry day/ I am Shure That I should not be able to go to all the places in a yeare/ I am your loveing Husband

till death doth us part James Manning

PS   the Barrer [bearer, "Mr Gates"] is wating/ I dont Exspect to write any more/ I have not Reciev'd a line senc I Came away/ I stay'd one Saboth in St. John wateing to here from home/ I have wrote three times senc I Came from home/

MANNING'S JOURNAL
[two leaves missing]

[SAINT JOHN]⁹⁵

[**Sunday, 2 August 1801**] .[. . .] did heare and here sow as to live/ Some Sines of both kingdoms was to be desarned [discerned]/ Some opposition appear[ed] which ever to me is a good sine & Several frinds Came in to See me and it seamed as tho we felt Some thing like the Desciple[s] when there harts burn[ed]/

[**Monday, 3 August 1801**] the next day I spent in visiting Some frinds/ some times my mind would be stole away after GOD and at other time darkness wou'd role in on my mind and overwhelm me but the day brakes and my soul breathes her native are [air]/

[**Tuesday, 4 August 1801**] tuesday evening I went to here the Methodest and I Could not help for runing from such Darknes/ Good LORD deliver us/ Such a ja[r]gan of nonsense/ I went to my lodging where a few of our frinds got to geather/ we talked with grate freedom a[n]d we sang and pray[e]d/

[**Wednesday, 5 August 1801**] Wednesd[a]y I felt Indesposed in body but a sellemnty [solemnity] on my Sperrit/ I met with several frinds from up the River which pres't me to go up the river/ I oft times would feal my mind stole away to my little famaly in Nova S[c]otia/ oh how strong a Creature Love strik[e]s the Sence wheth[e]r [whither?] the warm affections moves nor Can we drive them thince [thence]/ Wednesday evenin had another Meatin and a Grate number Gave there attendance and a very grate Sollemnity Cloth'd the Congration [congregation]/ the Ange[l] of God stood by me/

I [had] freedom in prayer . . . . [torn]
in speacking . . . . [torn]
Meatin the . . . . [torn]

a nother .... [torn]
acomidat- .... [torn]
and woma- .... [torn]
oute in- .... [torn]
home .... [torn]
and I Co- .... [torn]
son of pea- .... [torn]
and Could .... [torn]
Come .... [torn]
Earth as .... [torn]

[Thursday, 6 August 1801] Thursday I was Invited to meet with a number of women to tea and I fealt some thing of the Saints Everlasting reast [rest]/ I had a meatin at Six Oclock and I

[torn] .... lead to speake of man
[torn] .... depravity and his
[torn] .... -overy by Christ
[torn] .... so free as I
[torn] .... before I
[torn] .... -stress in my
[torn] .... that ____
[torn] .... that he that
[torn] .... go into
[torn] .... kills
[torn] .... be kil[le]d
[torn] .... is very
[torn] .... nature

[Friday, 7 August 1801] Friday evening thare was a lecture[96] and the day is lay'd out to visit diffarant persons/ many ware [were] my Exceruse [exercises?]/ I had some sense of [the] lost world and Desires to be more engadged/ that night I felt a good degree of liberty in speaking/ the People was very attentive/ the same [some?] were pressing for my staying/ the little few who know the truth seam'd very much encouraged that the Lord is aboute seting down the foot of his tower/ the[y] Came more and more to here [hear]/

[**Saturday, 8 August 1801**] Saturday I felt so well/ I could say with the poet I find my self a stranger here and seek my home and am not here/

[**Sunday, 9 August 1801**] Met a Sonday morning as usual/ the people gave a very good hereing/ as our afternoon meatin did not go in till five Oclock I went to here Dr Boile [Mather Byles][97] and I can truely say he was the best that I ever heard/ he spake very well on the nagat[i]ve and in the general on the possative [positive]/ my going to Church[98] brought a grate many to meatin/ I felt a good Deal of freedom/ in the evening [after the meeting] I happen[ed] in Conversation with one who held to free will and I believe a good man at hart but he felt him self Confused and declined advanceing any farther/ took my leave of [him] for that night/ he was to have a meatin the next night/

[**Monday, 10 August 1801**] Monday I felt destress'd in my mind/ walked from place to [place] but was not left all toget[her]/ I felt some doors open and felt freedom in Speackeing/ at night I went to here the man for mention'd but he was very much Shut up and brocken/ I endevored to pray for him that GOD would derect him/

[**Tuesday, 11 August 1801**] the next day I went up to the mash [Hazen's Marsh][99] and had meatin and all tho [although] thare was not a grate many to meatin GOD was there to fulfill his promis/ the few which new the truth felt Glad in there God/ I felt my mind a Good Deal lead [led] to Speacke of Christian Exspearance and it had a good affect and [on?] people in general/

[**Wednesday, 12 August 1801**] Stay[e]d all night and next morning Came to town very much Sunk in mind/ had meatin in the evening/ felt some help from God/ the people seam'd desireous for another meatin/ I notif[i]ed the people That I would Speacke the next night/ I went to my lodging/ felt rather unwell in body/ took some Cold [?]/

[**Thursday, 13 August 1808**] the next morning felt very unwell/ I felt Sore all over till I went to prayer/ oh for more faith to lead me on my way _____/ in the Corse of the day I felt very much Exercised with bodily pane which affected my mind/ it seamed a Cross to go to meatin but knowing my feeling was not to be the standerd it was with mee as it was often before/ thare happen[e]d to be tow [two] Quakers[100] in town and they Gave thare attendance and after I had don speackeing one of them spocke and gave oute a meatin the next Day/ the 5th hower [hour] of the day I went home to my lodgeing and my good friend M'rs [Daniel] Lovit[101] got me herb drink and warm'd my bead [bed] but I felt a wake to GOD and sleep departed from me/ I had Some Sence of GOD and felt gratutude to my Heavenly Father/ oh that I might allways feal Such a sence/

[**Friday, 14 August 1801**] next morning Brother E Brooks [Elijah Estabrooks][102] Came in from Passmquday and his Countenance planely shew[e]d that he felt the Sun shine of the Gosple/ he brought Good news/ he inform[e]d us how many of the dear Children of GOD Came forward and wase Baptized and how Broth[er] Murphy [James Murphy] felt his Chains fall of[f] him/ he told me that he purposed gowing to novascotia which Eased my mind as I was so uneasy about home/ I hoped I should not stay any longer/ [*one leaf torn out*]

[**Monday, 17 August 1801**] a munday had no meatin/ spent the day in visiting the people/ Some destres in my mind for none of my oponants would give me oppertunity to talk with them/ I see more of my own nothingness/ some times I truely felt a stranger on earth/ I was maide to pray that GOD would derect me to dow [do] his will/

[**Tuesday, 18 August 1801**] a tuesday I went among the Soldears [at Fort Howe] w[h]ere I found a number that newe the lord and I cou[l]d See the Lord was kind to his Poor desciples/ tow [two] poor women Confin'd to there beads [beds] rejoic'd in the Lord/ I coul[d] say it was a good visit/ I Could Call on his name and Cou[l]d find him

103

answer my request/ that Evening had meatin at the [Reversing] Falls[103] w[h]ere a grate number of people Came to here and I think I never saw any people Behave better perticularly a number of officers/ I stay'd all night/ my mind was so much awake that I Could not Sleep any that night/

[**Wednesday, 19 August 1801**] next morning had some oppertunity to Converse with those of different Sentiments to my Self/ it took all my appilite [ability]/ the Lord stood by me and I belve [believe] Some good was dun/ Wedensday evening I had meatin [in] town wher[e] a grate number gave there attendance I belve [believe] for good/ the people seemed to be hungary for the word/ I gave oute meatin the next night among the black people/

[**Thursday, 20 August 1801**] I felt very unwell all the day/ it seam[e]d as tho I shou[l]d not be able to speacke but I went to meatin and the Lord was my strength/ I went home with my friend M'r [George] Harding. [104] went to bead [bed] but got but little sleep/ felt a good deal wandering in my mind/ my thoughts stray'd to my Famaly and from one thing to another but the night passed a way and the day brooke and a Sun without Clowds/ I felt some releece in my mind but week in body/

[**Friday, 21 August 1801**] Confin[e]d my self to the house perty much the day being very warm and as I was to have a meatin that night att the [Reversing] fall I maid [made] these minets and read some/ oh that all my life might be a serious[?] of watchfullness and prayer/ I gave my attendance a cording as I had appointed and spacke with some freedom and the people seam'd to be very ____/ I walked in to town that night/ felt some wary [weary] after speacking and walking so far/

[**Saturday, 22 August 1801**] A Satterdy I felt glomy and distrest/ a Seterday night I felt the bofiting [buffeting] of Satan/

[**Sunday, 23 August 1801**] I arose arely [early] the next morning and got ready to attend to administer Baptizm and oh what a number of people got together altho the day was very desagreeable/ I felt very much freed in my mind/ went at the ushal [usual] our [hour] and I dont no when I felt the Gosp[e]l run so free/ it was a good day and likeways in the afternoon/

[**Monday, 24 August 1801**] Got some Cold/ did not feal sow well a mond[ay]/ wrote Some leaters to my frinds and maide these minits/ I gave oute a lecter [lecture] a monday night and a Wed[ne]sday night and was undetirmin'd wheather I should go home or Stay or go up the river but I hoped the lord will open the way that I should go/ had meatin munday night at M'r [George] Hardin[g']s and all tho I felt very unwell in Body the Lord spacke by me/ the people Seamed to give very Grate attention/

[**Tuesday, 25 August 1801**] the next day Rain'd very hard and [I] felt unwell/ I pay'd Several Visits in the Corse of the day/ in the afternoon I went to a frinds House according to appointment to meet with a number of frinds and we had a very good time/ we stay'd till 10 oclock/ went to prayer before we parted/ went home to my lodging/ felt very unwell with my Cold/ took some drink and had my bead [bed] warm'd/

[**Wednesday, 26 August 1801**] felt a little better the next day/ in the after noon met with a number of my frind[s] and I fealt the Son of peace to my Soul in deed/ after tea went to meatin where a grate number of people and I felt Some freedom to Speacke to them/ this was the last meatin I Exspected to have had but while I was speackein it Seamed to be wright to stay longer and I gave oute tow [two] leckters in the week and a Saboth/ oh that I might feal more engadged in his Bless'd Cause/

[**Thursday, 27 August 1801**] felt not so well/ felt both body and mind indesposed but attended acording to appoint[ment] and felt some freedom to speack to the people/ many felt there harts affected and it seamed to think that never man spocke as I did altho I did not feal as

105

much devine life as att other times but I was lead to speacke of the trials of the real seeker makeing some destingson [distinction] betwixt the tow [two]/ felt very unwell with a very bad Cold/ went home to my lodging and took some herb drinks/

[Friday, 28 August 1801] next day felt some better/ pay'd some visits to people that I had not before/ went up to the [Reversing] falls where I had appointed a meatin and was Bless'd with Some good degree of liberty and the people seamed to pay very Grate attention and I believe one day or other the[y] will tell of Conviction under my Speacking/ Stay'd all night/ got a prety good night rest/

[Saturday, 29 August 1801] got break fast and then went into town desireous to here from home as I Expec[te]d the packet in but when I found no letter I was very much sirprized at the Carlessness of my frinds assperaly [especially] Mrs Manning not sending me word how my little Son was but I Concluded that he was better or else I should [have] had a letter at all avents [events] and Concluded that my letters had not Come to hand and from those Considerations I Concluded to go up the river/ Exspected to meet with a number of frinds in the after noon/ met according to appointment/ felt very much shut up/ it Seamed as thare was no possabillity of Saying one word aboute Religion but how short sited Creatures we are/ GOD make[s] way where ever he sees fit/ I put a question to one of the Company and the Conversation began and I did not no how to leave of[f]/ I was lead to tell my mind very freely/ oh that I might be faithful in the Descharge of my duty till my dieing breath/ I went home to my lodging and very dark in my mind and and shut up in my mind/ went to bead [bed]/ got Some Sleep in the fore part of the night but felt very uneasy in the latter part/

[Sunday, 30 August 1801] in the morning felt still shut up and felt a Cross to Speacke but thanks be to god who still helps me in all things and in all places/ [He] Sent his angel with a life Cole [live coal] from his alter and tought'd

106

[touched] my lips and the dere [dear] people of god felt there harts melt under the word/ darkness flead away and I felt an all mighty arm to deliver my soul from death and unto life/ in the entermisson I was desir'd to go and see a sick woman/ I went acording to promise and pray[e]d with her and I belive shey felt the truth and rejoiced in the Lord/ meet in the after noon and a very Grate number Came oute to here [hear] and it was desearnable [discernable] to every Eye/ I took my leave of the people/ felt some tried in my mind wheather it was right for me to go up the rive[r] or go home but upon the [w]hole I Concluded to go up the river/ Sat oute from the [Reversing] falls aboute ten Oclock with little or no wind and gat a Cross the grand bay before before [*sic*] the flood/ jest as the flood maide we got in[to] the long reach and the wind began to blow/ never stopt but once till we gat to Long Island/ had little or no sence of GOD/ felt rather sick till I got to the Hous[e] where I desind [designed] staying and·all at wance [once] my mind awoke and the first thing I [k]new I was a Singing and all tho it was an open boat I never felt the least Cold/ the people was in bead but the[y] Soon got up and gat Supper and I truely felt my self at home/ I went to prayer in deed it was answered in some answer when the woman of the [house] brooke out Rejoicing and blessing the Lord for Sending the[m] his Sarvant wance more/ She afferm'd [affirmed] that the Lord would wance more Stir up his people/ they sayd that for ten days she felt such distress that no tonge Could not tell/ her Son a young man felt his Chanes fell of and he Saide that he did not want to go to bead/ we went to bead but did not Sleep much for I Exspeted to Set oute arely [early] the next morning for fredericton with the posst [post]/

[LONG ISLAND]

[**Monday, 31 August 1801**] after breackfast next morning the man of the house tooke me to the publick house where I wated [waited] but all to no purpose for the post went a long in the night but the people did not no it/ I felt very uneasy as I had appointed gowing along and not Stoping [here] till I did return/ I walked up and down the fields Concluding Some times not to go any farthe[r] but found no light there nor in any thing Else/ a[s] blind as a bat/ onely Could Say the Lord [k]nows [my] mind/

[Tuesday, 1 September 1801] September the first maid thes[e] minit/

[WATERBOROUGH]

[Wednesday, 2 September 1801] next morning Concluded to Stay at long Island over Sabouth as thare was no bote [boat] Came to hand/ felt very uneasy in my mind/ gave out word that I should be thare on Saboth and three lecters in the Corse of the week/ I was jest gowing over the [River] to the main[land] and finden [a] Cannow a gowing up the Contry/ I gave up my Engadgements and Sat [set] oute up the River/ gat up to Waterboroughy a little before sundown and Brother E Brooks [Elijah Estabrooks] thought it Best to have meatin and I Could not say that I would not speacke all tho I felt very unwell/ the peopl[e] came togeather and the LORD meet in the midst/ Stay'd at M'r Rings/[105] sat up till 12 oclock/ Could not sleep/

[Thursday, 3 September 1801] Next morning Sat oute to go up the Contry attended by B[rother] Elijah E Brooks [Estabrooks] & Brother [Zebulon] Easty/[106] Stopt at Several frinds/ Stopt at Capt [Thomas] Peaters[107] to Deaner where we Recived this worlds goods/ Rode to St Stans wher[e] we had a lecter and I was lead by the skilful hand to Speacke to the harts of the people/ I felt my message from GOD/ Stay'd at my werthy frind M'r Rans/

[PRINCE WILLIAM — QUEENSBURY]

[Friday, 4 September 1801] Wrode [rode] 5 miles before breckfast to my worthy frind M'r [George] Sifers/[108] wrode to the french Vilige felt a good deal unwell in Body which maide me ride past several houses/ did not stop till I got to Brothe[r] [Albus] Coles[109] where I was kindly Received/ Stay'd till we got deaner [dinner] then wrode [rode] Several miles/ Stopt at M'r Hamon[d']s[110] where we [were] recev'd with very Grate frindship/ did not entend Staying all night but we Could not get away/ Stay'd all night/ we Convers'd with grate freedom abought the thing[s] of the Kingdom/ sang and pray[e]d and went to bead/

[Saturday, 5 September 1801] next morning got Breckfast/ we sang and pray'd and the glowry fild every hart/ the unity of the Spirit and bond of peace was felt/ attended at a Conferrance meatin[111] whare a grate number of true belivers meet in Covenantes love/ I Could bless the LORD for the blessed oppertunity/ oh what hart melting was among the dear people of GOD/ a number told the Dealling of GOD with there Souls/ after meatin went over the River to Capt [Ebenezer] Browns[112] where Every attintion [was given]/ felt rather unwell went to bead after prayer/ did not get much sleep thinking of the dutys of the day/

[Sunday, 6 September 1801] meet at half after nine for worship/ I spock some of the order of Gods House and jest as meatin tow [two] Came forward and told the dealling of GOD to the Church and after preaching [we] Repard [repaired] to the water and [sic] and tow Came and told there Exspearance/ oh it was Easy to pray and easy to sing/ it was a happy time/ not one I belive that Came forward but felt the Holy Spirrit/ they Sang from the water to they House and there I think the Supper was administe[re]d/ oh what a Glowry appeard in the Holy ordenances/ Glowry to GOD for all those means of Grace/ it was a good Glowryous day to many to many [sic]/ I belive Grate Good was dun for the Cause/ after meatin I went home with a M'rs [?] [Nicholas] Whealar[113] whose heart was warm'd with the love of God/ we sat up till the middle of the night talking abought the things of GOD/

[BEAR ISLAND]

[**Monday, 7 September 1801**] next morning before I was up a young woman Came to See me that was Converted when I was Convert'd/ Shey told her Expearance and it was the means of blessing to all preasent/ we Sang and pray'd and oh what an awful sallmnty [solemnity] rested on every mind/ the Lord Came in a Small still voice/ I took my leave of them and went over the river to Capt [Ebenezer] Browns and took our horses and wrode up the river/ Stopt to dinner at Brother [John] Manzar/[114] after dinner went up to bare [Bear] Island to attend a lecter where a grate number Came to here the word all tho it was Harvest time/ bless'd be god it Seammed to be harvest Spirritually/ oh how the harts of the people wept and lean'd on the bosom of the dear redeamer/ the little Children praysd [praised] they [the] worthy name of the worlds restorer/ went home with one that was a grate opozer [opposer]/ he would not leat any of his famaly [seek religion] but now he seam'd to pay every attention and all the famaly had Exspearance [experience] of the way of life and Salvation/ stay'd to teay [tea] and conversed freely aboute the thing[s] of another world/ the man of the house went with me where I was agowing to Stay all night/ oh how it affected my hart to See how GOD was geathering in his Elect/ he Stay'd till after pray[e]rs/ the man of the house got talking and seam'd as tho Sleep had departed from us all for after we went to bed we Could not go to Sleep/

[**Tuesday, 8 September 1801**] next morning I felt quite unwell when first I got up but after I pray'd in the famaly I felt better/ got our Hors and Sat oute on our jurney as we ware to have a meatin in the afternoon/ Stopt at Several

110

frinds and a good deal of freedom appear'd in Every place/ Thare [were] Several diniers prepar'd for us but we did not stop till we got to the place we were to have meatin when gladness appear'd in Every Countannance/ I spocke and there was a word with in a word/ oh how the tears flow'd from all most every one/ we stay'd all night where the time was taken up in Singing and praying/

[WOODSTOCK-NORTHAMPTON]

[Wednesday, 9 September 1801] next morning we Sat oute to Go up to the opper Settlement [Woodstock]/ we left our horses and went in a bote/ it raned in the morning till breakfast time/ then it Clear'd of/ I Could not help noticing how favorable the weather was ever Since I left St Johns/ oh that I may be ever desposed to sarve my GOD and my fellow men/

[Thursday, 10 September 1801] Wednesday [*sic*] September the 10th 1801/ at night [on 9 September] got to my frind Dows[115] where gl[a]dness appear'd in every Count[en]ance/ Thare was a meatin gave oute next day [10 September] aboute 3 oclock/ I went in the fore part of the day I went among the people and found Some engadgment in the minds of the people but a good Deal of preadegise [prejudice] in many/ how it did make me feal for the Cause of God/ how to proseed I did not no/ I though[t] with in my Self that god wou'd in his Good time/ the people flock'd to meatin and the LORD Stood by me and gave me liberty to preach his own Gosple/ the people seamed very much affected after meatin/ a num[ber] of the y oung people oute dores got Rejocing/ oh the[y] Extol'd the worthy Jesus/ the[y] soon cal[le]d the people to geather/ after meatin I went home with M'r [George] Hartly[116] which was in a black Sleden [backslidden] State/ we sat up very late/ we pray'd and went to bead/

[Friday, 11 September 1801] next morning felt grate freedom to pray for the famaly/ after that I felt destress'd in my

111

mind/ Cal[le]d at several houses as I went to the place I was to have meatin and the Lord stood by me/ I felt a Spirrit to pray and to preach/ the people aspeacking/ The young people was alive like a be[e] hive jest ready to swarm/ I stay'd after meatin at the house and while the[y] was Geating tea a young man Came in and told me how M'r [Amos] gates[117] was to set oute next morning for novas[c]otia/ I sat down and wrote to M'rs Manning and after Supper I wrote these minites/ Stay[ed] all night/

[Saturday, 12 September 1801] next morning went to breakfast to brother [Samuel] Mores/[118] payd tow or three visits before dinner and in the afternoon had a Church [conference] meatin/ the meatin was open'd by Singing and prayer/ acording to there order the[y] Chose me as moderatur/ the Church open'd there minds very freely to my Satisfaction/ there was some small differances but the[y] for gave and made [up]/ 13 Came forward and told there Exspearances to the Church and I think some of them told as clear [an] Expearance as any that ever I heard/ my heart was Like a cup flowing over/ oh that I might all ways feal as I did/ backsliders was brought back/ oh what hart Repentances appear'd/ after meatin I went home with a young marrid Cople [couple] which loved the Lord which had not been baptiz'd so we spent a very Good evening/ I felt a heart to pray that GOD might Give them strength to Come forward and join the Church/ I got my answer that the[y] would obey the Lord/

[Sunday, 13 September 1801] went to meatin where a large Company Came to here and see the ordanance [of baptism] administer'd/ I preach'd in the forenoon and after meatin Repar'd to the water where the Lord appear'd by his Holy Spirrit/ I Baptiz'd 13 not only in the name but in the Spirrit/ Sang up from the water/ then gave the [Lord's] Supper after I had pray'd with the Candidates and gav[e] theme the right hand of fellowship and a Charge as to there duty/ oh bless'd be the name of GOD/ it was a Glowrious day/ I took my leave of the people/ oh what a affe'g [affecting] Sight it was to See the dere [dear]

Lambs of God all in tears bid[d]ing me farewell many a tear was Shead/ that evening I went to See three Famalys/ Return'd to my lodgens where a number had Collected as I was a gowing away next morning/ we Sung Several hyms and young Converts went to prayer/ oh how it affected my hart to here the young lad Confess his faults to all mighty GOD and promise to be for the Lord and none else/

[PRINCE WILLIAM — QUEENSBURY]

[**Monday, 14 September 1801**] next morning we arose with the Son and Several of the neighbours Came to here prayers/ The[y] Sang the fare well hym and it Seam'd as tho the angels came down to men/ I prayed for the blessing of GOD to Rest with them/ Came down [the River] aboute 3 miles/ Stopt at a poor mans and got denner/ after denner went down in a Connow [canoe] about 7 miles where we left our horses/ got Some Refres[h]ment/ The[y] press'd us hard to Stay all night but we thought best to Ride Seven miles to brother [Amasa] Coys[119] where we ware Receiv'd with open arms/ Stay'd all night/ felt a good deal tir[e]d/ had but little sence in prayer/ got but little Sleep/

[**Tuesday, 15 September 1801**] got up next morning and pray'd with some freedom after breakfast went across the river/ had a long Spell of Conversation/ walked 2 miles to see my frind M'r Johsling[120]/ Stay'd all day & it being a very hurri[e]d time [ie, harvest] I Could have no time to Converce before night/ Spent a very agreeable time that evening/ sat up very late/ talk'd very freely/

[**Wednesday, 16 September 1801**] Next morning took my leave after prayer/ went a Cross the river to attend a lecter for the last [time] in that place where a grate number for a week day gave their attendance/ I felt grate freedom to preach the Everlast[ing] Gospel/ the people was very much affected/ after meatin Several told there Experance and wished to be babtized before I went a way/ we

113

attended and the Lord gave his Preasense/ Sung back from the water and I maid a Prayer at the house and bid theme fare well/ I shuck hands with old and young/ took my Horse and Rode 4 miles to Capt [Ebenezer] Browns with my frind E[s]q'r [Zebulon] Easty and the[y] ware very glad to see us/ after prayer went to bead/ got one nap/ after that Slept no more/ we got a talking/ Got up and attended prayers/

[**Thursday, 17 September 1801**] we went after breakfast to see one of the neighbours/ there was but little freedom to talk aboute the Soul/ I felt very much Shut up and destress'd in my mind/ Returned and Got dinner/ after dinner got our Horses up and took our leave of my frind/ we swom our horses a Cross the River/ Cal[le]d at brother [Nicholas] whealars and had some Conversation with Sister [Ruth?] his wife a dear Child of GOD/ they press'd us hard to Stay all night but as we had several places to stop at we beged to be Excqused/ after Calling at the places that we desi[g]ned that after noon we went to brother [John] Barkers[121] where we desi[g]ned to Stay all night/ I felt indespos'd in body and I lay down till tea was ready and then I got up and entering in to Conversation I felt better/ one of the neighbors one of the Church Came in who acted as a Clark [William West][122] and [as] the[y] were [a] young [church] the[y] wanted Brother [Zebulon] Easty to Give them some Insite [insight] in Keeping there Record and after there business was over we Sang and pray'd and the people of the house went to bead [bed] all but the man of [the house]/ he and [I] Sat up tow hours after the famaly went to bead/ then I went and Strove to get asleep but it Seamed as tho' all Sleep had departed from me/ I dont think I Slept one half hower all night/

[**Friday, 18 September 1801**] got up in the morning and felt Some indesposed/ oh that GOD might Cause his face to Shine upon me his unworthy Sarvant for I more and more see without his preasence I cant do any thing/ we took our leave of the famaly/ Pay'd Several Visits and in the after noon held meatin at M'r Lowtrip Hammons [Lathrop Hammond]/ Preach[ed] with Some freedom/ Stay'd all night/ Convers'd with Some freedom and gratest frindship appear'd in all the famaly/ I got a very Good nights rest/

[KINGSCLEAR CHURCH GATHERED]

[**Saturday, 19 September 1801**] next morning I arose praysing [praising] him that gards our Slumbring moments/ pray'd with the Famaly/ took my leave and went down to the vilidge/ stopt at tow or three Houses and found there minds Engadged to go forward in Church order/ met at Brother [Albus] coles and held Conferance meatin where the Power of GOD was Clearly Seen among the people/ a number as many as 32 Embody as a Church of Christ/ a grate number of those told there Expearancs/

[**Sunday, 20 September 1801**] on Lords day a very grate Congragation Collec't from all parts of the Contry/ I was oblidg'd to Preach oute dores and the LORD be praysed/ I think I never felt better to preach in my life/ the people of GOD appear'd like a morning withoute Clowds/ after I had dun preaching one man told his Expearance and then repar'd to the waters/ Sang as ushal [usual] and pray'd and then spocke to the people/ baptized 13 on the profession of there faith/ oh what a Salimnity Cloth'd the people/ as the place of administration was near by we sang to the house and proseed'd to brake the bred/ the number that Serounded [surrounded] the bord [*ie,* table] of GOD was about 60/ it was a happy season/ after meatin went home with Mrs Bidole[?] and if I was an angel the[y] Cou'd not [have] pay'd more attention and a number of yo[u]ng people Came in/ I sung and pray'd and then went to M'r John Easty[123] to Stay all night/ fell in discourse with the woman of the House which was fil[le]d with horrid delusion/ talk'd a grate deal and her talk seamed so horrid [that] after I went to bead I Could not go to sleep/ I felt allmost destr[oy]'d/

[**Monday, 21 September 1801**] Got up by day light and went to Mr Coles before the[y] ware up/ it seam'd as tho I had got

115

into a new world/ a number of the dear Children of GOD we Sang and pray'd with [had] some sence of the grate Redeemer/ took my leave of the people/ pay Some visits in the fore noon/ Convers'd with a yo[u]ng woman from the States and I belived that the Lord would Converte her/ went to Brother Thomas Everrats[124] to denner/ a number of Christian men talk'd about Church order/ after denner when I was taking my leave of the Famaly I felt tenderness of hart and the oldest daughter felt her heart brack [break]/ the woman of the House went to the next house and had some happy moments Conversation a bought the Kingdom of the dear redeemer/ it Seamed as tho we Could not part/ I went to see a poor sister which lost her husband/ Shey [she] was a widow indeed/ I went to Brother Jeorge Everott to Stay all night and [met] a number of Christian frinds/ we Convers'd freely aboute Church order and the ordanances of the Gosple/ we Sang and pray'd with and for the Company then preasant/ I got a very Good nights Sleep more sow than I had for several nights/

[**Tuesday, 22 September 1801**] next morning, I pray'd and felt a good deal of liberty in my mind/ Came down to Brother [George] Sifers before dinner and after dinner wee went over the River to M'r John Nevers[125] where a number of the op[po]sing world came to here/ I was lead to Speake very plane/ I thought I was lead very perticular/ after meatin Came back over the River where we spent the Evening Singing and pray'd before we parted/ got a very good nights sleep/

[FREDERICTON]

[**Wednesday, 23 September 1801**] next morning I felt very Sollom/ had some sence of the necessity of having GOD to be our Supporter/ I felt Strong ties of nature/ it appear'd as much as ever it did that man and wife was no more twa[i]n but one flesh/ oh that I might Ever do my duty at home and abroad/ after denner we rode to town

116

[Fredericton] where we had meatin/ a grate number
Came to here/ I felt my mind some engadg'd to Seet [set]
life and death [before them]/ Some Came down ten
miles/ Stay'd all night at M'r Ran/[126] up very late/

[**Thursday, 24 September 1801**] next morning I went to
Breack[fast] at M'r Mcenturs [McIntyre's?]/ felt some
Engadgement of Soul for thire Souls redemtion/ Some of
the neighbours I pray'd with them and for them took my
leave of my frinds/ got my horse to go over the river/
stopt at M'r Nevers [in Maugerville] and the[y] would not
let me Come away till we got Dinner/ The man was in a
deep Decay not long for this world/ his wife had a very
tender mind/ I trust shey will be found with a Robe of
rightiousness/ oh that my life might be Spent in the Cause
of GOD/ after dinner I went over the feray and rode
Seven miles and then got a boate and went over the river
[to Lincoln] and had a lecter at Mr Glashers [Glasier's][127]
where a grate number of sensere people [met]/ I felt the
Lord indeed/ oh how the young lambs of Christ drew
near/ I did not exspect to Satay [stay] after meatin but the
people would not take any denial but I must have
another meatin/ I gave out for another meatin at night
and the house was Crowded/ I felt the Lord—/ I felt after
meatin very much wore out/ I could not slee[p] any all
night/

[**Friday, 25 September 1801**] next morning I got up earely to
get across the river but the man would not let me go till I
got breackfast/ then I walked three quarters of a mile
then Cross'd the river/ after[wards] walked three miles
[to] where my horse was keept/ I felt a good deal fitegude
[fatigued] the day being very warm/ Stopt at Several
houses/ wrode down to Waterborough/ Stay'd all night
at M'r Rings/ I felt very unwell/ I thought I was a gowing
to be sick but the grate phisian [physician] Stood by me/
Brother E Brooks [Estabrooks] and a number of frinds
came in and the Evening was spent in talking aboute the
things of the Kingdom/ we sang and pray'd/ got a prity
good nights rest/

117

[Saturday, 26 September 1801] next morning I felt the Lord both Sin[g]ing and praying/ payd some visits in the fore noon/ in the afternoon attended a Conferance meatin where a number of the dere Children of God meet to hold Conferance/ I pray'd to open the meatin/ I felt my Soul affected with a Sence of GOD['s] Eternal love/ after meatin I rode up to Sheffeld where I was to hold meatin on the Lords day/ Stay'd with M'r [John] Wason[128] a man which had been Confin'd to his house in a very strange way but jest began to go aboute his Bisness/ he says that he Exspe[c]ts he was Converted before he Came from the States/

[Sunday, 27 September 1801] Sunday morning I went to Deacon Smiths[129] to breackfast and then went to meatin/ I felt very unwell/ I was allmost affraid to go to meatin/ I felt dark in my mind/ every thing appear'd dark/ The methodest had meatin Close at hand/ I thought they did it on porpose because I was to preach that day as it was give oute Some time before/ the[y] Sent all the way to St John for M'r James man[130] to Gard the flock but the[y] ware disapoint'd and so was I for the darkness of my mind was Clear'd away and the people Came from all parts/ the house was full/ I felt that I was dowing the will of GOD/ I Could desarn [discern] light to brack oute on the right hand and on the left as so many notes/ in the entermision I went home with Esq'r Burphey/ attended on the after noon with a grater number to heare/ I gave out three lectters/

[Monday, 28 September 1801] A Munday I had meatin at M'r [Evan] Monrows[131] [in Maugerville] where a very solom aud[i]ance gave there attendance/ after meatin I went home with Capt Thomas Peters where I meet with the gratis[t] frindship/

[Tuesday, 29 September 1801] next morning I took my leave of the Famaly/ payd Several visits as I Came down [to Sheffield]/ had a meatin at M'r [Samuel] Upton['s][132] where I felt the holy oile of gladness/ the harts of GODs people felt the rock and God of there Salvation/ Stay'd all night/ Converc'd very freely and feelingly/ did not rest very well not because I had not good lodging but my mind got roveing/

[Wednesday, 30 September 1801] next morning went to breackfast [in Sheffield] to M'r Coperthets [Hugh Cowperthwaite]¹³³ people which favour'd the Frinds [Quakers] but was very frindly/ then walk'd down three miles to M'r [Samuel] Brideges¹³⁴ were I stay'd to get dinner/ after denner we went a Cross the River [to Burton] where I was to have a lecter where a number of people Came to here [hear] the word/ I did not feal so much freed as at other times/ after meatin I went home with Capt [Ebenezer] Hatherway¹³⁵ a bout a mile frome the place that I had meatin/ I rode his horse and he went a foot where I Spent a very agreeable evening/ they ware of the Congregational order/ we talked very Freely aboute the ordanance of Baptizem but no ways hard/ Sang and pray'd and Retir'd/

[GAGETOWN — WATERBOROUGH]

[Thursday, 1 October 1801] next morning a rose Soon after sun rise/ went throw the duty of the famaly/ after brackfast took my leave of the famly/ pay'd several visits in the Corce of the day/ felt Some destrest in my mind/ warid of my Jurney but not altogether With oute Some sence of GOD/ got to Esq Eastys [Zebulon Estey of Gagetown] where the people Express'd all sines [signs] of frindship/ I Sat down and wrot[e] these minits/

[Friday, 2 October 1801] in the morning I went to the Ship Yard where there was a number of those which Christ Chose oute of the World/ I went from house to house/ I felt my mind a good deal ingadged in Conver[sing] with both Saint and Sinner/ Return'd to M'r Eastys to dinner/ after dinner I went to See an acquantance to spend the after noon/ I Could say in Some degree the Son of peace

119

was there/ after tea we went over the River to Waterborough to attend a lecter where a grate number Came to here the word/ [At] the first singing the LORD appear'd and likeways the first prayer/ I Could Say with Thomas my LORD and GOD/ did not feal So much in Speacking/ after meatin some frind[s] stay'd/ We sat up till mid night/ pray'd be fore we parted/ got some Sleep which Refress'd my waresom [wearysome] body/ in the morning I felt Some Sence of that God that gives me life and Streng[t]h/

[Saturday, 3 October 1801] after breackfast went to brother [Benjamin] newcoms[136]/ Convers'd very freely abought the grate thing[s] of GOD and a nother world/ Exspe't [expected] to Spend the day in visiting my frinds/ oh that my Speach might allways be as becomes my grate profession/ oh for a more lively sence of Jehovah/ I went to dinner to brother [David] Currys[137] a dear Child of God/ in the after noon took tea with Brother Kines [Kinney?][138] with a number of frinds/ went to Brother [John] Mashs[139]/ Spent a very agreeable Evening/ lodged with D'r [Charles] Gunter[140] a dear Brother in Christ/ he Came 25 miles to be at meatin on the Lord['s] day/

[Sunday, 4 October 1801] next morning before it was day I lay awake as I allways do but lay still/ The dockters hart was fild with love to GODs eternal Son/ we got up and went to prayer and Lord appear'd/ then I went to breackfast to a M'r harts[141] who has pretended to preach one who is very aronias in prensiables [erroneous in principles]/ we talked very freely/ we agreed to disagree/ then went to meatin/ I got to the meatin house before any body got there/ it being a very Stormy day the people did not attend as soon as the[y] do in the general/ I preach[ed] with Some devine assestance/ the people Gave very grate atendanc[e]/ I administered the Supper to [a] number of true Communicants/ after meatin I went home with Brother Loden and a number of frinds and got tea/ after tea I went to Brother [John] mashes to attend a meatin where a grate number Came to here/ I felt as tho I Should not have one word to Say but the Lord stood by me/ it seam'd as tho the people Could not get away/ after meatin I went to a frind['s] house to Stay all night/ felt a good deal wore oute/

[Monday, 5 October 1801] next morning went to take breackfast with a nother frind/ felt my mind Some engadged with GOD/ Cald at several houseses in the Corce of the day/ Some times I Could [think] that I was waried [wearied] with my jurney and long'd for my releace/ oh for paytiance [patience] to wate the time/ oh that my guide might allways be with me/ throw [through] him I Can do faliantly [valiantly]/ as I was on my way of the river I had to Call at every house and had meatins every day which Caused me to feal allmost wore oute/ I Easpect [expect] to have a lecter over the River at Mr Kiers [?] and as I was a gowing over the river I felt my mind awake with Some Sence of GOD and all tho it was in the Evening and dark I belive thar was tow Hundred people Came to here the least of all Saints Speacke/ I felt God to Be my Strength/ oh what an awful Sence of GOD Struck the people/ GOD appear'd in Singing and in prayer and in Specking/ I Could Commend my Self to all there Consiances [consciences]/ the last singing was alittle resemblenc[e] of Heaven/ I took my leave of the people and lay'd down there duty to both Saints and Sinners/ I went home with Br [Zebulon] Easty/ Stay'd all night got a good nights rest/

[Tuesday, 6 October 1801] next morning after breackfast took my leave of the Famaly/ thare was not one but was affected/ Mr Easty Sat me over the river and engaged to attend me in the after noon to a lecter down the river/ Stay'd [at] Mr Ring['s] to dinner then payd t[w]o or three visits and took my leave of the people and it Seam'd very affecting for the tears flood [flowed] very plentifully/ a number attended me to the meatin/ Stopt at Brother David Curry['s]/ then [we] went to the place of Worship where a number of the dark world Came to here me that never did before/ I felt dark at the first of the meatin but before meatin was Concluded the LORD appear'd and

121

preached his own Gosple/ Stay'd all night where I had meatin/

[**Wednesday, 7 October 1801**] in the morning Sang and pray'd before I Came away/ went to the mans mothers an old Christian woman to breackfast/ Sang and pray'd/ then went over the river to another of hir Sons a dear Brother in the Lord/ Stay'd to dinner/ after dinner went down the River three miles and attended to meatin to Brother Petters[142]/ felt not so much freedom as at other times but not all to geather with oute some sence of GOD/ Stay'd all night and was kindly entertaned/ We talked very freely as we Ware old acquantenc[e]s/ the night was far Spent before we ware aware/ went to bead betwixt 12 & 1 oclock/ got one nap/ Exspected to go over to gadgetown the next day but that night there was a vessel Came down from fredrictown and Came to anker Jest at the door and [**Thursday, 8 October 1801**] the next morning by day the[y] Sounded there horn and I got up and got abord/ the[y] landed me on long Island/ went to see several frinds and the[y] Sat me on the mane Land where the people see[m]'d very Glad/ Stay'd all night at Brother Lawranc[e]s where a good many of the neighbours Came in/ I felt very free to Converce with them of Christian duty/

[LONG ISLAND CHURCH GATHERED]

[**Friday, 9 October 1801**] next morning I went over [to] the other Side of the river to Brother [Clement] Lukes[143] where gladness [was] plain in every Countananc[e]/ Stay'd to dinner/ after dinner atten'd a meatin whare a number of Senseare Soles Came to here the word/ Brother Theodore Harding [of Horton] preach'd on his way up the river St Johns with Some freedom/ after meatin we sang several hyms and felt the divine preasence/ Conversed aboute the ordore of GOD['s] house and the necesissity of GODs people attending to the desepline of the Gospel/ went home to Sister Chase/ appointed a Conferance meatin the next day at M'r

Clarks[144] on the other Side of the River and on the Sabouth on the Long Island/ Stay'd all night att Brother cases/

[**Saturday, 10 October 1801**] next day we went to Brother Vanwarts to dinner where the gratest frindship appear'd in Every Countanance/ it was Somthing like the gates of Heaven/ the people was those that I was made the Enstrement [instrument] of there Conversion [in 1793]/ after dinner we went across the river where a grate number of people Came to geather on the Occation/ Brother [Charles] Lewis preach'd before Brother [Theodore] Harding and my Self and I Could Say I was pleased to heare [the] Engenity [ingenuity] and Simplosity of the dear man/ I witnessed to the truth and so did M'r Harding and pray'd/ then a number told there Exsperances and I we [*sic*] Sang and I pray'd and after meatin we went home to M'r Cases/ Stopt at Brother Vanwarts/ Stay'd to tea and the house appear'd something like the gates of Heaven/ then we went to Mr Cases/ Stay'd all night/

[**Sunday, 11 October 1801**] next morning being the lords day attended meatin on Long Island at Brother Gerows[145]/ M'r [Theodore] Harding preach'd in the fore noon with freedom and in the after noon I preach'd and the glowry of the [Lord] Shone all around/ We appointed a Conferance meatin at M'r Elithay Clarks[146] and appointed preaching in the morning/

[**Monday, 12 October 1801**] I preached and then a number told their Exspearances and then Brother harding administer'd Baptism to 12 persons/ a very grate number came as Spectators/ then retur'd to the house and proscee'd [proceeded] to forming a Church/ those that Came forward then and before Stood by them Selves and Brother Harding pray'd and lay'd hands on the Church and gave them the right hand of feloship and then I gave them the Charge before the Congregation [*ie*, the "society"] and likways [likewise] there many dutys/ then we Sang and I pray'd and Brother Harding dismist the

123

people/ then I gave oute meatin the next day and the day following at several plases and on Sabouth at Wickham at Brother George Cases[147] and that the LORDs Supper Should be administer'd/ Went to little river [in Hampstead] that night/ Stay'd all night at Brother Lawrances where a number of the dear Children of God Some [of] which [had] followed of the Lord Jesus in Baptism Sung and pray'd/ got a good nights response/

[Tuesday, 13 October 1801] next morning went to Brother [Marcus] Palmors[148] to breackfas and in the forenoon went to see several frinds and in the afternoon attended a lecter/ Brother [Theodore] Harding preach'd/ the people seamed very sollom/ I pray'd with Some freedom/ after meatin we went to the other Side [Wickham] of the River/ went to M'r [Clement] Laces/ Stay'd all night/ felt glomey and some destresst in my mind/ felt no better all night/

[Wednesday, 14 October 1801] remain'd So the next morning/ after breackfast Got our horses and went up the Wasademoeck [Washademoak]/ Crossed the ferry and went to Esq'r Colwells[149] and held meatin Where a very Sollom assem[b]ly attended to here the word/ a number of the people that attended was brought home to GOD by my Enstramenty [instrumentality]/ the[y] wanted very much that I Should Stay longer with them but I dast [dared] not Stay for I felt very uneasy aboute home/ nothing but the Cause I trust that I am engadg'd in would Keep me so long as I have been from home but I told them if the LORD Shew'd me that it was his will I would Stay longer/ Stay'd all night at M'r Colwells/

[Thursday, 15 October 1801] next morning M'r [Theodore] Harding after breckfast got his horse [and] Sat oute on his Jurney up the River/ we parted in good frindship and the[y] Sat me over the river whare I was to visit whare I was to visit a number of my [heavenly] fathers Famaly/ took dinner at M'r Merrits/ he was not a Christian but his wife was one that loved Christ in deed and in truth/ the[y]

124

wanted me to Stay all night but as I had engadged to Stay that night at M'r Clarks I Could not Stay/ I bid them farewell/ Stopt at several houses on the way/ som[e] of those that did not profess to no Jessus but the[y] seammed to shew the gratest frindship emmagin'le [imaginable]/ Came to my frind Clarks where I stay'd all night/ Convers'd very freely/ the old man and his wife both loved the LORD indeed and in truth/ got a very good nights rest/

[Friday, 16 October 1801] next morning read and pray'd in the famaly/ took my leave of the dear old people not Exspecting ever to see them before I saw them in a world of Spirits/ Stop'd at M'r Sans[150] a Christian man/ Stay'd Some time there and then he Sat me over the river/ I felt my mind very solom not much Engadged but rather destress'd/ went to Brother Gerows where the[y] ware a good deal hurid [hurried] in the world/ I read the bible more then I had for some time/ thought a good deal aboute home/ Stay'd till night/ then got set over the river/ the wind blow'd very hard So that the people were afraid to go over the river/ I felt some dissapointed as I had promis'd to be thare that night but jest at night thare Came a tow mast[ed] boate from wasademock [Washademoak] by/ I asked them if the[y] would set me over the river and the[y] Saide the[y] would if I Could get a bord/ I waided of[f] to my [k]nees and had to do the Same on the other Side/ I could not help vi[e]wing the hand of GOD that derects all things for the best/ got to my entended lodging where we spent the Evening in frindship/ did not rest so well as I had for some time/ I felt troubled aboute geting home as I had been gon[e] so long/ oh that GOD might grant me paytiance in all thing[s] that I might have a single I [eye] to do his will/

[Saturday, 17 October 1801] next morning I wrote these lines for the Satisfaction of my dear partner at home/ oh that the king of Glowry might seport [support] her in all her trials as it is hir lot to have a travelling preacher/ in the fore noon went with my frinds to one of there Sons to dinner/ Spent the day Somethin in a wor[l]dly Sence till

125

Evening/ a little before we came away the man Parants desir'd that I Should pray before we parted/ that open'd a door not onely to pray but to Speack/ after tea we went to a nother of there Sons where I was to Stay all night as I was to have meatin the next day there/ we spent the evening Conver[s]ing about the thing[s] of a nother kingdom/ I felt some distress in my mind and rather indesposed in body/ got but little rest all night/ aboute 2 oclock it began to rane/

[**Sunday, 18 October 1801**] and kept on till day and all day showery but not so hard as it did in the morning/ it being Sacrement day and it being the first [for the Long Island church] I Exspect'd a grate Many to give there attendance but the lord Saw better than his unworthy sarvent did but bless'd be his holy name he brought his dear Children togeather and a grate many more and the blessed Lord Spocke by me his unworthy Sarvent/ I preach'd twice and then administ[er]'d the LORDs Supper to a number of real broken harted Souls/ the people as well as the Communicants was Very much affected/ after laying down the many fold [manifold] duties to the people I took my leave of them all/ after meatin I with a number of frind[s] went to brother Vanwarts and spent the evening/ felt some Sence of the good hand of GOD which was with us throw [through] the day/ I pray'd before we part'd then went home with brother [Charles] Leweus/ after we went throw [through] the duties of the famaly I went to bead/ Got one nap and I Slept no more/ my mind was very much tossed all the night/ I belive if I had wings I Should Speed my way/

[**Monday, 19 October 1801**] next morning Brother [Samuel] nickland¹⁵¹ Came to wate on me to St Johns/ went down the [River] a boute tore miles/ Stopt at brother Joneses¹⁵² to bid them fare well but he was not at home/ his wife and the Children lay'd in that I should stay all night as the wind was right a head/ upon the [w]hole I Concluded to stay and have a meatin/ the[y] Sent word aboute to the people and a grate number gave thare attendance and the Lord gave me to feal Some Sence of there State by nature to be dreadful without Christ/ after I had dune speaking the people Stood and Seamed as tho the[y] Could not go away/ I spocke to them for Some time and I trust that Good was dun in the name of the holy Child Jesus/ after the people all went to bead the man of the house and my Self Sat up till half after one and when I went to bead I Could not Sleep/

[**Tuesday, 20 October 1801**] next morning we Sang and pray'd and [I] took my leave of the famaly/ the[y] ware all in tears/ oh what love appear'd throw out the [w]hole famaly/ the wind being ahead I thought I would [go] Some of the way/ at the first I walked fore miles and then I got in the boate and the wind being so much ahead that the man maide but little head way/ I helpt him row as much a[s] I Could for several miles and it was so Cold on the water that I felt very de___/ then I got oute and walked seven miles/ got down to the fals [Reversing Falls] a good deal benum'd/ walk'd into town and when I Came to Sit down I felt very much beate oute but the Lord was pleased to order that I had a good nights rest/

[SAINT JOHN]

[**Wednesday, 21 October 1801**] next morning went to see a number of frinds/ gave oute meatin next evening at M'r [George] harding['s]/ felt a little Sence of GOD who upholds his people in the midts [midst] of all danger/ Something very shocking happen'd in town/ a man which had been awakin'd in Some degree under my visits and fell in with the methodist fell into Some awful Condery [quandary]/ he was working on board the mast ship/ he threw himself over bord and refused to take [help]/ went home with M'rs [Daniel] Lovit/ Sat up for Some time with a few more frinds/ went to bead after prayrs but did not sleep much/ felt my mind a good deal destrest [distressed] on the acounts of Some news I heard from home/

[Thursday, 22 October 1801] Spent the next day in a dark and
Sollitary Manner/ I was not fit Company for Saint or
Sinner but as I had given out a meatin at Brother George
harding['s] went but it seamed to be a Cross to nature but
oh the goodness of GOD/ how I was disapointed/ I had
not felt so well for many a day/ it was no less than the gate
of heaven and the house of GOD/ I thought I Could
Spocke all night/ Stay'd Some time after meatin and
Conversed very freely/ then went home to my lodging
acompane'd [by] Mr Ensly [Thomas Ansley] from
Canibacases [Kennebecasis] a person I never saw before
one of GOD['s] dear Children/ we sat up very late/ the
dear man would [have] talked all night but we went to
bead and I got one good nap but after that I Could not
Sleep no more/

[Friday, 23 October 1801] as soon as he [Thomas Ansley]
awoke he began to tell his mind where he left of[f] the
night before/ we got up and sang and pray'd and felt some
freedom/ after breackfast I went oute and purchesed
Some thing that I had to get for my famaly/ oh what a
death appear'd in every thing of wor[l]dly kind/ I felt a
good deal tried in my mind wheather I Should go home a
Cross the bay with Mr Taylor or stay and go with the
packet after Sabouth as the people was So very desirious
for my Staying longer/ I could say onely the Lord derect
me for I more & more see that my ways are not as his ways
nor my thoughts as his thoughts/ oh for more likeness to
GOD/ went in the after noon to a house where I
Exspect[ed] to have met with oposion [opposition] but I
ever Experanc[e] that I dont [k]no[w] allways what is
best/ I Could Say he was kind/ he stood by me indeed/ I
felt Every thing taken oute of the way/ the man of the
house gave me a general Envation [invitation] to his
house/ while we sat at the tea table he and his wife Could
not help Sheading tears/ then I went to here a methodest
preacher and oh the darkness might be felt/ it Seamed to
me that he was Closing up every Ear and eye/ I felt
distres to See the horred delution [delusion] and many

128

tow [too] found [fond] to have it Sow [so]/ I gave oute
meatin a satterday night/

[**Saturday, 24 October 1801**] I felt all day a good deal destrest
[distressed] in my mind but the Lord stood by me/ I
preached to a very attentive Congr[eg]ation/ the Lord
appear'd in the midst of the people/ one woman
Exsperienc'd the love of GOD/ we sang after meatin
Some hyms and with the Spirrit and the understanding/
went home to my lodging/ felt Very Sollom in my mind/
did [not] get much Sleep/

[**Sunday, 25 October 1801**] in the morning I felt a good deal
indesposed in body and mind as I thought/ attended
publick worship and GOD appear'd with his Spirrit and
his word/ a number of the Christians began to look above
the things of time/ had but one meatin/ in the day[time] I
went to here a Church [of England] minister/ I did
Exspect to have heard D'r Boils [Mather Byles] but a Mr
Norse [Robert Norris]¹⁵³ Spocke but he Soon Shew'd to
my Sattisfaction what he was/ went home and got tea/
then attended meatin where a grate number Came to hear
the Word/ numbers felt much brokin down/ felt some
more Comeposed in my mind/ a number of frinds
stop[ped] after meatin/ had some profetable
Conversation/ I retir'd and blessed be GOD I got a good
nights rest more so than I had for some time/

[**Monday, 26 October 1801**] after I arose I Sat down/ I went to
see several frinds in the Corce of the day/ felt Some Sence
of GOD and in the evening I had meatin and the Lord
appear[ed] in the midst/ the people seam'd Sollom/ I
gave oute to have a meatin and the Lord appear[ed] in the
midst/ The people seam'd very Sollom/ I gave oute to
have meatin a Wednesday evening at the same place/

[**Tuesday, 27 October 1801**] a tusday I Spent in paying visits a
mong my frinds/ the Exercise of my mind was betwixt
Cloude and the Sun Shine/ my mind was a good deal
tos[s]ed very much as I was wateing [waiting] for the
packet/ Everyday Seamed a week/ the time Seamed

tedious/ oh that my Way might be prosper'd/ oh that the angel of GOD might be all ways in my view to stre[n]gthen me/

[**Wednesday, 28 October 1801**] as the pa[c]ket did not go as I Exspected we had a meatin and a number of people from the Contry Came withe the people of the town/ had a Good meatin/ the fire of GODs love was desarnable [discernable] to be in [the] Countanan[ces] of the people/ as I was not shure the packet would go oute the next day I gave oute meatin on Condessions [conditions that] if the packet did not go that I would attend/

[finis][154]

NOTES FOR CHAPTER TWO

1   The original church covenant (from an early copy, with only eight signatories, all male), dating from c1762-63, is printed in James Hannay (ed), "Documents of the Congregational Church at Maugerville," in (1894) 1 *Coll NB His Soc* 119. In view of the disjointed nature of the documents in Hannay's edition, the great sensitivity of events in the early history of this church and Hannay's low credibility as an historian it had been rather suspected that the printed documents were bowdlerized. Inspection of the originals, lately deposited at PANB, reveals that they were not censored, although they might have been more carefully and comprehensively edited.

2   The complicated history of the Sackville Six-Principle Baptist church and the Sackville Calvinist Baptist church is authoritatively discussed in Robert Gardner, "Early Baptists in Sackville, New Brunswick", an unpublished 1980 manuscript deposited at Acadia. Gardner's compact study replaces all previous work on the subject. One source in addition to those in Gardner is the obituary of Sarah (Estabrooks) Seamans in *Am Bapt Mag* (September 1819), p. 189. Joseph Crandall's recollection that by 1797 there remained "only one [person] in that whole Parish [Sackville] who had been immersed" cannot be taken at face value: J.M. Bumsted

(ed), "Autobiography of Joseph Crandall," in (1973) 3 *Acadiensis* (#1), p. 85.

3   Far the best historical writing on the settlements on the Petitcodiac is that of Esther Wright in *Samphire Greens: The Story of the Steeves* (1961) and, especially, *The Petitcodiac* (1945). These pamphlets are dated in tone but students ignore them at their peril.

4   Another region of pre-Loyalist settlement in New Brunswick was Passamaquoddy Bay. Its role in the course of religious dissent was distinctive but minor. It had begun by 1770 when James Boyd, a justice of the peace under Nova Scotia, was regularly preaching to a congregation of Dissenters on Indian Island: William Owen Journal, II, p. 230, 239: GRE/3, National Marine Museum, Greenwich. Further comments on the role of religious dissent in the Passamaquoddy region are offered below in the context of James Manning's career and in Chapter Three.

5   The best source on Noble's early career is Noble to Wheelock, 12 July 1773: Wheelock Papers, Dartmouth College Library. I think an exploration of the references in this letter would prove that Noble was not a Newlight. On Noble's advent to Maugerville, see Lucius Boltwood, *Descendants of Thomas Noble* (1878), pp. 202-12; James Hannay, "The Maugerville Settlement, 1763-1824," in (1894) 1 *Coll NB His Soc* 63, pp. 73-78; J.M. Bumsted, "Seth Noble," in (1983) V *Dict Can Biog* 627.

6   Noble to Dewey, 7 February 1776, in Boltwood, *Thomas Noble*, pp. 203-04.

7   Hannay, "Maugerville Settlement," p. 74, states that Noble had correspondence with Washington, but Bumsted could find no such letters. Mary Coy recalled that, "after the English and Emerican War broak out M'r Noble Menafested a Great zeal to have a hand in it And Imprest upon the minds of the people that it was their duty to be ingaged in the Cause:" "Reminiscences

of Mrs. Mary Bradley:" New England Historical and Genealogical Society, Boston. This Bradley manuscript is important and differs substantially from (but does not contradict) her well-known published *Narrative* (1849). Bradley was, however, a child during the Revolution, and her credibility is somewhat undermined by the fact that she depicts her father, Edward Coy, as a steady Loyalist, while a contemporary account calls him a "rebel committee man": James Hannay (ed), "Sunbury County Documents," in (1894) 1 *Coll NB His Soc* 100, p. 104. Another little-known account of this complex period on the St John is in Charles Jadis to Treasury, 30 March 1787: T1/644, Public Record Office, London.

8 Mary (Coy) Bradley gives a child's-eye view of these great events:

> then the Men [Goold's] came on shore. We ware greatly fright[e]ned. The Room was full of them. They were very plesent and seem'd to wish us not to be afraid of them. They talked with the children and gave them toys to please them — and our fears soon left us. After ward we were inform'd of their Business which was to ketch M'r Noble and the Other Gentlemen that were unighted with Him.

9 Noble was to serve as one of Henry Alline's pall-bearers at North Hampton in 1784. Early in the 1790s Noble visited the St John but was forbidden from preaching by provincial authorities. His purpose was to leave two of his motherless sons to be raised by their Barker uncles. One of these sons, Benjamin Noble, became in 1830 the first deacon of New Brunswick's only considerable Free Will Baptist church. In 1841 it joined the Free Christian Baptists: Bradley, "Reminiscences"; [Saint John] *Religious Intelligencer*, 15 June 1860; [Limerick, ME] *Morning Star*, 6 October 1830; 24 March 1841.

10 "Notes on New Brunswick History," c1803: W.O. Raymond (ed), *Winslow Papers* (1901), p. 508.

11 The principal documents quoted here are: James

133

Beverley & Barry Moody (eds), *Life and Journal of the Rev. Mr. Henry Alline* (1982), pp. 100-03, 106-09, 114, 128-29, 193-97, 206; James Hannay (ed), "Documents of the Congregational Church at Maugerville," in (1894) 1 *Coll NB His Soc* 119; Gordon Stewart (ed), "Records of the Church of Jebogue in Yarmouth," in *Documents Relating to the Great Awakening in Nova Scotia, 1760-1791* (1982), pp. 94-99.

12   Perhaps one of the reasons that the St John townships were so receptive to Alline is that there were at least eighteen families there recently arrived from parts of Nova Scotia (chiefly Cornwallis) in which he had already preached. This statistic is only for townships neighbouring Maugerville. There are no comparable data for Maugerville itself.

13   Interestingly, Alline refers to his church as having been "settled according to the plan of the gospel," a phrase suggestive of his subsequent use of the term "gospel church".

14   "Memoir of the Rev. Elijah Eastabrooks," in (1829) 1 *Bapt Miss Mag* (#10) 289, p. 290.

15   In addition to his references to the "church" in Maugerville Alline distinctly refers to religious "societies" lower down the river. It was probably to the "society" in Gage that Alline preached his great 1782 sermon on Elijah's translation and felt his own soul "bore away to the realms of eternal felicity".

16   An account of this feat was provided by the Wesleyan preacher Joshua Marsden in his *Narrative of a Mission of Nova Scotia, New Brunswick, and the Somers Islands* (Plymouth, 1816), p. 64.

> It had been built upon a litigated lot of land, and the people having a glebe five miles lower down the river, it was agreed to get the whole settlement to assist in removing the chapel, which being a frame building large enough to hold 800 people, with a

spire steeple, required some difficulty. More than 100 yoke of oxen, besides horses, were employed on the occasion; and after the chapel was raised with levers from the foundation, immense beams were placed under the whole length; to these, the oxen were yoked with iron chains, and at a given signal, each man standing by his yoke, the chapel was drawn down the bank of the river, and so long to the appointed place ... .

This Congregational church, like John Payzant's at Liverpool, survived to enter the United Church of Canada in 1925.

17   Richard Parr Journal, 8 October 1820: PAC. This remarkable journal was brought to Canada through the efforts of Roger Nason, by whose kindness I was able to consult it. For a similar assessment of the Anglican effort at St Andrews in 1823 see William Leake, *History of Lord Seaton's Regiment* (1866), I, pp. 393-96.

18   For example, Bishop Inglis' journal for 17 July 1792 contains the following report on the inactivity of James Scovil, rector of Kingston (PAC Reel C-2227).

Half way up Long Reach. The people of this house complained that Mr. Scovil had not visited this part of his parish for upwards of a twelvemonth, of which neglect the methodists [especially Abraham Bishop] had availed themselves, and were very assiduous in making proselytes. Church people offended at Mr. Scovil's neglect, and officiousness of the Methodists, who do much injury to the country.

Even more pointed accounts of the sloth of the Anglican clergy are found in John Mitchell Journal, 12 August 1804 (Oliver Arnold): PANS, and *Mass Bapt Miss Mag* (February 1807), p. 269 (Samuel Andrews).
    Four Anglican clergymen settled in New Brunswick did not exercise their vocation except in

special circumstances. The two non-Anglican clergy who came to New Brunswick as Loyalists are not known to have preached: Michael Kern (German Reformed) and John Martin (ethnic Presbyterian).

19 The phrase is Bishop John Medley's, in W.Q. Ketchum, *Life and Work of the Most Reverend John Medley* (1893), pp. 89-90, echoing Tocqueville. It was the arrival of Medley, New Brunswick's first bishop, in the 1840s which transformed and thereby saved Anglicanism in the province and gave it, in time, a rich, self-confident and authentic presence in the lower St John valley that was the equal and opposite of the unique and self-confident Baptist culture of the upper St John valley.

20 The principal sources for this section are: Beverley & Moody, *Alline's Journal*, pp. 173-81, 197-98; Brian Cuthbertson (ed), *Journal of the Reverend John Payzant (1749-1834)* (1981), pp. 28, 30-31, 40; George Rawlyk (ed), *New Light Letters and Spiritual Songs, 1778-1793* (1983), pp. 46, 101-25.

21 Note also William Black's early encounter with the Steeves in T.W. Smith, *History of the Methodist Church of Eastern British America* (1877), I, pp. 124-25. According to the obituary of his son-in-law (the preacher Robert Colpitts), Christian Steeves

> was converted under the labors of Mr. William Black of Cumberland, was a devoted Christian and frequently held meetings and taught the people. Mrs. [Rosanna (Trites)] Steeves was converted under Henry Alliene; she was the first person converted on the Petitcodiac river — and at the time was considered *insane: Religious Intelligencer*, 16 November 1855.

See also R.H. Hutchinson, *Early Methodist Connection of the Steeves Family* (1981), pp. 7-9.

22 George Levy (ed), *Diary and Related Writings of the*

Reverend Joseph Dimock (1768-1846) (1979), pp. 87-88.

23 Marsden, *Narrative of a Mission*, p. 49; Job Seamans Journal, 14 August 1803: New London Town Hall, NH; John Mitchell Journal, 7 August 1804: PANS; Howard Temperley (ed), *Gubbins' New Brunswick Journals* (1980), p. 17 (16 July 1811); Ingraham Bill, *Fifty Years with the Baptists* (1880), pp. 579-80. A further instance, the "Babcock tragedy" (1805), is discussed in Chapter Three and Appendix X.

24 J.M. Bumsted (ed), "Autobiography of Joseph Crandall," in (1973) 3 *Acadiensis* (#1), p. 79.

25 Wright, *Petitcodiac*, pp. 62-63. An invaluable and little-known 1803 list of households in most of what are now Westmorland and Albert Counties is printed serially in *Generations* (the quarterly of the NB Genealogical Society) beginning with the issue of June 1979. I use the 1791 date for Pierson's removal from Horton because that is what all the secondary source give. In mid-1793, however, Pierson was reported itinerating through Liverpool: C.B. Fergusson (ed), *Diary of Simeon Perkins, 1790-1796* (1961), III, p. 241.

26 Bumsted, "Crandall's Autobiography," p. 86.

27 Saunders, *History of the Baptists*, p. 75.
     Just what occurred in Crandall's home neighbourhood of Salisbury is less clear. The denominational historians give 1800 as Salisbury's organizational date. Crandall's "Autobiography" does not mention such an event, but that was the date he gave in another context: *Christian Visitor*, 17 May 1848. In the only two early Association annual minutes to survive (1802 and 1809), Salisbury was described as merely a "branch" of the Sackville church, suggesting that it was not organized independently. Not until the minutes of 1811 was Salisbury listed completely separately.

28   Levy, *Dimock's Diary*, p. 72.

29   Wickwire to Manning, 30 October 1799: Manning
     Papers, Acadia. Note how this letter has been radically
     falsified in the version given in Saunders, *History of the
     Baptists*, pp. 78-79, to read as if the events described had
     occurred on the St John rather than the Petitcodiac.
     Moreover, none of the six melodramatic sentences on p.
     79 is in the original.

30   Hannay, "Documents of the Congregational Church,"
     p. 124 *et seq.*

31   The (false) rumour was to the effect that on his primary
     visitation to New Brunswick Inglis had infected Sarah
     Craig, a prostitute, with venereal disease. It is well
     documented: Inglis to Canterbury, 13 September 1788;
     28 January 1789; 13 March 1789; Inglis Journal, 21
     January 1789: Reel C-2227, PAC; Peters to Breynton, 3
     February 1789, quoted in Kenneth Cameron (ed),
     Church of England in Pre-Revolutionary Connecticut
     (1976), p. 280. The libel was put into circulation by John
     Caleff, a Massachusetts Loyalist who had been one of
     the pallbearers for George Whitefield.   His recent
     biographer says Caleff served as part-time chaplain at
     Fort Howe (Saint John): A.G. Condon, "John Caleff,"
     in (1983) V *Dict Can Biog* 134. Condon suggests that it
     was he who caused the Countess of Huntingdon to send
     James to New Brunswick, but in their petition of 22 May
     1792 the Sheffield Congregational society asserted that
     it was they who had sent to England for James: see
     Appendix III.

32   "Reminiscences of Mrs. Mary Bradley". At the same
     time the church still enjoyed the favour of the general
     community, for more than eighty adult males
     subscribed the salary of John James. The US Baptist
     Isaac Backus was also favourably impressed by James,
     who appeared "to understand the gospel well": W.G.
     McLoughlin (ed), *Diary of Isaac Backus* (1979), III, p.
     1318.

33 The first Methodist preacher in western New Brunswick
    was the Saint John slave Edward Morris. The *Saint
    John Gazette* for 13 May 1784 carried a notice of
    Morris' escape, describing him as

> an elderly negro about five feet five inches high, by
> trade a mason, has a remarkable wound in his
> forehead which shews a hole resembling a bullet
> shot, is a celebrated methodist preacher among the
> Negroes, was bred at Fairfield in Connecticut.

Thus the first Methodist and the first Baptist preachers
on the River St John were Black. When Abraham
Bishop visited Saint John in 1791 he found that the
Blacks had already been awakened "under the ministry
of one of their own color". This has usually (and I think
correctly) been taken as a reference to the work of David
George, but it is possible that Morris had also preached
or exhorted.

34 The principal sources for this section are: Smith,
    History of the Methodist Church, I, pp. 220-29, 256-63,
    266-68, 304-06, 309, 320-21, 323-24, 326, 341-42;
    Stephen Humbert, *Rise and Progress of Methodism, in
    the Province of New Brunswick, from its
    Commencement until about the Year 1805* (Saint John,
    1836), pp. 1-33. This last item, a 43-page imprint, seems
    to be unknown to recent Methodist historians, probably
    because T.W. Smith's monumental *History of
    Methodism* purposely did not mention it (Humbert
    having set up a separate meeting about 1805 and
    supported another in the 1820s). Humbert was early
    Saint John's leading Wesleyan and an important figure
    in Maritime musicology. In 1845 it was said that a
    typical settler's library consisted of a Bible, an almanac
    and "Humbert's Union Harmony, the province manual
    of sacred music, of which they are most particularly
    fond": Frances Beavan, *Life in the Backwoods of New
    Brunswick* (London, 1845), pp. 31-32.

·35   Smith, *History of the Methodist Church,* I, pp. 309-10, suggests that Boyd withdrew from the Wesleyans because he married.

36   Mann to [Fidler], 19 July 1795, in Goldwin French (ed), "Papers of Daniel Fidler", in (1959) 12 *Bulletin: Records and Proceedings of the Committee on Archives of the United Church of Canada* 3, p. 16.

37   George Patterson, *Memoir of the Rev. James MacGregor* (1859), pp. 343-44, 351.

38   This section is based on: "Memoir of the Rev. Duncan M'Coll", in *British North American Wesleyan Methodist Magazine* (May 1841), pp. 333-34; (August 1841), pp. 460-61; Smith, *History of the Methodist Church,* as cited *supra:* David George's "Memoir", in David Benedict, *General History of the Baptist Denomination in America* (1813), I, pp. 287-96; "Memoirs of Jarvis Ring", pp. 9-37: Acadia; Hannay, "Documents of the Congregational Church", p. 145; John James to ___, 18 October 1792 (transcription supplied by Dr G.A. Rawlyk); Hubbard to Winslow, 29 May 1792, in Raymond, *Winslow Papers,* p. 391; Patrick Campbell, *Travels in the Interior Inhabited Parts of North America* (1793) (1937), pp. 255-56; Walter Bates on Religious Dissent: MG23 D1 vol. 71, Book 3, PAC; Rawlyk, *New Light Letters,* pp. 175, 179; Philip [Griffin-]Allwood, *Atlantic Baptist Roots* (1980), p. 6 (as corrected).

39   The version of George's Memoir printed in *Bapt Ann Reg* (1790-93), I, pp. 473-84 makes no reference to George's ordination. Certainly George acted as though he were ordained. George's activity in New Brunswick is always dated at the summer of 1792 because his licence to preach from the provincial government (printed in his "Memoir") is so dated; but by then George was in Sierra Leone. No doubt the correct date of the licence is 1791, which accords with both internal and external evidence.

40   To label the Lunt and Hammond party New

Dispensationalists seems a natural extension of the term being used simultaneously in Nova Scotia; yet I know of no contemporary use of the term in or with reference to the St John valley. Hummondism in Waterborough more closely resembles what is now loosely called a cult (*ie,* like Cochranism in Maine, it had a separatist impulse) than the form New Dispensationalism took in Nova Scotia. Perhaps this difference explains why Edward Manning, who in Nova Scotia was at least a fellow traveller with the New Dispensationalists, later recalled that he had been deeply shocked by what he saw in the St John valley in 1793. (It must, however, be added that the two famous letters he wrote about his New Brunswick trip indicate that he gloried in, rather than recoiled from, what he found there.) Perhaps the most important point to be made is that New Dispensationalism was just a local name for antinomianism: the notion that the convert was in such an immediate relationship with God that he might disregard the precepts of ordinary morality and boldly follow the lead of the spirit; and from this perspective the irregularities of the 1780s, 1790s and 1800s in Nova Scotia and New Brunswick are part of the same phenomenon.

41 The Congregationalists of Sheffield seem to have placed the outbreak of dangerous tendencies within the reformation a little earlier. Writing about the close of 1792 a committee of the church suggested that towards the end of 1791 "there appeared to be a very considerable religious concern on the minds of many persons at no great distance [*ie,* Waterborough?] intermixed with great commotions Some arregularities and false notions". They were, however, writing for a purpose unconnected with the subject of this passage; perhaps, therefore, one should not put much weight on so general a remark.

42 It must be emphasized that this incident occurred in the late summer or early fall of 1792. Maurice Armstrong mistakenly dated it at 1791: *Great Awakening in Nova*

Scotia, 1776-1809 (1948), p. 128. Such an error would confound the attempt to piece all the scattered fragments of evidence into a plausible narrative.

43   Early in 1837 Edward Manning revisited the field of his early success above Fredericton. In his Journal he described Abigail (Estey) Hartley as "the Fruits of my Ministry 44 years ago", and Solomon Parent as "called by my Ministry 44 years ago", as well as some Hagermans. Parent and the Hagermans were Loyalists. Abigail Hartley was a pre-Loyalist married to a Loyalist. On the same occasion Manning described himself forty-four years earlier as having been "the first dissenter that even visited them": Edward Manning Journal, 26 January, 1 & 2 February 1837: Acadia. This is probably correct. The first Wesleyan to preach in the parishes above Fredericton was Daniel Fidler in the spring of 1796.

44   Some idea of Saunders' worth as a faithful witness to Baptist history will be had by comparing the versions of these two Edward Manning letters in Rawlyk, *New Light Letters,* pp. 175-76, 179-80 with Saunders, *History of the Baptists,* pp. 37-38. For a similar exercise with Cramp, compare *New Light Letters,* pp. 175-76 with *New Light Letters,* pp. 291-92.

45   Dimock to Bennett, 9 December 1793, printed in John Davis, *Life and Times of the Late Rev. Harris Harding* (1866), pp. 234-35.

46   Supreme Court Circuit Minute Book: RS36A, PANB. The jury for the trial of the Garrison rape charge were: James Peck (foreman), John Watson, Asher Vail, Anthony Baker, John Townsend, Joseph Nickerson, David Cowperthwaite, Lewis Mitchell, Robert Cox, Caleb Stivers, Elijah Smith, Joseph Dixon. The jury for the trial of the Hammond rape charge were: Joseph Holland, Anthony Baker, Henry Sharpe, Alexander Montgomery Jr, Robert Cox, James Peck, John Titus, Abiel Briggs, Joseph Nickerson, William Spencer,

Lewis Mitchell, Jordon Cock.

The court minutes also make reference to the following proceedings: R *v* Lathrop Hammond, R *v* Joseph Garrison and R *v* Abijah Garrison. No such cases were tried; probably these references merely evidence formal undertakings to the Crown to appear at court (as potential witnesses) rather than criminal charges.

The Garrison family, most of whom figure in the Lunt-Hammond trials, is notable in several other respects. From Chapter One it will be recalled that Eliza Garrison (Sarah's sister) is the only person known to have been immersed by Henry Alline. Abijah Garrison, in addition to his supporting role in Hammondism, earned a footnote to history in 1811 when he was presented by the Queens County grand jury on the denunciation of Peter Forshay for offering a public toast in the following tenor: "May the Eagle of America shit on the Crown of Great Britain and wipe it off with the Lillies of France". Another Garrison brother, Nathan, was clerk of the first Baptist church gathered in Saint John (1810).

47 Bates portrayed the result of the Lunt-Hammond trials very differently from that disclosed in the Supreme Court minutes.

> At this [Queens County] Court I was myself present the whole trial. Lunt was indicted for an attempt to commit a Rape and Hammon for an accessory: from witnesses before an impartial Jury I head them pronounced Guilty, and sentenced by the Court to fine and imprisonment in the common Gaol of the County. However for certain considerations parts of Hammons imprisonment was respited on bail for good behaviour. Lunt at the end of his punishment fled to the United States, leaving to Queens and Sunbury Counties their Hammonites, Hartites and Brooksites with travelling preachers occationally.

Bates "heard" no such thing, but his distortion is probably attributable to lapse of memory (writing forty-six years after the event) rather than pure malice. What Bates remembered correctly was that Lunt and Hammond were imprisoned; what he forgot was that the imprisonment occurred between the time of their arrest and their trial, rather than as a result of the trial. Two other sources confirm the fact of imprisonment. Duncan McColl recorded that "they went on from bad to worse, until the authorities took them up, and put Messrs. H[ammond] and L[unt] in prison, and kept them there for several months": *British North American Wesleyan Methodist Magazine* (May 1841), p. 334. And, from a child's perspective, Jarvis Ring recalled that:

> At last thair Was a Bench Ret [writ] Issued for Lunt and old M'r Hammond. They ware taken to Gage town and Loked up in the Gaol. . . . Hammond and Lunt had thair tryal after laying in Gail sum time. By Giving Security for thair Good Behaviour under a havey pennelty they ware let gow: Ring Memoir, Acadia.

As to Bates' concluding reference to the "Hammonites, Hartites and Brooksites," it is obvious that "Hammonites" are the followers of Archelaus Hammond and John Lunt, "Brooksites" has reference to Elijah Estabrooks (presumably the junior) and "Hartites" probably has reference to Samuel Hartt of Waterborough, who is known to have preached occasionally in the early 1790s. Either he or some other Hartt is mentioned as "pretending" to preach in James Manning's journal for 4 October 1801. (The "Hartites" were certainly not the followers of Horton's Theodore Harding, as Maurice Armstrong was misled by Saunders into suggesting: *Great Awakening*, p. 128.) More problematic is the list offered by William Hubbard on 29 May 1792: "Hammonites," "Palmerites," "Brookites" and "worst of all the "Pearlyites or Burpeites". It must be stressed that these labels do not represent distinct sects but simply prominent preacher-exhorters. For example, at the time Hubbard wrote the Hammondites and the Brooksites were still united in the Waterborough Allinite society. "Palmerites" may simply be a contemptuous characterization of the Sheffield Congregational church, in which David Palmer was an elder. Israel Perley and David Burpee, members of the Sheffield Congregational society (although not the church) may be the originals for the last two labels, although it is not quite clear why they would be "worst of all". "Pearlyites" might also have reference to Thomas Perley of Waterborough, one of the Hammondites, but in that case it would not be evident why Hubbard offered "Burpeites" as an alternative label. Hubbard's contemptuous terminology for unordained preacher-exhorters is explicable in part by an ongoing dispute between local Anglicans and Congregationalists over possession of the Sheffield parsonage lot. See Hannay, "Documents of the Congregational Church," pp. 146-47; L.M.B. Maxwell, *History of Central New Brunswick* (1937), pp. 124-25 and Appendix III.

48   William McLoughlin, "Free Love, Immortalism, and Perfectionism in Cumberland, Rhode Island, 1748-1768," in (1974) 33 *Rhode Island History* 67; [Ephraim Stinchfield], *Cochranism Delineated* (Boston, 1819); Klaus Hansen, *Mormonism and the American Experience* (1981), pp. 155-66.

49   The only source for this incident, the memoir of Jarvis Ring, indicates that it took place when William Black and John Mann were in Waterborough. I cannot find such an occasion, but if Ring means Black and *James* Mann, then the time may have been towards the end of 1795.

50   McLeod to [Fidler], 17 January 1800, in French, "Fidler Papers" (1960), pp. 45-46. One of the causes of decline was removal of several families to Upper Canada.

51 Early in 1799 Duncan McColl encountered an "Antinomian preacher" and "many" Antinomians in Saint John: "Memoir of Duncan M'Coll" (August 1841), pp. 460-61. This may have been James Innis, James Murphy, Gilbert Harris, Thomas Ansley or even Daniel Shaw. By "Antinomian" McColl may well mean Calvinist.

52 Nicholas Pierson lived in Hopewell but did not preach. Strictly speaking, he may no longer have been considered as a minister.

53 Here I make no distinction between "Baptists" and persons who had merely been baptized by immersion. Assuming the latter amounts to the former, there would have been some Baptists in Sackville, among the pre-Loyalists on the St John (migrants from Nova Scotia) and in Charlotte County (remnants of a company of Baptist Loyalists, to be noticed more particularly below). Joseph Crandall encountered one Baptist among the St John River Loyalists early in 1800: the wife of Elisha Case who, significantly, was from the Baptist stronghold of Rhode Island.

54 So argued in D.G. Bell, *Early Loyalist Saint John: The Origin of New Brunswick Politics, 1783-1786* (1983). By the "loosening" of the Loyalist consensus I do not mean that religious dissent did not remain defensive and apologetic (especially as compared to Nova Scotia); merely that it no longer seemed impossible.

55 This section is based on Bumsted, "Crandall's Autobiography," Jarvis Ring's Memoir and the Waterborough Churchbook, Acadia.

56 On both this and his next visit to Waterborough Crandall fell so ill that his life was dispaired of. Illness seems to have been remarkably common among Newlight and Baptist itinerants. Was the drama of preaching despite illness another way in which this generation unconsciously imitated the consumptive Alline?

57   This twenty-year existence as a society is not, however, a record. The Allinite society at Millstream existed for upwards of twenty-five years before becoming a church (in 1833).

58   Estey to Manning, 4 May 1800: Manning Collection, Acadia.

59   Saunders, *History of the Baptists*, p. 90. I state that Crandall attended the 1800 Association because his "Autobiography" and the version of the minutes printed in Saunders so state. However, a week before the Association opened Crandall wrote Edward Manning from Sackville to apologize for not being able to attend: Crandall to Manning, 16 June 1800, Manning Collection, Acadia.

60   The earliest membership list and other documents relating to the church are printed in Bill, *Fifty Years*, p. 596. It will be noted that the church is called the "Waterborough" church only as a label of convenience. Presumably it drew its membership from a fairly broad area on both sides of the River. Its clerk called it "the Baptist Church of Christ sojourning at Waterborough and adjacent villages [*sic*] in New Brunswick".

61   We know little of this Norton church. In addition to Crandall's "Autobiography" there is John Francis' history of the Norton church in the *Christian Visitor*, 17 May 1848. For the Sussex church, see note 66 below.

62   Late in life Manning recalled "a general revival and I baptized 40 persons" on this occasion (Edward Manning Journal, 2 February 1837: Acadia). The higher number formed into the church includes some of Crandall's Kingsclear baptisms.
     This church is commonly spoken of as having been in Prince William but it embraced a much wider area. Its record book (Acadia) refers to it as "the Church of Christ in Queensbury & Prince William".

63   The church in Woodstock existed by the time of James

Manning's visit in the fall of 1801. This means it was gathered either by Edward Manning late in 1800 or by Elijah Estabrooks in about February or about May 1801. Of these I lean towards Manning because it was he who had been the first to visit this region in 1793 and the Woodstock people were spoken of as his converts. It was only natural that he would revisit them in 1800 and, if so, he may well have organized the church.

The Woodstock church is one of those about which least is known. Its geographical centre was not within the present parish of Woodstock but in that part of the pre-1833 parish that is now the parishes of Canterbury and Dumfries and in the opposite parishes of Southampton and (upper) Queensbury. Its principal figure was either Enoch Dow or his son Amos. The Dows were pre-Loyalists, but most of the church would have been Loyalists.

64 James Manning Journal, 20 September 1801: Acadia. Some of these would already have been baptized by Crandall and Edward Manning. Some would also already have belonged to the church in adjacent Prince William and presumably would have received dismission for the purpose of uniting with the new Kingsclear organization. (The Prince William churchbook confirms this, but does not give dates.) Presumably some of the Christians in what is called the Kingsclear church were actually from the Keswick area across the River.

65 James Manning Journal, 10 October 1801: Acadia.

66 Gilbert Harris (b1765-dafter 1814) is one of the ordained Baptist preachers who have been written out of Maritime Baptist history. His family appears to be that outlined in Arthur Eaton, *History of Kings County* (1910), pp. 691-92. On 9 August 1789 he was baptized in connection with the Horton Baptist church. Five years later he was an itinerant preacher: Fergusson, *Perkins' Diary*, III, p. 274. Towards the end of the following year

(1795) the Horton church "admonished [him] for erregler practisis," probably something to do with New Dispensationalism. In 1798 he "confessed his falt" to the church's satisfaction. According to Edward Manning (writing in 1812) Harris:

> moved to Sussex Vale and was ordained over a church in that place in 1801. But [he] continued in fellowship with them but a verry short time. Possesses small Talents and Ill Fame: Notes on Baptist Ministers, Manning Collection, Acadia.

The Sussex church was gathered between 22 September 1800 (the date of Innis' ordination) and 2 December 1800, the date Innis wrote Edward Manning apparently apologizing for helping to gather the church: Innis to Manning, 2 December 1801: Manning Collection, Acadia; *Christian Visitor*, 26 April 1848. The church then gathered is said to have consisted of forty members. Presumably Innis, Theodore Harding and Joseph Crandall officiated.

After Harding's departure Gilbert Harris arrived, triggering another reformation. On Harding's next visit which must have been late in 1801 or early in 1802 — the very time Edward Manning specified — the church applied to him to ordain Harris. According to the church's historian, Harding "with other brethren, advised that Mr. Harris' ordination should not take place at that time". Apparently, however, the church insisted that the ordination go forward, and Harding and James Innis complied. James Dougan and William Freeze were ordained deacons.

Harris' further adventures are outlined by the county's sheriff, Walter Bates:

> [H]arris . . . told the people he had come to them by an irresistable call from heaven, to offer salvation in Sussex that night . . . for now was their accepted time, now only was their day of salvation offered in Sussex. To which many gave great heed and were converted, espetially one respectable member of

the Church & his son [Ozias & Thomas Ansley] who had been disappointed [by Bishop Inglis' refusal to ordain Thomas Ansley]. [M]any followed them in preference, dividing Harris' congregation until he repented he had ever offered salvation in Sussex . . . : MG23, D1, vol. 71, Book 3, PAC.

Bates says that Harris then removed into Norton parish, married a couple illegally and, mindful of the fate of James Innis, fled to the United States. This is partially confirmed by the fact that a criminal process was commenced against him in Supreme Court on 12 October 1811: Crown Office Minutes, RS30B, PANB. In 1812 Edward Manning thought Harris somewhere near Eastport.

Because Baptist denominational historians would not mention Gilbert Harris, references in documents to his work have erroneously been attributed to David Harris, James Manning's successor at Lower Granville: Fergusson, *Perkins' Diary*, III, p. 274n; Grace Aiton, *Story of Sussex and Vicinity* (1967), p. 84; Rawlyk, *New Light Letters*, pp. 341-42.

67 (1835) 2 *Bapt Miss Mag* (#5) 169.   This devastating apology must be read to be believed.

68 Edward Manning's comments are written over part of an undated letter in Alline's handwriting which begins "[To the] followers of Christ scattered [abroad]:" Manning Collection, Acadia.

69 The basic source of the Manning's background is John Duncanson, *Falmouth: A New England Township in Nova Scotia, 1760-1965* (1983 edn), pp. 311, 316-17, supp 53.   The exact date of James Manning's birth is unknown.   His only local obituary states that he died "in the 54th year of his age", *ie*, at age 53, suggesting that he may have been born as late as 1765: *Acadian Recorder*, 13 June 1818.   The notice of his death in *Am Bapt Mag* (November 1818) p. 467, states that he died at age 54.

Edward Manning liked to recall theatrically that his parents were Roman Catholics. Perhaps they had been early in life, but by the time of the 1770 census (taken when Edward Manning was three) they were Protestants: Bernice Richard (ed), *Nova Scotia 1770 Census* (1972), p. 9. Note that the version of the census in Duncanson, p. 68, is a partial edition rather than a literal transcription.

70   The relevant documents are in the Chipman Papers, PANS. They were discovered by Allen Robertson. Edward Manning's extensive autobiographical musings do not mention this searing event. More remarkably (in view of his ample reason for bitterness towards the Manning sons) neither does John Payzant's published memoir.

71   The standard account of Edward Manning's conversion is that printed in Rawlyk, *New Light Letters*, pp. 287-89. The conversion of the Manning sons is also mentioned in Cuthbertson, *Payzant's Journal*, p. 43.

72   Cuthbertson, *Payzant's Journal*, p. 47.

73   Edward Manning to Bennett, 10 October 1793, in Rawlyk, *New Light Letters*, p. 179.

74   The Jarvis Ring Memoir speaks of him on this occasion very affectionately.

75   All biographic accounts of the Manning brothers mention labours in Charlotte County in the mid-1790s. The nearest direct evidence of this is Edward Manning's 1836 recollection that he had preached in the St George area "39 years ago", *ie,* in 1796 or 1797: Edward Manning Journal, 12 February 1836, Acadia. On the same theme, an 1847 history of the "Cause of God in Charlotte County" by William Hall contains the following:

The first minister of Christ in Connextion with the Baptist [*sic*] denomination who visited the County

151

was Elder Edward Manning ... in the year of our Lord 1796; his labours were much blessed in the conversion of souls ... . [S]hortly after, Elder James Manning visit[ed] the place [and] a great revival of Religion took place, and many sinners were converted to God. The following year, Elders E. Manning and Henry Allen [*sic*!] again visited Saint George, when the cause was much revived ...: *Christian Visitor,* 8 December 1847.

All that one can confirm is that James Manning was in Machias and Eastport in 1795 and that he, Edward Manning and James Murphy were in the same places in 1796. The Wesleyan Duncan McColl reported a great reformation in St Stephen and St David in 1795 or 1796 but did not mention Newlight opposition: "Memoir of Duncan M'Coll", in *British North American Wesleyan Methodist Magazine* (July 1841), p. 415.

Hall's historical account suggests that the Mannings preached specifically at St George, and Edward Manning's 1836 recollection confirms this. St George was for several decades the centre (perhaps too strong a word) of what little Baptist activity there was in Charlotte County although, of course, the Mannings of the mid-1790s were Allinites not Baptists.

To some it may seem curious that the Mannings are not known to have preached in Beaver Harbour, where a company of more than eighty Baptist Loyalists had set down in September 1783. As this Baptist group has attracted little attention compared with the (ever-fashionable) Quaker company that settled Beaver Harbour with it, I give here the names of the heads of household, together with former home, where known. The names come from the "Return of Loyalists called Anabaptists ... actually embarked on board the Armed Ship Camel", 29 August 1783: WO 60/33 pt2, PRO. The "former home" data are from an earlier and shorter version of the same list in the same source. A complete list (not just adult males) of the Baptists and Quakers is in the *Camel* musterbook: AD36/9430, PRO.

Caleb Barrett (Cumberland Co, NJ), Benjamin Dunn (*ibid*), Jacob Stewart (Middlesex Co, PA), Joshua Wilson (*ibid*), Aaron (or Asa) Wilson, (*ibid*), Jarmen Davis (Cumberland Co, NJ), Amos Stedham (*ibid*), John Burges (Chester Co, PA), Benjamin Parker (Jersey), John Parker (*ibid*), Samuel Parker (*ibid*), Jonathan Parker, James Pierce (*ibid*), Adam Smith, Samuel Caman, Nicholas Hilier, Anthony Rickman, Thomas Dunham, Zachariah Barclay, Michael Stump, Gershom Alexander, James French, Robert FitzRandolph, Jonathan Parker (another?) (Jersey), George Ryan, Thomas Bullock, Isaac Woodward, Peter Whitman, William Harrison, Henry Gardiner

The Beaver Harbour community soon declined. At the provision muster of 14 May 1784 the Baptists numbered only 63: T1/609, PRO. On 8 September 1785 twelve of them (Albert Rickman, Peter Rickman, Anthony Rickman, Jonathan Dunn, Jeremiah Dunn, Benjamin Dunn, Adam Smith, Joshua Wilson, Benjamin Parker, Samuel Parker, Jonathan Parker, and the widow Sophia Barrett) signed a memorial stating that they were "now of Campo Bello" and asking for land on Moose Island (the site of Eastport). Moose Island was one of the disputed islands that was eventually held to be in Maine. Except perhaps in the confused mid-1780s, New Brunswick's jurisdiction never practically extended there, although the British occupied it militarily during and for a time after the War of 1812. In 1790 the remaining settlement of Beaver Harbour was wiped out in a forest fire. These are indications that the Baptist group scattered at an early date and help explain why the Manning brothers are not known to have preached in Beaver Harbour in the mid-1790s.

Little is known of the Beaver Harbour group's character as Baptists. Presumably they came together in British-occupied New York, although some clearly knew each other in their former homes. We do not know whether they had fellowship with other Baptists at New York, whether they formed themselves into a church or whether they held religious meetings or heard preaching in New Brunswick. Frederick Burnett and Robert Gardner have discovered that Caleb Barrett and several others of the New Jersey people were members of a Seventh Day Baptist church and that surnames of some of the others suggest a connection with the same group: see Gardner, *Baptists of Early America* (1983), p. 351. There is an historical sketch of the Seventh Day group in New Jersey in David Benedict, *General History of the Baptist Denomination* (1813), II, p. 420.

76 Except as otherwise noted this section is based on: James Manning to Edward Manning, 9 July 1795; James Manning to ⎯⎯, 10 June 1796; Jones to Edward Manning, 31 October 1796; Edward Manning to Jones, 11 November 1796; Jones to Edward Manning, 19 November 1796: Manning Collection, Acadia; John Ahlin (ed), James Lyon, *Saint's Daily Assistant* (1983); William Kilby, *Eastport and Passamaquoddy* (1888), pp. 70-72, 313-14, 342-43; George Drisko, *Narrative of the Town of Machias* (1904), pp. 25, 199; Jonathan Greenleaf, *Sketches of the Ecclesiastical History of the State of Maine* (1821), pp. 206-7; Joshua Millet, *History of the Baptists in Maine* (1845), pp. 294-95, 338-41. There are minor variations among them which need not be resolved in this context. There is also confusion as between Newlight and Baptist. These sources should, however, be used in preference to Henry Burrage, *History of the Baptists in Maine* (1904).

77 Like Gilbert Harris, James Murphy has been silently excised from Maritime Baptist history. An orphan, probably the offspring of New Brunswick Loyalists, Murphy received his spiritual awakening in Woodstock under the Mannings, presumably in 1793. He preached a little in the St John valley and, if the American sources (cited above) are correct, he was already preaching at Eastport in 1794. (This may be indirectly confirmed by the fact that the Eastport meeting-house was erected

that year, although the place had no religious organization.) If Murphy was at Eastport at this early date then it was he rather than the Mannings who established the Allinite beachhead in eastern Maine. American sources further suggest that in 1796 or 1797 Murphy settled over a Baptist church in Steuben (near Machias) and that he continued there until 1800. It is, however, questionable whether Murphy was a Baptist and unlikely that he was ordained at so early a date. Probably the religious exercises in Steuben were of a Newlight character.

On 21 August 1800 the town of Eastport voted whether "to give Mr. James Murphy, of Steuben, a call to settle in said town as minister of the gospel, and maintain him by a town tax". A majority rejected such a call but Murphy removed into Eastport (or Lubec) anyway and began regular religious meetings. He was, however, already experiencing heavy spiritual trials. In June 1801 he wrote Edward Manning (proposing an exchange of pulpits) declaring that, "I have been upon the decline in Spiritual health this some time and the Spirit of the Lord has departed from me": Murphy to Manning, 7 June 1801: Manning Collection, Acadia. Later that summer James Manning recorded in his journal the cheering news that, "Broth[er] Murphy felt his chains fall off[f]". But Jarvis Ring of Waterborough (who had known Murphy in his youth) visited Murphy in December of that year, finding him foppish in dress and puffed up with spiritual pride.

By mid-1801 Murphy was almost certainly a Baptist. A year later, on 8 August 1802, Elijah Estabrooks of Waterborough ordained him over a newly-gathered church of fifty-seven members at Eastport (drawing support from adjacent Deer and Campobello Islands). In early 1804 Murphy made a tour of eastern Charlotte County, probably the first Baptist ever to preach there: Murphy's letter, 12 March 1804, in *Mass Bapt Miss Mag* (September 1804), p. 88. He also made a tour of eastern Maine but bad reports followed him on his return. In 1805 he was dismissed (or

155

excluded) from the Eastport Baptist church, but he continued to live there and evidently established a separate meeting. The latter is disclosed in an extract from a letter by the Congregationalist Ephraim Abbott, dated 19 September 1811.

> There is in this town [Eastport] considerable superstition among some aged people ... . Their prejudices I believe have been strengthened by the preaching of Mr Murphy who deceased a little before I came to this town. Mr Murphy taught that a man ought never to know his text before he entered the meeting house; then he said if the preacher was sent by God he would be taught what to say ... . Those who are opposed to preaching with notes, are also opposed to having a bass viol in the meeting house: Kilby, *Eastport*, p. 331.

Further information on Murphy will be found in Case's letter, 27 September 1806, in *Mass Bapt Miss Mag* (February 1807), p. 268 and the Jarvis Ring Memoir, Acadia.

78 *Supra*, note 68.

79 Early in 1796 Jacob Bailey, rector of Annapolis, remarked that among the dissenting preachers he had lately married was a "congregational monster," presumably a reference to Manning: Bailey to Peters, 10 March 1796: Bailey Papers, vol 94, PANS.

80 Saunders, *History of the Baptists*, p. 85. Most Baptist historians mistakenly give the date of Manning's ordination as 1796.

81 Manning to Manning, 29 August 1799: Manning Collection, Acadia.

82 Isaac Case, 18 May 1808, in *Mass Bapt Miss Mag* (September 1808), p. 74.

83 When David Harris assumed the pastorate there were

only twenty-five members: Charles Tupper, "History of the Baptist Churches in Nova-Scotia" (1828) in (1829) 1 *Bapt Miss Mag* (#10), p. 318. Edward Manning commented, "May Brother Harris have a more comfortable ministry among them than . . . [James] had": Edward Manning Journal, 1 November 1821: Acadia.

84 Halfyard to Manning, 4 June 1817: Manning Collection, Acadia. By this time, however, he himself is said to have "a Handsome little property unincumber'd". Six years after Manning's death his eldest son sold the family farm for £120: Lawrenctown Registry Office, BK 21, pp. 176-77. (I am grateful to Dr. Barry Moody for this information.)

85 Jarvis Ring Memoir, Acadia.

86 Manning to Manning, 29 August 1799: Manning Collection, Acadia. Fanny was about ten years younger than James. Together they had at least five children, the first in 1799 and (it would seem) the last — a daughter — on 11 November 1814, when Fanny was forty.

87 The 1835 "Memoir" in the *Bapt Miss Mag* seems to be the only source to mention this important point. As Edward Manning never refers to it I question whether it is true.

88 Manning to Manning, 29 August 1799; Manning to Manning, 9 November 1816: Manning Collection, Acadia.

89 Manning to Manning, 11 April 1817: *ibid.*

90 Edward Manning Journal, 1 & 13 June 1817; Halfyard to Manning, 4 June 1817: *ibid.*

91 Edward Manning Journal, 18 July 1817; Manning to Manning, 9 November 1817: *ibid.*

92 Quoted in J.M. Cramp, "Baptists of Nova Scotia" (a series of newspaper articles published early in the 1860s

and made available in a standardly-paginated edition by Acadia), p. 135 (Article *XXIX*).

93 *Minutes of the . . . Baptist Association* (1818), p. 8.

94 "Every Brother ought . . . to keep a Diary:" (1829) I *Bapt Miss Mag* (#10), p. 291. Interestingly, Charles Tupper also referred to his journal as "minutes:" Bill, *Fifty Years with the Baptists*, p. 691.

On the purposes for which journals were kept, Joseph Dimock offered the following:

> I have not had time to write any so long that much is lost that would be well worth remarking — it would have done my heart good to have wrote it down & hereafter been joy to have read it: Levy, *Dimock's Diary*, p. 46.

95 Saint John was New Brunswick's principal settlement and commercial centre. Founded by Loyalists in 1783 and incorporated as a "city" in 1785, the place cannot have had more than four thousand inhabitants by the time of Manning's 1801 visit. Settlement was then chiefly on the Parrtown peninsula on the east side of the harbour, the settlement on the Carleton (west) side having much decayed.

An 1802 traveller described Saint John as built on rocks but well laid out and with an excellent harbour. He added that, "The City has at present one large handsome church [Trinity] and a county court-house in a handsome square near the water, and (to their honor) several schoolhouses". "Back of the City on a rocky eminence is a fort [Fort Howe] and a block-house": [Charles Turner], "New Brunswick in 1802," in (1907) 7 *Acadiensis* 128 (27 August 1802).

Of Saint John's spiritual state a Presbyterian preacher recorded these impressions in 1804:

> There are a great number of Inhabitants in this City but only two Ministers, a Church [of England] man [Mather Byles] and [a] Methodist, and from what I could learn vital goodness is a great rarity in this

place. . . . [T]he religion that is cheapest is considered best: John Mitchell Journal, 15 August 1804: PANS.

Wesleyan Methodist preachers came and went so fast that it would be difficult to know to whom Mitchell refers. The Wesleyan society was an active one. Its leading figure gives a good description of it in Stephen Humbert, *Rise and Progress of Methodism, in the Province of New Brunswick, from its Commencement until about the Year 1805* (Saint John, 1836).

At the town's founding the principal religious minority was ethnic Presbyterianism: see D.G. Bell, *Early Loyalist Saint John* (1983), pp. 67, 81. In 1787, for example, the rector reported a "great number of Scotch Dissenters" but added that they were "moderate, and regularly attend at Church during the Winter": Bisset to SPG, 4 July 1787, summarized in SPG Journal, 19 October 1787: PAC Reel A-157. (Similarly, at St Andrews the rector found that the "greater Part" of the inhabitants were "Scotch Presbyterians" : Andrews to Peters, 21 July 1786: Peters Papers, American Church Historical Society.) This early strength in the ethnic Presbyterian (as opposed to Congregational Presbyterian) community is emphasized because it has never received scholarly attention and, at least at Saint John, seems not to have given rise to a significant organized religious community. In John Moir's *Enduring Witness: A History of the Presbyterian Church in Canada* (1975) New Brunswick is scarcely mentioned.

The presence of a Calvinist Methodist party among Saint John Anglicans was noted earlier in this chapter. There cannot have been more than a handful of White Baptists at Saint John by 1801.

96 It is not easy to distinguish between a "lecture" and a "meeting." My sense is that a meeting always featured preaching (an exercise defined as exposition of a Biblical text), whereas a lecture was something less. Perhaps a lecture was akin to a combined Bible study

159

and prayer meeting. I presume a lecture was understood to have a relatively definite length whereas meetings were indefinite in length.

97 Mather Byles (1734-1814) was descended from a respected succession of Massachusetts Congregational divines. He left the Congregational ministry for that of the Church of England, serving as rector of Christ Church, Boston. A Loyalist, Byles became the second rector of Saint John (considered the most important parish in British America) in 1789. In the wake of Manning's 1801 visit Byles wrote that:

> I have myself never condescended to mention to you the Methodists & New-Lights, because they give me but little Disturbance, & their influence in my Mission is very inconsiderable. I have always viewed their enthusiastic vagaries, & their malignant attempts to injure the established Church with the Contempt which they deserve. I am much more seriously apprehensive of the secret growth of Infidelity & the artful Dissemination of French Principles: Byles to SPG, 24 December 1801: PAC Reel A-184.

The most accessible of many sketches of Byles' life is in (1983) V *Dict Can Biog* 127.

98 Church of England services at Saint John were held in the first Trinity church, finished *c*1791 and destroyed in the Great Fire (1877). A rare photograph of the chaste and rational elegance of the old Trinity is printed in T.R. Millman & A.R. Kelley, *Atlantic Canada to 1900: A History of the Anglican Church* (1983), facing p. 99.

99 A 1792 traveller described Hazen's Marsh as:

> a large meadow, consisting of some thousand acres, formerly overflowed by the sea . . . . This immense tract of meadow produces a quantity of hay, that the city and all the neighbourhood consume only a

small portion of its produce, and it is sufficient to supply ten times the demand.

Those to whom Manning preached were likely poor tenant farmers: Patrick Campbell, *Travels in the Interior Inhabited Parts of North America* (1793) (1937 edn), p. 258. The Wesleyan Duncan McColl preached and baptized at the marsh in late 1798 or early 1799. Here he encountered "an Antinomian preacher".

100   Apart from the well-known company of Quaker Loyalists who settled Beaver Harbour with the Baptists, little is known of Quaker activity in New Brunswick. There were said to be two Quaker preachers visiting Saint John in 1786, and Bishop Inglis encountered a Quaker preacher (an Evans from Haddonfield, NJ) who had been at Saint John in 1795: Byles to Winslow, 2 August 1787, in W.O. Raymond (ed), *Winslow Papers* (1901), p. 345; Inglis Journal, 7 August 1795: PANS. By 1800 there was an "exempt" company of Kings County militia, formed of those who (like Quakers) were otherwise excused from militia service. It is, however, almost impossible to believe that there was any significant number of Quakers in the St John valley.

101   Wife of the prominent pre-Loyalist ship owner, Mrs. Daniel Lovitt was aunt to the young Baptist preacher Jarvis Ring. Ring recalled of her at this time that she was "a grate person for Metings".

102   Elijah Estabrooks, ordained over the Baptist church in Waterborough less than a year earlier, was returning from what was probably his first preaching tour outside the St John valley, undertaken in connection with a visit to the annual Baptist Association. James Murphy's history at Eastport has already been given.

103   I take this to be a poor neighbourhood (at the Indian House?) on the east side of the River at the point of portage around the Reversing Falls. I think it possible that the Lovitt family Manning mentions lived at the Falls.

104 Jarvis Ring's memoir states that at this time in Saint John "Metings was held at M'r George Hardings; he with his father [Capt William Harding] were Baptist". The Hardings had arrived at Saint John in a company of New Jersey Loyalists.

105 Either Zebedee Ring (father of the preacher Jarvis Ring) or his brother Levi, pre-Loyalists. Both had been "Brooksites" (Zebedee was a brother-in-law of Elijah Estabrooks) but neither joined the Waterborough Baptist church (although two of Zebedee's sons did).

106 Zebulon Estey (d1806), a Gagetown pre-Loyalist, was clerk of the Waterborough Baptist church and probably the most prominent Baptist layman in early New Brunswick.

107 Probably Capt Thomas Peters, a New York Loyalist shown on an 1801 jury list as living in the parish of Maugerville.

108 George Cyphers was a Loyalist disbanded from the 2nd New Jersey Volunteers. Henry Hale preached at his house in Kingsclear in 1809.

109 Probably Albus Cole, formerly a corporal in the Kings American Dragoons. He was one of the initial (1800) members of the Prince William Baptist church, although he subsequently joined that in Kingsclear. I have already speculated that it was his wife who was Joseph Crandall's first immersion above Fredericton. In 1809 Henry Hale preached at their home in French Village, Kingsclear.

110 Many of the Hammonds had removed from Waterborough to Kingsclear or Prince William. Among them were Archelaus Sr, Archelaus Jr, Simon (who joined the Prince William Baptist church in 1802) and Lathrop (who joined in 1807 and was ordained the church's pastor in 1810). Manning would have known them from his sojourn in Waterborough during the Hammondite horrors in 1793.

111 Conference meetings were generally held one Saturday a month and almost always on the day before communion was to be administered. A conference meeting was the forum in which members of the "church" (people merely in the "society" would not attend) enquired into each other's spiritual health, discussed cases of discipline and did whatever secular business needed to be attended. It would have singing and prayer but not preaching. It was presided over by a "moderator" elected anew at each session rather than by the pastor (although the pastor was often chosen moderator). Conference meetings were also held in preparation for formation of a church. Church record books reflect Saturday conference meetings rather than Sunday services. The practice survives in the few Free Baptist churches but not among the United Baptists.

112 Many Loyalist Browns settled in the general area. Perhaps Manning's most likely host was Ebenezer Brown, formerly captain in the Guides and Pioneers. He had joined the Prince William Baptist church only three months before Manning's visit. The Wesleyan Daniel Fidler preached at his house in 1796: Smith, *History of the Methodist Church*, I, p. 316.

113 Several Wheelers lived in the area but this is likely the Loyalist Nicholas Wheeler, who joined the Prince William Baptist church in 1802 just after the Manning visit. A Ruth Wheeler, perhaps his wife, had been among the church's original (1800) members.

114 A Loyalist in the 2nd DeLanceys, John Manzer was the first deacon of the Prince William Baptist church. In 1805 he "removed up the Nashwalk".

115 Either Enoch Dow or his son Amos Dow, pre-Loyalists.

116 A sergeant in the disbanded Kings American Regiment, George Hartley married the pre-Loyalist Abigail Estey (presumably the niece or daughter of Zebulon Estey), whose sister was the wife of John Dow.

163

117　This is presumably the Annapolis pre-Loyalist Amos Gates. In 1792, when he married the pre-Loyalist Margaret Larlee, he was apparently living in the parish of Woodstock.

118　The Loyalist Samuel Moores was an original (1800) member of the Prince William Baptist church. The churchbook states that he died 30 May 1803.

119　This is presumably one of the pre-Loyalist "Brooksite" Coys, probably Amasa Coy, one of the original (1800) members of the Prince William Baptist church. His brother Edward was deacon of the Waterborough Baptist church and his brother John would by 1807 be deacon of the Nashwaak Baptist church. The memoirist Mary Bradley was a sister. In 1814 Amasa Coy became one of the original members of the Fredericton Baptist church. He was also a founder of the Bank of Fredericton. In 1809 Henry Hale preached at "br Coy's" in Queensbury.

120　Although there was a Moses and a David Joslin in the area, this is probably a reference to the Loyalist Isaac Joslin, one of the original (1800) members of the Prince William Baptist church or to the Loyalist Andrew Joslin, who joined just after Manning's visit. The churchbook notes that at some point Isaac Joslin removed to Saint John. There is presumably a connection with Lathrop Hammond, who in 1803 married Bathsheba Joslin. Henry Hale preached at "br Joslins" in 1809.

121　The pre-Loyalist John Barker, formerly of Sheffield, was one of the original (1800) deacons of the Prince William Baptist church.

122　The Loyalist William West was the first clerk of the Prince William Baptist church.

123　This may have been the John Estey who was brother to Zebulon Estey.

124 Both Thomas and George Everett were Loyalists. In 1812, when the Keswick Baptist church re-organized itself on close communion lines (the earliest surviving record), Thomas Everett was a member.

125 John Nevers has a distinctively pre-Loyalist (Maugerville) surname but I can learn nothing concerning him.

126 Jarvis Ring speaks of him simply as "a M'r Ran from N. Scotia".

127 Stephen and Benjamin Glasier were brothers of Beamsley Glasier, one of the principal land speculators on the St John in the twenty years before the arrival of the Loyalists. Just after James Manning's visit both Glasiers joined the Waterborough Baptist church although they lived in Lincoln. Rebecca Glasier, who married Hammond Estabrooks (Elijah's brother), was presumably a sister..

128 John Wasson was a Sheffield pre-Loyalist. He was married to an Estey. Seth Noble's account of his religious experience was quoted at the beginning of this chapter.

129 This "Deacon Smith" was not a member of the Waterborough Baptist church. He was likely Nathan Smith, who as late as 1796 (the latest available record) was ruling elder of the Sheffield Congregational church. Smiths were also prominent in Sheffield Wesleyan affairs, but the tenor of Manning's remarks suggests that he was not breakfasting with a Wesleyan. Nathan Smith is probably also the "Mr. S____" mentioned in George Patterson, *Memoir of the Rev. James MacGregor* (1859), p. 343.

130 There is a biographical sketch of James Mann in (1983) V *Dict Can Biog* 573.

131 Evan Munroe, a Maugerville Loyalist, is the only Munro on the east side of the River in the jury list for 1801.

132 Samuel Upton Sr and Jr were Sheffield pre-Loyalists. In 1796 one of them was a member of the Sheffield Congregational church.

133 Hugh Cowperthwaite was a Sheffield Loyalist from New Jersey.

134 Samuel Bridges was a Sheffield pre-Loyalist. He signed an 1802 Baptist marriage petition.

135 Ebenezer Hatheway was a Loyalist from Massachusetts living in Burton.

136 A pre-Loyalist, Benjamin Newcomb was one of the original (1800) members of the Waterborough Baptist church. He signed an 1802 Baptist marriage petition.

137 David Curry was a Loyalist.

138 Possibly Stephen Kinney, a pre-Loyalist signatory to an 1802 Baptist marriage petition.

139 A Loyalist, John Marsh was one of the original (1800) members of the Waterborough Baptist church. He married a sister of the preacher Elijah Estabrooks. In 1812 he appears to have joined the Keswick Baptist church when it adopted close communion. In 1813 he was among those dismissed from the Waterborough Baptist church to form the Fredericton Baptist church. He was a signatory to an 1802 Baptist marriage petition.

140 A German Loyalist, Dr Charles Gunter (1760-1835) was described in 1811 as "often embarrassed to get home his fees, of hay, salt fish, or banded pork, but I have seen him returning with boots": Howard Temperley (ed), *Gubbins' New Brunswick Journals* (1980), p. 26 (20 July 1811). Gunter, who lived in Fredericton, was host to Henry Hale in 1809.

141 Probably Samuel Hartt (of the "Hartites," so called). He was immersed in 1800 by Crandall but is conspicuously absent from the membership list of the Waterborough Baptist church. He was first married to a sister of the

166

preacher Elijah Estabrooks. Significantly, two sons of the marriage were named George Whitefield Hartt and Henry Alline Hartt. By his second marriage (to a sister of the preacher Lathrop Hammond) Hartt was the father of Samuel Hartt Jr, later one of the most prominent of Free Christian Baptist ministers — although his step-brothers were rigidly Calvinistic. Samuel Hartt Sr was one of the regular hosts of the travelling Allinite itinerant Daniel Shaw: Edward Weyman, "Notes Regarding Early Ministers," Acadia. He was also father-in-law of the Baptist preacher Jarvis Ring.

142 This cannot be the Peters of note 107. It is possibly the Peters who lived (kept a public house?) on Grimross Neck: Temperley *Gubbins' Journal*, p. 9 (11 July 1811). In 1795 a Mrs Pugsley, mother-in-law to such a Peters, complained to Bishop Inglis that Peters and his wife "were fond of the New-Lights & Methodists": Inglis Journal, 15 August 1795: PANS.

143 Pennsylvania Loyalists, both Clement Lucas, Sr and Jr, signed an 1802 Baptist marriage petition.

144 There are too many Clarks, Chases and Vanwarts in the area to name these with certainty. The last two families were Loyalists.

145 There were several Gerows in the area. The only one to sign an 1802 Baptist marriage petition was James Gerow, a Loyalist from New York. When Henry Hale preached "at br J. Gerow's" in 1810 he appears to have been in Kingston or Springfield.

146 Elisha Clark was a Loyalist.

147 George Case, presumably a Loyalist, signed an 1802 Baptist marriage petition. Henry Hale preached at his house, apparently on Long Island, in 1809.

148 Possibly Marcus Palmer, a Loyalist and signatory to an 1802 Baptist marriage petition.

149 A New Jersey Loyalist, John Colwell was one of the two Queens County justices of the peace to sign the 1802 Dissenters' marriage petition. An incident concerning him will be found in Walter Bates, *Mysterious Stranger* (1910 edn), pp. 42-43.

150 The name is sufficiently unusual to allow one to suggest that this is the Loyalist Stephen Sands.

151 Samuel Nicklin was a Pennsylvania Loyalist and signatory to an 1802 Baptist marriage petition. Within a few years he was leading an Allinite society in Hampstead.

152 Probably the pre-Loyalist John Jones, who lived at the head of Long Reach, in Upper Greenwich. Henry Hale preached at his home extensively in 1809-10. He also preached extensively at Stephen Jones', but I take this to be on Belleisle Bay.

153 An Englishman and former Roman Catholic priest, Robert Norris was missionary at Chester until his removal to the New Brunswick parish of Westfield and Greenwich in 1801. From 1806 he served in Cornwallis.

154 In loose pages once sewn into the back of the journal volume are verses covering five sides. One is written in someone's "best" handwriting, the other in a more cursive hand. At the foot of the verses are two versions of a "Rev'd James Manning" signature written in the same style and with the same instrument as the second of the two poems. As ministers do not normally style themselves "Rev'd," one would assume that the two signatures represent either a practice effort by James Manning or were written by someone else to attribute the verses immediately above to James Manning. While I will not venture to decide the question, I do think that all of the handwriting is consistent with that of James Manning. Both of the verses are clearly bad enough to be local. The first (I am advised by Frederick C.

Burnett) is connected in theme, and similar in metre, to
verses in the *American Vocalist.*

[FIRST POEM]

Meeting of Three Indians

Once more welcome dearest friends
Now at last our wandrings end
And tho hope did oft depart
Oft tho sorrow sped its dart
Let our griefs no more remain
Since we three now meet again.

2nd   Though remote we long have been
Many a toilsome day have seen
Through the burning zone we've trod
Or the Polar earth embraced
We have sweets from friendships ca- [torn]
Often of each other thought.

Let us seek that call [cool] retreat
Where we three oft used to meet
Where beneath the spreading shade
We have oft together strayed
And when last with anguished [heart]
We three friends were torn apart.

Ah! how altered is this bower
Where we first felt friendships power
How has time with ruthless blows
Laid its vigorous beauties low
Nought but this lone pine remains
And its naked arm sustains.

Are we now that youthful three
Who reclined beneath this tree
Men with verdant foliage crown'd
Now with moss and Ivy bound

Not more altered is this pine
Than our looks by wasting time.

Every feature then was fair
Nor was grief depicted there
Then our sparkling ey[e]s did glow
Then our cheeks with health did flow
Then the lamp of light was bright
Now it sheds a glimring light.

Though our mortal strength decay
Though our beauties waste away
Though our languied eyes are blear
And the frost of age appear
Still our friendships bright shall bloom
Far beyond the closing tomb.

[SECOND POEM]

Hark from the sky the trump proclaims
Jesus the Judge approaching nigh
See the creation wrapt in flames
First kindled by his vengful eye
When thus the mountains melt like wax
When earth and air and sea shall burn
When all the frame of nature breaks
Poor sinners whither wilt though [thou] turn
The ＿＿ey [tinney?] works which feeble men
Now boast or covet or admire
Their fancys and arts and treasures then
Shall perish in one common fire
Lord fix our hearts and hopes above
Since all below to ruin tends
Here may we trust obey and love
And their be found amongst thy friends
John in a ——— [vision?] saw the day
When the Judge will hasten down.

[here follow immediately the two
"Rev'd James Manning" signatures]

Chapter Three
THE JOURNAL OF JAMES INNIS,
1805-1811

THE JOURNAL OF JAMES INNIS, 1805-1811

I was Come to Cry against the altars of Baal.
James Innis, 1806

THE DECLINE OF THE BAPTISTS IN NEW BRUNSWICK, 1802-1810.

In Nova Scotia the reformation of 1798-1800 turned part of the pre-existing Allinite movement firmly in a Baptist direction. In that province the overwhelming majority of Allinites — and hence of Baptists — were of pre-Loyalist Yankee rather than Loyalist extraction. In New Brunswick, also, a good many Newlights of Yankee extraction entered the Baptist fold; and their leadership role in spearheading the Baptist drive can hardly be overemphasized. Yet there were relatively few pre-Loyalists in New Brunswick, and these few were concentrated along the Petitcodiac and in the Waterborough-Sheffield neighbourhood of the central St John valley. Even in 1800 it is likely that a majority of New Brunswick Baptists were Loyalists rather than pre-Loyalists; and the great majority of these Loyalist Baptists had formerly received their spiritual nourishment — to whatever extent — from the Church of England rather than dissenting sects. Thus, while the Nova Scotia version of the first Baptist reformation represented a move towards greater church discipline — and in that sense formalism — the same stir in New Brunswick was characterized by a movement away from formalism and towards spiritual vitality. For Nova Scotians, submission to the visible discipline of immersion symbolized their break with the religious anarchy associated with Allinism. But for New Brunswickers the same act, often performed before hundreds of curious onlookers, meant taking a bold stand in favour of vital spirituality in an environment dominated politically as well as religiously by the decorous formality of the Church of England.

The dramatic rise of Baptist sentiment — especially in the St John valley — was at the expense of its potential rivals: orthodox Congregationalism and Wesleyanism. While the Baptists may not have seriously cut into the numerical strength of these alternate vehicles of religious dissent (there being few areas of direct competition), they did effectively pre-empt opportunities for expansion. In the first decade of the nineteenth century there was only one orthodox (*ie,* non-Allinite) Congregational church in New Brunswick — that at Sheffield. In the 1790's the church retained a broad popular base, attracting the support of many local Loyalists (there being no Anglican service in Sheffield, except briefly during the John James affair). But from the mid-1790s to the 1820s the church was without regular preaching, a circumstance that brought on rapid decline. In that condition it was unable to lead what might otherwise have been a significant Congregationalist expansion in the St John valley as Loyalists sought a respectable alternative to the Church of England.[1]

The fortunes of Wesleyanism in the same decade were more complex. By the end of the eighteenth century Wesleyanism was the major vehicle of religious dissent in New Brunswick. (Presbyterians may actually have been more numerous but they were still unorganized.) Relatively the strongest sphere of Wesleyan influence was the Yorkshire-Cumberland ethnic base in Westmorland County. Early in the 1790s Wesleyans held two of the county's four seats in the House of Assembly. Yet by 1801 the Cumberland circuit (*ie,* both sides of the inter-colonial border, from Ramsheg to the Petitcodiac) numbered only 90. In 1804, it was 95, in 1808 it was 113 and by 1812 still only 135. In notably similar reports on the area William Black (in 1804) and Joshua Marsden (in 1805) explained that from a high of 200 members about 1780, the Cumberland circuit had been "continually apon the decline & scarcely any vestiges of the former work are now seen". This had occurred despite the presence of two local preachers and two chapels (one at Sackville and the other at nearby Point de Bute). Both Black and Marsden put the blame for the relative failure of Wesleyanism in the region on the tares sown twenty years earlier by Henry Alline. They might also have noted a lack of steady ministerial talent and the fact that one of the appointed preachers who did serve there (Thomas Olivant) was excluded for drunkenness (whereupon he fled to preach for a time in Cape Breton).[2]

A second area of relative Wesleyan strength was

173

western Charlotte County, bordering Maine. Here the unique combination of a fixed Wesleyan pastor (Duncan McColl) at St Stephen and the absence of organized opposition (the Anglican rector lived at St Andrews) gave the Wesleyans the kind of opportunity to attract support they did not enjoy elsewhere. By 1805 there were chapels at both St Stephen and St David. These chapels may have been often crowded, but the number who would formally submit to Methodist discipline remained constant in the first decade of the century. In 1801 the circuit numbered eighty souls, the same statistic reported in 1812.[3]

In the St John valley at the end of the eighteenth century there were perhaps six Wesleyan churches (Saint John, Long Reach, Sheffield-Maugerville, Nashwaak, Fredericton and, possibly, Grand Lake). But the churches above Saint John had so little contact with Wesleyan preaching that they go virtually unmentioned in the surviving missionary correspondence. In 1804 William Black thought there were about 200 Methodists in the whole valley. In 1812 the figure was 209. By 1805 there were chapels in Saint John, Fredericton, Sheffield and (if it was still in use) on the Nashwaak. Yet the regular Methodist ministry so completely deserted the St John valley (apart from Saint John itself) that the churches up the River were forced to engage the services of the Sheffield schoolmaster Thomas Olivant, who had formerly been excluded from the connection for his intemperance.[4]

During the first decade of the nineteenth century no new Wesleyan church was gathered in New Brunswick — certainly none in addition to those named above. Probably the only area of significant vitality was at Saint John. Here the Methodist meeting was the only religious organization in the town apart from Trinity Church. It is therefore not surprising that, despite the defection of the leading local layman (Stephen Humbert),[5] Joshua Marsden could boast in 1806 of a church of ninety and a congregation of 250. It was about this time that the congregation undertook the building of a large new chapel. This, and a small reformation in Sheffield in early 1807, were the only highlights in what was otherwise a decade of lost opportunity for the Wesleyans. While the Baptists were making great strides the Methodists were barely holding their own. William Black's 1804 admission of defeat applies to the whole decade.

> If this river [St John] had been properly supplied with suitable preachers, for 12 years back, all the entire country for 200 miles would have embraced the Methodist Doctrines. That time is now lost: they are deeply initiated into the mysteries of Antinomianism, which in some Instances [the Hammondites], has produced extravagances, hardly to be surpassed in the whole history of Enthusiasm. Most of those who were in connection with M'r Alleine, and here [are] commonly called Newlights, have lately both Preachers and people, assumed the name of Baptists and become somewhat more sober both in doctrines, and discipline. Their doctrines formerly were a strange mixture of Mysticism and Antinomianism. They have now adopted a looser kind of Calvinism than generally prevails in England.[6]

In suggesting to his undiscerning English readers that most New Brunswick Baptists had — like those in Waterborough and Sackville — passed through a Newlight stage, Black was simply mistaken. He was generalizing from the Nova Scotia experience in a way inapplicable to New Brunswick. But his basic point — that the swing to the Baptists had foreclosed opportunities for Wesleyan expansion in the province — was quite correct.

The statistical dimension of Baptist growth in the first decade of the nineteenth century is extraordinary. At a time when neither orthodox Congregationalism nor Wesleyan Methodism could broaden its New Brunswick base, the Baptists organized about twenty churches. Until the gathering of the Sackville church in 1799 the number of Baptists in New Brunswick cannot have exceeded one hundred. Yet by the middle of the first decade of the nineteenth century there were likely about 1500 Baptists and supporters in the province, approximately 8% of the Protestant population.[7] Baptist expansion was, however, heavily concentrated in the first half of the decade, suggesting both that the initial Baptist reformation lasted rather longer in New Brunswick than in

175

Nova Scotia but that, conversely, New Brunswick did not share in the spectacular Nova Scotia reformation of 1806-08.

BAPTIST CHURCHES IN NEW BRUNSWICK, 1799-1810

Date of Organization	Church
1799	Sackville
1800	Salisbury; Waterborough Norton; Prince William; Sussex; (*prob*) Woodstock
1801	Kingsclear; Long Island
1802	(*prob*) Springfield; (*prob*) Hampton; Eastport (Maine)
1804	Nashwaak; Wakefield
1806	St Andrews; St George; St David
1810	Carleton; Saint John

Here the qualification "probably" relates only to the year of organization, not to the fact of church formation itself. The St Martins (likely by 1805) and Keswick (about 1810-11) churches are omitted because of uncertainty over date of formation. The Springfield and Eastport churches are listed under their first rather than their second organizations (1809 and 1810 respectively). From this Table it will be seen that the initial Baptist organizational drive ended in 1804. Appropriately, it was in that year that the Baptist Association met for the first time in New Brunswick (at Waterborough). Further contours of the Baptist experience in New Brunswick during the first decade of the nineteenth century are best viewed from a regional perspective.

176

PASSAMAQUODDY It was preachers from the Maritimes rather than New England who introduced vital religion to the Passamaquoddy region. As noted in Chapter Two the campaign began on the Maine side of the border in the mid-1790s with the preaching of the Manning brothers and James Murphy, augmented in the early years of the nineteenth century by Daniel Shaw and Elijah Estabrooks. By 1796 there was an Allinite church in Eastport and an Allinite meeting in Machias. In 1802 Estabrooks ordained his friend Murphy over the Eastport Baptist church, which drew some of its members from the adjacent New Brunswick islands. Thereafter, the Maritime offensive on eastern Maine fell off sharply, except through the continuing residence of James Murphy. Maritime preachers still visited the region (Thomas Ansley[8] in 1805 and 1807; John Burton[9] in 1807; William Archer[10] in 1808; John Fay[11] and Joseph Crandall[12] in 1809; Edward Manning in 1810[13]), but not as part of the concerted campaign that had formerly made the region an outpost of Allinism. The declining Maritime presence in eastern Maine coincided closely with the disgrace of James Murphy and with the arrival of the first New England Baptist "missionaries", who would successfully claim both Washington and Charlotte Counties for the Yankee religious orbit.

Despite the early Maritime Newlight and Baptist drive in eastern Maine, Charlotte County was for many years left primarily to the Wesleyan form of dissent, as personified by Duncan McColl. But beyond his immediate neighbourhood of St Stephen and St David McColl travelled little, and only two other Wesleyans visted the county in the entire 1785-1810 period. As well, Jotham Sewall, a US Congregationalist, preached in Charlotte County in at least 1803 and 1805 but gathered no church.[14] In 1804 the Scot John Mitchell, an unordained Congregationalist/Presbyterian missionary from eastern Nova Scotia, laboured at St George.[15]

It was not until 1804 that the first ordained Baptist entered Charlotte County. That preacher was James Murphy, whose labours in Charlotte came on the eve of excommunication from his own Eastport church.[16] He was followed by the unordained Sussex Baptist Thomas Ansley, probably on the journey to Maine that would result in his ordination. Ansley's performance drew mixed reviews. The Maine Baptist Isaac Case later thought that his labours around St Andrews had "been blest in several places". "He met with some opposition", Case added, "being apprehended, and a young man with him, for preaching, and put under keepers for two days, but by some means they were let go, without receiving much injury."[17] The Wesleyan Duncan McColl had quite a different view of Ansley's work.

> In the fall [of 1805] a man of the Baptists ... came to St David's, and blew up the coals of the old new-light business ... . They boasted of [their intention of] converting thirty people of Mill-town, in St Stephen's [parish], and of breaking up this Church. They came in a body for that purpose — screaming and falling into fits &c., running into the water to be baptized. At last one of the magistrates took up Mr. A[nsley], who saw fit to run away from his keeper, and so left the country without converting any at Mill-town, or breaking any one off from us.[18]

Even a Baptist preacher thought the people of St David "had imbibed strange notions, and gone into wild extremes, the particulars of which I forbear to mention", although he did not attribute the confusion to Ansley.[19] In the same year as Ansley's tour (1805), John Still became the first American Baptist to labour in Charlotte County. Preaching briefly at St George, he immersed eleven but formed no church.[20]

The first major American incursion into Charlotte County — and, indeed, the Maritimes[21] — came in 1806, when three ordained Baptists (Isaac Case, Henry Hale, Robert Low) arrived in two waves. Drawn by word of Ansley's impact, they preached in every settled part of the county except, significantly, McColl's St Stephen and remote Grand Manan.[22] Within a week of setting foot on British soil Case and Hale gathered (on 1 August 1806) a Baptist church in St Andrews. By year's end membership stood at about thirty-eight. Two weeks later, on 16 August, they formed a church of about fifteen in St George.[23] On the evening of 31 December 1806 Case and Robert Low added a third church (at St David) to their tally. At the conclusion of their visit the St David church had twenty-six members.

The gathering of three churches in quick succession suggests that the Baptist organizational drive had spread from the St John valley to New Brunswick's southwestern frontier, but this was not the case. Politically Charlotte County was part of New Brunswick, but by 1806 the only New Brunswick resident ever to have preached the Baptist message there was the unordained Thomas Ansley. The gathering of the three 1806 churches was wholly unrelated to the fortunes of the Baptists in the St John valley. It represented a territorial gain for the New England rather than the Maritime Baptists. Ten years earlier eastern Maine had been a satellite of the Maritime Newlights. By 1806 the whole Passamaquoddy region, on both sides of the frontier, had been pulled into a New England orbit, where it would remain, with regard to vital religion, for several decades. Only in this corner of New Brunswick would the Yankee Free Will Baptists, Christ-ians, Unitarians and Universalists have any success.

Formation of the three churches also suggests a depth of Baptist interest in Charlotte County that is probably misleading. One suspects that Case and his contemporaries brought them into existence prematurely in order to justify their own continuance as paid emissaries of the Massachusetts Baptist Missionary Society. After this 1806 mission Case boasted of 205 immersions and organization of six frontier churches (including the three in Charlotte), but not one of them had access to regular preaching. They would, therefore, have had a hard struggle to retain a visibility. In the case of Charlotte County it is likely that all three churches died out within a few years of formation. The 1847 historian of the four-part "Cause of God in Charlotte County" had heard of only the extinct St George organization.[24] The latest evidence of the St David church is Henry Hale's report of the "shocking unhappy divisions reigning among them" in mid-1808.[25] The St George organization is last heard from in 1809, when it was duped by the "impostor" John Fay.[26] Isaac Case's remark late in 1810 that the St Andrews church had been "destitute of preaching for a long time" suggests that it still existed. But probably none of the three Charlotte County churches survived long thereafter. It must be significant that Edward Manning, Joseph Crandall and Theodore Harding all visited Eastport late in the first decade of the nineteenth century but none is known to have preached in Charlotte County. Indeed the only ordained Maritime Baptist (unless one counts James Murphy) known to have preached in the county at any time before 1815 is John Burton in mid-1807.[27]

SOUTHEASTERN NEW BRUNSWICK

Geographically Charlotte County was an extension of Maine. Its only practical link with the rest of New Brunswick was by water. It is, therefore, not surprising that Baptist development there was unrelated to developments in the St John valley. To a considerable extent the same is true of the Tantramar-Petitcodiac region of the southeast. Its settlers were a heterogeneous mixture of Acadians, Germans, Yorkshiremen, New Englanders and Loyalists. In religious terms it was the most volatile region of New Brunswick. Like Nova Scotia's Falmouth and Newport in the 1780s and 1790s, it was an area in which many religious novelties could gain a hearing but none could prosper. Connected to the heartland of the province by a long and arduous treck along the Kennebecasis, the whole trans-border region was geographically, ethnically and religiously more a part of Nova Scotia than New Brunswick.

The gathering of a Sackville Baptist church in 1799 and another in Salisbury the year following are two of the best-known episodes of New Brunswick Baptist history. Within two years, Joseph Crandall later recalled, each church had over 100 immersed members.[28] By 1803 the Sackville church had a meeting-house.[29] But having come this far, Crandall's autobiographical sketch falls silent as to the further travel of the two churches in which he served as pastor, and apparently with good reason. By 1809, when the next membership profile of the churches becomes available, Sackville was reduced to 52 members and Salisbury to only 40. In that year a visiting US Baptist declared the Sackville church "in a backslidden state". The earliest surviving entry in the Sackville Churchbook (1808) declares that "Zion['s] walls was broken Down" and the "church of christ" was "scatter'd".[30] Significantly, the church noted that in future "none but Baptised beleavers should be

180

received as members," signalling that it had at some point earlier retreated from its original Baptist constitution into Allinism.[31] The labours of Daniel Shaw, Jacob Peck and Matthew Fenwick[32] in the region also testify to residual Allinism, as does the predicament of Obediah Newcomb in neighbouring Shepody (Hopewell).[33] Newcomb preached the Baptist line steadily from at least 1803 until his ordination on 4 July 1811. Yet in all that time neither Newcomb (whose labours were always described favourably) nor Henry Hale (who laboured extensively in the region) nor the presence in their midst of Nicholas Pierson (formerly the Baptist pastor at Horton) could convince the Allinites of Shepody to go into the water. Consequently Newcomb had to be ordained an evangelist rather than a pastor.

Baptist fortunes in the region briefly revived at the end of the first decade of the century. The Sackville church started keeping its records in order and reasserted Baptist discipline, a small church was gathered in Amherst in 1809, Obediah Newcomb was ordained with a view to planting a Baptist church in Shepody, the Baptist Association held its annual meeting in the region (at Sackville) in 1810 and the Salisbury church had constructed a meeting-house by 1811 (perhaps earlier). This revival of the Baptist cause was led by a strong contingent of New Englanders (Amos Allen, Henry Hale, Job Cushman, Daniel Merrill) and Thomas Ansley of Sussex. Joseph Crandall seems to have had little to do with the campaign (he was often elsewhere) until he and Henry Hale triggered a reformation in the Salisbury neighbourhood early in 1811. In 1810 Salisbury had reported only 46 members to the Baptist Association; by mid-1811 the number was nearly doubled to 83. A year later it was 110, making Salisbury the second largest church in the Association.

Yet the rapid expansion of the Salisbury church merely restored its membership to the level of a decade earlier, and even this success was transitory. As early as 1810 the church declared itself divided by those who "stand opposed to the order of God's house" (*ie*, opposed to close communion).[34] While no immediate separation took place (at least none was reflected in the annual Association statistics) the crisis evidently came to a head in late 1813 or early 1814 when twenty-five members were formally excluded. And there are other indications that the apparent revival in Baptist fortunes in the region was only superficial. The new Amherst church, founded in 1809, remained with fewer than twenty members for many years, and the Sackville church actually declined, from 55 members in 1810 to 50 in 1812.

While there were probably more immersed persons in the Petitcodiac-Sackville region in 1810 than a decade earlier, there were actually fewer who were willing to be members of a Baptist church. Thus the first decade of organized Baptist presence in southeastern New Brunswick was in great measure one of failure and decline. A spectacular beginning was followed by a rapid falling away. Yet the Baptists were not suffering at the hands of the Wesleyans (the fortunes of which were stagnant), and the Church of England was scarcely known in the region. Equally clearly, the Baptist decline in the first decade of the century cannot have been just the result of the close communion controversy, for that was first evidenced about 1810, when the set-back was already pronounced. One is left with the inference that the Baptists, like the Wesleyans, were on the defensive to resurgent Allinism. It will be recalled that when the Wesleyans William Black and Joshua Marsden tried to account for the disheartening malaise in local Wesleyanism, they did not blame the Baptists. Each attributed it to the lasting influence of Henry Alline. Similarly, the Sackville Baptist church was gathered in 1799 as an organization of immersed believers; yet within a few years the church was admitting unimmersed members, so that its Baptist character had to be reasserted in 1808. Under popular pressure the Sackville church had for a time reverted to Allinism. In Shepody the steady labours of Obediah Newcomb, begun in or before 1803, were not enough to overcome the residual Allinite notion that immersion and church order were mere non-essentials.

A second factor which helps to account for the decline of the organized Baptists and the stagnation of the Wesleyans in the southeast region was the profound check given vital religion by the circumstances attending the 1805 murder of Mercy Hall. In the fall of 1804 a number of earnest Christians on remote Shediac Bay commenced meeting twice weekly for spiritual exercises. It is not known whether they were moved to do so under the stimulus of any visiting preacher, but the unordained Presbyterian John Mitchell had laboured in the neighbourhood in 1803 and Joseph Crandall is said to have been there in 1804.[35] At first these essentially Newlight meetings attracted general support among the English families in the neighbourhood, but when Amos Babcock — a poor farmer-fisherman of Newport pre-Loyalist extraction — turned preacher-exhorter, some recoiled at the "confusion" he generated.

In the early weeks of 1805 the neighbourhood was visited by the unordained Newlight preacher Jacob Peck of Salisbury.[36] Peck was a product of the Hillsborough pre-Loyalist Germans on whom Henry Alline had made so deep an impression twenty-five years earlier. In Shediac Peck preached an apocalyptic message, prophesied that Napoleon would overturn all the European monarchies and that the end of Time was near. Under his influence two of the young women in the Newlight circle — Sarah Cornwall and Mary Babcock — also assumed a prophetic role. Among those consigned to hell was Amos Babcock's sister, Mercy Hall. Under the stimulus of prophesies by Peck and the girls and weakened by the strain of prolonged, intense religious exercises, Amos Babcock lost touch with mundane reality and became attuned to what he believed were communications from heaven.

On the evening of 13 February 1805 Babcock heard a noise which, he at length concluded, was the metaphorical "Midnight Cry" of Matthew 25:6. Looking out a window he saw "Stars falling from heaven" and announced that "it will be But a few Minutes Before they will be here". Declaring that he was the Angel Gabriel, Babcock told his family that they need not be afraid. He anointed his children and told his wife to keep her eyes fixed upon him, presumably their means of salvation. Babcock's feelings about his brother Jonathan are less clear. He ordered Jonathan to remove his clothes, evidently intending to kill him, but could bring himself to make only "two or three Feints, with his knife, & Struck him with his Left hand". Babcock had less compunction concerning his "reprobate" sister Mercy. Having ordered her to "make herself

183

Ready" by removing her clothes, he "Walked a Cross the house & then flew a cross" to her, striking three mortal blows with his knife. Some hours later Babcock was arrested. At the next circuit of the Supreme Court he was tried for murder and on 28 June 1805 put to death — the first judicial hanging in the history of the region.

The Late-Romantic historians who first publicized the Babcock affair considered it as merely a "tragedy," an isolated gothic curiosity from the days before "Baptists" rendered themselves respectable; and there is something to be said for the view that this chilling episode, acted out in one of the remotest English settlements in New Brunswick, was qualitatively different from New Dispensationalism in Nova Scotia or even the Lunt-Hammond affair in Waterborough a decade earlier.[37]   Yet in another sense the Peck-Babcock reformation at Shediac was, except for its bloody climax, an archetypal Newlight exercise, and the chance survival of documents generated by the legal process against Amos Babcock may permit us to make it one of the "elucidating contexts" of Maritime Newlight historiography.   The Jacob Peck revealed in the documents printed here in Appendix X is as typical a specimen of the Newlight preacher as an Edward Manning.   The religious exercises of Amos Babcock and his circle probably differed from those of a local exhorter-preacher like Christian Steeves only in the one climactic particular.   When the young women of Shediac consigned their neighbours to heaven and hell (in a manner reminiscent of the young women of Salem a century earlier) they were asserting — as youths and as females — their claim to equality in the spiritual realm in a manner that had countless parallels in the contemporary Maritime Newlight movement.[38] When Jacob Peck and Amos Babcock sensed that they were living in the last days they were not betraying eccentricity or derangement.   They were invoking one of the most widely-shared Protestant conventions of their time.[39]   Three years earlier, for example, Elijah Estabrooks, the Baptist pastor at Waterborough, was himself listening intently for the "Midnight Cry".   Amid a gathering of Baptist preachers on Long Island preparatory to the ordination of Charles Lewis, Estabrooks rose at the conclusion of Gilbert Harris' sermon:

and asked the patience of the people, till he communicated his thoughts of the near approach of the milennium day, when Christ will reign a thousand years. Mr. Estabrooks had spoken but a few minutes before his mind seemed to awake in possession of the glorious day. A divine spark catched in the hearts of Mr. [Theodore] Harding, Mr. [Joseph] Crandall, and some others, and increased to a mighty flame. One sang glory, glory, glory to God in the highest, and others hallelujah, hallelujah, amen, so let it be; indeed, sir, the people were overshadowed with power divine.[40]

Finally, it can fairly be said that Amos Babcock's conduct was only an extreme example of the basic Allinite tenet that the convert could — indeed must — be in an immediate relationship with God. To those Allinites called New Dispensationalists, this meant that the Bible, the ordinances, church organization, the conventions of morality and the laws of the state must yield to the primacy of immediate revelation from heaven. It was one such revelation that cost Mercy Hall her life.

The murder of Mercy Hall was the kind of event that both the friends and enemies of vital religion had always feared. To Solicitor-General Ward Chipman, prosecuting on behalf of the Crown, Babcock's democratic conceit — that God would condescend modern revelations to illiterate peasants — was symptomatic of the dangerous popular enthusiasms that had ruined France and America and put religious and political establishments throughout the North Atlantic world on the defensive. Babcock's pretension, Chipman reminded the murder jury, was a symbol of "all the disorganizing principles of the present day". Edward Manning also saw the murder of Mercy Hall in its wider significance. In his 1812 summary of Newlight and Baptist history Manning singled out two episodes as crucial in finally frightening Maritimers out of New Dispensationalism: the Lunt-Hammond affair and, especially, the murder of Mercy Hall:

[I]n one place [Waterborough] the Bible was actually bur[n]t from a pretended Zeal for God. And in annother where a company of this description Resided a sort of a leader in a fit of Religious Phrensey Prepaired a Knife and actually fearfully mangled and stabbed his Aged Sister residing with him to the heart, for which he was apprehended, tried, condemned and executed in Do[r]chester Westmorland county, New Brunswick. The other Instance was in that Province. Since the above circumstances that description of People have been losing ground verry fast.[41]

Manning's point was that the Babcock affair gave New Dispensationalism its deathblow, not that it immediately reoriented the extremists towards the greater discipline offered by the Baptists and Wesleyans. The murder of Mercy Hall, like Hammondism in the 1790's, must have turned many against vital religion in any form. This, in part, helps explain the surprising decline of the Baptist cause in southeastern New Brunswick after so promising a start.

ST JOHN VALLEY In the St John valley, as in southeastern New Brunswick, the rapid momentum of Baptist expansion in the early years of the nineteenth century was not sustained. Geographically remote from the Baptist hierarchy in Nova Scotia, the churches of the St John region had only two ordained pastors settled among them for any great part of the first decade of the century — and one of these (James Innis) was not in fellowship with the Nova Scotians. Of fourteen churches in the valley region[42] only five were sufficiently integrated into the emerging denomination to join the Nova Scotia Baptist Association during the period: Waterborough, Prince William, Wakefield, St Martins, Kingsclear.

In general the St John valley churches declined rather than prospered in the latter half of the decade. Waterborough, it is true, ended the decade with a respectable fifty members; but it had constant pastoral labour from Elijah Estabrooks, and in 1812 even this church would report "a very dark and a Cloudy day".[43] But Waterborough's stability was unique. More representative of general trends was the case of Prince William, founded the same year. On 2 January 1802 — just after James Manning's visit — the Churchbook boasted a membership of "one Hundred ... and the gates of Zion still throng'd with Converts". But nine years later the church was reduced to a mere forty-three, and this despite the 1810 ordination of Lathrop Hammond to be its pastor.[44]

Little is known of the fate of the neighbouring Woodstock Baptist church, except that an 1809 visitor found "verry unhappy divisions among them" occasioned by the preaching of Daniel Shaw. On 3 May 1812 the Prince William church received Amos Dow of the Woodstock church under its watch and care, a clear hint that all was not well in the Woodstock organization. The following year, when Dow applied to join the Prince William church, the clerk recorded that the Woodstock church "was not in a state of fellowship to grant [Dow] a Certifycate" of dismission.[45]

Declension is also evident in Wakefield, the uppermost Protestant community in the St John valley. Gathered on 14 July 1804 with fifty-six members, the Wakefield church probably enjoyed a higher degree of popular support than any other Baptist organization.in the Maritimes. Yet four years later, during a visit by James Manning, only twenty-seven would renew their covenant. In 1809, when the church voted on the controversial issue of whether to hear preaching from the itinerant Daniel Shaw, only twenty-six members participated.[46] The 1810 Baptist Association minutes put its membership at twenty-two.

Even less is known of the churches in the lower St John valley. Long Island is not heard of after 1803.[47] The same is true of Springfield, which had to be organized anew in 1809 and probably again in the early 1820s. The Hampton (French Village) Baptist church was regathered in 1817. Sussex also lost its visibility (before 1810) and had to be regathered in 1823.[48] St Martins was reconstituted in 1819.[49] The Norton church may also have disappeared. There is no reference to it for a decade after its 1800 founding, although some of the Norton people did erect a meeting-house in 1814.[50] In 1818, when a Norton church finally joined the Baptist Association, it had only six members — all newly immersed — suggesting that there was no continuity between it and the organization of 1800.

That the decline of the organized Baptist cause in the St John valley preceded the disruption over close communion is

187

quite apparent. After the white-hot enthusiasm of 1800-02, some falling off in support was only to be expected in a region with little pastoral stability. The 1805 murder of Mercy Hall would have given backsliders an excuse to break with Baptist discipline. Outmigration from the St John valley to Upper Canada may also have cost the organized Baptists more support than has yet been realized.[51] But just as in the southeast, it seems likely that the major cause of tension, separation and decline in the organized Baptist churches of western New Brunswick was a resurgence of Allinism.

In Wakefield the division was sealed by the close communion controversy but seems to have arisen earlier, over the more basic point whether the church should be exclusively Baptist in its membership. This anti-formal impulse was also manifested in Sussex, where two Allinite groups separated from the Baptist church, either causing or as a result of its dissolution. The mixed Baptist and non-Baptist society formed in Upper Sussex was led by William Freeze, formerly deacon of the Sussex Baptist church. That centred at the Lower Millstream was led by the unimmersed Matthew Fenwick, (Freeze's son-in-law) and the immersed Henry Weyman. Yet another Allinite meeting was established in the Hampstead-Little River area (facing Long Island), led by Samuel Nicklin and (John?) Delong. Judging from their signatures to one of the 1802 marriage petitions they had formerly been Baptists; it may have been their secession which led to the dissolution of the Long Island Baptist church. Finally, there is a suggestion of an Allinite meeting within the territory of the Woodstock Baptist church.[52] Each of these Allinite societies arose in conscious opposition to a Baptist organization of the Nova Scotia variety and not in default of such an organization. Each represented a separation from or the dissolution of a Baptist church. Within twenty years each was transformed into an open communion Baptist church which, together, became the nucleus of the Free Christian Baptist denomination.

To claim to detect the formation of several 'Allinite' societies a generation after the preacher's death, in areas where (with the partial exception of Hampstead) he had never preached, among people who, with a few exceptions (Freeze,

Fenwick), were Loyalists may seem an extraordinary proposition. It would mean that at the very time Allinism was under intense attack in Nova Scotia in the second Baptist reformation (of 1806-08), it was experiencing a major revival in the St John valley and Sackville-Petitcodiac regions of New Brunswick. Yet the fragmentary evidence does suggest that these new religious societies represented a direct and deliberate rejection of the exclusivist Baptist organizations planted in New Brunswick only a few years earlier. In the Maritime context, a religious organization of mixed Baptists and non-Baptists indifferent to whether their Christian fellowship takes the form of a 'church' or merely a 'society' is incontrovertible evidence of Allinism.

One factor all of these Allinite societies had in common was occasional preaching from Daniel Shaw. Decades later, when Free Christian Baptists listed their denominational precursors, they singled out Shaw as a key transitional figure between Henry Alline and formation of (the forerunner to) the Free Christian Baptist conference in 1832. Shaw (1758-1838) was a Scottish immigrant to Nova Scotia. Judging from the Horton-Cornwallis Newlight Churchbook he joined that organization in the 1780s. By 1791 he was an itinerant preacher with some success, presumably in sympathy with the New Dispensationalists.[53] Thereafter references to Shaw's career are scattered and miscellaneous but suggest the broad geographical scope of his labours. In 1800 the Anglican rector of Gagetown (opposite Waterborough) on the central St John River spoke of him in these terms: "One of their teachers, by name Shaw, who ... it is said, does not articulate a single word, but when he holds forth, bellows like a mad ox in a field, is accounted among them as a saint of the first magnitude".[54] The following year James Manning mentioned Shaw as accompanying James Murphy from Passamaquoddy. In 1803 Shaw's chance encounter with Job Seamans, a New Hampshire Calvinist Baptist revisiting his boyhood home in Sackville, resulted in a description of his preaching style in essential agreement with that of the rector of Gagetown.

There was a Scotish man present by the name of Shaw, who made the last prayer and gave an exhortation. He talked very broken: and I think he appeared to be the

189

greatest flame of zeal I ever saw — a number of people soon left the house. Whether his sentiments were good or bad, I cannot tell; for his broge & zeal prevented me from understanding him. The people desired me to preach for the afternoon, and not open the door for him, by giving liverty which I did in the morning ... . I have since heard that friend Shaw's moral Character labours which I suspected.[55]

In 1811 Shaw was still sufficiently notorious in southeastern New Brunswick for an English visitor to be told that "a New Light preacher named Shaw has held forth that there is no sin in man below his heart".[56]

Shaw's Horton-Cornwallis church was also aware of reports that his "moral Character labours". The first complaint was registered against him on 7 May 1803, at just the time the Manning forces were marshalling to purge Lydia Randall and John Pineo. The specific charge against Shaw was that he had denied lying about his adultery. Curiously the church took the extraordinary step of calling a council of all the principal churches in fellowship with it to deal with Shaw's case — perhaps a tribute to his standing as an itinerant preacher. The following year the church voted to seek the advice of the Baptist Association (meeting in Waterborough) with regard to Shaw. The Association advised that Shaw be "cut of[f]" as "corrupt in principal & practice," which was finally accomplished on 9 September 1804.

The Baptist Association was so concerned about Shaw's activities that they thought it wise to report their adverse opinion on Shaw in letters to individual churches, even though there is no evidence that Shaw was himself a Baptist.[57] Accordingly, when in the spring of 1805 Shaw sought to preach in the Waterborough Baptist meeting the church voted not to hear him.[58] Yet three months earlier when Shaw and Peter Crandall (brother of Joseph Crandall) preached in the Wakefield Baptist church (not yet a member of the Association) the Churchbook recorded "a perfect Union".[59] Shaw is next known to have preached in Wakefield in the spring of 1809, but the churchbook does not mention the internal controversy surrounding him until the following August. Whether this was because he was again in Wakefield or because the Baptist Association had in the interim adopted close communion (of which Shaw was the leading itinerant opponent) is unclear. On this occasion the church voted 25 to 1 to refuse to hear Shaw (an an excommunicated person).[60] The vote against Shaw was impressive in its unanimity, but the total numbered less than half of the church's initial intake of members five years earlier. Later that year Shaw's labours caused "verry unhappy divisions" in the Woodstock Church. In the spring of 1810 Shaw again presented himself in Wakefield. This time only fifteen members of the church were named in the (somewhat incomplete) church records as pledging to leave the meeting if he attempted to speak. It may be that Shaw responded by holding separate meetings for those (perhaps the majority) willing to hear him preach against close communion.[61] So far as one can tell (from the now fragmentary state of the Churchbook) Shaw was back in Wakefield for his annual spring visit in 1811. He is not actually named in the surviving portion of the church records, but it is clear that the church was once again troubled over the propriety of hearing preaching from one guilty of "Bad practices," part of the standard description of Daniel Shaw.

Daniel Shaw lived until 1838, but the latest contemporary reference to him is the Wakefield fragment of 1811. He is not known to have been ordained or even immersed. He left no written memorial. He can be viewed only through the scattered comments of others, generally his detractors. Yet Shaw's role in providing occasional preaching in Allinite societies formed to oppose Baptist churches seems to have been crucial. Probably he also had a presence in John Pineo's Allinite church at Habitant. Whether he gave support to the Allinite groups in Chester, Onslow and Yarmouth is not known.

Shaw's role, if we correctly understand it, may have been unique in the New Brunswick context; but as an unordained preacher he was only one of any number active in the St John valley in the first decade of the nineteenth century. One class of Baptist layman — often overlooked — is that exemplified by the 'loyal' pre-Loyalist Zebulon Estey of Gagetown. In the 1780s and 1790s Estey carefully straddled the fence between the Allinite meeting in Waterborough and the more respectable Congregational church in Sheffield. Joseph Crandall found Estey the most vigorous opponent of his attempts to make the "Brooksites" Baptists en masse. Yet when the day for immersing arrived Estey was the first to go into the water.[62] In the short period between his 1800 immersion and his death in 1806, prosperous, literate "Esquire" Estey occupied a key position as clerk of the Waterborough church, the foremost Baptist organization in the St John valley. In this capacity he corresponded familiarly with the key Nova Scotia Baptists, and was even chosen to write the Association's Circular Letter for 1805. On James Manning's 1801 visit to the St John River he wrote his wife that, "Esq'r Easty has Rode with me as my Companion 75 miles up the River and found me a horce bridle and Sadle and stays with me till I Return". In 1802 Estey performed the same service for Joseph Crandall and Theodore Harding. There is no suggestion that he ever preached; yet the support of a sober, respectable patriarch like Zebulon Estey probably gave the St John valley Baptists much-needed stability and indigenous leadership in the crucial first decade of their existence.

At least five Baptist laymen are known to have preached in the St John valley in the early years of the nineteenth century. Peter Crandall, ordained in 1809, visited Wakefield in the company of Daniel Shaw in 1805.[63] Philip Mosher was preaching in his own St Martins neighbourhood as early as 1809.[64] That same year Lathrop Hammond of Prince William, ordained in 1810, was also preaching to the St Martins church.[65] Concerning the early preaching of Thomas Ansley and Benjamin Fairweather much more is known.

Ansley was the son of Ozias Ansley, a Sussex Loyalist and zealous Anglican (before he absconded to New York in defiance of his creditors). It was the younger Ansley who in 1794 gave the land on which the first Anglican church in Sussex was erected. In return he received "the ground or floor for the pew," which he continued to own even after his ordination as a Baptist minister.[66] The following year Ansley's religious impressions led him to apply to Bishop Inglis for ordination. Yet Ansley acknowledged that "he was unacquainted with the [classical] Languages; & prayed, that if he could not, on that account, be Ordained, he might be appointed a [SPG] Catechist — he now lives at Norton".[67] Ansley left this school in Norton in May 1798,[68] moving back to Pleasant Valley (Sussex). Whether he broke with the Church of England from this early date is unclear. It was, however, at this time that Ansley's father was drawn into Simon Baxter's campaign to ruin James Jones, the SPG missionary at Norton and Belleisle.[69]

Baxter had personally provided the Church of England with a glebe in the parish of Norton on condition that a missionary be settled on it within ten years. This prompted Bishop Inglis to shift Jones into Norton. But the domineering, officious Baxter, anxious to rescind his gift, charged that Jones was not a "soul-searching, soul-winning Minister" and, indeed, that he had been guilty of misconduct. That Jones was neither evangelical nor very energetic is not in doubt. At his earlier appointment to the "burnt-over" district of Sackville-Amherst Bishop Inglis characterized him as a "quiet, inoffensive man [who] will neither do much good or harm".[70] But as to Baxter's allegations of immorality against Jones, the Bishop's board of inquiry acquitted him completely.[71] This did not, however, mollify Baxter who, with Ozias Ansley and Caleb Howe as justices of the peace, accused Jones of having "lately committed the crime of Fornication with one Br[idge]t [Guthrie] and of Incontinency and attempting to commit the said Crime of Fornication with one Mary Golder and other Immoralitys and offences" and proceeded to use their offices to make inquiry. This irregular and improper proceeding led the Kings County grand jury to present Baxter, Ansley and Howe in 1798 for their "illegal," "malicious" and "unconstitutional" conduct.[72] The outcome of the affair is not known, but Baxter did successfully revoke his gift of the glebe (the deed not having been registered), and by 1804 Jones was preaching for the Wesleyans in Sheffield.[73] One of the motives for the senior Ansley's attack on Jones may have been the notion that his son would be a fit successor in the Norton mission.

This did not of course occur. About 1800 the Ansleys united with the Sussex Baptist church. Walter Bates recalled that, under the preaching of Gilbert Harris, Thomas Ansley himself was moved to come out as a preacher. Perhaps it was he who led the faction that drove Harris out of his Sussex pastorate and on to Ansley's former neighbourhood in Norton. Ansley's signature is present on the 1802 Sussex Baptist marriage petition but that of Harris is not.

On 22 October 1801 Ansley presented himself to James Manning at Saint John. Manning was very favourably impressed with Ansley; "the dear man," he recorded, "would [have] talked [about his religious experience] all night". Little is known of Ansley's other early labours, except that they must have been in the lower rather than the upper St John valley (he is not mentioned in the Wakefield, Prince William or Waterborough Churchbooks). In mid-1805 he and James Innis laboured together for two weeks in Greenwich parish. Later that year his adventures in Charlotte County (noted above) generated the first extended notice of his work. Although the date of Ansley's ordination is not yet known with certainty, it probably took place in Maine in 1806 or 1807.[74] Ansley was preaching a good deal in the Sackville region in 1809, although he still lived in Pleasant Valley (Sussex). At the end of that year and in early 1810 he staged his only well-documented campaign on the St John as he and Joseph Crandall rushed in to bask in the reflected glory of Henry Hale's reformation on the Belleisle.[75] Soon thereafter Ansley removed to Upper Granville where he had notable success while the neighbouring church under James Manning was entering its period of steep decline.

If Thomas Ansley is a rather familiar figure in Maritime Baptist historiography Benjamin Fairweather is obscure. A Connecticut Loyalist, Fairweather was among the anti-Administration dissidents whose votes were disallowed in the first Saint John election (1785). In 1798 Fairweather settled in the parish of Norton, just as Thomas Ansley was giving up his SPG school. Here Fairweather presumably united with James Innis' Allinite society, turning Baptist with the others in 1800. On 10 December 1801 he was deeded two acres of land for a Baptist meeting-house.[76] This was not the land on which the central Norton Baptist meeting-house associated with the Innis group was subsequently erected. The fact that it was deeded to Fairweather rather than Innis may indicate that there was already a division among Norton Baptists.

Fairweather is next heard of in 1803, by which time he had come out as a preacher. In January of that year Baptist

194

churches in Hampton and Springfield petitioned Governor Carleton to have Fairweather licensed to preach. Each church declared that Fairweather had been chosen as its pastor. (The petitions are printed in Appendix VIII.) Fairweather himself (not yet ordained) could not have gathered these two churches, although their members may have been his converts. Perhaps one of the three neighbouring Baptists ministers — James Innis and Gilbert Harris in Norton, Charles Lewis on Long Island — did the actual dipping. Yet it is remarkable that, in the midst of the greatest concentration of Baptist ministers in the two colonies and having already secured a pastorate, Fairweather could not procure ordination. This may have brought a temporary halt to his public labours and explain why the Springfield Baptist organization soon fell apart.[77]

By 1809 Fairweather was again active as a Baptist preacher. In February of that year Henry Hale found him labouring in the Kingsclear church. A few weeks later he was preaching in Wakefield where (in conspicuous contrast to Daniel Shaw) he was described in the Churchbook as "a Godly man full of the Grace of God".[78] Thereafter Hale mentioned Fairweather with some frequency, either as his host in Norton or as a preacher. It is clear that the American regarded his work as very acceptable, more so than that of James Innis. On 4 February 1810, for example, Hale and Fairweather were labouring together in the Long Island area.

> We met at br Benwart's [Vanwart's]. br Fairweather spake unto the people fr Luke 12.1. I then spoke unto the people for a short season and closed with prayer. This was a very solemn season. It was judged there were between 3 and 400 people present.

Later that year Hale attended one of Fairweather's meetings at Saint John.

The final known reference to Fairweather's preaching is a curious one. At the 1811 annual session of the Baptist Association the reconstituted church in Springfield "requested the ordination of Brother *Fairweather*". Fairweather was not, however, actually a member of the Springfield church (presumably because he lived in Norton). On that pretext the Baptist Association declined to ordain him, appointing instead

195

a committee "to enquire into their [the church's] standing". Neither the committee nor Fairweather is heard from again. The Springfield church, which in 1811 had fifty-six members, was reduced by 1813 to thirty. It had to be organized the third time early in the 1820s.

This sketch of early Baptist activity in the St John valley has concentrated on the role of unordained preachers because they were more important to early Maritime religious development than is readily recognized. Of the ordained Baptists resident in the St John valley in the first decade of the nineteenth century Elijah Estabrooks and Lathrop Hammond are too well known from the Baptist denominational histories to require comment, and the case of James Innis is discussed separately below. The rogue Gilbert Harris is last known to have preached in the St John valley in the spring of 1803, when he and Joseph Crandall were in Prince William.[79]

Charles Lewis (1762-1837) is a rather shadowy figure in the Baptist past. Son of a pre-Loyalist immigrant to Sackville, Lewis was a convert of Henry Alline. James Manning found him preaching on Long Island in 1801. On 8 February 1802 Crandall, Harris and Theodore Harding visited Long Island to ordain Lewis over the local Baptist church.[80] (Curiously, Lewis is not known to have joined the Baptist Association.) Edward Manning recalled in 1812 that Lewis "did not continue long with them and I believe the church is entirely desolved". Lewis removed to his father's neighbourhood in Salisbury, adjacent to Joseph Crandall and Jacob Peck. He is listed there, with a wife and six children, as early as the parish enumeration of 1803. Yet in the spring of the year following Lewis was in Wakefield, the remotest English community in the St John valley, triggering what was in local terms a major reformation. He was in Wakefield again in 1806, preaching with great success.[81]

Lewis was certainly living in Salisbury in January 1809, when Henry Hale preached in his house, as he did again in 1811. Lewis himself did not preach with Hale and, indeed, there is no evidence that he was still active. About the same time Edward Manning reported to David Benedict that "the last account I had of M'r Lewis he did not Preach at all".[82]

The most important of the ordained Baptists from outside the region to preach in the St John valley in the early

196

years of the century was Salisbury's Joseph Crandall. He is known to have visited the region in 1800, 1802, 1803, 1804, 1805, 1809 and 1810. It was probably he who formally gathered the Waterborough church (1800) as well as Norton and Sussex in the same year. He gathered the Wakefield church in the summer of 1804 and, likely, the Nashwaak church a few weeks later. Of the Nova Scotia pastors, Theodore Harding was preaching in the St John valley in 1800, 1801-02[83] and in 1805. James Manning visited in 1801 and 1808-09, and his brother Edward in 1800 and 1810.

A survey of Baptist preaching in the St John valley in the first decade of the nineteenth century would be incomplete without mention of the arrival of Baptist missionaries from New England, usually as representatives of the Massachusetts Baptist Missionary Society.[84] Much the most important of these was Henry Hale of Charleston Maine. Hale preached on the St John in February-March 1809, again in July-August, and then steadily for a full year from October 1809 to October 1810. Hale toured the whole settled length of the St John valley, from St Martins to Wakefield, even travelling up the Nashwaak. If one is to credit his own journal then he probably attracted the largest crowds ever to hear preaching in the Maritimes. On Sunday afternoon, 27 May 1810 he preached at Saint John "on the commons to above 1000 people". Three weeks earlier an assembly of "between 1000 and 2000" had collected to witness him perform three immersions.

From the fall of 1809 the centre of Hale's work was Belleisle Bay, in upper Kings County. Here he generated perhaps the best-documented neighbourhood reformation in early Baptist history.[85] The triggering event was the conversion on 30 October 1809 of Polly Davis, daughter of Caleb Davis (a member of the defunct Springfield Baptist church). In Hale's words:

> The last night I tarried at br Davis' about 2. o'clock in the morning Polly Davis a youth of about 20 years was brought to cry to the Lord for mercy. Thus she continued untill about 8. o'clock in the morning, when her soul was delivered into a glorious liberty of the gospel. From this time intill late in the evening the house was thronged with people and many of them

197

crying for mercy. The most of them was young people.

The conversion of young people always had a deep effect on their elders, and before long Hale was recording many "day[s] of Penticost" in Springfield. Characteristically Crandall, Ansley, Fairweather and Hale's fellow missionary Isaac Case soon arrived to share in Hale's success. A month after Polly Davis' conversion the Springfield Baptist church was formed anew, with twelve members. It would soon swell to five times that number. James Innis played an insignificant role in the Belleisle reformation but perhaps it was Hale's success which prompted him to renew his labours in Carleton. Here in the early months of 1810 he was able to gather a small Baptist church of eight members. A few weeks later Hale gathered another, across the harbour in Saint John.[86]

However extensive the American Baptist penetration of New Brunswick — first in Charlotte County, then on the Belleisle, then in the southeast — George Rawlyk is no doubt correct in judging that the Americans were less important in the New Brunswick context than in Nova Scotia.[87] In Nova Scotia they won over the Baptist leadership. In New Brunswick there was no Baptist leadership to win over. Hale's labours on the Belleisle and in Salisbury did, however, allow the New Brunswick Baptists to end the first decade of the nineteenth century on a temporary upswing. Fittingly, it was at the 1810 Association meeting (held in Sackville) that the organization's name was changed to include the word New Brunswick. In the wake of that session an American Baptist was moved to boast that there were now "nearly forty" Baptist churches in the Maritimes, half of which would have been in New Brunswick.[88]

Yet of the nearly twenty New Brunswick Baptist churches by 1810 only five (Sackville, Salisbury, Waterborough, Prince William, Wakefield) were members of the Association. St Martins and Kingsclear — still carried on the Association minutes in 1809 although non-reporting — were dropped altogether in 1810.[89] In that year the combined membership of the five Associated churches was a mere 210. In 1820, when the Baptist Association next met in Sackville, the combined New Brunswick membership of the Associated churches was 447 — and this after twenty years of Baptist activity in the province.

By 1810 the controversy over church constitution — whether to be Baptist or mixed Baptist and non-Baptist in membership — had already cost the organized Baptists dearly. Half a dozen or more Allinite fellowships had coalesced, most in direct reaction against exclusivist Baptist churches. And in 1810 the close communion issue was beginning to take its toll among those Baptists who did remain within Baptist churches, Associated and un-Associated. The result was the continued low fortunes of the Baptist cause in New Brunswick in the decade after 1810.

In January 1819 the Revd Duncan Dunbar, a newly-ordained Baptist endeavouring to re-establish the Baptist standard in Charlotte County, published a 100-page pamphlet on the *Origin and Principles of the Several Religious Denominations Existing at Present in the Province of New Brunswick*. The sober Dunbar candidly admitted the crisis. There were, he conceded, ":but *four* or *five* regular societies of the . . . [Baptist] order" in New Brunswick (a figure derived by counting only Associated churches actually reporting in 1818). Having devoted this single line to the regular Baptist churches, Dunbar took a full page to describe and denounce another group of New Brunswick Christians with whom the Calvinist Baptists were "too often confounded". This "set of enthusiastic professors" — which Dunbar thought held "the doctrine of Arminius" (*ie*, were anti-Calvinists) — were portrayed in familiar terms.

> They live by the frames and feelings of their heated imaginations, and prove their *faith* more by *these* than by good works — they attend to no discipline — they ridicule the administration of the *Lord's Supper* — they pretend to be moved to speak by the spirit, and their *Females* are generally the most active in this part of worship.[90]

Dunbar conceded that this deluded set contained "many *pious* and worthy characters" but condemned the whole as a dangerous distemper among New Brunswick Baptists. The newly-arrived Dunbar did not recognize that this anti-formal,

199

unsacramental, spiritually egalitarian contagion was Allinism.

At the very time Dunbar was preparing his text for the printer his nearest Baptist colleague, the Revd Thomas Griffin of Saint John, was also complaining bitterly of the continuing susceptibility of local Baptists to the tug of the Newlights. "If a man take a text," Griffin wrote,

> and totally forget it, speak in the most improper manner as to pronunciation, snuff at the nose as if nothing sho'd be lost, and dance with the feet like a weaver in his loom, contradict himself often, and speak so as you could not discern whether he be an Arminian [*ie*, a believer in freedom of the will] or not — this will do.

In another letter — the subject was heavy on his mind — Griffin complained that "they want to feel religion — ie, something to ferment like yeast and then as flat as water — something that will set them going tho they live in neglect of watchfulness, prayer and Gods ordinances".[91]

Like Dunbar, Griffin was lately arrived from England. As such he was peculiarly ill-suited to understanding the phenomenon he found so dangerous. Apparently he did not even realize that the "preacher of the name of Alline" whose labours provoked his outburst was the saintly, consumptive Clark Alline, nephew of the saintly, consumptive Henry Alline, who had himself preached in the "Loyalist City" at its founding thirty-five years earlier. Clark Alline (*c*1791-1822) made only two or three visits to New Brunswick before his early death. No more than Daniel Shaw can he be said to have 'organized' the Allinite counter-attack on the exclusivist Baptist churches. Yet like Shaw he would be remembered in New Brunswick as a key inspiration in transmitting the ideal that mere externals should not divide those who were "Newlights indeed" from Alline's day to formation of the Free Christian Baptist conference in 1832.[92] So potent was the Allinite ideal of Christian fellowship that no priests, creeds or platforms (other than Alline's hymns) were needed or wanted. So unappealing was the rival Associated Baptist ideal of close communion exclusivity that after ten years — indeed after twenty years — its very survival in New Brunswick was still in doubt.[93] Whether the purist impulse of the Allinites or the pragmatic denominationalism of the Associated Baptists would prevail was — even by 1820 — not yet clear.

JAMES INNIS
James Innis is one of the first generation of Maritime Baptist preachers about whom least is known. Born about 1743,[94] the earliest document relative to his life is the certificate of his 19 May 1764 marriage to Elizabeth Coghland. In it Innis was described as a "Soldier in Col. John Owens Regim't of Foot [*ie*, the 59th Regiment], & Capt [Alexander] McDonal's Company".[95] The place of the Innis marriage is not stated, but the fact that it was solemnized by John Reader "According to the Rites & Ceremonies of the Church of Ireland" suggests either an Irish or a Newfoundland locale; and, as the 59th Regiment was not shipped to America until 1766 and as no John Reader can be found among the Anglican clergy of eighteenth-century Newfoundland, it seems likely that the marriage occurred in Ireland.[96] This would indicate that Elizabeth Coghland was herself Irish; but Innis, as a soldier stationed in Ireland, might have been from anywhere in the British Isles.

Innis is next heard from in 1767 when his first child was baptized by the Anglican rector of St John's Newfoundland.[97] Other children were born in Newfoundland in 1769 and 1772. Innis' fourth child was born on 20 July 1775 in "Boston New England," indicating that his unit had been sent to the defense of that city. After the evacuation of Boston Innis was shifted to Nova Scotia and, probably by late 1776, to Fort Cumberland (near Amherst). (It was here that the child born in Boston died.) It is uncertain whether Innis was actually present at the 1776 siege of Fort Cumberland but his journal indicates that he was present during the subsequent pacification of the region.

Innis' last three children were born on the River St John in 1779(?), 1780 and 1782, indicating that he was part of the Fort Howe (Saint John) garrison under Gilfred Studholme. Whether he was at Fort Howe as part of the Royal Fencible Americans or the Royal Highland Emigrants (84th Regiment) is unclear. He is mentioned in a local trader's account book in 1780 and 1782.[98] He was likely the same "Inness who kept the Provision Acc'ts" for Fort Howe, who was said late in 1784 to have been "for some time past out of His Senses," but was recovering.[99]

Towards the end of 1783 Innis was disbanded. In the middle of the following year he and two of his sons were listed among former Royal Fencible Americans at Letang Charlotte County, but it is doubtful whether he settled there.[100] That same year (1784) he was granted a lot at Saint John. In 1785 Innis was among the first to be admitted as a freeman of the "city," in his capacity as a "merchant". Just what his business was supposed to be is not clear. From surviving court records it is, however, known that on 13 June 1784 he lost (and subsequently had to sue to recover) "one Gondolo and three oars". Later that same year he loaned "a certain boat with One Mast rigged as a Sloop compleat with Sails and four oars" to Joseph Cutler for a voyage to Passamaquoddy, on which trip the sloop was lost.[101]

By the fall of 1786 Innis had shifted his location to the north side of the mouth of the Miramichi. Here he was among (but not a leader of) those engaged in a long dispute over marshland. This, however, was to prove only a temporary speculation, for the focus of his activities was soon the fertile Kennebecasis valley of Kings County. On 1 August 1787 "James Inness Gentleman" was commissioned a lieutenant in that county's militia.[102] Probably it was about the same time that he settled on a farm lot near the Baxter tract in the (then) parish of Sussex. On the 1793 petition for erecting the western part of Sussex into the parish of Norton Innis' signature comes fourth, indicating a respectable standing in the neighbourhood.[103] In the 1790 assessment of his section of Sussex parish Innis' wealth was rated ninth (out of fifty-seven landowners).[104]

Innis had opportunity to hear Henry Alline preach on all of his visits to the St John valley. It is natural to wonder whether he was the "one soldier" whom Alline adjudged a Christian in 1779.[105] One can, however, be reasonably certain that Innis had not come out as a preacher by 1787 or he would hardly have been given a militia commission. Yet by the end of the 1790s Innis, like Joseph Crandall in Salisbury, was holding Newlight exercises. When the newly-ordained Crandall arrived in Norton on his first mission to the St John valley

202

early in 1800 he found that Innis already "preached in his own house". Crandall may well have been the first Baptist preacher Innis had ever heard.[106] By the time of his ordination by Crandall and Theodore Harding on 22 September of that year Innis had evidently experienced Baptist enlightenment, as had the seventeen others who were gathered into the Norton Baptist church.[107] Probably these new Baptists were former members of Innis' own Allinite fellowship.

Little can be said with certainty of the course of Innis' ministry, even with the aid of his 'journal'. Soon after ordination he was at Sussex, probably assisting in organizing that church.[108] He was also active on the Belleisle late in 1800.[109] In 1801 he is thought to have assisted in the ordination of Gilbert Harris over the Sussex church.[110] It may have been about this time that Innis carried the Baptist gospel to St Martins.[111]

By 1801 Innis' activities were sufficiently notorious to come to the attention of Joshua Upham of neighbouring Hampton, one of the judges of the New Brunswick Supreme Court. In a long and rhetorical letter to the preacher, Upham referred to rumours that Innis was "railing" against the Church of England and "reviling and traducing" its ministers. Upham warned Innis to moderate his language and comply with the provincial statute requiring all preachers to take an oath of allegiance and be licensed for itineracy.[112] There the matter evidently rested.

Nothing whatever is known of Innis between 1801 and the commencement of his journal in 1805. If he was active his itineracy must have been modest. His name is not found in any surviving Baptist churchbook. In the spring of 1805, when he travelled with Joseph Crandall to nearby Long Reach, he noted that he had never been there before. His journal mentions a total of three visits to Long Reach (twice in 1805, once in 1809), one to Belleisle (in 1805, with Thomas Ansley), two to Carleton (1809-10) and one to Lower Millstream (1808). Hale's journal mentions him preaching only once in the Belleisle reformation of 1809-10. Innis made only two preaching visits to Nova Scotia. In 1805 he went by boat from St Martins to tour the Annapolis valley. In 1811 he made a shorter tour overland through Westmorland County, preaching principally in the Chignecto Isthmus.

No doubt Innis' journal does not tell the whole story of his itinerant ministry. The fact that in 1808 he was "Sent for" from the Millstream and that he was on familiar terms with the Allinite preacher Matthew Fenwick indicates that he was well known to the Newlights of Sussex parish. Yet in general Innis was probably not very active as a Baptist itinerant. There is no information on his work between 1801 and 1805. In 1808 he confessed in his journal that he had not performed an immersion in upwards of three years. Sheriff Walter Bates recalled that after his 1812 release from gaol Innis did not preach at all.[113] This may not have been strictly true (he is known, for example, to have preached a funeral on 18 April 1815),[114] but I do not doubt that it was generally correct. On his release from gaol Innis was about 68, probably the oldest ordained Baptist preacher in the Maritimes.

If Innis' itineracy was modest then were his labours in his own Norton parish highly successful? In Baptist terms it is reasonably clear that they were not. The visibility of the Norton church is low, even by New Brunswick standards. In 1800 the church was gathered with 18 members. In 1818, after Innis' death, a new Norton Baptist church was gathered — entirely from persons immersed that year.[115] There was, in other words, no link in personnel between the church in which Innis laboured and the organization of 1818. It is also remarkable that we do not know the name of a single member of Innis' church (other than the preacher and his wife), that none of the Baptist petitions printed here as Appendices appears to have Norton support and that Henry Hale's journal of extensive labours in Norton in 1809-11 never mentions a Norton church.

Is one to infer, therefore, that Innis was temperamentally unsuited to a settled pastorate (hardly unusual among Newlight Baptists) and that the Norton church disappeared almost as soon as it was founded? The religious contours of Norton parish are too complex to permit such an easy generalization. Nothing, for example, is known of the relations between Innis and his near neighbour Gilbert Harris or the other Baptist preacher in the parish, Benjamin Fairweather. Fairweather's case is particularly interesting. It was he (rather than Innis) who in 1801 was deeded land for a Baptist meeting-house; and at the end of the decade he seemed to be working well with Henry Hale (suggesting that, unlike Innis, he was orthodox on the close communion issue). The fact that in 1814 yet a second Norton Baptist meeting-house was erected, this one in Innis' own neighbourhood (Bloomfield), invites the inference that both Innis and Fairweather had Baptist meetings in Norton. Yet this would not necessarily mean that these were rival meetings or that the Baptist cause was thereby divided and weakened. Indeed one wonders whether Fairweather's meeting-house — located in Norton, but near the Hampton and Springfield parish lines — was intended primarily for the Baptists in those latter parishes, who by 1803 had elected Fairweather their pastor (see Appendix VIII).

The fact that Baptists in the section of Norton in which Innis lived could erect a meeting-house in 1814 but were wholly unrepresented in the version of the Norton church David Nutter gathered in 1818 is another puzzling feature of the Norton religious scene. Here Edward Manning's 1812 notice of Innis' work may provide a useful hint. Manning told David Benedict that Innis:

> was ordained . . . over a Small Infant and unexperienced church with whom he never travild in Gospel order, for Like People Like Priest. They were all unskillfull. But the old Gentleman having obtained more information I understand he is quite ortherdox in sentiment and correct in morrals, and tho a Man of Small Talents is useful in the cause of Religion.[116]

It is notable that Manning speaks of the Norton church as though it was already (in 1812) a thing of the past. Manning also emphasizes the church's non-conformity with "Gospel order". At the very least this means that the Norton church did not practise close communion. This, however, would be a strange complaint to make of the church at its 1800 founding and for several years thereafter, when all but a few Maritime Baptist churches practised open communion. Manning may, however, mean that the Norton church was never truly Baptist; *ie*, that it never effectively abandoned its Allinite constitution

205

(of admitting both Baptists and non-Baptists) or that (like the Sackville church) it reverted to Allinism. There is much to be said for this line of speculation. It would explain why Innis' circle was strong enough to erect a meeting-house in 1814 but wholly unrepresented among the close communion Baptist organization four years later. It would also explain why Clark Alline was drawn to Norton to preach in 1818.[117]

There is yet a further puzzle in the record of the Baptists of Norton. The final entry in the Innis journal (for June 1811) records his sorrow at being instructed by "the church" to apply on its behalf to join the Baptist Association. The "church" in question is not actually named. No doubt it was the Norton organization, although this is the only allusion to such a body in the whole journal, and the Norton church did not, in fact, join the Association in 1811.[118] But how does one account for the fact that a church which Edward Manning thought (the following year) did not exist and which I have speculated had relapsed into Allinism would seek to ally itself with the close communion Baptist Association? Part of the answer, no doubt, is that the labours of Henry Hale (perhaps with the assistance of Benjamin Fairweather) had stirred up a close communion party in Norton. Perhaps even Innis, disoriented by his long encounter with the law and under pressure for the first time from close communion preachers, had himself assented to the plan. This would account for the fact that he wrote the Association on behalf of the Norton Church and explain why Edward Manning could subsequently claim that Innis had become "quite ortherdox". Yet why the close communion majority of 1811 should be completely unrepresented in the Norton church of 1818 is a mystery. As for Innis, the relevant journal entry indicates that he much regretted the move to close communion. Perhaps it was this, the hardships of his imprisonment and his very advanced years which put an end to Innis' active itinerant and pastoral activities.

To Edward Manning and the Baptist 'Denominational' historians James Innis was a preacher rather to be forgotten than commemorated. Too much of a Newlight to be numbered among the Maritime Baptist saints, Innis was remembered only because his prosecution for unlawful solemnization of

206

marriage gave the denomination one of its rare martyrs. Two legislative enactments circumscribed the activities of dissenting preachers in New Brunswick and Innis fell foul of both. The first was the 1786 *Act for Preserving the Church of England, as by Law Established in this Province, and for Securing Liberty of Conscience in Matters of Religion.*[119] Its purpose was to regulate the clergy of the Church of England and give the provincial executive a degree of leverage over the activities of dissenting preachers. The Act provided that no one might officiate at a public religious exercise in the colony without having taken the oath of allegiance and that no one could lead a religious exercise *other than where he was the elected pastor* without licence from the governor. The oath of allegiance requirement was probably unique to New Brunswick. The prohibition on unlicenced itineracy had precursors in some of the old colonies.

The intent of the *Act for Preserving the Church of England* was not to prohibit religious dissent. It was designed to put dissent on the psychological defensive — to signal clearly that dissent would be merely tolerated, not treated equally. Its primary motivation was political rather than religious (a distinction which would not generally have been made in 1786). The Act was grounded on the assumption that religious organizations not aligned with the state created independent poles of social authority that could ultimately disrupt the colony's political constitution. Democracy — independent thinking — in religion tended to democracy in politics. As James I had acutely observed, "No Bishops — No King".

The 1786 law did, however, reflect one genuinely religious concern. In the eighteenth century the terms "teacher of religion" and "minister of religion" were used almost synonymously. The essential ministerial function was to "teach" religion in a setting in which many had no other source of religious instruction. Thus Bishop Inglis considered the question of licencing preachers under the New Brunswick legislation in terms of their competence for "the office of a Public Teacher" (Appendix VI). One class of dissent (orthodox Congregationalism) called to its ministry only those who were able, learned, orthodox and whose competence for the public "teaching" of religion could not be questioned. But the Great Awakening of the 1730s and 1740s had thrown up a quite different cast of dissenting preacher — the Newlight — who regarded his call from God as the only requisite for a public ministry. This class of preachers, wrote Inglis in 1801,

> are generally common labourers or mechanics, without any liberal education, or even tincture of learning — scarcely able to read a chapter in the English Bible; being also of the very lowest orders of society, they have no respectability of character to qualify them for a public and responsible situation.

Requiring itinerant preachers to be licensed under the 1786 Act would allow the New Brunswick executive a measure of control over the class of Dissenters allowed to "teach" religion in the colony. Bishop Inglis would have confined the privilege to only those whose "literary attainments" as well as "Political Principles" were satisfactory.

The importance of the *Act for Preserving the Church of England* was in helping set the tone of repression in Loyalist New Brunswick. Its passage was intended to signal that religious dissent, like political opposition, was unnatural and unwelcome. The question of the actual application of the Act has yet to be fully explored. Preliminary research indicates that the Act was in some sense invoked (licence granted, licence denied or, usually, lack of license asserted) more frequently than has been realized. I count thirteen such occasions, the earliest 1791, the latest in 1812.[120] Six of these occasions involved Wesleyans, five involved Baptists (one twice), one a Newlight and one a Congregationalist (Seth Noble). In most cases no legal action resulted. In only one case (the last) was there a successful prosecution for a violation. Most invocations of the Act were by a local magistrate, by way of intimidation.

In practical terms, therefore, the 1786 enactment was not used as an active weapon against religious dissent. Rigorously enforced, it would have barred all Americans from preaching in the province (they would not have taken the oath of allegiance) and severely curbed the activities of other itinerants. In fact it was violated a hundred times for every one occasion when it was invoked. The Maine Baptist Henry Hale's 1810 experience perfectly captures the provincial executive's attitude towards enforcment.

> Monday 16 [July 1810] this morning called on his honor the president [Martin Hunter] for licence to preach the gospel and was refused without submiting to the following prerecisites, viz., be examined respecting my education. 2ly be confined to a particular parish, then take the oath of elegious [allegiance]. Then I should have liberty to preach in one Parish. Not being [willing] to submit to the above, the President gave me verbal liberty in the presence of Doc. [Charles] Gunther to preach as I had done untill I should hear farther from him.[121]

The Act accomplished its primary purpose simply by existing. It warned preachers like Hale to take care not to offend the colony's essential political and religious constitution. The fact that actual enforcement was almost never even attempted was as much a measure of its success as of the fact that by 1810 the time for practical enforcement had long since passed.

Under the *Act for Preserving the Church of England* James Innis received the 1801 admonition from Judge Upham; but he was subsequently to have the distinction of being the only person ever successfully prosecuted under New Brunswick's 1791 *Marriage Act*. The first "Marriage Act" (introduced in the General Assembly in 1787 but not enacted) would have given the privilege of solemnizing marriage to those in Anglican Orders and to all justices of the peace, with Quakers, Blacks and coloureds allowed to intermarry after their own fashion. This liberal proposal aroused great opposition from Bishop Inglis.[122] As a result the Act that finally became law in 1791 was more rigorous. It confined solemnization of marriage to clergy of the Church of England with only two classes of exceptions. In parishes where there was no Anglican clergyman a justice of the quorum might perform marriages; and, where both parties to the marriage were Quakers or of the Kirk of Scotland or the Church of Rome, they might be married according to denominational usage.

Protests against the narrow scope of the *Marriage Act* began almost at once by Congregationalists (Appendix II) and Wesleyans (Appendix V).[123] The first Baptist petitions came early in the nineteenth century (Appendix VII). All were unsuccessful. Yet, in marked contrast to the *Act for Preserving the Church of England*, there is no evidence that the *Marriage Act* was violated until the James Innis affair.

Two of Innis' unlawful marriages came to the notice of public authority. On 17 September 1809 he married Ebenezer Vaughan to Hannah Brown, both junior members of St Martins families who had emigrated from Newport. Brown was related to the Dimocks and the Baileys; and Vaughan, to the Crandalls. The following February Attorney-General Thomas Wetmore formally filed an Information against Innis alleging violation of the *Marriage Act*.[124] The preacher was not, however, arrested until the summer, lodging in Kingston gaol for a night of drunken song until his sons arrived to post bail.[125] Innis then travelled to Saint John to engage Charles Peters as his counsel and attented court but, as he recorded in his journal, the authorities refused to "bring on" his case for trial. Such a tactic was not unusual; it parallels the handling of the Peck case five years earlier. It signals that the Crown's concern was to intimidate Innis and other dissenting preachers, not to do them a favour by persecuting them. There matters would probably have ended had not Innis been so headstrong as to marry yet another couple. In October 1810 the Kings County grand jury indicted Innis for "solemnizing Marriage between Farquhar McKenzie and Margaret Pack without legal authority".[126] This explains why Innis' journal records that he was again arrested and required to give bail about the end of 1810. As this prosecution, unlike the first, was in Kings rather than St John County it suggests that McKenzie and Pack — although they probably lived in St John County — travelled to Innis to be married.[127]

The Kings County process seems not to have gone further but Innis' repetition of the marriage offence did prompt the Crown to reactivate the suspended Vaughan-Brown prosecution. In February 1811 the attorney-general filed a new Information against Innis and later that year a St John County jury convicted him. On 11 October 1811 he was sentenced to be imprisoned for twelve calendar months in the Gaol of the City and County of Saint John, to pay a fine of fifty pounds, to the King, and to stand committed untill the Fine with the costs of prosecution be paid.[128]

This very severe penalty was in fact the minimum possible under the *Marriage Act*. Innis' supporters paid his fine and costs and the prisoner was released from Saint John gaol after serving only a portion of his sentence. No doubt part of the reason for this remission was Innis' age, but Sheriff Bates remarked on his "disgraceful and ridiculous" conduct while in gaol. Grace Aiton suggested that this offensive carrying on consisted of preaching through the cell window.[129]

* * * * *

All the published notices of James Innis are derived from the notes which Edward Manning prepared for the use of the historian David Benedict. Manning had no reason to think favourably of Innis, either personally or for his Newlight tendencies. Yet the happenstance of Innis' prosecution under the *Marriage Act* meant that he had to be brought to Benedict's notice as a martyr and, accordingly, that his heterodoxy must be disarmed. Hence Manning's decision to portray Innis as the "old Gentleman" who suffered from want of "information". Befuddled old eccentrics could be forgiven their doctrinal peculiarities if they made acceptable martyrs. All subsequent treatments of Innis adopted this interpretative tactic.

One who approaches the Innis journal from such a perspective will be surprised. Although the document here printed begins when Innis was 61 and ends when he was 67 there is nothing feeble about the *persona* it depicts. If Innis was troublesome and embarrassing to his preaching brethren it was for reasons more substantive than the generation gap. Innis' literary production is called a 'journal' only as a term of convenience; it is essentially a series of memoirs recording his itineracies. The personality it reveals is sensitive, insecure, defensive, petty and altogether more complex than that of, for example, James Manning. The difference in tone between the two journals is striking.

Innis constructed his various memoirs in a

211

'confrontational' mode. On nearly every page Innis presents a foil — either a person or a situation — against which he exercises superior discernment or judgement. The three principal confrontations — those with Theodore Harding, Edward Manning and Charles Peters — hold such fascination that it is easy to miss the more basic insight that Innis liked to assure himself that he had a greater measure of the spirit than almost anyone else. He boldly lectured widow Dimock; he self-righteously rejected Rebecca Elder's advice to keep a purse of donated money; he dramatically prophesied good concerning Peter Martin; he walked directly to the right house to keep an appointment, without knowing the way.

The chief significance of the Innis document is in the conflict it presents between a 'Newlight Baptist' who saw himself as continuing the work of Henry Alline and a new breed of Baptist, oriented towards Boston, who wanted desperately for the world to forget Henry Alline. Innis' tour of the Minas townships was virtually a pilgrimage among the sisters and brother of Henry Alline. He embraced every opponent of Harding and Manning he could find. Repeatedly he invoked the name of "my Brother Allen". Theodore Harding (who had ordained him) and Edward Manning were each denounced as priests of the altar of Baal. Innis served Christ's "church" but Harding and Manning served Satan's "chapel". Harding was a "hirling". Manning was a power hungry formalist and an enemy to vital religion.

That James Innis preached a Baptist message is not in doubt. He was not a pure Allinite and certainly not a New Dispensationalist. Yet Innis also clearly stood for the proposition that Baptists need not cease to be "New-lights indeed". He had nothing but contempt for the retreat into denominationalism, safety and respectability that he saw in Harding and Manning. If his own account is to be credited, he bitterly denounced them to their faces. This 1805 confrontation between two possible types of Baptist is a crystalization of the fundamental division in the Maritime Baptist movement throughout the nineteenth century. Was the spirit of Henry Alline to be cultivated — or eradicated?

What follows is the complete text of the Innis 'journal'. Capitalization and spelling are as in the original text.

212

Punctuation and paragraph structure have often been editorially supplied. As there are so few dates in the journal I have italicized those which do appear. The first document printed below is Judge Upham's 1801 cautionary letter, taken from the *Christian Visitor*, 17 May 1848. Then follows the Innis journal proper.

[Joshua Upham's letter to James Innis, dated 13 July 1801 at Hampton]

Sir — As a Justice of the Supreme Court, and a Civil Magistrate, bound by solemn oaths of office to support, as far as in me lies, the mild, liberal, and indulgent constitution and Government under which we live, and *particularly* to protect the established National Church, I feel it to be my Indispensable duty to call upon you to answer and explain by what authority you assume the character of a *Dissenting Teacher*, preach sermons and lectures, and officiate in the celebration of divine service and administration of the sacraments, and to let me know whether you have been approved and licensed so to do by His Excellency the Lieutenant Governor, under his hand and seal, conformable to a law of this Province, entitled, "An Act for preserving the Church of England, as by law established in this Province, and for securing liberty of conscience in matters of religion."

It is indeed with great reluctance I interfere in a matter of such nice delicacy, and in doing which it is possible I may be supposed, by persons of weak and jealous minds, to bear hard upon the rights of private conscience, which I confess I hold sacred and unalienable, and "to the scruples of which" (in the words of the late learned and eminently liberal Judge Blackstone) "our present laws have shewn a very just and christian indulgence, for undoubtedly all persecution and oppression of weak consciences, on the score of religious persuasions, are highly unjustifiable upon every principle of natural reason, civil liberty or sound religion. But (adds the same good man) care must be taken not to carry this indulgence into such extremes as may endanger the National Church, there is always a difference to be made between

213

toleration and establishment."

That great law writer and law Judge adds further on the same subject, as follows, viz: "The sin of schism, as such, is by no means the subject of temporal coercion and punishment; if through weakness of intellect, through misdirected piety, through perverseness and acerbity of temper, or (which is often the case) through a prospect of secular advantage in herding with a party, men quarrel with the Ecclesiastical Establishment, the Civil Magistrate has nothing to do with it, unless their tenets and practice are such as threaten ruin or disturbance to the State, he is bound indeed to protect the Established Church."

These sentiments accord perfectly with my own. For your non-conformity to the worship of the Church, you are by no means answerable to me, as a Civil Magistrate, but for railing against the Church, for reviling and traducing the characters of reverend, grave, and respectable clergymen, duly authorized, and regularly approved and licensed; for dissuading persons from going to Church, and treating it with contempt and rudeness, which no Establishment can tolerate; for speaking in derogation of the Book of Common Prayer, and discouraging the use of it; and for acting in defiance of the law of this Province, in the character of a Dissenting Preacher, I conceive you to be unquestionably amenable to the Civil Magistrate, and particularly to the Supreme Court, or any Court of Oyer and Terminer or gaol delivery in this Province. I do not wish you to be exposed to the heavy penalty of the law, which cannot be less than fifty pounds, nor more than a hundred — of which it is possible you may be ignorant.

When you have given this cautionary letter a candid and dispassionate persual, I shall expect either to see you or hear from you, and that you will give some satisfactory account of yourself, as a Dissenting teacher, particularly with respect to the above heavy charges against you, which, if true, are highly criminal and unwarrantable.

It will give me pleasure to find your conduct has been misunderstood, and that you have no criminal intention of opposing Church or State, or of violating the King's laws of Government. The law of this Province above cited has been approved by His Majesty, our Gracious King and Sovereign,

214

who is the Supreme Head both of Church and State. "Fear God and Honour the King." [*etc*]

PS If you are not approved and licensed, as I strongly suspect you are not, I advise you, if you wish to approve yourself a good and faithful subject, either to relinquish the character of a Dissenting Preacher, or to apply decently to His Excellency the Lieutenant Governor for his approbation and license in due form, which, if you can be well recommended, and found properly qualified, will most undoubtedly be granted.

Submit yourself to every ordinance of man, for the Lord's sake, whether it be to the King, as Supreme, or unto Governors, &c.

INNIS' JOURNAL

[SMITHTOWN — GONDOLA POINT —
LONG REACH — GREENWICH]

Sent [set] out about the *15the may 1805* for little River [Smithtown][130] where I had freedom in Sum degree, but not as formely [formerly], yet I Baptized four and Spant the hold [whole] night in conversation with them and orthers to the no Small Comfort of our our [sic] Souls/ When [*ie,* then] I and Brother [Joseph] Crandell laft them in love, and want to Gundalaw point [Gondola Point] where I was Received with great Joy borth by young and old/ hear we Called a Meeting and give out a Church [Conference] Meeting [of the Hampton Baptist church][131] one [on] Sataday and want to the longreach where I had naver been [to preach] before & the first house we Come to Recieved·ous with Joy of heart where we dined, after which two woman Carried ous to their house where I found freedom all [?] and hild meeting that Night in the Smal[l] house to the Joy of meny a heart after which give out meeting the orther Side the River [Greenwich Parish] where I Stayed all night/

in the morning they asked me to pray with them and orthers/ I asked and [an] young man that was there to Stay untill after prayers was over but he went away with Scorn — but the Goodness of our God was Such that he Caused me to Remamber the young man in my Prayer/ Meeting was Give out lower down the Reach next night and I Got in to a boat to attend it with a number of women & an old Man but the wind and water was so high they did not think it Prudant to Parceed/ So we turned back, and went to the house where the young man lived who would not Stay for Prayer in the morning — but the lord Brought him home in the evening and I delivered to him what I Recieved from the lord with freedom and pleasiour and laft them in the hands of a marcyfall God/

hear I want from house to house a Breaking my bread with Singelness of heart to the Comfort of my own Soul and orthers and I would gladly have Stayed untill after Sunday but for my apointment at Gundalow point [Gondola Point] which we attend[ed] when a daughter of our late Sister Oileys[132] Came forward for Baptizam — one Sunday after which I administred the Sceacerment [sacrament] to a number of prasious [precious] Souls/ at Gaundalow point long reach and lettle River [Smithtown] the Christains all appeared varey Boughtfull [beautiful] to me indeed/ I leaft them in love and Return'd to little River where I meat with My old frind [Andrew] Shearwood[133] which I had not for three years before been so near [to] as to Spake/ we had a long Conversation to gether/ at last he asked [w]ho ded the lord send/ I said Ballams ass/ once this day I fealt a learge Stone Rol[l]ed from the door of Israel and I fealt satisfied for all my leabour/

June 16th [1805] wrote two latters to my dear Christain frinds which May the lord of his Marcy Conway [convey] with a Blessing to their Prasious Souls/

23th June [1805] this day o lord thou seeist and Knows the Need I Stand of they [thy] Mightty Power at all times to defand me from the enemy of My Soul which are great and many and are to[o] Powerfull for me but not for thee that Says a man Shall not be tempted More then he Shall be inabled to bear/ o lord are not the Cattle one [on] a thoushand hills all thine and thou Sees lord how those Comited to me are abused by this Baxster[134] and o lord he is thine allso and lord Vangence is thine likwise/ o lat [let] it be in marcy o lord I Pray thee and o that thy Name may once More be a Prayse in this land/ Many times this day as my heart fealt Happy/ glory be to God in the Highist/

July 2d [1805] wrote a latter to My frind [Andrew?] Sherman[135]/ may the lord grant it a Blessing/ after which I heard Brother Hansley [Thomas Ansley] was going to the longreach & wanted me to go with him — and I feal free to go but will the lord go with me, and grant me a Happy time or at least grant that it may be for the Honour of God and the advancement of his Kingdom/

[BELLEISLE BAY — LONG REACH —
KINGSTON]

the *6 July* [*1805*] Sat out with Brother Hansley [Ansley] for Ballile [Belleisle] where we [felt] Sum freedom in Meating Sataday & Sunday and in the family we Stayed with — whom we leaft Happy in the lord — and sat off for the longreach/ towards evening we Called at Brother and Sister Browns[136] and they datained [detained] ous all night — and we where all Happy to gether/ Next day whey [we] Callerd meeting where but fue Christians Come and we Could not Gat another Meeting untill Sunday with the Christians — but in talking with a M'r Curry the lord tuched [touched] his heart and he applyed for Baptizam at which I asked him to lat ous [us] preach in his House and invite his Neabours to Come which he dad and meny Came to heare for the house was full and a women said I had no form for what I delievered/ the lord give it [to] me/ Sataday whe [we] had meeting at M'r Sharp's where we again had freedom in meeting & in the evening and morning for I Stayed their all night — when two indians Came in with whome I talked with freedom — and it Seamed to take Sum imprassion one [on] their minds·— which may the lord grant may work for their good/ on Sunday we attended the meeting we [had] apointed where we borth [both] preached with freedom after which we want to the water and Baptized Brother Currey Brother Kemble & Sister Kemble and the lord Graced his own ordennance with his prasance in Such a manner that we Could arderley [hardly?] leave the waterside/

hear my beloved Brother [Thomas Ansley] leaft me & want home [to Pleasant Valley]/ hear I past a way towe [two] days and nights in two differant houses — Much to my Satisfacttion Loath to Leave the peopel and the peopel to lat me go/ On Weddansday I Came to Kingston to attend my apointment but the enemy of man was before me and Sowred the mind of the people, or weather fear of man — So as none attended — all tho I Come to the House and Sent for them — but I leave them in the hands of him that made the[m] and Returned home after a leabour of 13 days Much to the Comfort of my poor Soul — with Brother Hansley [Ansley]/

on or abought the *6 of August 1805* Come hear [Norton] Brother and Sister Vaughan[137] [and] Sister [Elizabeth?] Marand[138] from Saint martains Sister Smith Sister Odall and M'r Odall[139] from lettle river [Smithtown] and the *7 aug't* Brorther [Thomas?] Brown[140] from S't martains and with these and my own family I Spant Sume time Varey agreeabely — for we Meat in love and Parted in the Seam after Promisen them to Come to S't Martains in fourteenday[s] and Go with them up the Beay [of Fundy], but will the lord in marcy Condescand to Go with him thy Sarvent and grant him a prosprious Jurney — and that the time he Spands may be to the Glorey of his God, and that he may have Much fruite/ o lord thou knows the leabour of My mind ever since I Promised to go to Quaco [St Martins] and up the Beay — and all for fear that thou o lord are not a sending me and will not go with and Bless me and give me fruite — but o lord I have ever found three [thee] Prasent in time of need/ Good lord Bless the week indevours of they Servant I Pray this *19th Aug't 1805*/ o lord thou Knowist I leave all that is Near and dear to me, not knowing where I am a going or when I Shall Return or what may Happen to me but o My lord and my God, I trust it is for the advancement of they Cause — and by they Command, or why this truble of Mind ever since I Consented to go/ o my God Keep they Sarvent and all his Concearnes in the Hollow of thy hand and late [let] his Jurney be Prospirous, and lat him have much fruite, that they Great Name may spread & be glorified theirby/ lat [let] the Angal of the Covernant go befor and Prepear the hearts of the Peopel — and go thou with thy Sarvent and guide his feet where it Seamath good in thy Sight and lat him Brak[e] his Bread with Singleness of Hart to they Honour and glory — and thine shall be the praise/

[ST MARTINS][141]

on or abought *22nd of Aug't 1805* I Set out for Saint Martains agreable to my appintment with Brother [Ebenezer] & Sister Vaughan/ in my 1[st] day Preached at Lettle River [Smithtown] where the power of the lord was Prasent to heal/ Next day want to Saint martains/ hear I

219

Preached freakquantly while waighted [waiting] for a passage
a Cross the bay [of Fundy] with freedom but Could not
Rejoi[c]e in Spirit for I See a dark time a Coming one [on] the
Cristains & My mind was varey Much Exarcised in deed
Concarning My Crossing the bay — and Brother & Sister
Vaughan Halped my mind to Sink that was Ready a Nauff
[enough] its Self — for they give over the thought of going with
me — but Said brother [Philip] Moshar[142] & wife [Elizabeth]
was going and that would do for they Could not bear the
thoughts of my going a lone/ I Said I was not a going a lone for
all the lord See feet [fit] Should go with me — but I was not __
arme of Flash [flesh] — but my Cry was for the lord to go with
me and it was all I wanted/

 hear I Baptized five and at Least [last] they all Give up
Going with me — but Said they would pay my passage for me
— but I tould them no I would Bagge [beg] my Passage/ th[e]y
Said [James?] merand would not take me without money/ I
Said he would take me and be glad for I knew where the lord
Put his dart in him/ with that I want to his house — and tould
[told] him I wanted a passage Cross the Bay and if he wanted
pay he must Charge to the Lord — for I had no money/ he
Said I was wellcome to go Brakward and forward as offen as I
wanted while he had a Vassel and that he would find [ie, board]
me to[o]/ O lord Remamber this for good to him I Pray/ in
Preaching my fearwell Sarmond [sermon] their was a Judge
[Daniel] Bless[143] that leaft [left] the meeting but the lord Soon
brought him back a Gain/ he was waighting [waiting] for the
wind to be feair [fair] for to go in the Seam [same] Shipe with
me and as Soon as the meeting was out a women Broke out in a
Rejoicing Spirit and Sayd go my brother for the god of
Heaven and earth is a going with you/ I know it my Sister I
Said and the wind turned feair [fair] in a moments time and in
less then two hours M'r [Philip] Mosuhar, [Ebenezer]
Vaughan, [Thomas] Brown, Black and Smith with Mises
[E l i z a b e t h] M o s h u h a r, V a u g h a n, [E l i z a b e t h]
Brown, Black and lettle girl whent one Bord and Emeadeatly
Sail'd/ the Ruast [rest] of the Christians Remain'd one the
Beach untill Night hide them from our Sight/ this was about
the *25th Septem'r 1805/*
 when we got a lettal in the Bay I tould the woman they

had Batter have tea now before we wear all sick/ when the kettle was biled [boiled] we all Seat down to gether/ Judge [Daniel] Bless Lying in his Cabbin Cast his eye towards ous & Said you lock [look] as if you all belonged to one Family/ I Said we do for we have but one Father all tho we Have meny mothers/ he Said he wished he Could Joine our/ I Said he was Welcom and it was as free as the water that Run by ous — but I hear he is Since dead and made his apperance befor that God that do him Justise/

[FALMOUTH]

a lettle after Sun Rise We Come an anker and I, Captain marand, [Ebenezer] Vaughan and his Sister [Elizabeth Brown] want a Shore and Came to their Brother [James] Smiths[144] house — which was the first house we Come to/ hear I was inabled to Say the House was mine and all that was in it/ Smith want to the Cubbord and Showed Me where their was borth Meat and Drink and Said you Say [see] the house is yours/ lat me See that you use it like your own by making free to halping yourself to aney thing you want — and if you want a meeting hear I will warn the peopel and provide the Seats/ I tould him I ded that night — for I Came for that purpose/ this is the man that his own Wife Judged Varey heard [hard] and Said She ded not believe he ever would be Seaved but with God their [is] Marcy/

hear I had 3 meetings and give out a meeting at the Schoolhouse a four miles off/ their a Number Come and I found freedom with them/ give out a meeting on Sunday at the Church [of England] where a greater Number attended who wanted me to go in to the Pulpiet/ I said my master want in to none n[e]ither Sould I and the lord had giving me my tongue to be Spant in his Searvice/ after Half hours intermishen had a nother meeting — but while th[e]y wear gathering of Money which they give to me — a women Come to me and asked me if I would not take Sume Refreashment befor meeting/ I thanked her & Said no/ then M'r Wilson asked me to dine with him after meeting which I ded but ded not find that freedom their I wanted/ I asked the name of the women that first

221

invited me/ th[e]y Said her name was Smith and that She lived [in] the Next house/ I Said I would go and See her/ I went/ as soon as I see her I knew her — and She Said I was wellcome and Said I Should not go from her for that night/ I Said if She was willing to Ceep me I was willing to Stay/ I talked to her and husband her Son and towe Daughters — and they wear much affacted all the while/ at night I Prayed and [the] man Said he never heard Such a Prayer in his life before/ he leat [led] me to bead/ in the morning I Prayed again and th[e]y where all much affacted a gain/ I tould him I had a feavour to aske him/ he Said he Should be glad to oblidge me in aney thing/ I Said I wanted two neak [neck] and one Pocket Handchefer [handkerchief] and for them young women to make them for me and for his wife [to] By them for me/ th[e]y Said th[e]y would do it a wellcome/

hear I meat with a Mr's [Priscilla] young and Mr's [Abigail] porter[145] Borth [both] the Sisters of Hanrey Allan — with whom I had Sweet Conversation — for our minds was as free as water to gether/ th[e]y ware of great Strangth to me and I to them/ Praise God o my Soul and all the powers within praise his Holey name — that Sant me out both to Teach and to be taught/ hear I tould my Exprance [experience] Meny times and found great freedom a mounge the Peopel — and Got an invatation at M'r [John?] Godfareys[146] outside win[d]sor to Preach at his house which I dad to a Number of Peopel where Sume where much affected and hear I found Smith and Walless, who attend evrey Meeting Notwithstanding what his wife had Said/ I Preach in win[d]sor to a house full of Peopel with freedom and th[e]y tould me their was more outside then their was in/ Sume Bla[c]k Peopels faces Shoune [shone] with love/ one of them asked me to Go with him to Parsborough/ I Said I could not now/ he asked me to Sat a time and he would till the Peopel — but I Could not — for my mind was searching to know and do the lords will/

[NEWPORT]

hear I was Sent for with man and horse to Preach in Newport one Sunday which I fealt to be of the lord and So I

Said and tould the young [man] to till his master so — but I
Could not go for I had apionted meeting in win[d]sor — and
after that I Should be there one [on] munday if the lord
parmited/ on Munday I Seat of[f] — and Come to the forden
please [fording place] to go over and whent to the house —
where I found a Number of wemen and but one Boye — with
whom I talked a good While but th[e]y Said Nothing but I
asked them if th[e]y Kecpt a feary/ th[e]y Said th[e]y dad but
th[e]y Could not lance [launch] their Boat — for th[e]y had no
men at home Nor no horse at home/ I asked them if I Could
ford it/ th[e]y Said I Could — So I walked over alltho the
water was Coule — but Blessed be to God he fitts the Back for
the Burden/ the first man I meat asked me if I was not M'r
Innis/ I Said yes/ he asked me to Come and See him/ yes Said
I if the lord will/ hear I Past by a Publick House alltho I had
money and wanted a lettle Sparits of Sum Kind to Comfort
and Strangthen Me yet I see it was good for me to denie myself
the gratefacaten my Flesh wanted/ hear I was a Stranger in a
Strange land — and not one face that I Knew/

    So I travaled for a lone time/ at Last I mist my Road
and fealt I had after I got a but [about] a half mild [mile] out of
my way/ I meat a Man [w]ho Seat me Right/ then I Called at a
house and asked the women to give me a Drink of water — who
Said She had none and had a long way to Bring [it] — So I lift
her without any but thought I would try again the Next House
I Come at/ a bought a half an hour after I See one a fealt
[afield?] but I thought to have past it and gon further but the
lords ways are not mens — for in this house was Brother
[Philip] mosuhar, B[rother] [Ebenezer] Vaughan, Sister
[Elizabeth] Mosuhar, Sister Vaughan, S[ister]
[Elizabeth] Brown and orthers who Come to the door and
asked me if I was a going past/ I Said I dad no Know but I
Should if th[e]y had not Come to [the] door/ they asked me if I
had been to dinner/ I Said no but I want a Drink more then I
wanted aney thing to eat/ they Said to the women of the House
give him Sum Sparits water & Sugar & gat him Sum dinner
which She Soon got & they paryed [prayed] that the wind
would Change for the[y] Dad not want to go Since I was Come
but they Laft [left] me — but when the last want out which was
M'rs Vaughan a weaping Spirite tuck old [took

223

hold] of me — which Caused me to Said to the woman of the house — this is not for me but for you to lat you Know that God is with me/ We all attended meeting that Night ware a Number Came to See what the Babler had to Say, and not to find the lord/ if th[e]y had th[e]y would have found him for he was their and I found freedom to pray and Preach to and in Spirite Recieve Sume Christains/

l want [went] to See George Dimick[147] which I found Buried up in the world/ I asked for the widor [Deborah] Dimick[148] his mother — but the world would not lat him go all [the] way to her house but Just fear a Nuff to Point it out to me So as I Could find it/ when I had got Batter [better] [than] Half way I see a Child Coming towards [me] about five or Six years of age/ when we Meat I Said to him ware are you a going/ he Said you are a Going to See my graney and I [k]new you was a Stranger and I Come to Shew you the way/ my dear Said I [w]ho Sent you/ nobody Said he/ I Come of myself/ I Ceam [came] to the house and She Read Sum latters and talked a bout her Sister Brawn [Sarah (Bailey) Brown] — and Complained of herself for being cearless [careless] while she had her husband [Daniel Dimock] with her but thinks if she had him a gain, She would Emprove her time Batter/ well Said I God has Sent me in his Room for a few days/ make good use of me while you have me/ we Sang and Prayed together and the lord inabled me to talk to them all which was herself 2 Sons and two Daughters and her grand Son untill the[e]y ware all in tears/ o my Soul how Shall I Praise the lord for all his goodness to me — for though [thou] Knows how meny times — for the nine weeks I Stayed there I was inabled to Leave them in the Seam fream [frame] of mind/

I preached all maust [almost] evrey Night — and want from house to house for many Miles Round amoungth all Sorts of peopel and groley [glory] be to God not in Vain to none So Much as with the Baptize [baptists] [of Newport] [w]ho ware tied down to their Note Books and outward forms and modes and wanted to ple[a]se the world more then our God/ hear I want to a house where the Man had a Spirite of Dispear/ the women Said the glorey of the lord Shines Round you for you Bring a Blessing where aver you go/ hear I See a woman that dad not appear to me to be long for this world/ I fealt that for her that was Stronger then Death which Caused me to invite her to meeting that night without knowing for what — but She Said She was Just going to See her mother for the last time, for she was afraid of the Least Drope of Due to tuch her Body/ if it dead [did] She Should be Brought to death's door if not to Death/ I Said if you Cannot trust your body with the lord How Can you trust your Preasious Soul/ the Soule is of more Vallow [value] then the body with a great dele [deal] more that past — but we parted — and I want to preach at the mans house that Give me the first invertation/

after meeting one Said M'r Burgas wanted Me to preach at his house to Morrow at three oClock/ I Said he Should be Searved with the will of God — if I Could find his house — but none offered their Sarvice So I want a lone/ only the lord that I knew was with me/ I want three mild [miles] and the first house I See Sumthing Said that is Burgass house — So I turned out of the road and want to the house [and] Knocked at the door/ they said Come in/ I Come for that Parpose/ before I See aney body belonging to it and in a moments time I fealt the house to be the lords, and Said does M'r Burgast live hear/ th[e]y Said yes/ I Said I thought So and Said Blessed and Happy for all of the Name of Burgast — for I Shall have them all — before I leave the Place and begun to talk with a women in love — but She fought but Could not Stand it long — when a young man invited me to dinner and when I asked a Blessing I Expacted to have Seen them fall under the Table/ I fealt the Power So great but it ded not Stur them/ it was the Seam in Returning thanks/ O My Soul you was then Crying to the lord for Strangth who naver Leaft you destetute — as yet/

the peopel be gon [began] to Come and a Moungth [among] the Reast [was] an old man [James Harvey][149] that was Varey light and trifelling in deed/ he Said he Had an arrent [errand] this way So I thought I would Come to meeting/ yes Says I to hear what the Babler had to Say/ yes Says he for I am a Reaget [rigid] Prisperteran [Presbyterian]/ you are a Reaget [rigid] nothing Said I and if you die So you must aternely [eternally] Parish and Walked out of the door — whare I See a Varey good looking man for whom I had a Fellowshipe for but Knew he would pursecute me and Stand against the Work of God/ their was a great meny Peopel

225

Come/ I opened the meeting — and the Power ot God Sheaked [shaked] this old light man and this man that I feared in a wonderfull manner — and their was meny tears flowed/ after the meeting the old man and the one I feared talked to gether/ the old man asked the orther What he thought of the Stranger/ he tould him I was the Sarvent of the lord and Said that [which] you have heared to day is the gospel that Redeemed my soul from aternel who [woe] —. and who be to them that Say one Word against him — and borth Come to me, and asked me, if I was ingaged on Sunday/ I Said I was at the Scotchs Village — because Said they we want you to Preach inther [either] at my house or M'r [James] Harveys which was the name of the old man/ I Said aney time after Sunday that th[e]y would appoint I Should attend — if the lord See feit [fit]/ hear the work of the lord began — and the peopel be gun to Say is his a good man and orther [people] Said no but he Decieves the Peopel/

I want to my appointment — an a great Number attended from all Quarters — and many invatations for Horton Cornwallis and Rouden [Rawden] and Recieved in Spirit a great Number that I naver tuck by the hand — and their was a great number Varey wicked/ two men taking [taken] up for Dead in Six days by the means of horse Reasen/ Sum of my frinds Said they wondered the Peopel ded not Kill me for being So pleain with them/ I See them meny times in meeting that they Could have eat me with a grain of Salt — but the lord would not Suffer them even to Spake one word to my face/

I attended meeting at M'r [James] Harveys where I had great freedom in prayer/ hear I Cast my Bread one [on] water and Must leave with the lord/ Preached a gain at Burgast who Could not bear that I Should leave him for the lord had got in to his heart — and the hearts of a number more of his frinds and orthers — and they be gon to inquar [inquire] for Baptizam — and I layed it before the [Newport Baptist] Church who Said bring them hear/ no Said I it is your duty to Come to them and try the work —weather is it of God or no/

while I was Employed hear Satan Employed the man I Feared to Sow discord a moungth [among] the young Convarts which give me Strangth in the work — for I Knew where Christ would have a Church Satan would have a

Chappell a long side of it — but [w]ho Can Discribe my Feailings but they that have fealt the Seam for I thought I must have died for I Fealt So for three days together and then it all Leaft me but glorey be to our God for his Goodness to the Children of men/ our meeting lasted all night for their was no parting with the young Christains/ at for oClock in the morning they would Call one [on] me to Pray when it Seam[ed] to me Emposable for me to Pray or Spak — for weekness of body and Lowness of mind — but what Says the lord/ open your Mouth and I will fill it/ o my soul Praise the lord of life and glorey/ no sonner ded my mouth open then the fountain opened in my heart — to the Joy and Comfort of meny Prasious Souls as well as my own — and Cause[d] the old mother [Hannah] of these Burgasses,[150] w[h]o Hanrey Allan had Baptized [th]is day to Say She never See Such times in her life before/ o how Good [it] was to my Soul to hear her grand Children Say to her why Graney you have Renewed your Strangth and your age to[o] for your Face Shines like the Sun — but it is not in my Power to Discribe the goodness of our God to his peopel/

hear I meat a man one [on] the Road who tould me their was a Sick women on the Halifax Road that wanted Me to Come and See her and have meeting in her House/ I Said She Should be gratefied if I Knew her Name/ he Said her name was Dier[151] — but he ded not [k]now ware She lived/ I said I had a tunge [tongue] and I Could find her out — So we Sat [set] a day and I Got a horse and the horse want straight to the door/ when I Com in I found the Seam women I had befor invited to meeting/ I asked ware M'rs Dier lived/ She Said hear/ it was I that Sent for you/ I asked her if the peopel knew of [the] Meeting/ She Said they ded: but if they had longer notis their would more Come/ the house was Soon full of all Strangers to me Except a fue [few] Baptize [Baptists]/ the Rast ware matherdus [Methodists] but the lord inabled me to preach to all Sorts/ glorey be to God/ he give me freedom of mind and a longing Desier for her because She was Sick and to all parance [appearance] Could not Stay hear long — but I Could see her gat nothing all the time of meeting/ after it was out She and her husband began to Name over a Number of Peopel with Pleasour that they See much afacted [affected] that they never

227

See So before/ well Said I ded you get nothing yourself for my Soul longed for her Happyness/ She Said no/ what Said I Can you Rejoice at the Happyness of your Neabours and you got Nothing/ this Cannot be for Satan Could not Rejoice at the work of God — for their was Nothing he heated [hated] So much as the Edvancement of Christ['s] Kingdom/ We Spant the evening in talking of our Fathers Kingdom untill varey late/ they treated me Varey Kind/

[RAWDON]

I laft them to attend the appointment I had made after Giving out a nother meeting — but it is God only [who] Knows what I weaded [waded] through at this time for I fealt as if I must Die and Could not live much longer — but M'rs [Deborah] Dimmick Said She would Soon Coure [cure] me for She had offen Coured [cured] her husband [Daniel] but I tould her their was nothing Could Coure [cure] me but the hand of God — that I knew was on me for Sumthing I knew not then — but after I had got to Cantecock [Kennetcook] I found the enemy of man had go amongth the young Christians and th[e]y all got Round me and Said I had Recieved a latter [letter] from my family that they wear all Stearving [starving] to Death — and if I dad not make east [haste] I Should not See one of them a live and that they would never Come to hear me aney more if I dad not Clear up the matter to them/ I tould them I dad not want aney to Come to hear me but Such as the lord Sent for if a thoushand Come and the lord dad not Send them they Could not hear me — nor I Could be of no Sarvice to them/ it is true I have a wife and Children — but th[e]y are not mine but the lords — and if he will feed the young Reavens [ravens] and let them die what am I/ [152] I Shall Stay untill my work is Done and then I Shall lieve you in the hands [of] God — and opened the meeting when the lord Soon fullfiled his Promises by making the Crocked [crooked] Straight and the Ruaff [rough] Smoth — for Parfact love Cast out all fear/

I Stayed hear with freedom and Comfort of mind for Sum days and then attend my appointment one [on] the Halifax Road — whare their was a greater number then

228

before/ I found libe[r]ty and freedom of mind to Sing Pray &
Preach and after wards to go from House to house and Brak
my Bread with Singleness of heart — and believe their was
good done in the name of the Holley Child Jesus — but I Could
See no Rise in the mind of M'rs dier and her body Growing
weaker/ I Could but till [tell] her her time was but Short hear
as I thought and talked as the lord Lead me untill he and his
Children were Much affacted/

   want [went] to the Baptize [Baptist] meeting House
where I leaboured Heard [hard] for but lettle frouite [fruit] —
but I B[less?] God for a lettle/ want a gain to my appointment
at Cantecock [Kennetcook] — where the lord was Still at work
in the heart[s] of [the] Children but Seeing his Children was
beging [beginning?] to trust to[o] much in the arme of flesh I
thought it time to leave them in the hands of a Marcyfull God
— but How to leave them I knew not for our Souls was So neat
[knit?] to gether by the Spirit of God that we was no more
Twaine by [but] one for time and eternety/ I Could not preach
a fearwell [sermon] to them but was forarst [forced] to
Discemble [dissemble] with them and [leave] a Number of my
things with them to make them believe I Should Come a gain
— but dad not [k]now weather I Should or not/

   about this time M'rs dier [Dyer] died and her Brother
being a young Convart Came for me to Preach the funearel
Sarmon/ I asked him if She Leaft aney witness of her futher
happyness be hind her/ he Said none but Died heard [hard]
Bagging of them all to Pray for her but he Said there [was] no
body their that Could Pary [pray] one word for her/ What
Says She Can none of you Pray for me — for God sake go for
M'r Innis and he will Pray for me/ they tould her the night was
Dark and it Rained heard [hard] and they dad not think I
would Come which when I heart it truabled me much/ I tould
him he had done rong in not Coming for me altho says I I dont
[k]now weather I might be Suffered to Pray or not but I
Should have tryed/ I asked where She was to be Burried/ he
Said at His Fathers — where the funeral would be Preached/
acordeley [accordingly] I attend where a Great number from
all Part of all [religious] Sociateys attend and Could See Gods
Children with each one for God was pleasd to grace our hearts
with his presance which Caused meny tears to Drope in to the

lords Bottle, and it was a glorious day with meny but Satan was their all so and Reaged much because I landed her in abraham['s] Bossom but I ham [am] not Sent to Please man but God/ it would Cause a heart of Stone to mealt to See M'r Dier and all his Children looking in to the grave as if th[e]y ware leaving their all behind them/

Hear I Leaboured for 9 week[s]/ [at] the Last Sarmon the powers of Darkness give way in this Pleace and a Number of Souls that was naver Seeing [seen] Rejoice before Rejoiced Now for a long time/ one Sister Preached two hours and Come to me and Said you Leaboured amongth ous in tears of Blood But we would not have it/ I Said glorey be to God that you have got it at last/ Glory be to our God that give ous a Parting Blessing alltho I Could tell them So/ there was a Number Stay late that night that dad not Profeas to know the lord that will not easely for get it/ this is a Small Part of the ways of God with his Children/

beeing offen Sent for from Horton and Cornwallis to Come their I Strove to Shoun [shun] it for the Cross was heavey for I Knew the life and Power of God was trampled under feet by his oun dear Children — for Ch[r]ist is and allways was wounded in the house of his frinds/ [153] hear I got a horce to Carry me to win[d]sor where I Preached a fue times and want to fallmouth intending to Stay a fue days and then go to horton but my frinds would not Consent for me to go untill after Chrismass [of *1805*]/ I want from house to house with freedom and Preached in Sum places where they Said no Preachers had been befor/ hear I found an old man that wanted to make me think he was a Christian and began to till me what Hanrey Allen had Said to him Twentey years a go in a Varey Better [bitter] Spirite — but I tould him that My Brother Allen had tould him the truth and that what he had allready Said to him would be a Seavour of life unto life or of Death, with much more/

[I] attend[ed] meetings allmost Evrey night and Twice a Sunday/ the young Peopel flocked from evrey Quarter and Sum of the young Christain[s] from Cantecock [Kennetcook] one Sunday morning after I had give out meeting for the afternoon got up & Said frinds & neabours I would thank you if you would Put sumthing in your Pockets to give to our

230

Brother that is one [on] his Jurney to B[u]y himself a wascoat [waistcoat] or aneything he may want/ o how my Nothingness appeared to me but [I] was glad that the lord had giveing [given] the young men Such a heart/ the meeting was opened a gain and the hat went Round and it appeared to me Sumthing Said within me See you give the Half of what you got to day to [Daniel] Walsh/[154] I Said to Walsh, and it Came again as above but I Said nothing to aney body alltho Walsh was their and I walked with him along way the Seam [same] passing through me/ Next morning I want to Sister alders [Rebecca Elder][155] and tould her the first what had past through me and asked her weather Walsh was poor or not/ through me and asked her weather Walsh was poor or not/ She Said She dad not know his Sercomstance But believed him poor a Nuff [enough]/ Well Said I God [h]as Commended [me] to give him half what I Got yesterday: but I will give him all and I give it to her to Send to him but She tould Me I had lost the hearts of the young peopel/ they Said they would Never give me a nother Copper/ Brother and Sister [Thomas] Young[156] furnished me with a horse and Socks and their own Son to Conduct me to horton and to Carry me to her Sister Coaleles [Coldwell] which was the first house I enterd/ this was in *Jeanavery 1806/*

[CONFRONTATION WITH THEODORE HARDING]

their I bless God I fealt free/ to aney that would Lat me I talked of the things of God and inquiard if I Could have a meeting their/ She Said it would not look well to have a meeting their & M'r H [Theodore Harding] have one So near/ I Said my Command was to Cry aloud and to Spear [spare] not and to Selute no man by the way, and for me to go wear the meeting was I Said I would if I Could find it/ the young man that Brought me their Said he would go with me/

turning my eyes towards the bed I See a man Lying/ I asked her if that man was Sick/ She Said yes/ is he your husband/ She Said yes/ is he a Christian/ She Said no/ yes Says I he is/ Said She he ant [ain't] nor never will be/ if he ant I Said he never will be — but he is as much of a Christian as I

231

am/ I asked her if She thought he would Recover or not/ She Said he would Seatainly [certainly] die/ I Said he would but not now/ Says She he will never go out of that door untill Carried out feet formust [foremost]/ I Said he will walk out yet and you will [h]ear him Rejoice in the lord to the Comfort of your own Soul — with a Deal more/ he tould [her] to give me his new Socks and asked me to Pray for and with him which I dead [did] to the Comfort of my own Soul and orthers and then want and tuck him by the hand for the first time the lord being before in heart/ the tears feall in Showers/ he asked me to Return after meeting which I dead and was glad he asked me/

We Came to the house [for the meeting] which was full of peopel but not one I knew but M'r H [Theodore Harding] which Set in a Room with meny more and heared him Say their is M'r Innis/ he Come to me & Said I Must oppen the meeting/ I Said I Come for that purpose — and with that I Rose and want to the Table — and opened the meeting as I was Deracted [directed] Song [sung] and Prayed/ when I Leaft off another tuck it and So it whent untill Seaven or Eight had Prayed when I opened my Bibill and gave out a teaxt when all the Peopel Rose up with all their Eyes feasend one [on] me/ a women that Stood Close by me Roared out & feall at full leangth one [on] the flour Crying for Marcy and Beating the flour with her hands/ M'r H[arding] Said it was Gods work and God was their of a truth the peopel all Rejoicing in the lord in [a] wonderfull manner for a long time/

after meeting they all wanted me to go home with them but I [s]aid I Could not for I was promised to a Sick man/ they asked me to their Church meeting Next day — which I Promised to attend if I Could find the pleace/ their was a number that offered their Sarvice/ accordinly I attended where a Number Come that I had never Seeing before — when I was asked to open the meeting/ We Song and the lord had marcy one [on] me and give me a Spirite of Prayer that Reached meny hearts and Brought meny tears and Cased [caused] a sister to Breakout in praises to God that Sent that old Jentle man with a Blessing to her Soul and the Souls of orthers/ meny Backsliders was heaild [healed] and Saven Came forward & tould their Exprince/ Six they Recieved but

232

would Not Recieved one that was of Coller [colour] which
Caused Much Contansion between me and M'r H[arding] and
Church allmost allnight/ at las[t] I tould her She had don her
duty/ She had offered herself to the preast [priest] but he
would not Recieve her — but he Could not Shut the gates of
Heaven against her — and if I meat her one my was as phillipe
ded the Uneck [eunuch] I would Baptize her and lat her go/
hear I tould M'r H[arding] he was nothing Better then anirling
[an hireling]* — and to lat the people go free or I Should hold
him up in Publick — for I was Come to Cry a gainst the alters
of Baal — and asked whare is your first love/ then you wanted
no Pullpett or Perse for the People — but Now he was like the
world with more/ he Said I must Preach and he would
Baptize/

a Great Number asambeled to See the Baptizing after
which the house was as full as it Could hold — and the lord
inabled his worm to Sing and Pray — after which M'r
H[arding] Published the Bans of Mattremoney and wounded
me in a tender Part Not Knowing We Could not Save [serve]
God and the world at once — but Blessed be to God that Never
leaft me appeared a gain and inabled me to Leaft [lift] a
standerd to the houner [honour] of his own great names and to
the Comfort of meny Preasious Soul[s] Prasent which made a
day long to be remambered by me & orthers/

from this [place] M'r H[arding] and I want to New
Canaan to a M'r allen [William Alline][157]/ when the People
begon to asamble the lord inabled me to take anumber by the
hand and bed [bid] them God spede in their leabour of love —
which Much astonish[ed] them to See Me owen them that dad
not See them befor/ they all Seat together/ I Songe and
Prayed with great Power after which M'r H[arding] Prayed
and Said he ded not [k]now if he had done right or wrong/ I
Said he had done [w]rong: after which I named a taxt/ the
marcys of God So fillded the house that all th[e]y that
fallowshipet Rejoiced and Shoutted that is the Blessed gosple
that Redeemed my Soul with much More/ then I Said the
house was free for I fealt it so/ then Sister Stokes[158] Said She

* John 11:13: "The hireling fleeth, because he is an hireling, and
careth not for the sheep."

233

was not asheamed of Jesus or [h]is Cause/ then M'r H[arding]
& Sister Stokes begon to talk and he asked her and her young
Convarts to Come to the Meeting house for God Knows Said
he their is much Need — for gatting the word of the lord/ lat
the d[e]ad burrey the d[e]ad follow thou me &c &c/ he Said he
heated [hated] Devisions/ I Said I only Come to gather What
he had Dreaven [driven] away/ I tould him I had a roving
Commission/ he whant [went] with me from house to house
for meny miles where I prayd a[nd] talked with great freedom/

at last we Come to where their was a women with a large
family of Children/ She Said heant [ain't] you one of these
pardisternearens [predestinarians] in a Chiding way/ I Said
yes — but you had better Call your Famely to Gether that we
may Pray to Gether and after that I will ansouer any Questin
you may aske me/ o Says She I Can hear you Pray/ I dont
[k]now that Said I/ We Song & I Prayed and tuck the women
by the hand the lord heaven her heart and hearts of all her
Children & M'r H[arding] allso/ the tears flowed in Streams
and our Souls Rejoi[c]ed in God our Seaviour — & M'r
H[arding] Said he never So See it befor/ I turned to the
women & Said if you have aney thing to Say now & to me Say
on/ She Said for Gods [sake] Come again when my Husband
is at home for I want you to See him/ M'r H[arding] Brought
me to See a sister [Rebecca Davison][159] of Hanrey Allans/
after talking for Sume time I was going but She Said I Should
not untill I Prayed/ I Sayed it was a great thing to Pray — but
if She would Call her family to gether I was willing to try/ after
prayer I was lead to take a Peter Marten[160] bey [by] the hand
and Prophercy good Concearning him and his — and our Soul
was Neat [knit] to Gether like Jonathens and david/

I leaboured hear for a bought three weeks without
much froute [fruit] to allapreance [all appearance] and thought
to leave them — but when I See the peoples minds was after me
I Stayed three weeks more before I want to Cornwellis alltho
Manney times invited — and thought to go from thence to
Pa[r]trage island with Brother [Peter] Martian who Could go
to the ends of the earth with me and I with him/ the People in
general was Varey kind to me and I feal them Near to my heart
and ever Shall and long to See them a gain but God only knows
how that will be/

Brother [Peter] Martain and I Seat [set] of for Cornwallis to gether and he Brought me to his Brothers house in abbetant [Habitant] Street where we was Kindly Recieved — and we want from house to house in Breaking my Bread with Singleness of heart to the glorey of Gods Name I trust and much to the Comfort of meny Souls for Some time and then was invited to go to Scotchbay with martain and [John] Pinyo[161] where a number Convained together and had a happy time in Breaking our Bread with Singleness of heart Borth in Publick and in Privat/ after a Stay in Sumdays all the Satalment [settlement] Come to gether — a number of them Being at Swords points to gether and had not spoke to one another for Sume time/ our God in tender marcy Sant down his Reaconciling Spirit in to hour [our] hearts which Quikly made Peace Between Br[o]ther and Sister Father and Child and all the house — which Strak [struck] four Irish familys that was their with Such Power that the tears Run in Streams and Blessed are th[e]y that Sow in tears for th[e]y Shall bring their Sheaves with Joy/

[CONFRONTATION WITH EDWARD MANNING]

I dined Next day with a la[r]ge Family in great Comfort — and we Parted in peace greaving most of all for fear we Should not See one anothers faces any more one [on] the acting Side of eternety — but I leaft them in the hands of a kind and marcyfull God and Came to Cornwallis again where I meat with M'r [Edward] M[anning] who thought that evrey Sheaf Should Bow to his Sheaf but I tould him my orders was to Selute no man by the way but to go as I was Deracted by the tender Sp[i]rite of God for he Seamed to think I aught to go as he deracted me but that was not by Busness — and I Came to Cry against the alters of Baal/ our Convarsation was not lick [like] two that was ingaged for the advancement of the of the [sic] dear Redeemer['s] Kingdom — for he thought himself Sumbod[y] but I was nothing and less then Nothing — but our God knows ous [us] borth & will Render to evrey man according to his works/ it greaved My Soul to be oblidged to till him I See the day that it was his delight to go from one Smokey Cabben to another and if he Could Court but one

235

Soul to the Bleeding armes of Jesus it was Better to him then Counting over gouild [gold] — but Now he Could Spake a gainst the life of God in the Soul of man and Bleamed [blamed] me for making Christains befor God had made them — but I Said he aught to thank me for I only tuck them up he had [been] throwing [them] away/ he [k]new not that the Spirit that would Seaprate [separate] Christ from his Children would Seapreat God from his throne/ o lord Prasarve ous [us] from evil/ hear I Contuned [continued] between four and five weekes with my Sword in hand and my troul [trowel] in the orther/ lord have marcy on ous [us] Poor Creatures for we have none apon one another — for I find that Christ is Still wounded in the house of his frinds/

[ANNAPOLIS-GRANVILLE]

hear I was offered house mony or Cloas or aney thing alse I wanted only to Stay but I Sat of for home by way of Annapolis Contrey [contrary] to the mind of God as I think — for he Seamed to leave me as it Where in Sume degree — for I Could not guat [get] a meeting for a long way Untill over taken by a man one [on] the Road who asked me to Ride as fear as he was going which was about two mild [miles]/ one [on] our way he asked my name — So Carried me home where I found my mind free/ he asked for a meeting which I tould him was my Business from home/ Next day we want to the house appointed — where I was asked if I was a newdispanasioner [New Dispensationer]/ I asked if he had heard any thing that way/ he Said no bu[t] he Should [k]now when I Preached/ I tould his wife I Should never for get her/

they wanted to keep me longer but he Conducted me to Annapolis where he lift me and I want to Granville where I had two or three meeting/ heard M'r [Thomas] Chipman Preach one Sunday in the meeting house but dad not See him Come in/ when he had done he Said is that M'r Innis/ I Said yes/ he Said Pray Spake or Sing/ I Said I knew that to be the house of God for I Brought him with Me with much more — and Prayed and [gave] out meeting for the Evening — and Blessed be God their was one that owened the gosple that had Redeemed her Soul/
236

[MILLSTREAM]

one [on] or abought the *16 August 1808* — being Sent
for by Bangemain Ceasterd [Benjamin Keirstead][162] who is
under great temptasion at the [Lower] millstream — I want
Notwithstanding my mind was low where I had meny Happy
meeting[s] and I want from house to house a Braking my bread
with Singleness of heart, to the Comfort of meny Souls and
Batized two women, the first for upwards of three years and
leaft the peopel happy in God and Retterned *23d Aug* home/

[SMITHTOWN-GONDOLA POINT]

October the 12 [*1808*] whent to pay Gunderlowpoint
[Gondola Point] a Visit/ Stopted at lettel river [Smithtown]
and called a meeting alltho it locked Varey discorageing for the
minds of the People was Scarterad [scattered] Much but Gods
Ways are not our ways — for he bring[s] light out of darkness
and turns Better [bitter] into Sweets which was now the Cease
[case], for the people meat [met] and the lord appeared and
watered his flock with the dew of Heaven untill twelve at night
to the Joys of our Hearts/ [I] Give out a nother meeting and
invited the people to their dutys when one tould me he See it to
be his duty to be Baptized and Recieve the lord['s] Supper:
which Caused me to give out Church [conference] Meeting [of
the Hampton Baptist church] on Saterday week and want
[went] to Gondalow point where I meat with the peopel
Seavral time to the Joye of Meny heartes, alltho between the
meetings I want through great tryals and Strogals in my own
mind for the Powers of darkness worked much with me/ Still I
Visited evrey house and was glad to be there/
Returned to my apointment at lettle river [Smithtown]
when the people Meat to gether and the lord in the meadist
[midst] and give ous [us] a glorious night which will not be
forgot and three Came for ward for Baptizam — and we
pearted in love/ one [on] Sabathday we all meat a gain and the
lord with ous [us] and Conducted in to the water, and gracesed
[graced] his own teable with his Most glorious Prasence — So
as to inable ous [us] to Sing one of the Songs of Sion with a

237

glad heart after Baptizen [baptizing] Jas: [Jos:?] and Searth [Seth] Pickels/

[LONG REACH]¹⁶³

Longreach *18th Feb'y 1809* —
My dear and ever loving wife and Sister in the ever B[l]essed Jesus/ I embrace this oppertunety to let you Know that I am well — borth in body and mind — as I trust these will find you and our dear Children, and our God Knows that I fieal you all as Near to me as my own Soul many times Since I last See you — but I dont [k]Now what to write to you for I am a poor weak and a feable Creature — but I trust that our God will Guid[e] my Pen to the glory of his own great Name, and to the Comfort of your evrey Soul for it is all I wish is that you may injoy the Smiles of our God while he is Passing through the land — for hear where I am is a masadoning Cry [Macedonian Cry] of What Shall I do to be Seaved/ me thinks it would Cause your hearts to Rejoice to hear the Saints Shouting Praises to their God — and it would Make your Varey hearts to bleed, to hear Sinners Crying for Marcy — and See them Coming from every Quarter in Such Numbers that their houses Cannot hold them to Stand in with Comfort/

last night was the greatist Meeting [that] ever was Knowing one the longreach, where many Rejoiced in the lord — and meny Cryed for Marcy to allmighty God in the Better Pangs of the New Burth and Seavral of the old Saint[s] feainted away the Power of God was So great — and orthers Preached untill all their Strangth was gon inviting Sinners to the Bleeding arms of a Crusefied Seaviour — while the enemy of Sion was Reaging — and meny Brought to make their Choice of life or death/ the meeting lasted from early Candel light untill between twalve and one oClock in the morning — when I leaft them Crying for marcy/

May the God of Angels Comfort you My dear and well-beloved untill we meet on Canans Happy Shore/ dont morn for your onworthy worm — but for the God of the worm — and may I weep between the porch and the alter for the inabetants of time, is the wish and Disier of your Sincear frind husband Father and Brother in the lord Jesus Christ/ hear I Stayed Seavn [seven] days longer the work of the lord going one in a wonderful manner/ Sabathday the ice was Cut two feet for water whare I Baptized Seavn who Rejoiced in the lord in a wonderfull Manner — after which I adminstered the Scacrement to a Great number/ Still as wonderfull as before/

[CARLETON CHURCH GATHERED][164]

Janavery 28the 1810 or there abought — I leaft my lettle hall [all?] in the Hends of the lord — and want to S't Johns — but Could get no meeting then — wherefor I went to Carlton[165] [west Saint John] where I had leaboured before — to See if I Could get a meeting there or not for the mathoudus [Methodists] had got a good meny of them in to their Pound but glory be to God that never feails them that [put] their trust in him/ he alone inabled me to become allthings for the Good of his Church the work being his oun/ he opened the eyes of his Childrens understanding to See their Way More Clear to Chose for themselves/ but o My God how Shall [I] Praise thy Great Name for thy great goodness towards me a Poor Creature that Lead me thrught [through] that I never Expreanced before/ o lord will it for ever be that thee must be wounded in the house of your frinds/

hear I Visited a Sick women and Prayed with her after which I talked with her She all beathed [bathed] in tears — which I trust is now in Abrahams Bossom/ after I Visited the widder Clark [and] offered to Pray with her — but She Refused to lat me/ after a while I came to See her a gain and tould [her] I Come to till what I thought I Should want when I Come to ly as She then Leay/ all the while I was Spaking She Reaised her Hands as if I was Spaking to her Cease — but [she] Said nothing — but after a while She Sent for Me again and asked me to Sing and Pray with her which I ded much to my Satisfacttion/ I Preach[ed] her funeral — and trust the lord was marcyfull/ I leaboured here untill I Baptized four and orgarnized a Church and Administered the Scaerement to Eight mamber[s]/ Visited S't Johns and the [Reversing] falls frequantly for three month/ the Work is more than tunge or pen can Express/ 239 on or abought the *10 July 1810* [I] was taking [taken] out of My house — and put in to [Kingston] gaile [gaol] at the Ruisk of my life — for one kee [key to the gaol] was half a mild [mile] from the orther/ Next day my Sons Come and was oblidge to give four Hundrad Pound Baile for My apperance at the Nixt Court which Caused me to go to Town [Saint John] for Counseal — but after giving four doller[s] I found but lettle to my Sattisfaittion only a promise to be Kept from aney onlawfull Proceedence against me — and to give me timely Notise before my tryal Come one/ acordenly he Wrote me — to Employ one to argue for me which Caused me to go to S't Johns the Second time and indevoure [endeavour] to throught [throw] myself one the Crown & Cleame the Prevalage of his magestys Crownasion orth [Coronation Oath] with the Benafact [benefit] of the acts of Perlement that I thought where in feavour — and anchent [ancient] laws sturards [?] of the Provance of Novascota for I would not be tryed by their truspes [trespass] act that was Contreary borth to the law of God and man one less [unless] th[e]y Could Prove a turspes against me/

I asked lawyer [Charles] Peters¹⁶⁷ what was his fee/ he Said five guains [guineas] which I paid him/ [I] give him my Papers my discharge from the army my call to the minestry and my Cardanciels [credendials]/ he asked if th[e]y whare Called off/ I Said th[e]y where but that [publication of banns] was not Scriptural/ ded you use the [marriage] form of the Church of England/ I Said no/ how then ded you marry them/ by following the leadings of the Spirit that Says what two or three Shall bind upon earth Shall be Bound in heaven and the [w]Hole meeting Said aman — for I am a bibel Christian for by the word we Shall be justefied and by the word we Shall be Condamed/ he Said I mean if I Can to denigh the marige [marriage]/ if you do I will acknowledge befor the Court I ded it — for it is only just & right so to do if aney orther have and I think I aught to Sue Sombody which I think to be the Bishope [Charles Inglis] — for the Church [of England] Cleagey are keeping ous from our Pravelage which his Majesty [h]as Granted — by his Proclamasion to the Royallist and

240

Disbanded Soldiers/ he Said what Proclemasion/ what Said I
have you not Got it/ he Said he never heard aney thing
abought it/ I Said it was strange that they in the orther
Provence [Nova Scotia] Should have it a[nd] we not, and that I
Could go their and marrey and not be malested/

the[n] he Showed [me] Whitmore['s] [Attorney-
General Thomas Wetmore] dacklereation [declaration, ie,
indictment] as he Called [it]/ I Said his Dacleratasion was not
true/ he Said where in/ I Said where he Said knowenly and
willingly/ I Said knowenly I ded it but willingly I ded not/ he
Said why then ded you do it/ I Said God had made a law and
Put it one my right hand and man had made law and Put it on
my left hand and Put me between them Borth and Said one of
these you must Brak/ Now Sir Judge which I aught to brak —
the law of God or the law of man/

this is a Part of what Past between he and I for Eight or
nine days/ at last he advised [me] to leve the town in all east
[haste] and not the town only but the County and not be Seeing
for five or Six days/ I Said he Sarprised me/ I Never Run
from the face of Cannon and I was not agoing to Run from the
face of a man but Should attend Corurt — which I ded but
Could See they ded not whant to bering one [bring on his case]
as I thought — but it is our God that knows only the truable of
heart and Sorrow of mind I weaded [waded] through Sum
month[s] that are parst — Least I Should wound the tender
Cause of Christ Knowing my oun Weakness a[nd] ignorance in
evrey degree but glory be to him that Says I will feat the back
for the burden and I have ever found him in time of need — and
he knows the need I have of him Now — and if he leaves me
now it will be the fir[s]t time/

abought the last of this year *1810* [I] was again taken
and had to give two hundrad Pound Bail for my apprance at
the Next Court which Caused me to to [*sic*] Sat of[f] for
Novascota the *firs*[*t*] *day of the year 1811*[168] — with a
Sorrowfull heart and a truabled mind — because I was
Searound[ed] with enemys borth within and without for my
heart was as heard as a Stone and as Dark as Midnight — and
my Christain frind[s] Much the Seam Sume Saying on[e] thing
and Sume another as if Leaft alone to Sink or Swam — and So
I want for Sum days untill Come to Christain Steves[169] — when

241

in bead I found the God of all the earth was with me then but Soon with drew again Untill I Got to Tentremar where I found a tempted Child of God whom I talked with and his Exprance [experience] for him the Moust of the Night & Ceam to amist [Amherst] and dead [did] the Seam with a Nother and was asked to heave [have] a meeting which [I] had in the evening with Sum freedom and was invited to a Nother at the river flipe [River Philip] the Nixt Night — but it being Dark before I Got their I could not find the house So was oblidge[d] to Put up in a tervren [tavern] for that night and thought to Steart early in the morning and make the Bast of my way for Cobegate [Cobequid] where M'r Hurable lived for he was uppermost in my mind for I Wanted that freed from the burden it was Leabroun [labouring] Under/

I Rose early in the morning/ alltho it Stormed Rode ten mild and then Called for my Brakfast and ordered my horse to be fead with Hay and oats and Expacted to have made a Great Jurney that day but M'r Purday for that was the landlords Name Said Sir are you the Gentelman that Spake at M'r [Richard] Pipes[170] on Sunday/ I Said it was/ he Said you had better [stay] with me to day as it Storms — and lat us have a Meeting hear to Night/ I Said God had Called [me] in to his Vinyuard and I dear not Refuse to Spake aney Where the peopel was willing to hear/ he Said he would Keep me and horse as long as I would Stay, which I locked on as the lords doings, and was mearvalous [marvelous] in my Sight for while talking their Ceam in two women which [I] talked with and found to be Christains/ one of them invited me at my Return to Stope and geve them a meeting at her hourse which I Promised I would/ in the Evening we all attend[ed] meeting for the lord had given me all their hearts, wherefor th[e]y Could not Stay [ie, resist?]/ their was a great meny that attend[ed] all tho they had but Short Notis — and the lord enabled his worm to Reach there hearts which Caused me to give out a Nother Meeting to morrow evening, which I attended with great freedom, and Could Heardly leave them for they was Near my heart/

[ONSLOW]

M'r fountain and M'r Parmer want with me Naxt day from Cobagate [Cobequid] Mountain to Cobagate where M'r fountain Enterduced me to four women and two out of the four Said th[e]y had Seen me befor/ I asked them where/ th[e]y Said in Horton/ We had meeting their that Night/ was treated well by all in the house and when taken my Leave of them was invited again at my Return/ M'r fountain and I Sat of for onslow it beeing Sataday where we got Sum time befor Sun down/ hear — Glory be to our God I fealt a weaping Spirit & Could not Refreain from it — without Knowing for What it was Sent/ the first house I want to was M'r John Heggens[171] who offered to Keep borth me and Horse as long as I Stayed in Onslow and and [sic] desiered I would have a meeting that night which which I had with freedom/ hear I found it to be my duty to Render a Reason for my being Baptized by way of amarsion [immersion]/

Next day being Sunday I attend meeting up the North River three times Twise in the day and at night — when I was tould M'r Huarable was going for Harlifax on Tusday and advised to attend him on monday — which I dead with two Christain frinds — with whom I found a great deal of freedom to till him My Cause/ he tould me he See the Bishope [Charles Inglis] was at [the] Head of this — but thought he had had a Nuff [enough] of that in the Cease of M'r townan [Enoch Towner][172] which Pleaded & gained and Said he understod much [more] Now then he ded then/ I tould [him] I Should [be] glad if he Could undertake [my defense] — for I wanted him if I Could not obtain My freedom hear to lay it befor the King and Pailement/ he Said he would gladly do it for me but Busness was So Great that he Could not find So much time — but Said he was a going to Halifax to morrow and he and M'r Robey [Simon Robie] would Consult to gether and th[e]y would do evrey thing for me th[e]y Could — but Says he I believe I have so much infleuance with the Bushope as to with Draw the acttion/ I tould him I ded not want that with out the freedom/ no Says he I Shall take good Cear [care] of that — for I Shall till [him] if he had not a Nuff [enough] at the first tryal I will Now See it out with him Now/

243

[I] tould him I was willing to pay him for his truable/ he tould me he must have three or four dollers for M'r Robay [Robie] fee three or four more for himself/ I give [him] Twalve dollers with an offer of More but he Said it was a Nuff [enough] at the present and wrote a letter to M'r Botsford[173] to undertake for for [sic] Me — with a Promise of my Recieving latters from him from Halifex by the Twenth of Fabrary and invited [me] in to his house interduced me to his wife and treated me with Brandey & tould me not to be uneasey for he would be vary Cearfull of my Buseness which I was forst [forced] to believe for I leaft a Varey great lode [load] with him — and Could not but love him and tould him he aught to be a preacher/ this is but a Samll [small] Part of What Past of What Past [sic] Between him and I/

hear the Peopel was Near my heart & I Could have Stayed along time with them but for the Devision their was amongth themselves/ hear Brother Danil Blear [Daniel Blair][174] had the freeist and Priatist[?] mind I See this [these] meny days/ I tould him he had yet to Preach — and Could have tould [him] he had a Battle to fight yet for the lord but I dead not/ I Stayed with him one [on] monday Night and Came to Cobagate [Cobequid] mountain a gain one [on] Tusday and give out meeting one [on] Wadensday Night When th[e]y Ceam from one end of the Mountain to the orther — borth this Night [and] thusday Night when I was takeng Sick with the fatuage of the Jurney and the Coulness of the weather — but the lord had Provided me with two good Nu[r]ses who tuck good Cear of me Borth Night and day/ one [on] Sunday Evening I attended Meeting at M'r Purday['s] and we had a Happy time of it which made it heard to Part/ Next day I attended my appointment at at [sic] River flipe [Philip] with three Slay lodes of Peopel who Stayed all night/

[CUMBERLAND]

Next morning th[e]y Returned home and I for amist [Amherst] and Stayed at M'r [Alpheus] Morss[175] first Night when M'rs [Theodora] Morss Brought that to light that I had forgot — for She Said when I had her Husband a Prisoner [at

244

Fort Cumberland in 1776 or 1777] and ordred to leave [the] Pleace [place] She had not one Mouthfull of Vitals to give her Children and She tould her Child to take that tray and aske me for a lettel flour when I tould her to bring the largest thing She had/ that that [*sic*] is lost to me [but] is not lost with our God/ Glory be to his great name for that [which] a men Sows of the Seam Shall he Reape/ o that man would believe this/ hear I waited for M'r [Matthew] fanwick[176] three days Untill Sunday/ hild Meeting twice this day in amist [Amherst] Court house where I had a gain to Render a Reason of my Baptizem by a Marsion [immersion] with life and freedom which meny felt to the Joye of their hearts/

Now I wanted to go for home more then Any orther Place but Recieved Word from M'r [Matthew] Fanwick Not to Go without him/ there for on monday I want to find him at Meacan [Maccan] River Sixteen mild of where I found him holding but one Meeting in a week/ I tould the people I wanted one Tusday Night — which I attend[ed] and found Great freedom — which Caused Sum to Say th[e]y [had] not had Such a Meeting this fourteen years/ had meeting Nixt night with more freedom/ fealt the people to Come Nier & Nier — and So I Continued to have meeting untill Sataday and one [on] Sunday a Great number Meat to Gether — but locked varey while [wild] and Cearless but I had not Spake long befor th[e]y where Varey Sollom indeed and was Vary lorth [loathe] to let me [go] and [I] was oblidged to Give out a Meeting at Napann River on monday Evening which I attended and Nixt morning Sat of one [on] my Jurny for home/

I Called to M's [Mrs] Freemons[177] for my things that I leaft intending to Sat off Emmedietly for M'r Coals[178] but She ordered My horse in to the Stable and to be fead with Hay and oats and would not lat me go untill after dinner — When I leaft in the hands of a marcyfull God, and the lord Reward her for the kindness She Showed to me/ I Come to M'r [Jonathan] Coals a bought Sun Sat and the old man and woman was varey glad to See me of a truth and Said th[e]y was afraid th[e]y Should naver See me any more in this world and Could not bear that I Should go with out having one Meeting which I Consented to and So thought to have Stayed another Night with them/ at the Meeting the old gentle man Said he had the good Supper but the People would not lat me go with M'r Coal that Night but I want with those I naver See befor and Sat up the most of the Night and talked with freedom/

    5 March [*1811*] and no latters from Halifax but glory be to God I fealt this morning that my enemy Shall fall/ *14 March* Received a latter from M'rs [Messrs] Robie & archibald which Brought Varey lattle Satisfacttion to me and Mine but a deail of truable for I preavseave [perceive] that I am feast [fast] in the enemys hand — and no arm Can Deliver me but the mightty God of Jacob, and now I Must go to Town a gain not Knowing what to do or what will happing [to] me/

[CLOSE COMMUNION]

    June 11th 1811 Wrote a letter to the Conferance Meeting [of the NS and NB Baptist Association, meeting at Onslow] by order of the [Norton Baptist] Church[179] wishing to Join them in full Communion and fellershipe — but o the Sorrow of my heart no tunge Can till/ it Seams as if all the Powers of darkness was Let lous [loose] up[on] me and no way for my ascape was Leaft me and yet I know the lord is with me/

[FUNERALS][180]

Preached the funerals for the following Names —

a Child of Burnats
Martin Feay [1801]
a Child of armstronges
Jam's Ramsay
Will'm Righit
George Hays
M'r [John] darinton [1807]
a man that died at Hays
M'r [Christopher] Rubart [1810]
M'is Rubart
John Noblet
M'is Stover
M'r Foster

M'is Mcleod
M'is Mcleod [sic]
M'is dier [1805]
M'is Greeno
M'is Olley
Will'm Banson
George Teabour
Widor Clark [1810]
Jam's Beha [1809]
a Child of M'r Clark [1810]
M'is Freazes
Joseph Bickels Child
Hanry Rubart Child

NOTES TO CHAPTER THREE

1 On the low fortunes of the Sheffield Congregational meeting, see James Hannay (ed), "Documents of the Congregational Church at Maugerville," in (1894) 1 *Coll NB His Soc* 149-52. On the church's considerable Loyalist support in the 1790s see Appendix II. Although no new· Congregational churches were gathered in this period, a group of migrants from Sheffield did form a small society on Keswick Ridge, apparently in the first decade of the nineteenth century: Evelyn Gordon & Harry Grant, *On the Ridge* (1975), pp. 129-30.

2 This section is based on the annual Wesleyan conference minutes for 1801, 1804, 1808 and 1812; Black to WMS, 17 September 1804; Black to WMS, 10 October 1804; Marsden to WMS, 11 March 1805: Wesleyan Missionary Society Reel A-258, PAC; T.W. Smith, *History of the Methodist Church . . . of Eastern British America* (1877), I, chs 14 & 15.

3 Smith, *Methodist Church, ibid*; McColl to WMS, 6 August 1805; annual conference minutes for 1812: Wesleyan Missionary Society Reel A-258, PAC.

4 Smith, *Methodist Church, ibid;* Black to WMS, 10 October 1804; Black to WMS, 24 October 1814; annual Wesleyan conference minutes for 1812: Wesleyan Missionary Society Reel A-258, PAC.

5   Outlined in Stephen Humbert, *Rise and Progress of Methodism in the Province of New Brunswick, From its Commencement until about the Year 1805* (Saint John, 1836).

6   Black to WMS, 10 October 1804: Wesleyan Missionary Society Reel A-258, PAC. As noted in the text, Black's impression of the sudden rise of the Baptists is correct. His suggestion that they had formerly been Newlights is, in the main, not correct. Yet it must be said that his remarks have the support of two other observers. As a result of an 1805 tour of the Petitcodiac and St John rivers the Presbyterian James MacGregor wrote:

> The Chief part of the people are New Lights, whose principles are a mixture of Calvinism, Antinomianism, and enthusiasim.... The rest of the people are Wesley's Methodists, who are rather on the decline. On the other hand the New Lights are increasing, and I suppose rather improving in their principles, and they have now changed their denomination from New Lights to Baptists: George Patterson, *Memoir of the Rev. James MacGregor* (1859), p. 351.

Similarly a year earlier the unordained Presbyterian Congregationalist John Mitchell wrote the following while touring the Petitcodiac:

> [The English] are all Methodist and New-lights. The people who call themselves new-lights in this country in general Deny the divine right of Infant baptism [and are antinomians].

As regards the Petitcodiac Mitchell's remarks are true enough; but then, when moving on to the Loyalist Kennebecasis valley, Mitchell implausibly recorded that "the people in general call themselves new-lights": John Mitchell Journal, 7 & 12 August 1804: PANS.

Clearly Black, MacGregor and Mitchell were deeply impressed by the surge towards the Baptists in New Brunswick during the first decade of the nineteenth century. But why did all three portray it in 'Newlight to Baptist' terms when this was in all likelihood *not* the case for most of those who became Baptists? No doubt part of the answer is that all three lived in Nova Scotia and all three were writing for a British readership which would hardly have been concerned about the differing religious contours of New Brunswick and Nova Scotia. Perhaps, then, it is not surprising that they would generalize the Nova Scotia experience to include New Brunswick. Surely another reason is that all three men viewed New Brunswick through the filter of their impressions of the Petitcodiac-Tantramar region (rather than the St John valley), and in this southeastern corner of New Brunswick the Nova Scotia analysis did indeed fit. Black had formerly lived in the region. MacGregor and Mitchell — both Scots — lived on the Isthmus of Chignecto so that, physically, they entered New Brunswick via the Petitcodiac region. How natural then that when the three thought about the religious character of New Brunswick, their views were disproportionately coloured by what they saw in the southeast, which was simply an extension of a pattern they knew in Nova Scotia. It must, therefore, be emphasized that as regards New Brunswick Baptists in general — the great majority of whom lived in the St John valley -- the analysis offered by the three preachers was mistaken.

7   It is generally said that at the end of the eighteenth century New Brunswick had about 25,000 inhabitants: Graeme Wynn, *Timber Colony: A Historical Geography of Early Nineteenth Century New Brunswick,* (1981), p. 3; W.S. MacNutt, *New Brunswick: A History, 1784-1867* (1963), p. 118. Neither historian admitted that he drew the statistic from James Hannay's *History of New Brunswick* (1909), I, pp. 290-91.

By the time of his *Atlantic Provinces: The Emergence of Colonial Society* (1965), p. 118, MacNutt had lowered his guess to 20,000 as of 1803. This nearly corresponds with the contemporary speculation of

William Black, who advised in 1804 that New Brunswickers numbered "not more than twenty thousand or at the farthest twenty five thousand": Black to WMS, 17 September 1804: Wesleyan Missionary Society Reel A-258, PAC. Assuming Black's median figure of 22,500 represents the New Brunswick population in 1805, and allowing 4000 for Acadian and the few English Roman Catholics (Black was probably not counting Indians), then Baptists would have numbered eight percent of Protestants.

On the Acadian population in 1803, see the excellent statistics in F.E. Rameau de Saint-Père, *Colonie Féodale en Amérique* (1889) II, pp. 255-56. Little is known of the few English-speaking Roman Catholics in Loyalist New Brunswick. It is, therefore, of considerable interest that among the earliest petitions to Lt-Gov Carleton by communities of religious Dissenters was one on behalf of Roman Catholics. The document itself is undated, but the formal answer it received was dated 6 May 1793. The text of the petition (from F67, NBM) is as follows:

Memorial in behalf of the Catholicks of this Province

Most humbly sheweth:

That there are many of the Inhabitants of this Province of the Roman Catholic Religion, who ardently wishes to have a Pastor of their own Persuasion.

They therefore humbly represent to your Excellency that many of the above description have removed from the Province to other parts, where they might enjoy the exercise & benefit of their Religion.

That numbers still remain (tho unknown) who look up to your Excellency on the present occasion, that have large growing Families, whom they sincerely wish to train up in the Religion of their Forefathers.

That far the greatest part of those Catholicks served His Majesty as good Soldiers and Loyal Subjects during the late American Rebellion.

Memorialists with all due submission to your Excellency and the Honorable Council, humbly hope that you will be pleased to take this Case into Consideration & grant them the Toleration they most earnestly desire, and Memorialists [*etc*].

> Tho's Sealey
> John Sinnot
> Roger Cooper
> Charles Brannen

[Provincial-Secretary Odell's reply: 6 May 1793]

I am directed by His Excellency the Lieutenant Governor ... to assure you that all such Inhabitants of this Province, who wish to have a Priest of the Roman Catholic Communion settled among them may unite in making the application proposed to Bishop [John] Carrol [of Baltimore] for that purpose, in the fullest confidence that they will at all times enjoy as ample toleration and protection under this Government as in any other part of His Majesty's Dominions. [reply directed to Charles Brannen]

8   "Memoir of Duncan M'Coll," in *British North American Wesleyan Methodist Magazine* (September 1841), p. 492; *Mass Bapt Miss Mag* (February 1807), p. 268; Henry Hale Journal, 26 November 1807 *et seq:* Maine Historical Society, Portland.

9   *Mass Bapt Miss Mag* (March 1807), p. 14.

10   Henry Hale Journal, 31 July 1808 *et seq:* Maine Historical Society, Portland. About all that is known of Archer is given in Brian Cuthbertson (ed), *Journal of the Reverend John Payzant* (1981), pp. 98, 100, 123. In 1809 Payzant thought Archer a Baptist preacher, but a year earlier the US Baptist Henry Hale had written of Archer in Newlight terms.

251

[H]eard Mr. Archer attempt to preach [at Eastport] fr Neh. 5.5. I could but think his discourse resembled the world in Chaos, Land and Water, undivided, and darkness over the whole. I felt some desire that he might be convinced of the differences between the leadings of God's spirit, and the running of a wild immagination.

11 Fay's adventures are noted below in connection with Charlotte County.

12 Henry Hale Journal, 5 September 1809 *et seq:* Maine Historical Society, Portland; J.M. Bumsted (ed), "Autobiography of Joseph Crandall," in (1973) 3 *Acadiensis* (⫫1) pp. 92-94.

13 Edward Manning Journal, 1 September 1810 *et seq:* Acadia; *Mass Bapt Miss Mag* (June 1812), p. 166.

14 Jotham Sewall, Jr, *Memoir of Rev. Jotham Sewall of Chesterville, Maine* (1853), pp. 131-147. Sewall made another extensive visit in 1811.

15 John Mitchell Journal, PANS.

16 *Mass Bapt Miss Mag* (September 1804), p. 88.

17 *Ibid,* (February 1807), p. 269.

18 "Memoir of Duncan M'Coll," in *British North American Wesleyan Methodist Magazine* (September 1841), pp. 491-92. McColl then added:

> It was dreadful to see the end of the new-light work: whoredom, adultery and the abolishment of all law, both divine and human, was the end of it. S----- S------, one of their preachers, and S------'s daughter produced fruit. He soon after left his wife and family; and his wife, a high professor, took up with another man. Several others of the most flaming professors among them followed the same example. This proved a bad stroke both to the religion and the morals of the people of St David's.

I took abundance of pains with that unstable people, and saw but little satisfaction among them.

Fifteen years later St David became the only New Brunswick locale to support the unitarian version of the Christian sect (Smithites). Perhaps the root of this eccentric religious behaviour lies in the fact that the parish had been settled by the Cape Ann Association from Massachusetts.

19   *Mass Bapt Miss Mag* (May 1807), p. 301.

20   *Ibid*, (February 1807), p. 270.

21   There is evidence of at least three ordained American Baptists preaching in the Maritimes between Alline's time and the arrival of the first representatives of the Massachusetts Baptist Missionary Society in 1805-06.

An unnamed "close Baptist" in the Cumberland area in 1783 or 1784: .Cuthbertson, *Payzant's Journal,* p. 31.

William Van Horn was authorized in 1787 to go to Nova Scotia as a representative of the Philadelphia Baptists Association, in response to an "application from Shelburne": *Minutes of the Philadelphia Association* (1951), p. 229. (I am grateful to Philip Griffin-Allwood for this reference.)

Job Seamans paid a short visit to his former home in the Cumberland region in 1803: Seamans Journal, New London Town Hall, NH.

22   *Mass Bapt Miss Mag* (February 1807), p. 268; (May 1807), p. 301.

23   Among the initial members of the St George organization were Stewart Seeley, Rebecca Seeley, Dominicus Millikin, Nancy Millikin, Charlotte Millikin, John Oliver, Deborah Oliver, Polly Baldwin and John Haycock: *Christian Visitor,* 8 December 1847.

24 *Christian Visitor,* beginning 8 December 1847.

25 Henry Hale Journal, 2 July 1808: Maine Historical Society, Portland. Hale does not actually refer to the St David church but one infers that it still existed.

26 John Fay was one of the almost numberless "imposters" who plagued every Protestant sect in the Maritimes in the post-Alline generation. They ranged from complete rogues like Fay and his celebrated fellow horse thief, Henry More Smith (who had been a Methodist preacher), to genuine ministers who turned out bad (like the Anglican James Jones and the changeable John James) to otherwise respected preachers who had given offence to one of their brethren (Edward Manning thought Theodore Harding an impostor). Fay, apparently a Maritimer aged about 26, arrived in St George in the spring of 1809. According to "Deacon Shaw," as paraphrased in a Portsmouth newspaper, Fay

> appeared to be a pious young man, and soon began to speak in public, and was very much approved of; he said he had lately left the Methodist society and had joined the Baptist, and was baptized [by whom?] after he came there. Soon after this took place he set out from Macadavie [St George] ... to go to Nova-Scotia; he went as far as St. John's and there took passage in the packet for Grenville, where he met with Elder Edward [James?] Manning, to whom he was introduced as a preacher, and shewed his recommendations [from "Col. McKay, Steward Sealey" and Deacon Shaw of St George] — he preached there a number of times, travelled with Elder Manning and was much approved of. He left those parts with a borrowed horse, to go to Halifax, and return again in a short time; soon after his arrival at the latter place, he sold his horse and went on board a vessel bound for Portsmouth.

Fay took with him a recommendation from Manning, on the basis of which — and a week of preaching in Elias Smith's Christ-ian church at Portsmouth — he was ordained. The next day he borrowed another horse for a short trip to Boston, from whence neither he nor the horse ever returned: *Herald of Gospel Liberty*, 13 October 1809. (The paper was edited by Elias Smith.)

27 *Mass Bapt Miss Mag* (March 1808), p. 15. For the sake of comprehensiveness one should note that about 1810 "a man of colour by the name of Miller" apparently staged a considerable reformation on Deer Island, formerly a "mere Sodom for wickedness": *Mass Bapt Miss Mag* (June 1812), p. 167. Possibly he was the same "collored man" preaching at Eastport on 5 September 1809: Henry Hale Journal, Maine Historical Society, Portland.

28 J.M. Bumsted (ed), "Autobiography of Joseph Crandall," in (1973) 3 *Acadiensis* (#1) 79, p. 90. Crandall's autobiographical sketch, written decades after the events described, is unreliable and must be handled with care. In the *Acadiensis* version the editing is, unfortunately, purely notional.

29 Job Seamans Journal, 25 September 1803: New London Town Hall, NH. (I am grateful to Dr. Robert Gardner for making available a photostatic copy of the original.)

30 "Minutes of the Nova Scotia Baptist Association . . . 1809": Acadia; *Mass Bapt Miss Mag* (May 1810), p. 298; Sackville Baptist Churchbook: Acadia.

31 This resolution might also mean that Joseph Crandall's description of the church's original constitution as open communion Baptist ("Autobiography," p. 86) was simply false, but I do not think so. The church was gathered by Edward Manning, Theodore Harding and Joseph Dimock at a time when they would probably have insisted that it be purely Baptist. I think, rather, that the Baptist church under public pressure had lapsed into Allinism.

255

32   Concerning Daniel Shaw: Job Seamans Journal, 14 August 1803: New London Town Hall, NH; Howard Temperley (ed), *Gubbins' New Brunswick Journals* (1980) pp. 17-18. Concerning Matthew Fenwick: James Innis Journal, *infra*. Jacob Peck is discussed in the text immediately below.

33   Obediah Newcomb was immersed and joined the Horton-Cornwallis Baptist church on 2 December 1798. In 1803 Job Seamans, visiting Hopewell, described him as "a baptist preacher" and "a promising young man": Journal, 26 & 27 August 1803: New London Town Hall, NH. In early 1811 it was said of Newcomb that he had laboured at Shepody "for several years; he is not ordained, but appears to be sound in the faith": *Mass Bapt Miss Mag* (September 1812), p. 203. His 1811 ordination is described in Henry Hale's journal, 4 July 1811: Maine Historical Society, Portland. The essentially Allinite character of Newcomb's neighbourhood (Alline himself had claimed success in Shepody) is confirmed by Edward Manning's remarks on Newcomb, written about 1812.

> Is sound in the Faith, of correct morrals, an acceptable Preacher. Labours hard; has a handsome property and Receves perhaps 160 dollars assistence from the people. He Received more when unordained. But when the Public knew that he was ordained upon New Testament principles [*ie*, close communion] many withdrew, which makes his income less, tho his comforts may increase: Notes on Baptist Ministers, Manning Collection, Acadia.

David Benedict listed a Shepody church among the unassociated Maritime Baptist churches but this was an error: *General History of the Baptist Denomination in America* (1813), I, p. 549. In 1817 Edward Manning was disposed to recommend Newcomb to the Baptists of Eastport as their prospective pastor, but the following year he was in Pennsylvania: Edward Manning

Journal, 1 March 1817; Newcomb to Manning, 18 August 1818: Manning Collection, Acadia. Newcomb is yet another of the early Baptist ministers omitted from Baptist denominational historiography.

34 *Minutes of the Baptist, Nova-Scotia and New-Brunswick, Association* (Halifax, 1810), p. 5.

35 As to Crandall, see the "Babcock Tragedy" article reprinted below in Appendix X. Unless otherwise noted all quotations are from the documents in this Appendix. As to Mitchell, his journal for 6 August 1803 notes simply, "Trav'led 15 Miles through the Woods to Shediak, where I preached in the evening to a number of English and French": PANS.

36 William Reynolds' *New Brunswick Magazine* article reprinted in Appendix X characterized the religious exercises in the Shediac neighbourhood as Baptist rather than Newlight. While that characterization is entitled to some respect as being based on sources I have not located (in this case, I presume, the memoir of William Hanington Jr.), I think it mistaken. The fact that Joseph Crandall preached in the neighbourhood in 1804 is no evidence of the religious character of the inhabitants. Admittedly, Crandall immersed rather freely in his early days and Jacob Peck was actually his neighbour in Salisbury. But nothing in the documentation in Appendix X suggests that the Shediac Christians were Baptists, and John Welling clearly recalled that the exercises in question (which he witnessed as a youth) were of a Newlight character, in the tradition of Henry Alline. Of Jacob Peck little is known except that he was the son of Martin Peck/Beck, a Hillsborough German. As such he was brother-in-law to the Newlight preacher Henry Steeves. In 1810 he was still living in Joseph Crandall's vicinity in Salisbury.

37 Such a view is expressed in G.A. Rawlyk, *Ravished by the Spirit: Religious Revivals, Baptists and Henry Alline* (1984), p. 101. There was a vaguely similar

occurrence a year later in Augusta Maine, when Captain James Purrington murdered his wife and seven children in the belief that the sooner they entered paradise the better: *Life, Experience, and Travels of John Colby* (Lowell, 1838), p. 198.

38 Rawlyk, *Ravished by the Spirit,* pp. 128-30; Rawlyk, *New Light Letters and Spiritual Songs, 1778-1793* (1983), pp. 27-29. The correspondence of three Anglican observers provides some less well known examples of the effects of Newlight stimulus on Maritime females. In 1790 William Clark of Annapolis wrote of:

> One of the [Newlight] tribe [who] took it into her head to live without Eating, Drinking or speaking and actually held out for nine days in defiance of force or persuasion — nature could hold no longer and she expired, leaving her husband and six children to follow her example if they choose; but he, good man, tired of lying alone for three weeks, has entered into a treaty of matrimony with another of the sisterhood: Clark to Peters, 5 June 1790: Bailey Papers, vol. 93A, PANS.

Across the river in Granville at about the same time a certain Sarah Bancroft came out as a prophetess. As Bishop Inglis recorded in his journal:

> The woman's name who prophecied that the Devil would carry off a man bodily is Sarah Bancroft, & the man that was to be carried off was George Morrison — the day on which she fixed for this adventure last Monday, being elapsed, & Morrison still remaining, the prophetess acknowledges her error — she is a girl of bad character & had been guilty of several deceptions & bad pranks formerly — Morrison had some time since declared himself a New Light & that he was Converted; but leaving that sect, this attempt against him is supposed to be the effect of revenge: Inglis Journal, 19 August 1791: PANS.

A few days later the bishop was still sufficiently titillated by this example of Newlight folly to record of Bancroft that:

> she lives at a Capt'n Shaw's in this vicinity — she lately told M'rs Shaw & the family that it was a great honour to them to attend & wait upon her, *as she* (the prophetess) *would be a pillar in heaven:* Inglis Journal, 24 August 1791.

Two years later he had the satisfaction of noting that "their prophetess, Sarah Bancroft, died suddenly — hereby they [the Newlights] have received a Check": Inglis Journal, 30 August 1793. Even the Anglican clergymen who stood most firmly against the errors of the Newlights could not always sufficiently fortify the female members of their household against the contagions of the day. An ironic case in point is that of Rebecca Bailey, 19-year-old daughter of the rector of Annapolis. Although provided by her brilliant father with what he described as the best education in the province she unaccountably became "a reader of novels & romances". Then, at the beginning of 1799 she was suddenly seized by the "religious prensy or disorder which then prevailed at Annapolis and Granville". This left her "more unsteady, more impatient of restraint and less attentive to her conduct than before". Finally in 1801 Rebecca Bailey suddenly absconded to Boston: Bailey to Parker, 13 November 1801: Bailey Papers, vol. 94: PANS. To her astonished and grieving father the novel reading, the flirtation with the Newlights and the rebellious flight from home were all aspects of a basic instability of character.

39 Brilliantly discussed in John F.C. Harrison, *The Second Coming: Popular Millenarianism, 1780-1850* (1979).

40 Estey to James Manning, 10 March 1802. This letter was apparently printed in the *Christian Visitor* about 1870-71, the clipping of which is preserved in the Fredericton Baptist Churchbook, p. 271: Acadia. I

think the same theme is suggested in Manning to Bennett, 10 October 1793, in Rawlyk, *New Light Letters*, p. 179. None of these views of the return of Christ is similar to that of Henry Alline; yet all of the preachers were in Alline's Newlight tradition.

41 Edward Manning, Notes on Baptist Ministers [1812]: Manning Collection, Acadia.

42 This count includes St Martins and Sussex as being in the St John valley but excludes Keswick owing to uncertainty whether it was formed in the first decade of the century.

43 Waterborough Baptist Churchbook, 16 August 1812: Acadia.

44 Prince William Baptist Churchbook, 2 January 1802; 1 June 1811: Acadia. The Churchbook may have been rewritten at a very early date for the purpose of removing references to the internal controversies that caused the dramatic loss of support.

45 *Ibid*, 3 May 1812; *c*November 1813; Henry Hale Journal, 10 August 1809: Maine Historical Society, Portland.

46 Wakefield Baptist Churchbook, 4 October 1808; 26 August 1809: Acadia.

47 We do not, of course, know how early the Long Island church disappeared, but Henry Hale made no mention of it in his visits at the end of the decade. On 19 February 1806 Charles Lewis was described in the Wakefield Baptist Churchbook as being "Minister of the Gospel over the Baptist Church in Long Reach," presumably a mistake for Long Island (above Long Reach). This might mean that a Long Island church still existed; but it might also mean simply that the Wakefield Baptists were too isolated to know what was happening on the lower River.

48 Griffin to Manning, 26 November 1817: Manning

Collection, Acadia; John Francis' letter: *Christian Visitor*, 26 April 1848.

49   George Levy (ed), *Diary and Related Writings of the Reverend Joseph Dimock (1768-1846)* (1979), p. 151.

50   Norton Baptist Churchbook (historical preface, 1840s-1850s). (I viewed this record courtesy of Josephine Innis McCready.) Azor Hoyt Journal, 2 April 1814: Kings County Historical Society, Hampton. As noted below in the context of Benjamin Fairweather, this may actually have been the second meeting-house erected in Norton. On 15 April 1810 Henry Hale preached at a meeting-house which appears to have been in Norton. I take this to mean that a meeting-house had actually been erected on the land deeded to Fairweather for that purpose in 1801.

51   No one has yet explored the demographic link between the St John and Upper Canada or its implications for the spread of Allinite, Baptist and Wesleyan principles. That the migration was substantial at an early date is evidenced by Edward Winslow's denunciation of the exodus in an 1802 letter to the *Royal Gazette:* W.O. Raymond (ed), *Winslow Papers* (1901), pp. 468-72. One of the questions Winslow commended to intending emigrants by way of self examination was, "Does anybody interrupt you in matters of conscience?". Winslow would have answered in the negative, but the fact that he raised the point at all — in the year when Baptists first petitioned for extension of the benefit of the *Marriage Act* — may be significant.

Concerning the Wesleyan migration to Upper Canada the best evidence is a footnote to an 1800 letter from Alexander McLeod to the preacher Daniel Fidler:

Jacob Barker is now in Quebec where he has been Sick near 5 Months in his return from Upper Cannada which Country he went to explore last spring when Mr. Ryerson, Mr. Mead & Robert McLeod from Nashwalk &c moved there: McLeod to Fidler, 17 January 1800, in Goldwin French (ed),

"Papers of Daniel Fidler, Methodist Missionary in Nova Scotia and New Brunswick, 1792-1798," in (1960) 13 *Bulletin: Records and Proceedings of the Committee on Archives of the United Church of Canada* 28, p. 46.

At about the same time that one or more of these Wesleyans was removing from the Nashwaak to Upper Canada, Titus Finch was taking his departure from the same neighbourhood. Concerning his religious sentiments in New Brunswick nothing is known except that his name seems to be on the 1786 Dissenters' petition printed here as Appendix I. Perhaps on the Nashwaak he was a Wesleyan. But after his 1797 or 1798 migration to Upper Canada he became a Baptist and was among those gathered into a Charlotteville Baptist church (on Lake Erie) in October 1803. Most of the others immersed on that occasion were his converts: Stuart Ivison & F.T. Rosser, *Baptists in Upper and Lower Canada before 1820* (1956), pp. 40-43, 98-99, 135-36; Rosser, *London Township Pioneers* (1975), pp. 127-29. (One suspects that Finch's group was a Newlight society which, as at Waterborough, turned Baptist en masse.) In 1805 Finch was ordained as the church's pastor. It is interesting to note the names of the other males who joined in the 1803 organization of the church: Lawrence Johnson, John Gustin, Peter Teeple, Oliver Maybee, Richard Lanning, Joseph Merrill, Samuel Smith, Robert Shearer, Abraham Smith, Andrew McCleish, Levi Montross, Peter Fairchild, James Corliss, Thomas Smith, Solomon Smith. Of these Lawrence Johnson, Peter Teeple, Oliver Maybee, Joseph Merrill, Samuel Smith, Abraham Smith, Levi Montrose and Thomas Smith are either demonstrably from New Brunswick (some from the Nashwaak) or are likely so. Possibly Peter Fairchild (ordained in 1806) was also a New Brunswicker.

Into this same western part of Ontario came another New Brunswick couple, Thomas and Sarah Hollowood. A Loyalist to New Brunswick, Hollowood was a member of the Wakefield Baptist church by 1805. A church meeting at his home on 23 February 1806 was described as "the Most Solemn Day that Ever was known in Wakefield," the clerk adding that "there was 136 People there besides infants": Wakefield Baptist Churchbook, Acadia. It is uncertain with which Baptist church the Hollowoods first connected themselves in Upper Canada; but in January 1819 they were dismissed from that organization to form a Baptist church at Bayham. It is notable that other New Brunswickers (and Nova Scotians) became members on that occasion and that at least two of the council of three who organized the church were former New Brunswickers: Ivison & Rosser, p. 119. Among the first Baptist preachers to visit this Bayham church after its formation was George Ebberson, pastor of the Baptist church at Gananoque. Ebberson would have been well known to some of the Bayham people from their New Brunswick days. He and his wife Zipporah were among the earliest members of the Prince William Baptist church. By 1806 they had moved up to Wakefield. On 18 June 1808 the Wakefield church instructed its clerk to

> [W]rite a Certificate for our Dearly Beloved Brother G Eberson and Zepporah Eberson his wife where in they Certified that Brother Eberson had Been Useful in his Improvements & which they Did and gave him as he was going to Upper Canada.

The reference to Ebberson's "Improvements" suggests that he was already an exhorter. Where he first settled in Upper Canada is not known. In 1812 he joined the Baptist church at Steventown and in 1817 he was ordained pastor over a church in Gananoque: Ivison & Rosser, pp. 90, 96-97, 133.

From these references (drawn to my attention by Frederick C. Burnett) it is clear that St John valley Newlights, Wesleyans and Baptists played a primary role in planting vital religion in Upper Canada, a role that well deserves to be explored. One final reference, from the Wakefield Baptist Churchbook, for 12 July 1806, indicates the dimension of the exodus.

263

In May and in June 1806 Brothers Jonathan Parks, John Stanley, and Jesse Baker and Sisters Abigail Baker, Lydia Baker that was Lydia Woodworth, Hannah Stanley, & Sarah Baker Left the Place. Abigail and Lyddia Baker Moved to St John. The Rest to Niagaria.

See also G.E. Reaman, *Trail of the Black Walnut* (1974), pp. 46, 63, 86, 117, 225.

52   The principal source is a one-page recollection by Edward Weyman (son of Henry Weyman) in the Weyman Collection, Acadia. In addition to the Allinite societies named in the text, Weyman locates others on the Oromocto and the Nashwaak. In another short reminiscence in the same collection Weyman gives further particulars of the Allinite society at Lower Millstream (in which he was reared).

At the commencement of the nineteenth century a few families that had moved from other localities to the Mill Stream, then a new settlement, united together to hold religious meetings, the Lord blessing them with his presence. Two of their number ... Matthew Fenwick and Henry Weyman, who were more gifted than the rest, appointed and led forward in their religious exercises. Henry Weyman [had been] a member of the First Baptist Church of Sussex; but, when the high tone[d] [Calvinist] doctrine was introduced among them, he protested against it and united his labours with Mr. Fenwick, who held Henry Allen's views on baptism, that is, [that it was a] nonessential; though they were much united in spirit till H. Weyman died in eighteen hundred and seven.

Matthew Fenwick from this time took the lead of the Religious meetings, at which Joel Daniels and family, the [Ezekiel] Foster and [William] Sipperell families were the principal [ones]... .

53   G.A. Rawlyk, *New Light Letters*, pp. 157-58.

54 Clarke to SPG, summarized in SPG Journal, 20 March 1801: (microfilm), PAC.

55 Job Seamans Journal, 14 August 1803: New London Town Hall, NH.

56 Howard Temperley (ed), *Gubbins' New Brunswick Journals* (1980), p. 17 (16 July 1811).

57 The Prince William church reported receiving such a letter: Churchbook, 7 July 1804, Acadia.

58 Waterborough Baptist Churchbook, 29 June 1805: Acadia.

59 Wakefield Baptist Churchbook, 9 March 1805: Acadia.

60 *Ibid,* 26 August 1809.

61 *Ibid,* March 1810; Henry Hale Journal, 10 August 1809: Maine Historical Society, Portland.

62 The event is recounted in both the Jarvis Ring Memoir (Acadia) and J.M. Bumsted (ed), "Autobiography of Joseph Crandall", in (1973) 3 *Acadiensis* (#1) 79, pp. 88-89.

63 Wakefield Baptist Churchbook, 9 March 1805: Acadia. Peter Crandall's ordination is described in the Henry Hale Journal, 28 June 1809: Maine Historical Society, Portland.

64 Henry Hale Journal, 15 October 1809: *ibid.*

65 *Ibid,* 5 July 1809. His ordination is described in the entry for 27 June 1810.

66 Grace Aiton, *Story of Sussex and Vicinity* (1967), pp. 20, 76, 79. There is a sketch of Ansley's life in Bill, *Fifty Years with the Baptists,* pp. 166-75.

67 Inglis Journal, 12 August 1795: PANS.

68 *Ibid,* 18 August 1798.

69   Simon Baxter (c1730-1804), a New Hanpshire Loyalist,
      was among the first to arrive in what would become New
      Brunswick. In 1782 he was granted a highly desirable
      tract on the Kennebecasis in what would become the
      parish of Norton. (James Innis subsequently acquired
      land on the edge of the Simon Baxter tract.) Already in
      1786 New Brunswick's attorney-general, making his
      first trip outside Saint John, could describe Baxter's
      place as "as good a Farm as any in this, or almost any
      Country in America": Bliss to Blowers, 24 August 1786,
      Bliss Papers, PANS. In 1792 Patrick Campbell thought
      Baxter "the most successful farmer in raising stock and
      clearing land in this province": *Travels in North
      America* (1793) (1937 edn), pp. 262-65. Baxter was an
      old-fashioned 18th-century gentlemen in his instincts;
      he was inclined to lusty vulgarity but with strong
      attachment to the social stability he associated with the
      Church of England. He had even intended one of his
      sons (as he said) "for a Cushing Thumper": Baxter to
      Peters, 22 February 1787, Samuel Peters Papers,
      American Church Historical Society. As early as the
      fall of 1782 he was writing to Jacob Bailey at Annapolis
      to "come over & Help us". There were, he reported, "a
      Grate Number of familyes in these parts, parfesers of the
      church of England & above 50 children Not Cristen'd":
      Baxter to Bailey, 10 February 1783, Bailey Papers, vol
      93, PANS. (As this was written when only a handful of
      Loyalist families can have been settled in the whole St
      John valley and as nothing known of the pre-Loyalists
      suggests that they were professors of the Church of
      England, one suspects that Baxter was counting
      children rather than "parfesers".) Something of the
      flavor of Baxter's character is suggested by the verses
      printed below at the end of Appendix XI.

70   Inglis to SPG, 4 July 1791: Inglis Transcripts, PANB.
      Before his time in Sackville Jones was chaplin to the
      Owen family of Campobello. After Sackville he was
      appointed itinerant missionary on the Miramichi. In
      this regard see W.A. Spray, *David's Kingdom: A*

History of the Anglican Church in the Parish of Chatham (1979), pp. 2-4.

71   Inglis to Baxter, 1 February 1797: Inglis Transcripts, PANB.

72   *R* v *Baxter et al:* RS42 (1798), PANB.

73   Wesleyan Annual Minutes, 6 July 1804: Wesleyan Missionary Society Reel A-258, PAC.

74   In his 1812 Notes on Baptist Ministers Edward Manning wrote that Ansley was

> Baptised [*ie,* immersed] about the year 1800. Ordained in Sedgwick, Ma[i]ne in about 1806. Removed to Annapolis in about 1809. Left a valuable property in Sussex vale, New Brunswick where he formerly Resided. Obtains about 300 Hundred [*sic*] Dollers from the church and Congregation where he [resides].

75   Extensively documented in the Hale Journal: Maine Historical Society, Portland. Concerning a 15 November 1809 meeting at Caleb Davis' Hale wrote:

> Br Ansley preached fr Acts 3.17. I believe he speak under the divine influence. After he had done a number of exhortations followed, and I believe the holy spirit decended in some measure like as it did on the day of Penticost. Many cryd out in keen distress of soul, and ten souls were hopefully brought into the liberty of the gospel. The people continued together untill 1 o'clock in the morning.

76   Ernest Graham, *History of the Anglican Church in the Parish of Springfield* (1983), pp. 23, 50; Abraham Baxter *et ux* to Fairweather "for the use of a Church Lot of [*sic*] the Baptist Society," 10 December 1801: Kings County Registry Bk G1, p. 345. (I am grateful to Ernest Graham for supplying this last reference.)

77   Graham suggests that Fairweather removed from Norton to Springfield about 1802 and that he sold his

Springfield land in the 1818-20 period. If Fairweather did indeed move to Springfield (as opposed merely to owning land there) then it becomes difficult to account for the collapse of the Springfield Baptist church (which had to be regathered in 1809) and the fact that Fairweather did not join in the eventual reconstitution of the church. The Henry Hale Journal provides clear evidence that Fairweather was living in Norton in 1809, so the inference that he had ever lived in Springfield may be mistaken.

78 Henry Hale Journal, 26 February 1809: Maine Historical Society, Portland; Wakefield Baptist Churchbook, entry following entry for 11 February 1809: Acadia.

79 Prince William Baptist Churchbook, 26 March 1803.

80 Estey to Manning, 10 March 1802: Fredericton Baptist Churchbook, p. 277: Harding to Manning, 17 February 1802: Manning Collection, Acadia. In the first of these letters Zebulon Estey relates that "the ordination was performed with great solemnity, before some hundreds of spectators".

81 Wakefield Baptist Churchbook: Acadia.

82 Edward Manning, Notes on Early Ministers [1812]: Acadia. Some time later Lewis resumed his ministry: Bill, *Fifty Years with the Baptists,* pp. 300-01.

83 Zebulon Estey left an account of part of this long visit: Estey to Manning, 10 March 1802, Fredericton Baptist Churchbook, p. 277: Acadia.

> The Sunday after the ordination [of Charles Lewis on Long Island], Mr. [Theodore] Harding and Mr. [Elijah] Estabrooks had a meeting at Fredericton. The meeting was held in the Play House; for Mr. [Cornelius] Ackerman had converted the Play-House into a meeting house, for the Baptist ministers to preach in... . [S]ome of the grandees

begin to listen, and others to threaten. Mr. Harding preached in the day to a very great audience, and immersed six persons, and Mr. Estabrooks in the evening — both with great freedom. It is my earnest prayer ... that Fredericton might be taken from the Prince of darkness; and some have faith that it will. That day that Mr. Harding preached, there was but five that attended the Church [of England] since. The next Sunday Mr. [Joseph] Crandall was there, the soldiers [of the garrison] were all ordered to attend to the Church [of England] service, and not to go to the meeting, which was very much against the poor soldiers wish. The next, or following Sabbath, Mr. Crandall preached at the lower village [of Kingsclear], and Mr. Harding at Prince William, at Mr. [Stephen] Young's [Jr], to a very large congregation. I think there was as many as when you preached there, when I had the pleasure of being with you [1801]. Mr. Harding baptized old Mr. [Stephen] Young [Sr], old Mr. [Mrs. Thankful?] Slocum, and Mr. Abraham Brown [and others].

Other accounts of these "Play House" meetings will be found in Harding to Manning, 17 February 1802: Manning Collection, Acadia, and in the Jarvis Ring Memoir, Acadia.

84   Two other US Baptists are known to have preached in the St John valley in the first decade of the century. Isaac Case was at Saint John for a week in March 1808: *Mass Bapt Miss Mag* (September 1808), p. 75. Case and Daniel Merrill joined Henry Hale in the work of reformation on the Belleisle in early 1810: *ibid,* (March 1811), pp. 36-37. In 1807 an Elijah Herrak?/Merrak?, "a baptist Minister from the States" preached in Wakefield: Wakefield Baptist Churchbook, 27 July 1807, Acadia.

85   In addition to Hale's detailed — although not entirely candid — journal at the Maine Historical Society there is an account of the Belleisle reformation by Daniel Merrill in *Mass Bapt Miss Mag* (March 1811), pp. 36-37 and a hostile account by Walter Bates printed below in Appendix XI.

86   Hale organized the Saint John Baptist church (12 members) on 25 May, 1810:   Hale Journal Maine Historical Society, Portland.   On 30 May 1811 Hale wrote concerning the Saint John church that:

> In the city of St. John's, the Lord has prospered his own cause the winter past. Brother Joseph Crandal has visited them, and baptized eight persons. Brother Thomas Ansley has also visited them, and baptized four.   So that the little church formed there about a year ago, has increased to thirty five members.   They appear to stand firm in the truth: *Mass Bapt Miss Mag* (September 1812), p. 204.

87   Rawlyk, *Ravished by the Spirit*, p. 102.

88   *Mass Bapt Miss Mag* (March 1811), p. 35.

89   Kingsclear and St Martins are sometimes said to have withdrawn from the Association because of its adoption of close communion.   While I do not doubt that close communion divided these churches, like the others, the fact that they did not report to the 1809 Association suggests they were already in a low state even before the close communion controversy.

90   Duncan Dunbar, *Concise View of the Origin and Principles of the Several Religious Denominations Existing at Present in the Province of New Brunswick* (Eastport, 1819), pp. 81-82. I am not sure what Dunbar means by "speak[ing] by the spirit".   If he means the phenomenon of unknown tongues, then this is the earliest known such reference in the Maritime context apart from Jarvis Ring's memoir of the Hammondites in the early 1790s. Henry Hale often referred to the day of

Penticost in connection with his Belleisle campaign but I do not take this to mean glossolalia. Those who read Dunbar's comments in their original context will note that I have omitted his attempts to link what I have no doubt is Allinism to the Free Will Baptists and to "the errors of *Elias Smith*". Although an intelligent young Englishman with some preaching experience in Kings County, Dunbar was new to New Brunswick. It is therefore not surprising that he would mistake evidence of residual Allinism for evidence of the penetration of novel religious notions from New England (*ie*, the Free Will Baptists and the Christ-ians or "Smithites"). This is the more likely because Dunbar lived in the only part of New Brunswick (Charlotte County) where there actually had been such a penetration.

The first Free Will Baptist to preach in the Maritimes was John Colby. On 28 August 1814, in the course of a visit to British-occupied eastern Maine, Colby preached on Grand Manan to "an attentive concourse". He was informed that it was the first preaching on the island in three years. In 1815 Colby again visited the region, preaching one Sunday on each of Grand Manan and Deer Island. On 24 March 1816 Colby was back on Deer Island preaching a Sunday service. On 11 April he preached at Chocolate Cove. His efforts on Moose Island (Eastport) triggered a reformation which attracted boats of enthusiasts from the New Brunswick islands. On 25 and 26 April he was again preaching on Deer Island. After a brief absence Colby returned to the area in the summer of 1816 and remained several months, again attempting to spread the gospel on both New Brunswick and British-occupied Maine islands: Colby, *Life, Experience and Travels of John Colby, Preacher of the Gospel* (1827 edn), pp. 220, 226, 322, 325, 328, 332, 339. Colby died within a year, having preached only on the southwestern margin of the province. He was likely the only Free Will Baptist to reach New Brunswick before 1825. Accordingly, while Dunbar's reference to Free Will Baptist sentiments may have a marginal relevance to Charlotte County they

271

have no application to the province in general.

In June 1817, less than a year after John Colby's departure from the region, Samuel Nutt, an ordained Christ-ian from New Hampshire, commenced preaching at St Andrews. The New England Christ-ians were unitarian Baptists. They were sometimes called Smithites, after one of their "founders" — Elias Smith. Among his correspondents was Edward Manning. Nutt had greater impact at St David where there was a "glorious outpouring of the spirit". This had been the scene of Thomas Ansley's early extravagance and evidently Nutt, too, had special success, for he seems to have settled briefly in the place. Also in the late 1810s the ordained Christ-ian William O. Grant was labouring on Deer Island: *Christian Herald*, September 1818, 19 January 1821, 25 May 1821, 29 August 1822, 26 July 1826. This invasion of "semi-Arians" was often and unfavourably noticed by Duncan McColl: "Memoir of the Rev. Duncan M'Coll", in *British North American Wesleyan Methodist Magazine* (January 1842), p. 8; (April 1842), pp. 122, 128; (May 1842), p. 164; (June 1842), p. 205. Given the sudden arrival in Charlotte County of something so alarming as a unitarian ("Arian") variety of Baptist it is not surprising that Dunbar was moved to include it in his compendium. But in implying that the anti-formal impulse he deplored in New Brunswick was inspired by New England Christians Dunbar was simply mistaken. It was part of the spiritual legacy of Henry Alline, now 35 years dead.

91   Griffin to Manning, 12 September 1818; 5 November 1818: Manning Collection, Acadia.

92   It was not, of course, this simple. What was formed in 1832 was the "New Brunswick Christian Conference". It became "Free Christian Baptist" only in 1847. (It had become Baptist in *fact* considerably earlier, though not in 1832.) The "New Brunswick Christian Conference" of 1832 is a complex and interesting phenomenon, but it would require a substantial essay to sort out its pedigree and give its history.

272

93 See, for example, Thomas Griffin's pessimistic reaction to the prospect of dividing the Baptist Association into separate New Brunswick and Nova Scotia bodies: Griffin to Manning, 12 September 1818: Manning Collection, Acadia.

94 Innis' tombstone states that he died on 17 June 1817 at the age of 74. This death date is likely correct as Innis' will (dated 27 February 1817) was probated 29 July 1817. (I viewed the Innis will courtesy of Josephine Innis McCready of Norton.) The brief notice of Innis in Bill, *Fifty Years with the Baptists*, p. 215 is evidently incorrect in placing his death in late August.

95 The marriage certificate is in the Kings County Museum, Hampton. Given Innis' Newfoundland connection it is natural to wonder whether his wife was the same Elizabeth Coughlan who was daughter to the Revd Laurence Coughlan, the Anglican priest regarded as the founder of Calvinist Methodism in Newfoundland. If Coughlan's biographer in (1979) IV *Dict Can Biog* 175 is correct and the Coughlan family arrived in Newfoundland in 1766, then this cannot have been the woman Innis married two years earlier.

96 W.C. Ford, "British Officers Serving in America, 1754-1774," in *New England Historic and Genealogical Register* (January 1894) 36, p. 39.

97 Innis' own record of his "Childrens Burth" is in his large Bible/Prayer Book in the possession of Josephine Innis McCready of Norton, by whose courtesy I viewed it. Innis recorded that his first child, John, was "Born Newfoundland 12 Feb'y 1767" but this is evidently a mistake as to the month, for the child was baptized in the Church of St. John the Baptist on 24 January 1767. (I am grateful to David Facey-Crowther for copying this record.) Innis and his wife had a total of four sons and three daughters. He was great-great grandfather of the economic historian Harold Adams Innis (1894-1952).

98 James White Account Book 6: Hazen Collection, New Brunswick Museum.

99 Studholme to Connor, 1 November 1784: MG23 D1, vol. 23, PAC.

100 "List of Men, Women and Children of the late Royal Fencible American Regiment in the District of Passamaquoddy," 2 July 1784: MG23 D1 vol. 24, PAC. The list includes Innis, James Innis Jr. and John Innis, none with dependants.

101 *Innis v Daniel Micheau; Innis v Joseph Cutler*: RS42 (1785) PANB.

102 The militia commission, among the earliest issued in New Brunswick, is in the Kings County Museum, Hampton.

103 RS24 S7 P5 (1793): PANB.

104 Grace Aiton, *Story of Sussex and Vicinity* (1967), p. 17.

105 James Beverly & Barry Moody (eds), *Life and Journal of the Rev. Mr. Henry Alline* (1982), p. 103. Crandall recalled that Innis "had been converted in the army" but Crandall is not always reliable, even concerning his own life: Bumsted, "Crandall's Autobiography," p. 87.

106 Crandall's Autobiography does not mention Innis' immersion, but either he or Harding must have performed it. If Crandall is to be believed then there is no doubt that Innis had not been immersed prior to 1800. John Francis, the first historian of the Norton church, wrote this of Innis:

> [H]is attention was drawn to the subject of believer's Baptism in conversation with a Mr. Medcalf, who was a member of a Baptist church, and one evening as Mr. Innis was returning home across the river near his own house, having been holding sweet conversation with brother Medcalf, he resolved [to be immersed]. Not long afterward Elder Joseph Crandel and Elder T.S. Harding passed through this place, and administered the ordinance of Baptism to Mr. and Mrs. Innis, who

were the first to obey our blessed Lord's command in this part of the Province: *Christian Visitor*, 17 May 1848.

I am inclined to think this story fanciful. I can find no Medcalfs in Loyalist New Brunswick, the nearest Baptist churches were in Waterborough and Salisbury and these were gathered almost simultaneous with that at Norton.

107 Innis' certificate of ordination over "the church of Christ, consisting of Baptists, in the township of Norton" is printed in *Christian Visitor*, 17 May 1848.

108 Innis to Manning, 2 December 1800: Manning Collection, Acadia. It is not clear whether Innis is using this letter to apologize for helping to organize or for not helping to organize the Sussex church, but I presume the former. That he should raise the matter in a letter to Edward Manning is surprising as Manning is not known to have visited Sussex. Perhaps Manning had heard of irregularities at Sussex and mentioned them in the letter to Innis to which this letter of 2 December was a response.

109 *Ibid*: "I have been to Bellile . . . and the Prasance of the lord was with Me: and the People Much affacted, where I was Constrained to Stand for the truthes of your God and mine a gainst Sum of My dear Bratheren." Earlier in 1800 Innis had guided Crandall to the Belleisle.

110 *Christian Visitor*, 26 April 1848.

111 The question of the origin of the St Martins Baptist church and of Innis' role in that process is a troublesome one. The earliest reference to the church's existance is the June 1809 minutes of the Baptist Association. But in 1809 the St Martins church was non-reporting, meaning that it had existed at least as early as the time of the previous (June 1808) Association meeting. Yet there was likely an organized religious presence in St Martins much earlier. It may well have started late in the 1790s

275

among the migrants from Chester and Newport. James Innis may even have preached there in his Newlight days. Certainly by the time of his 1805 'journal' Innis was on affectionate terms with a circle of pious friends at St Martins and the inference is obvious that he had preached (and probably immersed) there already. What is not so clear is whether by 1805 there was a Baptist church in St Martins and whether Innis had gathered it. But if Innis gathered the church then it is safe to say that it already existed in 1805. If someone other than Innis gathered it then (in my opinion) it is probable that it did not exist by 1805. An 1848 history of the St Martins church is probably not very reliable but is worth noting. It states in effect that the first Baptist to preach in the place was Elijah Estabrooks in the summer of 1801. Then:

> Elder James Innis of Norton was the second Minister that preached the Gospel in St. Martins. His preaching was attended with the blessing of God in the conversion of souls, and though he encountered some heavy trials and difficulties during his ministrations in this place, yet God was manifestly with him... . He baptized the first in this place that offered themselves as Candidates . . . : *Christian Visitor*, 11 October 1848.

The writer noted that Innis was more inclined to baptize and to administer the Supper than to form a church, implying that this was the case at St Martins. He then mentioned visits by Thomas Ansley and (it would seem) organization of the first St Martins church by Peter Crandall, with Daniel Vaughan as deacon. This, however, must be mistaken. Crandall would not have been in a position to organize a church until his 1809 ordination, and the St Martins church existed at least as early as 1808. This review of evidence surrounding the early history of the St Martins church clarifies little, but (as with so much in this volume) it at least sketches the contours of possibility. One final note: Edward Manning thought that Peter Crandall was immersed in

276

St Martins "in or about the year 1800," presumably by Innis or Estabrooks: Notes on Early Ministers [1812]: Manning Collection, Acadia.

112 The letter, from the *Christian Visitor* for 17 May 1848, is printed at the end of this introduction. The incident allegedly giving rise to it is detailed in this article and, evidently from another source, in Aiton, *Story of Sussex*, p. 85.

113 See Appendix XI.

114 Azor Hoyt Journal: Kings County Historical Society, Hampton.

115 The Norton Baptist Churchbook shows only six members in 1818 (including David Nutter, the new pastor) all immersed that year. The Association minutes for 1819 confirm that there were only six members in the church. Organization of a church with less than the "scriptural" number of seven male members was unusual.

116 Edward Manning, Notes on Baptist Ministers [1812]: Acadia.

117 Griffin to Manning, 12 September 1818: Manning Collection, Acadia.

118 The Springfield Baptist church did join the Baptist Association in 1811, but Innis (who had not participated in re-organization of the Springfield church) would hardly have been approaching the Baptist Association on its behalf.

119 Any number of historians have declared that the Church of England was "established" in New Brunswick in 1786: A.G. Condon, *Envy of the American States: The Loyalist Dream for New Brunswick* (1984), p. 185; John Moir, *Church and State in Canada, 1627-1867: Basic Documents* (1967), p. 38; J.M. Bumsted, "Church and State in Maritime Canada, 1749-1807," in *CHA Report* (1967), p. 42; W.S. MacNutt, *New Brunswick: A*

History, 1784-1867 (1963), p. 64. This was not the case. The 1786 enactment recited in its *title* that its purpose was to preserve the Church of England "as by Law Established," but the actual text of the statute did not do so. Nova Scotia, on the other hand, had a 1758 statute attempting to establish the Church of England in the most explicit language. The contrast between the New Brunswick and Nova Scotia statutes is striking. Just why New Brunswick's governing elite should have neglected to give the force of law to one of the central features of their grand 'Loyalist Constitution' is a subject too large for discussion in this context. The most obvious answer is that they (erroneously) assumed that they had inherited a legislated Anglican establishment from Nova Scotia — hence their act "for preserving" the Church of England; but I do not think it is quite this simple. That the Church was effectively established in a political and sociological sense is not in dispute.

120 1791 (Seth Noble, David George, William Black, Abraham Bishop); 1792 (William Grandin, William Earley); 1793 (Edward Manning); 1794 (William Jessop); 1801 (James Innis); 1805 (Thomas Ansley); 1806 (Isaac Case, Henry Hale); 1810 (Henry Hale); 1812 (Wiggins — a Wesleyan).

121 Henry Hale Journal: Maine Historical Society, Portland. Alternate accounts of the affair are offered in *Mass Bapt Miss Mag* (March 1811), p. 35, and in Walter Bates' memoir (Appendix XI). Interestingly on 31 July 1812 Hale called on the governor of Nova Scotia "for permission to continue in the Province," which he received. Hale's application was presumably prompted by tensions connected with the US declaration of war. But on general restrictions on itineracy in Nova Scotia, see David Benedict, *General History of the Baptist Denomination in America* (1813), I, p. 308.

122 Inglis' observations on the 1787 "Marriage Act" are in MG23 D1 vol 17, PAC. In them he warns that:

[T]oo much precision cannot be used in defining the persons who are publickly authorized to Celebrate marriages. New and Whimsical Sects are daily springing up and the Preachers, or as they call themselves, *the ministers* of those Sects will take advantage of the Law, where it is obscure or dubious, & undertake to Solemnize marriages, to the great Injury of Society. Several instances of this Sort exist in Nova Scotia at present.

123   In addition to the petitions against the *Marriage Act* printed in the various Appendices, one further production should be noticed, from RS24 S12 P1, PANB. In January 1798 13 male inhabitants of the parishes of St Stephen and St David petitioned the General Assembly to call attention to the "great Inconvenience" the inhabitants were under because there was no one locally qualified to solemnize marriage (*ie,* no Anglican olergyman and no justice of the quorum). As the petition expressed no religious concern and requested no alteration in the *Marriage Act,* it may only have been an oblique request to have one of the petitioners created a justice of the quorum. It cannot, therefore, be classed as a protest originating in a religious community. Yet St Stephen and St David both had Wesleyan societies and one of the petitioners (Robert Watson) was a leading Wesleyan. The possibility therefore remains that it had a latent religious dimension. The signatories were: Will'm Tyler, H.B.? Brown, Peter Cristy, Rob't Hitchings, James Cristy, Peter McCallum, Robert Watson, William Mabee, William Kennedy, Joseph Porter, Josiah Hitchings, William Moor, Robert Moore.

124   RS30B, PANB. Neither the Information itself nor any other substantive document regarding Innis survives in the Supreme Court records but a copy of the Information was preserved by chance in the attorney-general's precedent book: MG288 ms2C, pp. 26-34, PANB.

125 Innis' 'journal' and Sheriff Bates' narrative (Appendix XI) provide differing but reconcilable accounts of this incident. Was Innis' 1784 mental disorder a product of excessive intemperence?

126 *Royal Gazette*, 5 November 1810.

127 The version of the Innis affair included in Edward Manning's 1812 Notes on Baptist Ministers makes it unfortunately clear that Manning had no personal knowledge of the subject and but a very imperfect second-hand appreciation of what had taken place. Nevertheless, I have no doubt that Manning is describing the Vaughan-Brown marriage rather than the McKenzie-Pack marriage. For the geographically impossible "St George" one must read St Martins.

> The crime (if it may be called a crime) for which he was Imprisoned was Marr[y]ing a couple contrary to a existing(?) Law in that Province in the Parish of S't Georges [St Martins] about 40 miles from S't Johns and equally as far from Sussex Vale the nearest places where any of the Established clergy Resided. The couple was published [*ie*, banns] according to Law. It was at a Season of the year when the Roads were verry bad. The young Man Sent [for] the clergy man boath to S't John and Sussex Vale but neither would attend to Marry the couple tho [strong]ly solicited so to do. He indeavour'd to get a Majestrate to oficiate but in this he was disappointed. Brother Innis s'd as matters were circumstanc'd he would marry them and did, for which he was imprisoned. But is now out upon Bail.

When David Benedict gave his published account of Innis' experience he added that he was in gaol more than a year, that he was "now" (1813) out on bail, and that a petition was in preparation for alteration of the marriage law: *History of the Baptist Denomination*, I, p. 308. Presumably this is the document printed in Appendix IX.

128 RS30B, PANB. The following day an Information was filed in the Supreme Court against Gilbert Harris, presumably for unlawful solemnization of marriage. The case was not proceeded with because of Harris' escape into Maine.

129 Aiton, *Story of Sussex,* p. 85.

130 I identify Little River as what is now called Smithtown, on the Hammond River near French Village in the parish of Hampton, only with hesitation. The name does not appear in any gazetteer or map I have seen and must have disappeared at a very early date. The river in question is certainly the Hammond River, the earlier name of which was "Little Kennebecasis"; it is locating the neighbourhood called Little River that presents difficulty. The Innis journal indicates only that Little River was on a route of travel between Norton and Gondola Point and that a Sherwood, a Smith and a Mr and Mrs Odell lived there in 1805. The Henry Hale journal of a few years later adds that Little River was also on the standard route of travel between St Martins and Kennebecasis Bay, that a James Smith lived there, that coming from St Martins one reached Tabor's before Little River, and that after leaving Little River one came to Beveas, McCreadys and French Village. John Francis' historical article on the Norton Baptist church *(Christian Visitor,* 17 May 1848) adds one more datum: that Innis immersed a "Mrs. Bull, of Hampton, Little River". On this basis I think that Little River was the Smithtown neighbourhood.

131 I would tentatively suggest that the Hampton (parish) Baptist church had two centres of strength, one at French Village-Little River and this one at Gondola Point.

132 At the end of his journal Innis notes that he had preached the mother's funeral.

133 Probably Andrew Sherwood (1738-1823), a Loyalist from Long Island. He was father-in-law to the James

281

Beyea at whose funeral Innis preached. There is, however, a John Sherwood Sr among the signatures to the 1812 marriage petition.

134   The Baxter in question was one of the four New Brunswick sons of Simon Baxter (c1730-1804), the New Hampshire Loyalist whose misadventures over the Norton glebe were noted above in connection with Thomas Ansley. Some of the Baxters inherited their father's bawdiness without his sense of dignity. One (Benjamin) was convicted in 1810 of forgery and another (Abraham) in 1813 of "assault with intent to ravish Mary Sproule": Chipman Court Book, Milner Collection, NBM. The other two sons, however, had a known connection with the Church of England. Joseph was a warden of Christ Church, Norton, when records begin in 1811. At the same time local Anglicans were meeting in winter at Elisha Baxter's: Azor Hoyt's Journal (typescript), Kings County Historical Society, Hampton. James Innis lived so close to the Baxter grant that his dispute with one of the sons might possibly have involved a boundary; but the language of the journal suggests that the Baxter was "abus[ing]" local Baptists. It may be wholly unrelated, but less than a month after this entry Innis "resigned" his commission in the Kings County Regiment at Foot. His replacement was Joseph Baxter: *Royal Gazette*, 24 July 1805. About this time Gilbert Harris was probably living on the farm of one of the Norton Baxters, presumably as a tenant.

135   Probably the Loyalist Andrew Sherman.

136   In 1810 Henry Hale visited a Titus Brown on Long Reach.

137   The Vaughans may be Daniel (1747-1808) and Lydia (Harrington) Vaughan, of Chester, then Newport, then St Martins. After Daniel's 1808 death his widow was host to Henry Hale in 1809 and 1810. The male Vaughan may also be their son Ebenezer, who also hosted Hale on his 1810 visit to St Martins. If so the female Vaughan would be an unknown first wife. His

only known wife, Hannah Brown, did not marry him until 1809, in the ceremony that brought James Innis to legal grief. The Vaughans are an instructive example of how important "connectional" history can be in understanding the Newlight and Baptist network:

> Daniel Vaughan's daughter Rebecca married the preacher Peter Crandall (who was also her first cousin), brother of the preacher Joseph Crandall
>
> Ebenezer Vaughan's wife Hannah Brown was a daughter of John and Sarah (Bailey) Brown; she was thereby a niece of Deborah Dimock, wife of the preacher Daniel Dimock, and hence a cousin of the preachers Joseph and George Dimock; she was likewise a niece of the preacher Joseph Sanford Bailey who was, of course, first cousin of Henry Alline. Indeed, Hannah (Brown) Vaughan may have been a niece of Henry Alline's step-mother.

138   If this is the wife of the Captain Moran Innis mentions below then it is probably Elizabeth (Hamilton), wife of James Moran, rather than her mother-in-law Mary (Greer), wife of the blind Mattias Moran.

139   Possibly Abijah Odell; the Daniel Odell who signed the 1803 Springfield Baptist petition had died in 1804.

140   Thomas Brown was married to Elizabeth (Vaughan) sister to Ebenezer Vaughan (and thus had all of the connections mentioned in the note 137). Because of the Smith reference Innis makes below, I take these to be the Browns mentioned in the text. It should, however, be noted that in 1810 the US Baptist Henry Hale preached at a John Brown's in St Martins. This was probably a cousin to Elizabeth (McCumber) Mosher (introduced below). He was married to Sarah Bailey, aunt of the future wife of Ebenezer Vaughan, and sister of the preacher Joseph S. Bailey and also of Deborah, mother of Joseph and George Dimock. For the sake of

283

comprehensiveness it should be noted that on 21 October 1804 a "Jenny Brown of Quaco" received the sacrament in the Onslow Baptist church.

141 St Martins (also referred to by its older name, Quaco) was a dispersed community on the Bay of Fundy east of Saint John. At the time of Innis' visit the shipbuilding industry that would make it famous was in its infancy. The earliest known reference to a large vessel constructed there is in the journal of the New Hampshire Calvinist Baptist preacher Job Seamans:

> ran into a little River, where there was a Brig of 140 tons on the stocks. The Capt and I went on shore to the house of one M'r [Mattias] Morran, a blind man, who had been a Sargent in the British army, a man of good learning. He and his wife [Mary] and Children appeared quite obliging: Job Seamans Journal, 10 August 1803, New London Town Hall, New London, NH.

The St Martins area had been settled by disbanded Provincials (chiefly Kings Orange Rangers) in 1783-84, but the Loyalist presence soon declined. In 1796 the character of the community was fundamentally altered with the arrival of ten families from Newport NS, some of whom had formerly lived at Chester: article by Wellington Jackson in *Christian Visitor,* 1 October 1848. Among these were Moshers, Vaughans, Bradshaws, Melvins and Floyds: E.C. Wright, *Ships of St Martins* (1974), p. 6. The origins of the St Martins Baptist church are obscure: see note 111.

142 Philip Mosher and Elizabeth (McCumber) Mosher were among the 1796 migrants to St Martins. On 25 November 1810 the US Baptist Henry Hale recorded the following in his journal:

> Preached at br. [Ebenezer] Vauns fr. Duet 33.29. This was a good time. In the evening br. Mosier preached from John 10.27. I gave a word of exhortation &c. This was a refreshing season.

143 A Massachusetts Loyalist, Daniel Bliss (1744-1805) was settled in Lincoln. He was the senior justice of the peace for Sunbury and hence a "judge" of the Inferior Court of Common Pleas. He died two months after his encounter with Innis. Bliss was one of New Brunswick's executive counsellors. In 1798 he startled Bishop Inglis by applying to him for Holy Orders: Inglis Journal, 27 August 1798, PANS.

144 If I have correctly identified "Vaughan and his Sister" as Ebenezer Vaughan and Elizabeth Brown, then "Brother Smith" must have reference to James Smith of Falmouth, husband of Alice (Vaughan), who was sister to Ebenezer Vaughan and Elizabeth (Vaughan) Brown. Smith is not mentioned in John Duncanson's *Falmouth: A New England Township in Nova Scotia, 1760-1965* (1983 edn), but Edward Manning preached at his house in the "lower district" of Falmouth on 14 August 1814: Manning Journal, Acadia. And, when Smith's daughter márried William Fowns of St Martins he was described as "of Falmouth": *City Gazette,* 7 June 1820. If I have correctly identified Smith and he lived in Falmouth as early as 1805, then this answers the otherwise difficult question of where Innis landed. At the same time I should note that the US Baptist Henry Hale preached at a William Smith's in Newport and a Joshua Smith's in or near Windsor in 1808.

145 Now Innis is certainly in Falmouth. Priscilla (Alline) Young (1745-1826) was the wife of Thomas Young. Abigail (Alline) Porter (1760-1820) was the wife of Jacob Porter. In 1810 Priscilla Young, along with what appears to be another of Henry Alline's sisters (Mary Payzant) and Priscilla Young's son and daughter-in-law were purged from the Horton Baptist church for "corupt and avarious princepals". It is not clear what this means, but it does not appear that the offense was one of immorality. The timing suggests a disagreement concerning close communion. Mary Payzant's exclusion is particularly curious. She had presumably lived in Liverpool with her husband (John Payzant) for over a decade.

285

146 Probably either John or William Godfrey, who lived in Windsor, but possibly Elisha Godfrey, who lived about 30 miles from Windsor on the road to Halifax. Henry Hale preached frequently at all three houses in 1808 and later. John Godfrey's wife was Phebe (Payzant), a neice of John Payzant, brother-in-law to Henry Alline.

147 George Dimock (1777-1865) was a son of the preacher Daniel Dimock, brother of the preacher Joseph Dimock and cousin of the preacher Joseph S. Bailey. He himself was ordained in 1820.

148 John Duncanson gives Daniel Dimock's wife as Deborah (Bailey) (1746-1829) and says that she became his widow in 1804. George Levy gives her first name as Betsey and says that she was widowed in April 1805 (just before Innis' visit).

149 From the data Innis is about to provide, this appears to be James Harvey, whose mother was a Mosher.

150 Presumably Hannah Burgess, whose husband Benjamin had just died.

151 I cannot identify this Dyer woman but in 1812 Henry Hale stayed at "br J. Masters" on "Diers-hill," outside Windsor on the Halifax road.

152 One would hardly realize from this passage that Innis' youngest child was 23.

153 Innis means that he has hitherto preached in Newport, Falmouth, Windsor and Rawdon, where there was no Baptist pastor. In Horton and Cornwallis he would encounter Theodore Harding and Edward Manning.

154 Presumably Daniel Welsh, sometime deacon of the Horton-Cornwallis Newlight church, from whom the so-called "Welchites" had derived their name 20 years earlier (see Chapter One). This was the very time Edward Manning was trying hardest to push the church onto a close communion Baptist constitution. Welch, if still a member, was probably among those opposed to Manning.

155 Probably Rebecca (Jenkins) (*d*1809), wife of Matthew Elder of Falmouth, mother of the future preacher William Elder.

156 Presumably Alline's sister Priscilla and her husband Thomas Young.

157 William Alline (*d*1820), brother of Henry Alline and father of the preacher Clark Alline, had been the sprinkling ruling elder of the Falmouth-Newport Newlight church. Payzant (his brother-in-law) says that his New Dispensationalist opposition to "outward Forms" wrecked his attempt to reunite that church in 1786: Cuthbertson, *Payzant's Journal*, pp. 22, 39. At some point Alline moved to New Canaan in Horton, where he united with the Horton-Cornwallis Newlight church. Here he was a leading opponent of Edward Manning's attempts to make it a close communion Baptist body: *Payzant's Journal*, p. 81; Churchbook, 10 May 1800; 12 September 1803. It was in such a context that Innis visited him in 1805-06. The US Baptist Henry Hale preached at William Alline's on his first Nova Scotia visit (1807), and in 1812 Alline was immersed and joined the Horton Baptist church. This seems to represent an alteration in sentiments not only about immersion but also about the practice of close communion. (The only other William Alline to whom the Churchbook entry could refer was William Jr., who was old enough to join the church but mentally handicapped.) Perhaps, however, his sentiments soon changed again, for by the end of 1814 he and his son Clark were holding separate meetings (including on Sunday). It was here that the young Charles Tupper received his religious awakening: "Autobiographical Sketch," in *Christian Messenger*, 21 October 1863.

158 This is a clear suggestion that "Sister Stokes" held religious meetings on her own; hence the tensions between her and Theodore Harding. Possibly William Alline supported these exercises.

159 Presumbaly Rebecca (Alline) Davison, wife of Cyprian Davison. By 1803 Davison was a ruling elder of the Horton-Cornwallis Baptist church.

160 Peter Martin of Horton told his experience to the Horton-Cornwallis Baptist church in 1784 but was not immersed until 1789 (on the same occasion as Gilbert Harris). In 1793 the Church "agreed that Brother Peter Martin is blest with a gift that he ought to improve [*ie*, exercise] as the Lord shall call on him". That same year saw him preaching in Chester and Liverpool. In 1794 he was again at Liverpool, accompanied by Gilbert Harris and a Johnson. In 1800 Martin was at Barrington, prepared to be ordained over what one assumes was the church first gathered there under Alline's influence. The Horton-Cornwallis Baptist church agreed to send delegates but the Horton-Cornwallis Newlight church declined. He was finally ordained in Barrington in 1807. In that year he was also preaching at Liverpool. In 1808 the US Baptist Henry Hale spent an evening with him. He is said eventually to have become a "Free Baptist" (a term without precise meaning in Martin's time): Arthur Eaton, *History of Kings County* (1910), p. 744.

161 With this encounter with John Pineo (1753-1835), Innis completed his circuit of centres of resistance to Theodore Harding and Edward Manning. Pineo was the most trenchant opponent of Edward Manning's endeavors to make the Horton-Cornwallis Newlight church Baptist. By mid-1803 it was charged that Pineo "had not walk'd with the Church sometime past & now has separate meetings &c". Still essentially an Allinite with New Dispensationalist tendencies, Pineo thought that "the Scriptures was no rule without the teachings of the Spirit & that it was a dead matter": Churchbook, 12 September 1803. After this confrontation Pineo left the church; but the continued presence within the church of opponents of Edward Manning suggests that Pineo's following was not at first large. Pineo continued his separate meetings, from which the Cornwallis Congregational church evolved. The historian of the

church suggests that Pineo was ordained between 1807 and 1816: Jacob Cox, *History of the Congregational Church of Cornwallis, N.S.* (1900), p. 8. On 28 July 1808 John Payzant wrote to "my Christian Brethren at Windsor, Falmouth, Horton and Cor[n]wallis" (*ie*, the Allinites) advising them to "gather your Selves into a body, and if you have Got any that you look upon to be leading men to nominate them, than to write to us to Send you Such assistance as you Stand need of": Manning Collection, Acadia. This may have been the move that brought about Pineo's ordination.

162   Benjamin Keirstead was a Loyalist from Connecticut. His neighbourhood at Lower Millstream (near Sussex) was an early centre of Allinite/Free Baptist support. One suspects that this was the circle in which Innis preached.

163   This letter concerning Innis' success on Long Reach (presumably the Greenwich rather than the Kingston side) is part of the actual text of the journal. Innis' reference at the end of the letter to administering communion to a great number indicates the practice of open communion. Indeed, this is one of the few documented instances of an early Maritime Baptist administering the Lord's Supper where there was no church at all. It is worth noting in this context that the New England Baptist "missionary" Henry Hale had arrived for the first time on the River St John three weeks earlier, on 27 January 1809. In doing so he travelled past Innis' home (he had never met Innis) without stopping. Hale had, however, gone immediately up to Waterborough. He had not yet preached on the Long Reach, so Innis' success there was not a reflection of Hale's work.

164   Henry Hale's Journal adds some useful detail regarding Innis' work at Saint John and Carleton. Hale's first encounter with Innis was at Saint John on 21 March 1809: "heard old br Annes preach without a text". (Preaching without a text was considered a

contradiction in terms; see Charles Tupper's comments in Bill, *Fifty Years with the Baptists*, p. 695.) Hale also met Innis at Saint John (Carleton) on 9 March 1810, where he was favourably impressed with Innis' efforts. His only extensive observation of Innis was at Saint John-Carleton from 22 August to 23 September 1810. This suggests that Innis took advantage of a visit to his lawyer to engage in preaching. Innis' journal does not mention it.

165 Carleton is that part of Saint John on the west side of the harbour. In 1785, just after the initial Loyalist influx, it had upwards of 600 inhabitants (Common Council Minutes, 23 June 1785: NBM), but by the first decade of the 19th century it was an impoverished hamlet. In 1798 the inhabitants were said to be mostly "illiterate, & never having had any occasion themselves for learning, think that their money laid out in this way is lost; & indeed they pay little regard to their present or future welfare": Rule to SPG, 6 December 1798, summarized in SPG Journal, 3 May 1799, PAC Reel A-157. After the mid-1780s the only agent of the Church of England in Carleton was a succession of meanly-paid SPG schoolmasters. In 1797 it was said that schoolmaster John Rule "besides his other duties . . . [reads] the Service of the Church on Sunday to the inhabitants on that side of the river, & also Bishop Wilson's Sermons": Byles to SPG, 24 December 1797, summarized in SPG Journal, 20 June 1798, PAC Reel A-157. One of Rule's successors as schoolmaster and lay reader in Carleton, John M. Smith, was tried at the Saint John circuit of the Supreme Court in June 1806 for buggery with John Ketchum and James Stackhouse and with assault to commit the same on Stephen and Samuel Jones: RS36A, PANB. From the enormous number of witnesses called to testify one infers that the alleged victims were Smith's pupils. Smith was acquitted on the first charges but convicted, fined and pilloried on the second. Curiously, similar allegations were made against two other prominent Anglicans at about the same time. John James was charged by his former

Sheffield church with scandalous indecencies "not fit to be named among Christians," a (perhaps unknowing) invocation of the legal code words for buggery/sodomy: Hannay, "Documents of the Congregational Church," p. 145. It was, however, no accident that James Glenie attributed the same "Crime not N[atura]L" to Jonathan Odell: [Glenie], *Creed for St. John N.B.* (New York, 1800).

The Wesleyans seem to have had meetings at Carleton on Sunday afternoons as early as the 1790s. Stephen Humbert's first separate meeting was in Carleton, early in the 19th century: Humbert, *Rise and Progress of Methodism, in the Province of New Brunswick, From its Commencement until about the Year 1805* (Saint John, 1836), pp. 33-36. The Methodists, Innis complained in 1810, "had Got a Good meny . . . in to their Pound".

166   The general context of the marriage prosecution has been outlined in the text. Innis was lodged for a time in Kingston gaol, soon to be famous as the place of Henry More Smith's confinement. There is a good description of it, as of 1814, in Sheriff Walter Bates' *Mysterious Stranger* (1910 edn), pp. 61-62. Innis' reference to the keys suggests that, for security reasons, two keys were necessary to open the prisoner's cell and were kept by different people. Presumably his concern was over what would happen in the event of fire; the gaol itself was stone but the interior partitions were of wood. The £400 for bail would have to be secured, not actually paid.

167   By 1810 Charles Peters (1772-1848) had the most extensive law practice in the province. Subsequently he held the office of attorney-general from 1828 until his death. Shortly after his unsuccessful efforts on Innis' behalf Peters acted as counsel to Henry More Smith. There is a sketch of Peters' life in J.W. Lawrence, *Judges of New Brunswick and Their Times* (1907), pp. 396-98.

168   Innis may be mistaken as to the date of commencing his journey. On 2 January 1811 Henry Hale was at Innis'

291

house. Hale's journal mentions nothing of his host's absence.

169 As noted in Chapter Two, Christian Steeves (1753-1820) of Moncton had formerly been an Allinite preacher and is possibly the young "Dutch" exhorter referred to in Beverley & Moody, *Alline's Journal*, p. 198. By 1811 his brother Henry, also a former Allinite preacher, was prominent in the Salisbury Baptist church, but Christian is not known to have joined.

170 Presumably Richard Pipes of Napaan.

171 John Higgins was or had been a member of the Onslow Baptist church. Henry Hale preached at his house in 1808.

172 Enoch Towner's 1800 prosecution for unlawful solemnization of marriage was noted in Chapter One. His successful counsel on that occasion was Simon Robie, MHA for Halifax County: see Isaiah Wilson, *Geography and History of the County of Digby* (1900), p. 112.

173 This is probably a reference to William Botsford (1773-1864) rather than his elderly father Amos. Both were lawyers resident at Westcock, Westmorland County.

174 Henry Hale preached at Daniel Blair's in Onslow in 1812. He is presumably connected with the Blairs of the *New Light Letters*.

175 The family mentioned is probably that of Alpheus Morse (*b*1750) and Theodora (Crane) Morse. Apart from Innis' remarks, Morse is not known to have taken part in the Eddy rebellion. His widowed mother had, however, married William How, one of Eddy's lieutenants, and a sister was daughter-in-law to Eddy himself. In 1798 Alpheus Morse, as justice of the peace, attested a document verifying the losses of John Allan, another leading rebel. His own mother's property had also been forfeited for treason.

176 Matthew Fenwick (*c*1758-*c*1828) was a Yorkshire immigrant to Maccan Nova Scotia where he married a daughter of fellow immigrant William Freeze. About the turn of the century he removed to Millstream (near Sussex) where he became leader of an Allinite society (in an area in which Alline himself had never preached). Edward Weyman, whose father was this society's other leading force, distinctly recalled that Fenwick "held Henry Allens views of Baptism, that is nonesential": Weyman Collection, Acadia. Like William Freeze, Henry Weyman, William and Clark Alline, Peter Martin and John Pineo, Matthew Fenwick is demonstrably a transitional figure between Allinite and Free Baptist.

177 This could be the wife of either Samuel or Philip Freeman. Henry Hale preached at both houses frequently in the 1808-12 period.

178 Jonathan Cole of Cole's Island (an eminence on the Tantramar Marsh) was a member of the Sackville Baptist church.

179 This is the only place in his journal in which Innis alludes to his Norton church. As noted in the text, the Association minutes for 1811 make no reference to the letter Innis mentions. A Norton church is not listed in the Association minutes until 1819 (two years after Innis' death), and it seems to be unconnected with Innis' organization.

180 This list of funerals preached, obviously drawn from memory, is not in chronological order. Perhaps Innis compiled it as part of his defense, to show that he performed all the normal functions of the ministerial office.

APPENDICES

APPENDIX I

Queens County Dissenters' Petition For a Magistrate, *c*1786

This petition proposes the name of Thomas Hartt, a pre-Loyalist and a Dissenter, as justice of the peace for Queens County. At the organization of New Brunswick most of the pre-Loyalist settlement of the River St. John fell within neighbouring Sunbury County, where Dissenters would certainly have been represented on the magisterial bench. In Queens County, however, they were much less numerous, and it is probable that none had been appointed justice of the peace by the time of this petition. The actual date of the document was accidentally omitted, but it was located at PANB in a file of uncatalogued Executive Council documents dating from 1786. Whether the petition was successful is uncertain. In reciting Thomas Hartt's "moral Vertues Education and Experance in matters of Law" the petitioners neglected to mention that ten years earlier he had been "a rebel and one of the Committee for forming the Cumberland party": James Hannay, "Sunbury County Documents," in (1894) 1 *Coll NB His Soc* 116. Hartt was also brother to Samuel Hartt, of the future "Hartites". While the document does not actually style the petitioners as Dissenters, two-thirds certainly were and the others (Loyalists) were at least sympathizers. Titus Fitch/Finch, for example, was a Loyalist. He cannot be firmly documented as a Dissenter in New Brunswick; but when he arrived in Upper Canada about 1798 he was an "earnest lay preacher," and by 1802 he was a known Baptist: Stuart Ivison

& Fred Rosser, *Baptists in Upper and Lower Canada before 1820* (1956), pp. 98, 136. In short, it seems likely that all of these petitioners were essentially Dissenters at the early date of 1786.

[Text]

To His Excellency Thomas Carleton [*etc*]

The humble address of your Petetioners being fully convinced of your Excellencys gracious Disposition for the weai of the Province and knowing that as the happyness of a people touching borth Sivel and religous priveliges depend on being under the protection of good Laws, so it is an inestemable blessing to have them Exercised by men who will naturaly study the Good of the Community. We your Excellencies humble petetioners do therefore humbly recommend to your Excellency for a Majestrate M'r Thomas Hartt in Queens County whose moral Vertues Education and Experance in matters of Law are such as Convinceth us he will be a Grate blessing to the County Should your Excellency be Graciously pleased to Grant the Prair of your petitioners [*etc*].

QUEENS COUNTY THE 30 OF JULY [1786?]

Marmaduke Hutchenson
Amasa Coy
Edward Coy
John Walton
Andrew Harington
George Feriss
Bejamin Newcomb Jun'r
Nathaniel Cottle
Elijah Estabrooks Ju'r
George Fox
Thomas Goodspeed
Moses Cone
John Marsh
Elijah Estabrooks
Zebedee Ring

George Miller
Henry Miller
Thomas Jenkins
Isaac Gilburt
Daniel Mcneel
Titus Fitch
W'm Black
Jeremiah Frost
John Knockx
Moses Clark
Nathanill Churchill
John Coy
Edward Coy jun'r
Moses Clark jun'r
Aaron Clark

APPENDIX II

Sunbury County Congregationalist Marriage Petition, 1792

By the terms of New Brunswick's *Marriage Act* of 1791 the privilege of solemnizing marriages was confined to clergymen of the Church of England, with two categories of exceptions. In parishes where there was no Anglican clergyman resident, a marriage might be solemnized by a justice of the quorum; and, where both parties to the marriage were Quakers or in communion with the Kirk of Scotland or the Church of Rome, the marriage might be solemnized according to the usage of that denomination. Prior to the 1791 enactment there was no statutory regulation of marriage in New Brunswick. The Congregational Dissenters of Sunbury County may, therefore, have continued their earlier practice of marrying through means of a solemn declaration before the congregation, at least until 1788 when John James settled as their pastor: *eg,* James Hannay, "Maugerville Settlement," in (1894) 1 *Coll NB His Soc* 72. Under the 1791 statute the Dissenters of Sunbury were deliberately excluded from the privilege of solemnizing marriages, either congregationally or by a pastor. Hence the petition printed here, placed before the House of Assembly on 1 March 1792 by James Glenie, one of the members for Sunbury. Of the three justices of the peace whose signatures appear on the petition, two would have been supporters of the petition but the third (Hubbard) probably signed only to bring the document within the exception to the province's 1786 statute prohibiting petitions with more than twenty signatures. Of the remaining 62 signatories, 17 are

Loyalists and all but one or two of the remainder are readily identifiable as pre-Loyalists. Nearly all of the petitioners were among the 1788 subscribers for John James' salary: James Hannay, "Documents of the Congregational Church at Maugerville," in (1894) 1 *Coll NB His Soc* 139-41.

[Text]

To his Excellency Thomas Carleton [*etc*]

The Humble Petition of Sundry of the
Inhabitants of the County of Sunbury

Sheweth

That, by an Act of the General Assembly of this Province, Passed in the thirty-first year of His Majesties Reign, Entitled "An Act for regulating Marriage and Divorce, and for preventing, and punishing, Incest, Adu[l]tery, and Fornication" the Clergy dissenting from the Church of England (those of the Roman Catholic Church, and the Kirk of Scotland Excepted) are prohibited celebrating the Ceremony of Marriage, between persons of their own persuasion, and among their own Parishioners, A priviledge which Dissenters of all Denominations have ever Enjoyed in all His Majesties Colonies heretofore.

Your Petitioners therefore Pray, that an Act may be passed in Addition to or Amendment of, the Act aforesaid, permiting, & Allowing, all Ministers regularly ordained according to the Rites, and Customs, of Regular dissenting Churches, and who are Pastors of Regular dissenting Congregations, to solemnize, and celebrate Marriage, between persons of their own Communion, within the limits of their Respective Parishes. [*etc*]

The within Petition		
Consented to	D. Burpe	Justices of the
and Ordered by us	Jacob Barker	Peace for the
February 16th 1792	Isaac Hubbard	County of Sunbury

Febry 18th 1792

Moses Coburn
John Duncan
Zebulon Estey
C Mallery
James Chase
Stephen Coburn
Moses Foster
Benj. Barker
Jeremiah Burpe
Humphry Pickard
John Pickard
Sam'l Hutchison
Jesse Cristy
Jacob Barker jun'r
John Wason
Nathan Palmer
Daniel Palmer
Abijah Palmer
George Munro
William McKeen
Isaac Stickney
Richard Estey
Lemuel Woodworth
John McKeen
Syl Plumer
Nathaniel Underhill
John Russell
Jabez Nevers
Moses Pickard
Moses Coburn Jun'r
Moses Pickard j'r

Richard Webster
Jacob Loder
Samuel Upton
Eliphalet Olmsted
Hugh Johnston
Asa Perley
Benj'n Brown
Joel Daniel
Eph'm Deforest
Thomas Burpe
James Cristey
Joseph Reyerson
Joseph Bubar
John Barker
Conerord Stanist [?]
Joseph Barker J'r
Dominicus Sewall
Elijah Dingee
Daniel Jewett
Enoch Gerrish
Nathan Smith
Ezra Gates
Stephen Pine
David Ingles
Elihu Cogswell
Edward Burpe
Th's Langdan
Nath'l Gallop
Jed'iah Cook
John Bell
Ebenezer Briggs

APPENDIX III

Congregationalist Petition on the Sheffield Parsonage Dispute, 1792

It was noted in Chapter Two that the orthodox Congregational church was forced in 1789 to move its meeting-house from Maugerville to Sheffield after Maugerville Anglicans claimed the land on which it stood as a glebe. In its new location — Lot 15 — the meeting-house was finished with galleries and a steeple, although for some years the church met during cold weather in the public part of the adjacent parsonage house. It will also be recalled that in 1792 the pastor of the Sheffield church, John James, separated from his flock and commenced reading the service of the Church of England in the parsonage house — which he declined to give up. This strange circumstance emboldened Sunbury County Anglicans to form a vestry in the parish of Sheffield (where they were few in number), evidently for the sole purpose of applying to the Executive Council to have Lot 15 granted as their glebe. The documentation generated by the ensuing dispute between Sunbury County's Anglicans and Congregationalists is voluminous. Except as otherwise noted, all the petitions referred to here will be found in W.O. Raymond's careful transcriptions: MG23 D1 vols 71 & 72, PAC. The documentary part of the dispute began with a petition dated 10 April 1792 from Hugh Johnston and Israel Perley. It briefly outlined the Dissenters' title to the lot, their apprehension that James' conduct formed the basis of an Anglican attempt on the property and their request that the Executive make no decision until they could be more fully heard on the subject. Their fears were justified when on 2 May 1792 the Executive Council was petitioned by the newly-formed *"Wardens and Vestry* of the Parish of *Sheffield* and the lower part of the Parish of Burton". Reciting the urgent need to reclaim the "deluded People" of Sheffield to a "true sense of religion," the lack of an Anglican glebe in the parish, the actual occupation of Lot 15 by John James their candidate for holy Orders, and alleging that most of the improvements on the lot had been made by Loyalists (Captains VanAllen and Ryerson), the vestry prayed a formal grant of the lot.

The Dissenters responded with two further petitions. One was from "a number of the Inhabitants of Gagetown & Waterborough," reciting that its signatories were "associated with the Dissenters in the County of Sunbury in Supporting a Dissenting Minister in Sheffield". The document is interesting chiefly for its 13 signatories, several of whom were also members of the Allinite meeting in Waterborough (the "Brooksites"): Zebulon Estey, Edward Coy, Amasa Coy, Daniel ODell, Edward Coy Jr, Benjamin Newcomb Sr, Ephraim Tisdale, Lphraim Tisdale Jr, John Tisdale, Moses Estey, Issacher Currie, James McDiarmid, Nehemiah B. Estey. The second of the Dissenters' memorials to the Governor-in-Council is the long document printed below,· dated 22 May 1792. It is a detailed and lucid history of the dispute, important for its insight into the mentality of conservative dissent. Ironically it was this petition, incidentally deploring the effects of "vagrant & Ignorant Preachers," which precipitated William Hubbard's widely-quoted outburst against "the Hammonites, ... the Palmerites, ... the Brookites ... and worst of all the Pearlyites or Burpeites": W.O Raymond (ed), *Winslow Papers* (1901), pp. 392-93. A year later, just before Hammond and Lunt were scheduled to take their trial in neighbouring Queens County, the Anglicans of Sunbury addressed one further memorial to the Executive Council, with upwards of 125 signatures: printed in L.M.B. Maxwell, *Outline of the History of Central New Brunswick to the Time of Confederation* (1937), pp. 124-26. It was unsuccessful in procuring a grant of the land on which the Congregational meeting-house and parsonage stood, but the

302

Anglicans tenaciously continued in physical occupation of the parsonage, to the great chagrin of their opponents. On 6 August 1793 two of the leading Dissenters endeavored to turn the tables by availing themselves of an open door peacefully to reoccupy the parsonage, triggering the physical confrontation detailed in James Hannay, "Documents of the Congregational Church at Maugerville," in (1894) 1 *Coll NB His Soc* 119, pp. 146-47.

[Text]

To His Excellency Thomas Carleton [*etc*]

The Petition of the Protestant Dissenters within the County of Sunbury, Associated for the Support of a Protestant Dissenting Minister and Meeting House in Sheffield.

Respectfully Sheweth

That prior to any Settlements having been made by the British Government on the River St. John, the Grantees named in the original grants of the Township of Maugerville (now forming the two parishes of Maugerville and Sheffield, amounting to near Seventy dissenting Families) induced by His Majesty's Proclamation for encouraging the Settlement of Nova Scotia, became the first British Settlers on the River St. John.

That your Petitioners are many of them of that number, who were led to embrace the proffered Terms of Settlement (& to encounter all the Hardships and Difficulties, which your Excellency's Knowledge of this Province must convince you they have had to struggle with in obtaining a hard subsistence for themselves and families without any aids whatever but such as arose from their active and persistent Industry) and to this one of the strongest Inducements was, that being nearly to a man dissenting Protestants, the most liberal toleration was held out to them, with assurances of a reserved Lot for their minister pro tempore.

That your Petitioners in full confidence of the generous intentions of Government towards them unanimously selected and set apart Lot No 15 in Sheffield for the Residence of their future minister, which they have made large Improvements [on] and have built a good Dwelling House and Barn, and also erected a large Meeting House for public Worship.

That in these their Efforts for the Propagation of the Gospel and the rearing their Families in a decent and proper attention to public Worship, they have ever till very lately met with Encouragement and (in full assurance that the liberality of Government had enabled them by a reserve of Land for their Minister to provide for the reception and future support of a Pastor, whose education and abilities might qualify him to render them essential service) they applied to their Brethren in England for such assistance, by whom the Reverend Mr. John James, their late Minister, was sent out and for whom they made an ample and handsome provision amounting to about Eighty pounds p[er] year.

That latterly such causes of objection to the moral part of Mr. James conduct have arose as your Petitioners considered themselves in conscience obliged to notice, and Mr. James having (as your Petitioners have been informed) had previous intentions of obtaining Ordination in the Church of England, took this opportunity of resigning his Pastoral charge among them; and had such his resignation been conducted on fair and equitable principles, your Petitioners· conceive this present application to your Excellency would have been needless, but altho' your Petitioners had in writing under their hands firmly bound themselves severally to pay their yearly subscriptions to Mr. James's salary, and altho' those subscriptions were nearly all paid up, and Mr. James held in his hands ample security for enforcing his demands legally on those who might refuse to pay him, yet to the astonishment of your Petitioners Mr. James refused to resign peaceably the possession of the House and Land your Petitioners had allowed him for his accomodation and convenience during his ministry among them; His ultimate views by these unfair proceedures began at this period to unfold themselves, and Your Petitioners discovered that the same little interested policy (which had served him so well at their expense) had again enabled him to bring into his future views and designs a few inconsiderate or misguided people, who your Petitioners are informed have petitioned your Excellency to take from your Petitioners the said Lot No 15 in Sheffield, which your Petitioners have possessed undisturbed as a reserve for the purposes above mentioned upwards of 29 years, on which they have cleared and improved upwards of 30 acres & on which they have built a good Dwelling House and Barn and a Meeting House.

That your Petitioners here beg leave to request your Excellency's attention to the following incontestible facts. First that the Townships or Parishes (now Maugerville & Sheffield) were originally one only & called Maugerville. That it was considered as one parish & reserves directed & left therein for one parish only. Secondly, that the Church [of England] has had and retains the full extent of its claims for one parish [Maugerville], altho' no Vestry was formed or Church erected till within ten years past. Thirdly — that the Protestant Dissenters not only almost intirely hold the front Division of Lands in Sheffield but also a great part of those in Maugerville. That they were the original Settlers in both parishes. That they have had uninterrupted possession of Lot No. 15 in Sheffield for 29 years. That they have expended large sums in building and improving thereon & have paid all assessments levied on said lott. That the Lot was originally reserved as their portion of what was then only one parish, every previous reserve having then been made for the Church of England & still continued & confirmed to them: and that the Division of one parish into two should furnish a pretense for taking from them their possession, labor, buildings and improvements for a course of 29 years, is an absurdity so pregnant with injustice that the applicants, your Petitioners are confident must come under your Excellency's displeasure & more especially as a large part of the Lands in the parish of Sheffield are still unappropriated & ungranted, tho' perhaps their situation and state of improvement may not at present make them an object of consideration.

Fourthly — That the erection of a Church in Burton, the County Town of Sunbury, which has been long in contemplation, has always been considered as a sufficient accomodation to the very few church [of England] people in Sheffield who could not be better accomodated in Maugerville, and that no vestry was ever formed or any

Church ever proposed to be erected in Sheffield until after the differences between your Petitioners & their Minister.

Fifthly — That in the Township of Sheffield a Vestry has lately been formed apparently for no other purpose but that of wresting from your Petitioners the Lot in question, and that at the instigation principally of persons not even belonging to the Township. That in this very Township your Petitioners respectfully assert that there are not at present more than (in front) three Landholders members of the Church of England and —

Sixthly — That to crown the whole of their attempt upon the reserve in your Petitioners' favor with uniform absurdity, the new formed Vestry themselves are not all (for want of numbers sufficient) inhabitants of Sheffield, but several of them of Burton, under the specious pretext that the Inhabitants of Burton (who are *almost all Church people*) can be accomodated by the Church proposed to be erected in Sheffield, where they are *almost all Dissenters*.

That your Petitioners are apprized that they have been misrepresented to your Excellency as a sett of people unworthy of consideration, & torn to pieces by various opinions and puritannic principles, a charge the more injurious, as there principal object has ever been to enable themselves to provide handsomely for a resident minister of respectable abilities as the best security against the inconveniences resulting from vagrant & Ignorant Preachers.

That separated from the considerations above urged in support of your Petitioners claim to the lot in dispute, they respectfully submit one more which they hope will to your Excellency appear a sufficient barrier of itself against the rapacity of their opponents — and that is that all the improvements made and the buildings erected on Lot No. 15 in Sheffield (except a few small donations) have been made by the Petitioners, David Burpe, Jacob Barker, Nathan Smith, Daniel Jewitt, Sylvanus Plummer, Ebenezer Briggs, Moses Coburn, and Elijah Dinge, Trustees in behalf of themselves and the rest of the Association of Protestant Dissenters in Sunbury, and as no conclusive division has yet been made of their several shares under the original Grants, that the said Lot should in Equity be considered as part of their undivided shares as Tenants in Common, there having been only by Grant 100 Lots in Front, unto which an additional one 'has been made, which your Petitioners conceive they are entitled to hold as Tenants in Common in Virtue of their claim under the original grant.

Your Petitioners therefore humbly look up to your Excellency for that support and protection from the insidious policy of their opponents, which shall appear just and equitable under the circumstances above stated, and as a continuance of the disputed Lot under reserve for their use may leave an opening for future litigation, they respectfully intreat that your Excellency will be pleased to disperse those doubts which may otherwise damp their future exertions & improvements in consequence of the present contest by indulging them with a separate grant of the said Lot No 15 in Sheffield to David Burpe, Nathan Smith and Moses Coburn their heirs and assigns, in whom all your Petitioners have full confidence as to the further settlement of the same to such uses and purposes as to all your Petitioners will be satisfactory & agreeable to the design of its original appropriation [*etc*].

Sheffield 22d May 1792
Sam'l Peabody)
By order and Consent of David Burpe) Justices of
Jacob Barker)   the Peace

Israel Perley	Sam'l Upton Jun'r
Hugh Johnston	Eben'r Briggs
Samuel Upton	Jos'h Barker
Moses Coburn	Eben'r Hatheway
Jacob Loder	Samuel Bridges
George Munro	Nathanel Gallop
David Good	Simeon Porter
Stephen Coburn	Nathaniel Gallop Jun'r
Nathan Nevers	Edw'd Burpe
Moses Coburn Jun'r	John Pickard
John Upton	Thomas Burpe
Thomas Olmsted	Jacob Barker Ju'r

Moses Pickard S'r
Wesly Balch
William Stickney
Isaac Stickney
John Barker
Samuel Stickney
Jedediah Cook
John Marsh
Thomas Good[speed]
[illegible]
James Chace Jun'r
Joseph Barker J'r
Jeremiah Burpe
Lemuel Woodworth
Jacob Akerson
Daniel Jewett
Elijah Dingee
Stephen Gallishan
Enoch Gerrish
Alexander Brown
Moses Pickard
Benj'n Barker
Paul Smith
William Smith
Nathan Smith

John Wasson
Daniel Palmer
James Taylor
William McKeen
Jabez Nevers S'r
Caleb Mallory
Richard Estey
Thomas Taber
James Cristy
Jabez Nevers j'r
Sam'l Nevers j'r
John McKeen
Jesse Cristy
Robert McKeen
Tho's Perley
Ezra Gates
Israel Perley Junior
Oliver Peabody
Alexander Tapley
James Taylor
Asa Perley
David Morris
John Duncan
Joseph Bubier
John Hartt

APPENDIX IV

Wesleyan Petition for Licence to Preach, 1794

Under the terms of New Brunswick's 1786 *Act for Preserving the Church of England* no one except a Quaker could officiate at a public religious exercise unless he had taken the oath of allegiance and was either the elected pastor of that religious community or was licensed for that purpose by the lieutenant-governor. As elected pastor of the Saint John Wesleyan community the American William Jessop (*d*1795) was exempt from the licencing requirement, although he would not have been exempt as an itinerant to other parts of the province. Stephen Humbert, who preserved Jessop's memory in the spiritual song "Jessop's Lament," provides details of the incident that led to this 1794 application.

> One of his wicked hearers entered a complaint to the Clerk of the Peace [of Saint John], against Mr. Jessop preaching without a license. His complaint was made because Mr. Jessop did not always pray for the King: The fact was, that Mr. J. did not pray by form nor by imitation, but as the Lord gave him liberty: hence he sometimes did, and at other times did not pray for the King. However, Mr. Jessop waited upon the Clerk of the Peace, (who by the by had no authority in the matter,) and stated the business on which he came. Councillor [Elias] Hardy told Mr. Jessop that such complaint had been made, he appeared friendly, and said all that Mr. Jessop had to do, was to apply to Head

Quarters for a license, and take the oath of allegiance. Mr. Jessop [an American] replied, I am Sir, a man of peace, and have always had an aversion to taking an oath, and if I cannot remain without swearing, I can retire." Councillor Hardy said, "Sir, I shall not prosecute you on this complaint, you have only to apply for a license, and if in future any complaint is made, your application will silence such complaint": Humbert, *Rise and Progress of Methodism, in the Province of New Brunswick, From its Commencement until about the Year 1805* (Saint John, 1836), pp. 25-26.

Jessop's application was one of the earliest under the 1786 enactment. Either that or an extraordinary impudence must account for Jonathan Odell's modest proposal that Jessop apply first to Bishop Inglis. No doubt Jessop declined to do so and probably thereby remained unlicenced. It is, however, difficult to make very confident assertions about the fine points of early Wesleyan history, for the state of scholarship remains where T. Watson Smith left it a century ago. The source of the following documents is F67, NBM. I have omitted the brief certificate of Jessop's election as "Residing Preacher" of the Saint John Wesleyan congregation.

[Elders' Petition]

To His Excellency Major General Carleton [*etc*]

The Humble Petition of the Elders
of the Methodist Congregation
in the City [of] Saint John

Most humbly Sheweth —

That We your Excellancys Petitioners have for some time past enjoy'd great Privileges in being bliss'd with the liberty of conscience as British Subjects under your Excellencys clemency, and your Petitioners being truly sensible of the readiness which your Excellency have ever shewn to encourage every religious and civil Society: We

310

presume to lay our humble request before your Excellency, and do most humbly crave your Excellencys approbation to grant a licence to our Preacher R'd William Jessop whom we have Elected to Officiate in our Congregation. [*etc*]

Stephen Humbert
William Harding
George Kay
William Elton
John Kelly
S't John 11th December 1794   Lawrence Robinson

[William Jessop's Letter to Provincial-Secretary Odell, dated 12th December 1794 at Saint John]

As I have taken the liberty of inclosing to you, as Secretary of the Province, a Memorial to his Ex[c]ellency the Gov'r, I beg leave to inform you, that at a Conference of my Brethren of the Methodist Order, held in Nova-Scotia in June '94, I was recommended to take the Pastoral charge of the *Methodist* Society in this City, for a few Months; in consequence of which, I arrived here the 11th of Aug't last. Not being at that time fully acquainted with the Law of the Province, I did not make that early application for a Licence that I since learn would have been proper. I now hasten to rectify my Omission & flatter myself that as my delay has not proceeded from any disrespect, His Excellency will be pleased to grant the wish of the *Methodist* congregation in this city aforesaid.

I have been regularly ordained according to the Order of the Church to which I belong — certificates [of] which I shall forward, if required, for his Excellency's perusal.

I have offered nothing as to my Moral carrector, as I trust it has hitherto been unreprovable, & that I have always demeaned myself as a Minister of the Gospel. [*etc*]

[The letter is endorsed as having been answered on 5 January 1795 in the following tenor: "that his application should have been, the first instance, to the B[isho]p of Nova Scotia, who has episcopal Jurisdiction in this province".]

311

APPENDIX V

Two Wesleyan Marriage Petitions, 1795

Exclusion of the Sunbury County Congregationalists from the benefit of the 1791 *Marriage Act* was intentional. Exclusion of Baptists and Wesleyan Methodists may, in a limited sense, have been inadvertent. In 1791 their numbers in the province were so small that they scarcely warranted consideration. It is not surprising that the first Baptist petitions for extension of the *Marriage Act* did not come until 1802, when for the first time Baptists had a substantial presence in the province; but the better-organized Wesleyans· commenced their agitation shortly after the statute was passed. The first Wesleyan petition for alteration of the *Marriage Act* was probably generated in Westmorland County early in 1794. Because the petition is missing from the files of the House of Assembly nothing is known about it except that it was from the inhabitants of Westmorland and that it was tabled in the Assembly on 18 February 1794. The only plausible explanation for such a petition, however, is that it represented the views of the Wesleyans in the Sackville area. At the 1795 session of the House of Assembly two further Wesleyan petitions were presented, both by William Black (father of the preacher), one of the members for Westmorland. Neither of the documents has an internal date but both were placed before the House of Assembly on 13 February 1795. One of the petitions was from the Saint John Wesleyans. The other (that printed below) originated with the societies up the River.

312

[Text]

To the Honourable House of Assembly [*etc*]

The Petition of the Congregation Attending
Divine Worship, with the Methodist Preachers
in Sheffield, Maugerville, Frederickton, and
Nash-walk

Most respectfully Sheweth

That by an Act of Assembly of this Province, the
Preachers of the Methodist Connection are prohibited from
Marrying, which Creates a great Inconvenience and
Uneasiness amongst us. We beg leave to Observe, that none
are Admitted to Ordination in the Methodist Connection, but
who have first undergone three years probation, and are
afterwards regularly Ordained.

Also, that their Moral Conduct is Strictly inquired into
at the Annual Conference of the said preachers.

And that we are totally unconnected with any Other
Dissenting preachers.

Further, that a regular Register of the Baptisms and
Marriages is kept by the Stewards and Trustees of the Society.
Your petitioners therefore Most respectfully intreat, that the
preachers of the Methodist Connection, regularly Ordained,
be allowed to administer the Bonds of Matrimony in this
province. [*etc*]

Sign'd in behalf of the Society by the Stewards

> Duncan Blair
> Alex'r McLeod
> Ja's Stewart
> Daniel Ross
> Samuel Upton

[The second petition, from the "Methodist Society in the city of S't John," to the same effect but with different wording, was subscribed as follows.]

[Signatures]

314

APPENDIX VI

Bishop Inglis' Observations on Licensing Newlight Preachers, 1801

Pious historians of the Protestant dissenting groups routinely quote Anglican descriptions of Maritime Newlights as specimens of prejudice, hypocrisy and uncharity. That a few, at least, of the Anglican clergy lampooned "Newlights" (for Anglicans, a generic term) to amuse their English correspondents is certainly true. As the tide of history has run against Maritime Anglicanism it has been easy to discount all such observations a malicious gossip. It is well, therefore, to remember, that these comments were the conventional wisdom of the day, that they were confined in time to the 1780-1815 period, when dissent was a novelty, and that — far from being fabrications — they were in the main demonstrably true. They were not, of course, the whole truth, but historians cannot expect men to be angels.

Printed below are Bishop Charles Inglis' "Observations on the granting of Licences to Newlight Preachers in the Province of New Brunswick" pursuant to the *Act for Preserving the Church of England:* F67, NBM. As a careful articulation of an establishment view of the political implications of the public exercise of religion the document is of considerable interest. W.O. Raymond published an extract in his addenda to J.W. Lawrence, *Judges of New Brunswick* (1907) p. 458, but the document has escaped wider notice. Its timing (1801) corresponds with the dramatic rise of the Baptists in the St John valley. If Henry Hale's 1810 experience (noted in Chapter Three) is any guide, then the most onerous of Inglis' recommendations — posting a cautionary bond — was not implemented. In reading the document it must be kept in mind that, except as regards the oath of allegiance, the New Brunswick statute in question regulated only *itinerant* preachers. It had no application to those serving as pastors of congregations while they acted in that capacity.

[Bishop Inglis' Observations, dated 17 March 1801 at Fredericton]

The Governor of New Brunswick is solicited to grant Licences to New Light Preachers, by virtue of an Act of the Legislature for that purpose. As the exercise of the Authority thus vested in his Excellency, involves not only the interests of Religion, but also those of Order, Loyalty & Industry, great precaution, I conceive, is necessary in the grant of such Licences.

In Nova Scotia where this Sect originated, and where the New-Lights abound, their attachment to Government lies under strong suspicions; and they have occasioned much disorder and distress in several Districts, by drawing People ·from their necessary occupations and labour, and promoting idleness and the neglect of business. The Preachers are generally common labourers or mechanics, without any liberal education, or even tincture of learning — scarcely able to read a Chapter in the English Bible; being also of the very lowest orders of Society, they have no respectability of character to qualify them for a public and responsible situation. They are considered as Fanatics, Enthusiasts and Levellers.

The exercise of the above authority must unquestionably be discretionary; like that vested in Bishops to Ordain and Licence Regular Clergymen. If therefore an application for a Licence to preach, be made to the Governor, by a person whom his Excellency may have reason to deem incompetent to the office of a Public Teacher; or of whose political principles he is in doubt; He certainly has a right, as every Bishop has, to refuse a Licence to such Person, or at least to suspend the Grant of it, until the objection and doubts are removed. For if illiterate persons, without character or talents, and even vagrant strangers, who are unknown in the Province, are authorised, under the sanction of Government, to go about and disseminate their wild doctrines; the most pernicious consequences may be justly apprehended. On this delicate subject, his Excellency will doubtless take into consideration what is due to our gracious Sovereign, and to the peace and order of the Province, as well as to the Established Church, and the pure Religion therein taught. If after mature deliberation of those points, he should judge it expedient to grant Licences, I am humbly of opinion, that the following, or similar Regulations should, in all such cases, be uniformly adhered to —

1. That when any person applies for a Licence to Preach, some inquiry should be made into his literary attainments, moral character and Political Principles; and that no Licence should be granted when these are not satisfactory.

2. That if a stranger, a person from some other Province or country, applies for a Licence to Preach in New Brunswick, it be indispensably required of him to produce a Testimonial or Certificate of his good moral character, peaceable disposition, Loyalty to our Sovereign, and attachment to the British Constitution, signed by the superior Judge of the Court, and two other respectable Magistrates of the County from whence he came. Or if he be an Inhabitant of this Province, that he produce a similar Testimonial or Certificate, signed by three Magistrates, or other respectable Inhabitants of the District where he resides.

3. That each Person Licenced to preach, together with two other men of property and good character, be bound in a Penal Bond of — say £100 — for security of the Preacher's good behaviour, and that he will not utter, or preach, or do any thing injurious to the Government, or to the Established Church.

4. That the Oath of Alegiance be administred to every Licenced Preacher.

These precautions will attach some degree of responsibility to those Preachers, and may induce habits of caution and decorum in their behaviour. Hereby also the forwardness of self-sufficient ignorance & enthusiasm may, in some instances be repressed, and deterred from applying for Licences. Nothing should be omitted that may have a tendency to produce these effects; for perhaps no period can be named more eventful than the present — none which requires more vigilance in Magistrates, and in all to whom the superintendance and welfare of Society are committed, to counteract the Levelling Spirit that now so much prevails; which has been already attended with so many evils, and threatens the overthrow of all order and regular Government. It may not be improper to observe farther, that in doing this, decision [&] firmness are equally necessary with prudence and address. Hum[anity] dictates some regard to the feelings of others, however mistaken. Even Error should be treated with gentleness. And experience has uniformly evinced, that as harshness serves to irritate; so a timid, wavering Policy has scarcely ever failed to increase the number of disaffected Persons, and to make them more obstinate and perverse. In fine — the expedients here proposed, however necessary or proper, will rather mitigate than remove the evil. The latter would be most effectually done, by keeping those restless, turbulent People away intirely, were it practicable; and by an Increase of the Number, as well as of the exertions and vigilance of the Established Clergy.

APPENDIX VII

Three Baptist Marriage Petitions, 1802

These three petitions for extension of the right to solemnize marriage are important chiefly for the signatures attached. They reflect the supporters of four Baptist churches, providing in three cases the only membership profile available. The petitions are undated but were laid before the House of Assembly in February 1802. They were not triggered by any discernible event but by an accumulation of factors. One was the result of Enoch Towner's case in Nova Scotia in 1800, vindicating the right of dissenting pastors to marry their communicants. Another was the remarkable growth of the Baptist cause in New Brunswick, reaching nine churches by the time of the petitions. Third, by early 1802 there were five ordained Baptist ministers in the province — Crandall at Salisbury, Harris at Sussex, Innis at Norton, Lewis on Long Island, Estabrooks at Waterborough — so that it was for the first time practically possible for Baptists to be married by a Baptist minister. It will be observed that the petitioners do not characterize themselves as Baptist, but everyone whose religious sentiments is known was a Baptist. None seems to be a Methodist, and neither the orthodox nor the Allinite Congregationalists would have been in a position to claim they had a "communion" in the province or pastors to perform marriages if the privilege were granted. The petitioners represent Baptist support in four of the five areas of New Brunswick where there was an ordained pastor. There are, however, some surprising omissions. Only one of the five

319

ordained preachers (Charles Lewis, ordained 8 February 1802) is among the petitioners. While the Waterborough church is represented through the signatures of its two deacons and its clerk, the rest of the male membership is by no means fully represented. Completely absent is any contribution from James Innis' Norton church, perhaps an early indication of the cool relations between Innis and his preaching brethren. On the other hand, the absence of petitions from the three Baptist churches above Frederiction (Woodstock, Prince William and Kingsclear) is explicable both by their rather remote location and by the fact that none had a pastor.

Waterborough-Long Island Petition This petition was, strictly speaking, illegal. As a result of the tempestuous character of early Saint John politics, the General Assembly had in 1786 enacted a law prohibiting the gathering of more than 20 signatures to a petition for "redress of pretended grievances in Church or State" without the assent of three justices of the peace for the county. This first petition, unlike those which follow, has more than 20 signatories, but only two of them are magistrates. The petition is important because it gives an otherwise unobtainable view of the supporters of the Long Island Baptist church. Apart from the magistrate Zebulon Estey, most — or perhaps all — of the signatories down to and including Marcus Palmer were probably· connected with the Long Island church. Most of the remainder are demonstrably connected with the Waterborough church.

Sussex Petition This document provides a unique view of the male adherents of the Sussex Baptist church. Of the fourteen names only one (Graves) is that of a pre-Loyalist. All but two of the signatories are listed in the 1800 assessment for the parish of Sussex: Grace Aiton, *Story of Sussex and Vicinity,* (1967) pp. 31-33. The name of the pastor, Gilbert Harris, is notably absent from the petition, perhaps because he was not an "inhabitant" or had already moved on to Norton. One of the deacons (Dugan) is among the signatories but the other (William Freeze) is not. At least four of the signatories (Daniel, Sipperell, Weyman and Foster) would, like Freeze, soon separate from the church and form what were essentially Allinite societies that would eventually become identified with the Free Baptists.

320

Salisbury Petition Although this petition is said to represent both the Petitcodiac and Sackville areas its geographical scope is much more confined. Nine of the signatories lived in the parish of Salisbury by 1803: a "census" of the area is printed in *Generations*, beginning in June 1979. Of the 13 signers, four (the Blakeneys) are Loyalists, five are pre-Loyalists and the others are uncertain. One of the pre-Loyalists is the father of the preacher Charles Lewis. Another is brother of the soon-to-be infamous Amos Babcock. The surprisingly few signatures on the Salisbury petition (among the omissions is Joseph Crandall, who lived in the neighbourhood) may be explicable in part by the fact that another petition from the area was presented to the House of Assembly on the same day. This petition has not survived and is known only as the "Petition of James Watson, William Sinton and other inhabitants on the Petitcodiac River". This description (unlike those for the surviving petitions) does not suggest that the petition dealt with the marriage law, but the fact that it was presented at the same time as the Baptist petitions and that Sinton was deacon of the Salisbury Baptist church point in that direction.

[Waterborough-Long Island Petition]

To His Excellency Thomas Carleton Esquire [*etc*]

The Petition of a number of the Inhabitants
of Waterborough in Queens County
and Parishes adjacent

Humbly Sheweth

That your Petitioners (with many others of his Majesties dutiful and Loyal Subjects in said Province) are Dessenters from the Established Church of England who do not belong to the Communion of the Kirk of Scotland, of the Quakers or of the Church of Rome, therefore our Minesters however duly Elected and Ordained acording to the rites and customs of the Churches of our Communion are by an Act of the General Assembly of this Province passed in the thirty-first year of his Majesties Reign, debarred [from] the priviledge of Solemnizing Marriage agreeable to the forms and usages of the said Churches between persons of the same communion, a priviledge we enjoyed under the Novascotia Laws and which is still Enjoyed there.

We Therefore Humbly Pray that your Excellency and Honors will take the same into Consideration and by an Amendment of the said Act Authorise and Allow Ministers of any Denomination who are duely elected and regularly Ordained According to the Rights and Customs of the Churches in Communion with them, to Solomnize Marriage between persons belonging to there respective Societies under such Restrictions and regulations as effectually to Secure the Record of the Marriages so Solomnized to be safely kept. [*etc*]

Zebulon Estey Justice Peace
John Colwell Justice Peace

Clement Lucas Jun'r	Charles Lewis
James Gerow	Caleb Spragg
Elisha Case	John Clark
Aaron Clark	Marcus Palmer
Moses Clark	Benj'n Newcomb
Zophar Weeks	Edward Coy
George Case	Joseph Estabrooks
John DeLong	Thomas Olmsted
Stephen Kiney	Nathaniel Cottle
Clement Lucas Sen'r	Samuel Bridges
James Clarke	William Wade
Elias Secord	John Wade
Samuel Nicklin	John Marsh
James Chase	Joseph Abbett [Ebbett]
James Gray	Jarvis Ring

[Sussex Petition]

"The Petition of a number of the Inhabitants of Sussex Vale in Kings County and parishes adjacent"

[Text identical to Waterborough petition]

322

[Signatures]

Joel Daniel

James Dugan

W'm Siprel

Kiaher Casted [Hezekiah Keirstead]

Hugh Doyal

Tho's Ansley

William Nawdans

Marton Snyder

Henary Wayman

Jels [Giles] Godard

Ezekiel Foster

Isac Clavland

Wil'm Gravs

W'm Sprigs [Sprague?]

[Salisbury Petition]

"The Petition of a number of the inhabitants
Living in Pettecodac and Sackvill"

[Text identical to Waterborough petition]

[Signatures]

Young Shierman

Ring Shierman

Robert Smith

Fadric Babcock

Charls Cain

William Obrion

Mical Noddins

William Bleackney

Chalmars Bleackney

Jeams Bleackney

David Bleackney

Jacob Wortman

Benagh Lewis

APPENDIX VIII

Two Baptist Petitions for Licence to Preach, 1803

These petitions, located among the uncatalogued Executive Council manuscripts at PANB, are curiousities. They request the lieutenant-governor to license Benjamin Fairweather to preach, in compliance with the 1786 *Act for Preserving the Church of England.* In fact, however, as elected pastor of the churches in question, Fairweather was exempt from all the provisions of the act except the oath of allegiance. Perhaps the real purpose of the manoeuvre was to have Fairweather licensed for general itineracy. A second notable. aspect of the petitions is that they give the first indication of the existence of Hampton and Springfield Baptist churches. It is possible, but unlikely, that the petitioners were members of the same Baptist church. That would be contrary to the implication of the petitions, and is made even less plausible by the fact that the two parishes are not geographically contiguous. The uncertainty surrounding the origin of these churches and the vicissitudes of the preaching career of Benjamin Fairweather were noted in Chapter Three. It will be recalled that Fairweather had not yet been ordained; indeed, he was probably never ordained.

Springfield Petition All 12 of the petitioners are Loyalists. They were clustered on the upper reaches of Belleisle Bay. Most are discussed in Ernest Graham, *History of the Anglican Church in the Parish of Springfield* (1983) or the same author's *Mills, Hills and Early Settlers of Springfield Parish* [1983]. Caleb Davis was the father of Polly Davis, the

324

young woman whose conversion on 30 October 1809 under the labours of Henry Hale triggered perhaps the best-documented reformation for any Maritime neighbourhood. That reformation prompted the regathering of the Springfield Baptist church (which had evidently lost its visibility), presumably on close communion lines. Five of the 1803 petitioners were among the reconstituted church.

Hampton Petition All 12 of the signatories to the Hampton petition appear to be Loyalists. Most lived in Smithtown and French Village on the Hammond River. They are presumably the group Innis mentions visiting several times in his journal. I cannot determine whether any of the signatories lived at Gondola Point.

[Springfield Petition]

To His Excellency Thomas Carleton Esq'r [*etc*]

The Twenty Ninth of January 1803

The Memorial of the Members of the Baptist Church of Christ Inhabitants of the Parish of Springfield County of Kings and in the Province of New Brunswick, Most Respectfully Sheweth

That your Memoralist[s] claiming the privelidge of His Majesty's loyal Subjects and in Conformity to the Laws of the Province being destitute of a Gospel Minister, and beleving that the bearer Benjamin Fairweather is Called to preach the Gospel of God our Saviour have made a choice of him to be our Minister to Officiate amongst us. — And most humbly request your Excellency will please to grant his Licence [*etc*].

James Hughson	Jesse Gillies
William Harding	Jeremiah Dreak
William Gray	Caleb Davis
Thomas Walker	Daniel Odell
Caleb Spragg	James Drew
Edward Webster	Abraham Gray

[Hampton Petition]

["the memorial of the Members of the Baptist
Church of Christ Inhabitents of the Parish of
Hampton Kings County": 22 January 1803]

[Text identical to Springfield petition]

[Signatures]

Caleb birdzel
Robert mackee
W'm Crawford
Cornelous Mullereygh [Mallory?]
Jeams Smith
Gessey taber

John Macready
William Macready
Caleb Mcredy
Jeams Bea
El: yeamans
jessey taber jun'r

APPENDIX IX

Baptist Marriage Petition, 1812

James Innis was sentenced for unlawful solemnization of marriage on 11 October 1811. This petition, requesting extension of the benefit of the *Marriage Act* to dissenting clergymen, was tabled in the House of Assembly on 6 February 1812, when Innis was still in gaol. Its reference to the result of Enoch Towner's case and, especially, to Governor Charles Lawrence's 1759 proclamation track the argument in Innis' 'journal'. One would, therefore, expect that the petition was not only triggered by Innis' prosecution but that the petitioners were in some degree under his influence. Yet this seems not to have been the case. The petitioners were from Kings and perhaps lower Queens Counties. It is, therefore, surprising that the three justices of the peace who certified the petition were from St John County (Humbert was a leading Saint John Wesleyan). This would not have complied with the provisions of the province's anti-petition law and, accordingly, the document was illegal. The remaining 63 signatories to the petition are largely — perhaps entirely — from the Kingston and especially the Springfield shores of Belleisle Bay (including what is now Kars). There may be a few names, towards the end, from Long Reach and Long Island, but not many. There are few if any names from Norton and Hampton Baptists. In short, this petition is very largely the production of the reconstituted Springfield Baptist church.

[Text]

To the Honorable the House of Assembly [*etc*]

The petition of the undersigned
Inhabitants of the Province of New Brunswick

Humbly Sheweth

That by an Act of Assembly of this Province passed in the thirty first year of the Reign of His present majesty Chapter 5th Section 3d, It is enacted "That if any person other than a parson vicar Curate or some person in Holy Orders of the Church of England or some such Justice of the peace where there shall be no Parson Vicar Curate or other person in Holy Orders of the Church of England as aforesaid shall presume to solemnize or Celebrate marriage or shall officiate or assist in solemnizing or Celebrating or making any marriage or contract of present marriage between any persons whatsoever or if any such Parson Vicar Curate or other person in Holy Orders of the Church of England or any such Justice as aforesaid shall solemnize or celebrate marriage or shall officiate or assist in solemnizing or Celebrating or making any Marriage contrary to the provisions and true intent and meaning of this act every such offender who shall be thereof Convicted upon Indictment or information of His Majestys Attorney General before the Supreme Court of Judicature or any Court of Oyer and Terminer or Gaol Delivery shall for every offence forfeit and pay a fine to the King not exceeding one hundred pounds, nor less than fifty pounds and suffer twelve months imprisonment".

The said clause above recited then proceeds to except ministers of the Kirk of Scotland, Quakers and Ministers of the Church of Rome.

Your Petitioners beg leave humbly to suggest that in Nova Scotia in the Year 1759 at which time this Province was a part a proclamation was issued by His Excellency Charles Lawrence Esquire which contains the following words "Protestants dissenting from the Church of England whether they be Ca[l]vinists Lutherans Quakers or under what denominations soever shall have free liberty of Conscience and

328

may erect and build meeting houses for public worship and may chuse and elect ministers for the carrying on Divine Service and administration of the sacraments according to their several opinions and contracts made between their ministers and their Congregations for the Support of the ministry are hereby declared valid and shall have their full force and effect according to the tenor and condition thereof".

And your Petitioners beg leave further to state that in the Neighboring province of Nova Scotia at this Day Dissenters from Church of England are by the Laws thereof permitted to be married by the ministers of their respective Congregations without interruption or Molestation and when Your Petitioners settled in this Province it was in the full expectation of a free and unrestricted exercise of their Religious persuasions in the same [manner] as allowed in other of His Majestys Colonies and in the Mother Country, they therefore humbly conceive that the first recited clause prohibiting protestant Dissenters to marry is peculiarly restraining and hard upon your Petitioners; They therefore most humbly pray that the same may be repealed and that they may be permitted to enjoy similar priviledges with their fellow subjects in the British American Colonies [etc].

We the undersigned Justices of the peace
Do hereby Certify that we do approve of
the Contents of the within written petition and
that there is nothing contained therein
which is Tumultuous

Stephen Humbert JP
Thomas Hanford JPeace
Nathan Smith Just Peace

Ammon Fowler	Caleb Davis
Jesse Gilles	Hezekiah Scribner
John Sherwood sen'r	Philip Scribner
Joshua Hughson	Cornelius Nice Senior
James Hughson Jun'r	W'm Peter
James Hughson Sen'r	John Nice
Joseph Hughson	John Chadeayne
George Harding	Samuel Pears
Jacob Hughson	John Dann

Thomas Ganong
Jeremiah Mabee jun'r
William Mabee
Jeremiah Mabee
Samuel Peters
Joseph Erb
Hcncry Erb
Abram Gray
Richard Spragg
Samuel Spragg
David Odell
Abijah Odell
Caleb Carmon Odell
W'm Gray Esq'r
Charles Gray
Justus Gray
Isaiah Kairstead
John Drew
William Kenney
Aaron Fowler
Aaron Fowler jun'r
Daniel Veal
John Veal
John McDonnal

Robert Nobels
Christopher Willigah X mark
William Urquhart
Samuel F Curdy
Martain Record
Joseph Record
Abraham Downey
Stephen Jones
Jacob Vanwart
Isaac Vanwart
John Williams
William Williams
Jesse Jones
Daniel Urquhart
John Jones
Thomas Connor
Moses Jones
Moses Brundage
Michael Clark
Samuel Clark
Daniel Jones
Zabulon Jones
John Davis

APPENDIX X

Documents on the Murder of Mercy Hall, 1805

The first historical writing on what has become known as the "Babcock Tragedy" was Joseph Lawrence's unpublished 1884 paper (not extant) read before the New Brunswick Historical Society. The earliest printed narrative of the 1805 murder was William Reynolds' pseudonymous article in the October 1898 issue of the *New Brunswick Magazine,* pp. 214-22. All of the widely-circulated accounts of the affair to appear in the 20th century are reworkings of the *Magazine* article: J.W. Lawrence, *Judges of New Brunswick and Their Times* (1907), pp. 85-89; B.J. Grant, *Six for the Hangman* (1983), pp. 95-100; G.A. Rawlyk, *Ravished by the Spirit: Religious Revivals, Baptists and Henry Alline* (1984), pp. 100-101. About the same time that Joseph Lawrence was publicizing the Babcock affair in Saint John, a local historian of the Shediac area was preserving the reminiscence of John Welling who, as a lad, had been a neighbour of Amos Babcock. Welling's account, supplemented by material from court records also not used in the *Magazine* narrative, first appeared in J.C. Webster's *History of Shediac* (1928). Several other historians of the Shediac area have used Babcock material as derived from the Webster pamphlet.

Except as otherwise noted, the documents printed below are taken from file F55, NBM. They amount to most — but by no means all — of the sources on which the 1898 *Magazine* article was based. A reading of the documents themselves provides a more subtle and, I think, fundamentally more important view of the religious character of the Shediac proceedings than has formerly been available. Note also the recurrent sub-motif of Acadian-English tension.

A. The Religious Context

William Hanington was a neighbour of the Babcocks and the man chiefly responsible for taking the steps necessary to see the murderer brought to trial. In this key document he gives the best available account of the general religious context of the affair. Note that support for the reformation was at first general in the neighbourhood but that by the time of the murder itself there was — as at Waterborough a decade earlier — an emerging distinction between moderates and extremists. Note also that this account gives no reason to suppose that Jacob Peck was a Baptist, that the reformation had a Baptist character or that the Shediac English were converts of Joseph Crandall. It is true that Jacob Peck referred to himself as "John the Baptist," but this seems more likely to relate to the prophesies of the imminent return of Christ than to the manner of baptism he practised. The Hanington letter, written to Amos Botsford a week after the murder, was intended to initiate Peck's prosecution, although the writer did not quite· know for what. In it Peck is correctly described as being from Petitcodiac. Indeed, he was a neighbour of Joseph Crandall in the parish of Salisbury where, in 1803, he had been listed with a wife and two children.

[Text]

Shediack Feb'y 21, 1805

D'r S'r The melancholly affair that has Lately happened here, has induced me to Trouble you, with a Description of the Proceeding of a Jacob Peck of Petquodiack [Petitcodiac] previous to that misfortune. Last fall [1804] the People here met on Sundays & Thursday Evenings to Worship God. I attended Meetings as Long as they was Conducted with Propriety. But the unfortunate Man Amos Babcock turned

332

Preacher & so much Confusion took Place that I forbid any of my Family from attending — notwithstanding my wife Did go two or three times afterwards. The 6 or 7 Ins't [*ie,* February] Jacob Peck came here, & meeting was held at A[masa] Kilhams the evening of the 7th Ins't & I understood that J Peck said nothing amis. The evening of the 8th they met at Amos Babcocks & Did not go to Bed, & in the heights of their Confused noise they was alarmed By a Great noise as of something of a Great weight & force had fell on the Upper floor. Some of them thought the French was firing against the house, & they Stopped a few minutes. A[masa] Kilham Came home in the morning of the 9th & the other Company I am credibly informed, kept Praying in a Loud Manner, Prophesying Future events, & keeping up a continual uproar untill the morning of the 10th & Jacob Peck supported Amos Babcock in everything he Said or Did, & to Strenghten the cause Jacob Peck said the King of England had Prophesyed that there would be no Crown heads within ten years & that the news had come to S't John by Private Letter & that [a] great Reformation had taken Place in England & France. On the morning of the 10th meeting was held at John Wellings. Nothing verry Particular occurred only Amos Babcocks Daughter [Mary] said she had a spirrit of prophesy & Came to A[masa] Kilhams. The 11th I was sent for to see the girl. She was Laying on the Bed & Saying she saw the french all going Down to hell & Repeating Cannot you pray for their Immortal Souls. She Appeared to me not [to] be in her Senses. The 12th I was present & saw Amos Babcocks Daughter [Mary] & Sally Cornwell laying on their Backs on a Bed & Jacob Peck standing By the Bed side, Repeating I am Bound here; there is my Epistle; there is John the Baptist, as Loud as he possibly could, & Sally Cornwell Extending her arms upwards & her Eyes half open & Sometimes almost that Remained so 2 or 3 minutes & would then tell Some thing from heaven that she had seen or heard, & Jacob Peck would say she will Prophesy this or that, & she hearing what he said would fall into another trance, & afterwards Repeat nearly what he had said she would. I heard Amos Babcocks Daughter [Mary] Prophesy that this World would be Drowned in a short time & that another World would be made, & that 6 years after a Saviour would be Born of a woman & so on & said that she would Die then, & that 2 or 3 years after her Decease she should come (having Wings) & take her father to heaven, Condemned Several People to Distruction & said all that Did not join them in three days would go to the Left hand. Jacob Peck told Lucy Bramble that he had seen her sealed to Everlasting Destruction.

I have Related the Heads of things in a great Hurry, as I thought it my Duty to Both to [sic] King & Country to make it known. You will meet with many Improprieties & Bad writing which I hope you will Excuse, as I have Been Writing [a] great part of the Night & am now writin with out any fire as my house is full of people [etc]

PS   the gentlemen of the Jury are now
waiting for this Letter.

B. Blasphemous and Seditious Language

As a result of William Hanington's letter, magistrate William Black (father of the Wesleyan preacher) directed the immediate arrest of Jacob Peck. He was not gaoled but bound over to appear at the June 1805 sitting of the Westmorland County Circuit Court. Sureties for Peck's appearance were Leonard Peck of Salisbury and Reuben Mills of Dorchester. After hearing evidence from William Hanington, Amasa Killam and Dorcas Babcock, the grand jury voted to put Peck on trial for his "blasphemous & seditious language". It was intended that the trial come on at once (ie, on 15 June 1805, the same day as Amos Babcock's trial), but Peck asserted the absence of material witnesses. In consequence he was bound over to the next session of the court and ordered to find adequate sureties for his appearance. The sureties he provided were Henry Steeves (himself a former Newlight preacher) and John McDonald. Peck's case seems never to have been proceeded with, perhaps because the authorites thought it best to let the whole Babcock affair rest. There is no doubt that he continued to live in Salisbury and sign the usual public petitions. The grand jury's indictment against Peck, substantially reproduced below, gives a more extended version
334

of his offensive language than appears in Hanington's letter. The grand jury who presented both Peck and Babcock for trial were: Hezekiah King (foreman), Thomas King, George Chappel, Henry Stults, Pickering Snowden, Toler Thompson, Jeremiah Brownell, Thomas Wheldon, John Trenholm, Ralph Siddall, Thomas Anderson, Abraham Trites, Thomas Carter, George Wills, Christopher Horsman, Benjamin King, John Carter, William Tingley, Ira Hicks, Ebenezer Cole, Rosel Hunt, William Teakles, Daniel Tingley.

[Text]

The Jurors of our Lord the King upon their oath present that Jacob Peck ... being a prophane wicked and blasphemous man, and a wicked and base Imposter and perverter of the sacred Scriptures of the New Testament and contriving and intending to personate and to represent himself to be John the Baptist mentioned in the Holy Gospels of God, and also to terrify and deceive divers of the liege subjects of His Majesty ... with false denunciations of the Judgments of Almighty God and to bring the Christian religion and the doctrines thereof into derision and contempt, on the twelfth day of February ... [1805] ... in the presence and hearing of Samuel Cornwall and divers other liege Subjects of our said lord the King, to whom the said Jacob Peck was then & there preaching ... [did] declare ... these english words following:

> Here is John the Baptist ... there are my Epistles (pointing and alluding to one Sarah Cornwall Daughter of the said Samuel Cornwall and Mary Babcock then and there lying upon their backs upon a bed ...); from them ... I shall preach and take my text; she (meaning the said Sarah Cornwall) is no longer your ... child; she ... belongs to me ... and the Lord; ... she ... is an Angel of light; it is likely the end of the world will be this night; the Angel of the Lord is gone out to seal the people ...; you (meaning Lucy Bramble, one of the same liege subjects then & there present) are sealed for Hell... .

Also for that the said Jacob Peck being a pernicious and seditious man, and disposed to excite uneasiness and disgust among the liege subjects of our said Lord the King and to bring our said Lord the King and the British Constitution and Government into the contempt and derision hatred and dislike of the liege subjects of our said Lord the King on the eleventh day of February ... [1805] ... in the presence and hearing of divers liege subjects of our said Lord the King with whom the said Jacob Peck then and there was talking ... did ... declare ... these english words following ...:

> the King of England ... hath prophesied that there will be no crown heads within ten years... .

C. The Prophecies

The William Hanington letter printed above relates that its writer was present at Amos Babcock's on the days preceeding the murder and heard Mary Babcock and Sarah Cornwall prophesy. In the document which follows he gives a more extended version of the prophecies of Mary Babcock. In the opening sentence Hanington suggests that he was recording Babcock's words at the special request of the neighbours (perhaps because the "prophetess" was supposed to be dying). He dates the document at 13 February 1805 (*ie*, earlier on the very day of the murder), although his letter does not mention visiting the Babcocks that day. In any event it is clear from the document, as from the letter, that at least some of the prophecies were uttered on days prior to the 13th. In reading this and other documents it should be noted that three of the principals were referred to familiarly as "Masa": Amos (Masa) Babcock himself, his sister Mercy (Masa) Hall (the victim) and his daughter Mary (Masa) Babcock (the prophetess).

[Text]

I Do Certify that I was Called upon to take Down the Words of Masa [Mary] Babcock as it is Related By the

336

Following People this 13th Day of Feb'ry 1805. Masa Babcock Said in my Presence that this World would be Drowned by a Flood in a short time & that two people would be Saved in an Ark. When E[l]iz'th Welling had Been Praying to god that she might not utter any Thing But the truth & was going on Masa said her words Did not come from God & that it hurt her Soul. Her Father [Amos] Asked her who she meant. She said M'rs Welling. She was then Asked if it ws not Lucy [Brumble] she meant. After a short Pause she said it was Lucy she meant. Amos Babcock M'r Peck & I Believe M'rs Kilham told me she had Said, that after This World had Been Drowned Six years, a Saviour would be Born of a Woman & Laid in a manger in Swadling Clothes & that the next World, would Be Destroyed By fire. Mess'rs A Babcock & Peck told me she had said her Father & Mother & all the Children would be saved, But that her Aunt Masa [Mercy Hall] would not. She said she [Mary Babcock] should Appear to her father two or three years after her Decease (having Wings) & should find her father & his Children walking in the fields & should take him in her Bosom & Carry him to her heavenly Father. M'r A. Babcock & wife say she said — the Saviour that is to come will go out to preach at the age of 13 years & is to be Crucified with two others one on Each hand & an Angel at his head & another at his feet — & that our Saviour now in heaven will Come & take her Brothers & Sisters — & that all that Did not Believe in two or Three days would go to the Left hand & that Book[s] are to be Dispersed Throughout the next Earthly World.

Shediack [13] Feb'ry 1805   W'm Hanington

D. The Killing

Concerning the victim, Mercy Hall, little is now known. The published accounts suggest that she was separated from her husband rather than widowed, and that the Babcocks would not allow her to eat at table with them. Whether she was active in her brother's religious exercises is unclear, but of all the Babcocks she was the only one consigned by her niece (the prophetess) to hell. Solicitor-General Chipman, addressing the murder jury, stated that the "deceased was considered as reprobate" and alluded to a "former grudge," presumably one harboured against her by Babcock. The immediate motive for the murder seems to have been Babcock's impression that she should not be found among his household at the impending end of time. The only primary account of Hall's murder now known is that given by Jonathan Babcock, brother of the murderer and the victim, at the coroner's inquest. Nearly two centuries later it remains a powerful and chilling narrative.

[Text]

At an Inquest Taken this 20th Day of Feb'ry 1805 Before Gideon Palmer, Gentleman, one of the Coroners for the County of Westmorland, Touching the Death of Massa [Mercy] Hall —

Witness Examined — Johnathan Babcock — Says that on the night of the Thirteenth Instant [13 February 1805], he was at his Brothers Amos Babcocks house, & in the evening was grinding some wheat on a hand Mill, & he Desired him to Stop to pray for he was tired & Sleepy, & Insisted on his Staying all night. He then made his Children Relate Some Dreams & he then Related his Dream & went to Prayers. After Prayers he went out of Doors, & the Witness Began to grind again. He [Amos] hearing a Noise Commanded Silence, & the Witness supposed he wanted to Listen to Something & he went out to See. He was Standing & Looking upwards & Seemed to be Sniffing. He then came in & sat Down a few minutes, got up & Traversed the Floor, & Said there was Some great thing going to happen that night, & he should not Wonder if the Midnight Cry [Mat:25.6] was to be made that the Lord should Come to call the People to Judgment. He Appeared to be much Distressed in his mind & Groaned often. He Seemed to intimate that he was commissioned from the Lord to Reveal Some great thing. He then Pulled off his Coat & Tucked up his shirt Sleeves & took a Bark of Meal & Rubbed his Arms & feet with it & then went out of Doors, & Immediately Called to the Witness to Bring him a Towell, & he tied it Round his

Waist. The Witness then went into the house & sat Down & heard the Prisoner Repeat, Oh Lord not only My head & my hands But my feet also & would Frequently Pray a few words, & Just Before he Came into the house he said, I see the Stars falling from heaven, And then came into the house, & Told his wife & Children to be of Good Chear, that nothing would hurt them, & then Prayed a few Words, & to put their trust in god. He went to the Window & Said I see them coming & that it will be But a few Minutes Before they will be here. He then took out his knife & Sharpened it on a Stone, & then Laid them on the hearth, the Knife on the Stone & Said that [it] was a Cross. A short time after he Stamped on it, & then he Spit on all his Childrens heads & Rubbed it Down their hair, & Said he was Anointing them & named his Sons Gideons men. He then took up one of his Children about 3 years old, & Blowed his Breath into the Childs mouth, So that it was almost Strangled, & Then Throwed it with great force across the house against the Logs. He then Pulled the cap off the head of the Deceased [Mercy Hall], & said she must make herself Ready, & Told her to pull off her shoes. He then took up the Knife & Stone & Danced about the house. He then came to the Witness with his Knife, & Commanded him in the name of the Lord God of Israel to Strip, Saying he was the Angel Gabriel. He then turned to his Wife & ordered her to Look him Stedfastly in the face, & not to take her Eyes off, or Else he would Run her Through. She took her Eyes off him & he struck her with his fist, the Children all Standing in a Row as he had Placed them. He then turned [to] Witness & made two or three Feints, with his Knife, & Struck him with his Left hand. He then Walked a Cross the house & then flew a cross to the Deceased with the Knife in his hand and as the Witness made his Escape He heard the Deceased Screich out. The Witness then Alarmed the Neighbours.

E. The Arrest

Some of the particulars of Amos Babcock's arrest are provided below in William Hanington's letter to William Black Sr, dated 14 February 1805. There is, however, much more detail on this point in the 1898 *New Brunswick Magazine* account. Gideon Palmer, the coroner, finally convened the formal inquest at the house of Joseph Poirier on 20 February 1805. His jury were: William Hanington (foreman), Christian Steeves, Samuel Cornwall, William Sipperal, Ezekiel Peers, Amasa Killam, William Steadman, Malcolm McEachren, John Welling, John Beatty, Joseph Santis(?), John Williamson. Examination of the corpse disclosed the following:

> — in and upon the . . . Pit of the Stomach between the Breasts . . . one mortal wound of the breadth of two inches and of the depth of six inches
> — in and upon the . . . right side of the Belly between the Hip and Short Ribs . . . one other mortal wound of the length of six inches and of the depth of five inches
> — in and upon the . . . back part of the Head . . . one other mortal wound of the length of three inches and of the depth of half an inch.

On the same day as the inquest an inventory of Babcock's personal estate was made (located at PANB among the uncatalogued Executive Council papers for 1805). It indicates that Babcock was very poor indeed.

```
2 Beds, 2 Spinning Wheels,
1 Trunnel Bed, 3 Potts,
5 Chairs, 3 Netts [for] Herring
2 lines, Table all Included Valued at .............. 8/0/0
1 Cow at  ...................................... 4/0/0
2 yearlings ....................................... 3/0/0
1 Sow & 5 Pigs .................................. 2/0/0
4 geese & 5 Hens  .............................. 0/5/0
25 Bushells wheat by
    Estimation in the Sheaf
1 Plow Vally'd at  ............................. 1/0/0
                                            [£18/5/0]
```

[Text]

S'r I am Truly Sorry to Inform you that a Jacob Peck & Mansfield Cornwell, came to my house about one Hour Before Day Light, to Lett me know that Amos Babcock had Murdered his Sister. I Desired them to Alarm the Neighbours, & I got Ready as fast as Possible to go to Amos Babcocks, as I was afraid he Would Murder his Wife, Children or Himself Before I could get there (the Distance Being about Two Miles). A[masa] Kilham came to my house with Peck Before I was Ready & I Desired them to Loose no time & to Insist on the french People to go with them & Secure Amos. However they Stopped at Cornwells to Wait for me, which I did not know of & took my Snow Shoes & Cut a Cross the Bay as it was shorter & the Roads Bad. I Arrived at the French Houses Before any of my Neighbours & made four French Men go with me. I found the Prisoner Standing upright & his Wife & Children Seated in a Row. As he had no Arms I immediately Seized & we Bound him. As soon as he was Secured I asked his Wife if her Sister[-in-law] was Dead. She said she was. I then made no further Enquiry untill the English People Arrived — which I Believe was Something more than Half an hour. M'r A[masa] Kilham & M'r Jenks Can give you the full Account of the Proceedings Afterwards, So that I have no Occasion to commit it to paper, So shall Conclude this Melancholly News [*etc*].

> PS I forgot to Mention he had Dragged the Body of the Deceased out of his house & Burried it in the Snow. I have the Knife that he perpetrated the horrid Deed with, & it is Still Bloody.

F. The Trial

In June 1805 at Dorchester the same grand jury that presented Jacob Peck for his offensive language also presented Amos Babcock for the murder of Mercy Hall. On the following day, 15 June 1805, Babcock was put on trial. Solicitor-General Ward Chipman prosecuted for the Crown. A prisoner charged with a capital crime was not entitled to have legal counsel conduct his defence unless he were insane at the time of trial or stood mute by visitation of God. Evidently neither was the case with Babcock as no counsel was appointed to act for him. Babcock's petit jury consisted of: William Trueman (foreman), Aaron Brownell, Bill Chappell, Daniel Gooden, Christopher Carter, Thomas Estabrooks, John Chapman, Thomas Bowser, Oliver Barnes, Jeremiah Brownell, Eliphalet Reed and John Dobson. Unfortunately the editor of the foreman's journal deleted any reference to the trial: Howard Trueman, *Chignecto Isthmus* (1902). Eight witnesses testified: (for the Crown) Jonathan Babcock, William Hanington, Amasa Killam, Samuel Cornwell, Robert Keeler, Lucy Brumble; (for the prisoner) John Welling, Mary Babcock. The jury found Babcock guilty and Judge Joshua Upham sentenced him to be hanged 13 days later: Supreme Court Circuit Book, RS36A, PANB. Although surviving documentation of criminal proceedings in early New Brunswick is generally slight, in this case the notes of Solicitor-General Ward Chipman's opening address to the jury do survive: Chipman Papers, vol. 19, Lawrence Collection, PAC. Related documents will be found in vol. 9 of the same collection. Chipman anticipated that Babcock's only defense would be temporary insanity and addressed the jury with that in view. Apart from some routine opening remarks, Chipman's notes are fully reproduced below, with emphasis as in the original.

[Text]

If insanity is his defense, he must shew a total alienation of mind

That he has not voluntarily brought it upon himself

Drunkenness is no excuse, tho' it may make a man so mad, that he knows not what he does

Nor will any idle wild fanatic opinion, that a man may be so in a state of grace, that no act he commits can be attended with guilt

342

It is astonishing that the mild religion of the Gospel the Christian revelation designed, to give peace on earth and goodwill to mankind, should ever be so perverted and abused as to give rise to a doctrine calculated to reduce mankind to savages

If ignorant and weak minds by indulging in reveries of this kind, imbibe such principles and act upon them, however conscientous they may pretend to be, they must be answerable for all their conduct and suffer the punishment of their crimes

That there will be such delusions we are led from the sacred scriptures themselves to expect

With regard to those whose coming is after the working of Satan — because they received not the love of the truth that they might be saved — for this cause God shall send them strong delusion, that *they should believe a lie*

But such delusion will by no means lessen their guilt

It is to such delusions that all the disorganizing principles of the present day may be in a great measure attributed

But will it be said that the atrocious crimes that have been committed under the guise of conscience and duty can be palliated or justified by such pretences. God forbid and if among us we see the pernicious consequences of that same spirit it is our duty to check them and by just and condign punishment to put an end to such enormities

And for ourselves let us earnestly pray, "Lord — Lead us not into temptation"

To such objects — this Petition [*ie*, the prayer] may perhaps be supposed to be in a peculiar manner directed, when we attend to the events of the present day —

Madness must be a total alienation of mind — and whether permanent or temporary must be unequivocal & plain — not an idle frantic humour or unaccountable mode of action but an *absolute dispossession* of the free and natural agency of the human mind

343

In all very atrocious crimes there must be supposed a degree of derangement of mind

The law itself presumes it — The very introductory expressions in the indictment shew it — "not having [the fear of God before his eyes]"

In the present case I shall briefly state the facts, as I presume they will turn out in evidence — and shall then read to you some authorities upon the subject to govern your application of this law to the facts as they arise

I shall make no comments upon the facts after they are given in evidence —

This will be the Province of the Court who will guide you by their observations, in forming your opinion upon those facts, and will state to you the law arising thereon

State the conduct of the Prisoner from the friday preceeding

His conduct on the Wednesday respecting the Hay

His conduct on the Evening of the murder

The supposed former grudge. *with caution*

That the deceased was considered as reprobate

That the Prisoner might have thought under *his delusion*, that he was *doing right* as he express'd himself to Hanington

His conduct after the transaction — affectation of insanity — accidental discovery by Keeler

Read the Law authorities

Leave the cause with confidence that the Jury will do right

G. The Public Example

As noted in Chapter Three, Edward Manning viewed the Babcock tragedy as a symbol of the general failure of the

Allinite tradition. He recalled it as a landmark in finally turning Maritimers away from their volatile religious heritage and towards the comparative formalism of New England's Calvinist Baptists. Solicitor-General Chipman also regarded Amos Babcock's surrender to impulse and irrationality in significantly broader terms. In Babcock's audacious pretense of superior religious understanding Chipman saw a symbol of the "disorganizing principles of the present day" that had brought revolution to America and Europe and unprecedented attacks on religious orthodoxy. Probably either Chipman or the lawyer acting as clerk of the circuit court was responsible for the *Royal Gazette*'s report of the affair, printed below. To the reporter, the Babcock-Peck affair was important chiefly in the cautionary effect it might have on a public increasingly tempted to forsake the Church of England for religious dissent.

[*Royal Gazette*, 26 June 1805]

On Saturday the 15th inst. [June 1805] at a Court of Oyer, and Terminer and Gaol delivery, holden at Dorchester, for the County of Westmorland, at which his Honor Judge Upham presided, came on the trial of *Amos Babcock* for the murder of his sister *Mercy Hall*, at Chediac in that County, on the 13th day of February last; the trial lasted about six hours, when the jury after retiring half an hour returned with a verdict of *guilty* against the prisoner, he was thereupon sentenced for execution on Friday the 28th instant.

It appeared in evidence that for some time before the murder was committed, the prisoner with several of his neighbours, had been in the habit of meeting under a pretence of religious exercises at each others houses, at which one *Jacob Peck* was a principal performer; that they were under strong delusion and conducted themselves in a very frantic, irregular and even impious manner, and that in consequence of some pretended prophesies by some of the company in their pretended religious phrenzies against the unfortunate deceased; the prisoner was probably induced to commit the horrid, barbarous and cruel murder of which he was convicted.

The concourse of people at the trial was very great, who all

345

appeared to be satisfied of the justice of the verdict and sentence.

The above named *Jacob Peck* was on the same day indicated for blasphemous, prophane and seditious language at the meetings above-mentioned, and recognized with good sureties to appear at the next Court of Oyer and Terminer in that County, to prosecute his traverse to the said indictment with effect.

It is hoped and expected that these legal proceedings will have a good effect in putting an end to the strange and lamentable delusion, which made them necessary, and brought the unhappy culprit to such an ignominious death.

H. John Welling's Recollection

The importance of John Welling's brief memoir of the Babcock affair is that he expressly and authoritatively locates it within the Newlight tradition of Henry Alline. John Welling Jr was the son of a Loyalist and a neighbour of the Babcocks. Although this memoir rather implies that the Wellings merely witnessed the events described, the documents printed above show that the family were regular participants in Amos Babcock's religious exercises. The Welling memoir is drawn from a manuscript "Historical Sketch of Shediac" in F55, NBM. J.C. Webster published a version of it in his *History of Shediac* (1928) (1953 edn.), pp. 15-16.

[Text]

For many of these facts, the writer is indebted to the late John Welling whose vigorous memory even at a very advanced age was a store house of early incidents and occurrences. He possessed a vivid recollection of the circumstances attending the first murder trial in Westmorland. It arose out of the religious revival known as the "Newlight" movement. One of the multitude that Henry Alline had inspired was a farmer named Jacob Peck who visited Shediac in 1804 [*sic*] and commenced revival meetings from house to house. The people were wrought up to a great pitch of religious excitement. It culminated when one of the converted — a man named Amos Babcock, living at Shediac River — in a moment of frenzy set upon his sister with a sharp Knife and Killed her.

I. "The Babcock Tragedy"

William K. Reynolds' article in the *New Brunswick Magazine* for October 1898 (pp. 214-22) under the pseudonym "Roslynde" is the principal published account of the Babcock tragedy based on original documentation. An abridged version prepared by A.A. Stockton appeared a decade later in J.W. Lawrence, *Judges of New Brunswick and Their Times* (1907), pp. 85-89. Apart from the Webster history of Shediac noted above, all subsequent published accounts are reworkings of the Reynolds text. Reynolds had sources at his disposal that provide substantially more information than can be squeezed from the documentation printed above. One such source is the memoir of William Hanington Jr., a child at the time his father was swept up in the tragedy: see Lawrence, *Judges of New Brunswick*, p. 99. Another is the deposition of Babcock's wife (presumably given to the coroner) and probably that of Amasa Killam. On the other hand Reynolds had not seen some of the minor sources referenced here: the Supreme Court minutes, Solicitor-General Chipman's address to the jury, the inventory of Babcock's personal estate, the Welling memoir.

Because of its access to sources not now available Reynolds' 1898 *Magazine* piece remains essential reading. It is, however, curiously mistaken in its interpretation of the documents on a couple of minor points: Babcock is repeatedly styled "Amasa" rather than Amos, and his daughter (the prophetess) is styled "Sarah" rather than Mary. It is also mistaken in assuming that Jacob Peck still lived in Shepody (Hopewell). He was a Hillsborough Peck (son of Martin Beck/Peck) and no relation to the family of Abiel Peck in neighbouring Shepody; and at the time of these events Peck lived in Salisbury. Finally, I would again emphasize that one must be wary of the author's characterization of the religious exercises in question as Baptist rather than Newlight. Nothing in the documentation printed above suggests that Peck, Babcock and the whole Shediac society were other than Newlights in their essential religious character. One suspects that Reynolds (a Roman Catholic) would not have appreciated the difference between Newlight and Baptist and, if he had, that he would not have thought the distinction worth conveying to his readers. Yet the other sources at Reynolds' disposal may have justified the "Baptist" characterization. His article is reproduced below in full except for the *Royal Gazette* material that has already been printed in more complete form above.

[Text]

THE BABCOCK TRAGEDY

In August, 1884, Mr. J.W. Lawrence read a paper before the New Brunswick Historical Society, dealing with the Babcock tragedy at Shediac, in the year 1805. This paper did not become the property of the Society, and is not now available for publication. Through the aid of Rev. W.O. Raymond, however, the information upon which Mr. Lawrence based his paper has been secured, and with some additional facts the story is now told in more complete form than on the occasion in question.

In the year 1805 there were but a few English families in the parish of Shediac [*sic*: Dorchester], among whom were those of Amasa [*sic*: Amos] Babcock and his brother Jonathan. The principal man of the place was William Hanington, the ancestor of the now numerous family of that name in this province. Mr. Hanington was an Englishman who had, a number of years before, secured a large grant of land described as "adjoining the city of Halifax." Coming to the latter city, about 1784, to take possession of his estate, he was amazed to find that to get from the capital to his "adjoining" property meant a journey of about one hundred and seventy miles. This journey he accomplished on foot, in the dead of winter, going over the Cobequid Mountains and hauling a handsled containing a peck of salt and other

348

necessaries. Mr. Hanington made a later journey to Halifax on horseback, to procure a frying pan and some other essentials of housekeeping, for though there were stores at St. John at that time he probably knew little of the Loyalist arrivals, and chose Halifax as his most convenient base of supplies. His most remarkable journey, however, was when he went to Prince Edward Island in a canoe to get his wife, whom he brought back and installed in his home at Shediac. In 1805, Mr. Hanington had reached the age of 47, was the father of a family and was in prosperous circumstances. He was then, as he was all through his life, a very zealous member of the Church of England. There was at that time no Protestant place of worship in that part of the country, but the French had a small church at Grand Digue. On Sundays, Mr. Hanington used to read the Church of England service in his house, for the benefit of his own family and such of the other English speaking people as choose to attend. The service would be supplemented by the reading of one of the sermons of Bishop Wilson, of Soder and Man. In addition to the Babcocks, the chief neighbors were Samuel Cornwall, Simeon Jenks and Amasa Killam, all of whom were adherents of the Baptist denomination.

The home of Amasa Babcock was on the road to Cocagne, about three miles from the present church of St. Martin's in the Woods. It was a small block house, built by one Peter Casey, and by him sold to a Mr. Atkinson, who mortgaged it to a Mr. Barry of Halifax. The Babcocks appear to have been hard working men, of little education, and of the type easily moved to go to extremes on occasions of excitement. They worked at farming and fishing, and were in humble circumstances. Amasa Babcock was a man in middle life. His family consisted of a wife and nine children, (the eldest about twenty and the youngest an infant) and his sister Mercy, who had been married to one Hall, but was not then living with her husband. She was of a melancholy disposition and was not allowed to eat with the others of the family.

Mr. Hanington had taken a liking to Babcock, and had purchased for him the place on which he lived. Babcock was to repay him by catching gaspereaux, but had so far paid nothing of any consequence, and Mr. Hanington had sent some young cattle to his place to be fed and cared for during the winter, as a means of securing some of the amount due.

In the spring of 1804 a revival took place in the settlement, among the Baptist people. The meetings were held on Sunday evenings at first, but as the interest became greater they were held on Thursday night of each week as well. Towards autumn, the enthusiasm in the revival became more and more intense, and the people were wrought up to a high pitch of excitement. Many of them believed the world was coming to an end, and all kinds of interpretations were attached to the prophetic portions of the Old and New Testaments. Among those who came among the people was Joseph Crandall, a Baptist preacher, and later one of the members for Westmorland in the House of Assembly. Following him came two young men who were on their way to Prince Edward Island. They stayed one night at Shediac and held a revival meeting, which lasted until the next morning and was attended by the most extraordinary scenes of religious excitement.

In January, 1805, one Jacob Peck, another revivalist, came through to Shediac from Shepody [*sic*: Salisbury], and he appears to have exceeded his predecessors in the extravagance of his appeals to the excitable nature of his hearers. Indeed, his lurid declamation seems to have been all that was needed to drive a number of the people out of their minds. As a result of his work, Sarah [*sic*: Mary] Babcock, (daughter of Amasa Babcock) and Sarah Cornwall fell into a species of trance, and began to prophesy that the end of the world was at hand. The infatuated people believed that these unbalanced minds were inspired, and were anxious to have the prophecies preserved. As there was no one able to take down their words, a message was sent to Mr. Hanington, one evening, asking him to come and take their depositions, as they were supposed to be dying. Mr. Hanington, not being in sympathy with the methods adopted in the revival services, refused to go, saying, "It is all a delusion. They want madhouses rather than meeting-houses." The people were persistent, however, and the messenger was again sent to Mr. Hanington, after he had gone to bed, with the word that the girls had something to say *before they died*, and that they wanted it written down. Thereupon Mr. Hanington got up, remarking to his wife that he had better go, as perhaps he could convince them of their error.

It was then the middle of the night. Mr. Hanington found the girls lying on a bed and Jacob Peck walking to and fro in the room. "There is my epistle," said Peck. Mr. Hanington proceeded to inquire what the girls had to say, and to commit it to writing. The alleged prophecy was to the purport that Mr. Hanington was to be converted, and that Jacob Peck and the girls who were prophesying were to convert the French.

The excitement among the people continued during January, and in February the revival services were kept up, night and day, for a week. By this time Amasa Babcock and his household appear to have been wholly out of their minds and utterly indifferent to their temporal affairs. One Poirier, a Frenchman, brought Mr. Hanington word that the cattle which he had put in Babcock's care were suffering for the want of food. When Mr. Hanington questioned Babcock as to this, the reply was, "The Lord will provide." Mr. Hanington then threatened to take the cattle away from him unless he attended to their wants. This was on the 13th February.

When Amasa Babcock went home that night, he took his brother Jonathan with him to grind some grain in a hand mill. Jonathan began to grind, and as the flour came out of the mill Amasa sprinkled it on the floor, saying, "This is the bread of Heaven!" According to his wife's statement, Amasa then stripped off his shoes and socks, and though the night was bitterly cold, he went out into the snow, crying aloud, "The world is to end! The world is to end! The stars are falling!" After shouting in this way for a short time, he returned to the house.

The man had gone stark mad, and the others must have been out of their minds for the time being, as they assented to everything he did without appearing to think it at all strange. Then followed a most extraordinary scene.

Amasa Babcock, his eyes flashing with the frenzy of insanity, arranged his family in order on a long bench against the wall, the eldest girl being at one end near the fire and his wife and youngest child at the other end. He then took a clasp knife and began to sharpen it on a whetstone. Going over to his sister, Mercy, he commanded her to remove her dress, go on her knees and prepare for death, for her hour was come. She obeyed without hesitation. He next ordered his brother Jonathan to take off his clothes and the infatuated man did so. Nothing appeared surprising to that strange household of dcluded beings.

Amasa now acted as one possessed of a devil. He went to the window several times and looked out, as though expecting something to happen. Then he laid his knife down on the floor, on top of the whetstone, the two making the shape of a cross. Stamping on the whetstone, he broke it, calling out that it was the cross of Christ. Then he picked up the knife, went to where his sister was still kneeling and stabbed her with savage strength. She fell to the floor, the blood gushing from the wound, and died in a few moments.

This fearful act seems to have brought the family to their senses. As soon as Jonathan saw the blood flow, he rushed to the door and fled, naked as he was, in the darkness of that winter night, to the house of Joseph Poirier, a quarter of a mile distant. There he was supplied with clothing and went to Mr. Hanington's house, where he aroused the inmates by crying and shouting that his brother Amasa had stabbed his sister.

At that time there was no magistrate at Shediac, and Mr. Hanington at first refused to go to arrest Babcock, but on second thought he decided to act in the matter. Putting on snow-shoes, he started for the house of Joseph Poirier, senior, but in his excitement he found himself at the house of young Joseph Poirier, there being no public roads to follow in that part of the country in those days. He was after Pascal and Chrysostom Poirier, whose assistance he might require in making the arrest, and when he eventually found them at the elder Poirier's house they consented to go with him. It was then about two o'clock in the morning.

On entering the house where the tragedy had been committed, they found Amasa Babcock walking about with his hands clasped. Mr. Hanington told the Poirier brothers to seize him. Babcock resisted and asked what they were going to do. Their reply was that they intended to hold him a prisoner, whereupon he cried out, "Gideon's men, arise!"

On hearing these words, his two young sons, Caleb and Henry, jumped up as if to assist him, but were compelled to sit down again, and the prisoner was secured.

The body of Mercy Hall was not in the house, nor was it then known where it had been placed. When Mrs. Babcock was asked if her sister-in-law was dead, she simply said "yes". When some of the English neighbors reached the house about sunrise, search was made for the body, which was found in a snow drift where Amasa had hauled it. He had first disembowelled it, and having buried it in the snow he had walked backward to the house, sweeping the snow from side to side with a broom as he went, in order to cover up his tracks.

The prisoner, with his arms securely strapped, was taken to Mr. Hanington's house. While there he kept repeating, "Aha! Aha! Aha! It was permitted! It was permitted!" The statement of Jonathan Babcock was written down, and the necessary papers were prepared to authorize a commitment to prison. On seeing the papers, Amasa shouted, "There are letters to Damascus! Send them to Damascus!" It was evident that he was thinking of Saul's persecution of the Christians. Babcock was then taken to the house of Amasa Killam, who had been one of those prominent in the revival. There the prisoner became more violent in his insanity, and to restrain him he was placed upon a bed with his arms pinioned and fastened down to the floor.

The weather was then very stormy, and travelling, in the primitive condition of the roads of those days, was out of the question. By the third day after the tragedy, however, the storm had abated, and several of the men of the neighborhood started out to take Babcock to prison. Putting straps around his arms, they placed him on a light one-horse sled, and putting on their snow-shoes they hauled him by hand through the woods to the county jail at Dorchester, a distance of some twenty-six miles. Truly, one of the strangest winter journeys ever made in the wilderness of this country.

The slowness with which news travelled and found its way into print in those days is illustrated by the fact that the St. John newspapers contained no notice of this remarkable tragedy until after the trial took place, some four months later.

The following appeared in the St. John Gazette of June 24, [*sic*: 26], 1805: —-

[printed above]

On the trial of Babcock, Ward Chipman, solicitor general, appeared for the Crown, and his brief is believed to be still in existence. The prisoner was undefended. The court room was crowded during the trial, and it is said the verdict and sentence met with general approval. The unfortunate lunatic was hanged on the date appointed, and his body was buried under the gallows on what are still the jail premises at Dorchester. There is nothing available to show what became of Jacob Peck.

That a crazy man should be arraigned, tried and condemned without counsel for his defence seems incredible in the light of modern jurisprudence, as does the fact that he was hanged for a crime for which he was not morally responsible. In these days such a man would be sent to an asylum for the insane, but in those times not only were such institutions unknown in this part of the world but there was a wholly different spirit in the administration of criminal law. In the case of Babcock there was the undoubted fact that a person had been slain without provocation, and the court took the most simple method of dealing with the slayer, which was to hang him.   Roslynde.
[pseudonym for
William K. Reynolds]

354

APPENDIX XI

Walter Bates on the Rise of Religious Dissent, *c*1839

For several decades Walter Bates (1760-1842) was high sheriff of Kings County. He is known to history chiefly as the captor of Henry More Smith, whose story he perpetuated in the work now generally known as *The Mysterious Stranger.* A minor masterpiece first published in 1817 and still in print, it is probably the largest selling book in English ever authored by a New Brunswicker. Towards the end of his long life Bates produced a manuscript of between 30 and 40 thousand words. Much of the document — compiled *c*1837-39 — survives in F67, NBM, but the portion of greatest interest in the present context is now rather mutilated in the original and missing a major addendum. Fortunately, W.O. Raymond transcribed this section of the manuscript at a time when it was in much better condition; his work is preserved in MG23 D1 vol 71 (book 3) and vol 73 (book 13), PAC. Although Bates left his narrative in rough and unfinished form, it is clear that he intended the composition to develop along the following lines: an ecclesiastical history of Bates' native Connecticut arguing the link between democracy in religion (Congregationalism) and disaffection in politics; a history of Anglicanism in Connecticut, related to the Loyalist phenomenon; Bates' own sufferings as a Loyalist; the Anglican Refugee congregation at Eaton's Neck, Long Island; the 1783 evacuation of the congregation on the *Union* to what became Kingston; a history of the Anglican parish of Kingston; a narrative of the rise of religious dissent in Kings, Queens and Sunbury Counties and

355

the relative failure of the Anglican way. The theme of Bates' composition was the close relationship between Anglicanism and loyalty, and conversely, between a spirit of innovation in religious matters and novel and dangerous notions in politics. One of the last survivors of the initial Loyalist generation, Bates was issuing perhaps the final expression of the elite vision with which the Loyalist experiment in New Brunswick had begun. Oppressed by the spectre of rebellion in the Canadas and the possibility of conflict over the Maine boundary, and astonished by the fading fortunes of Anglicanism and the indifference of the younger generation towards the "Church," Bates framed a jeremaid against loss of the Loyalist vision.

Bates himself succeeded in publishing only the "Prospectus" for the work, but 50 years later W.O. Raymond printed much of it in *Kingston and the Loyalists of the "Spring Fleet" of 1783* (Saint John, 1889). In this, his first publication, Archdeacon Raymond carefully excised from the narrative Bates' pervasive theme of Anglican failure and all of his remarks on the rise of religious dissent. The result was a publication that has been the source of much misunderstanding. Just as the governing elite so lovingly depicted in Raymond's edition of *Winslow Papers* (1901) is wholly untypical of New Brunswick Loyalists in general, so the zealous churchmanship of Bates and his fellow Anglican exiles from Eaton's Neck to Kingston was absolutely unique. *Winslow Papers* is the key work responsible for the prevailing version of New Brunswick Loyalist mythology. Similarly, *Kingston and the Loyalists* is at the heart of the old myth that most Loyalists were ardent Anglicans. Raymond himself knew better, but by telling only part of the story he misled generations of less discerning students of New Brunswick history. Raymond seems to have referred to Bates' material on religious dissent only once, in a footnote to *Winslow Papers,* p. 392. Leonard Allison paraphrased a small portion in *Rev. Oliver Arnold, First Rector of Sussex* (1892), p. 11, and Allison's sub-transcription (A215, NBM) of Raymond's transcription was misused by Grace Aiton in *Story of Sussex and Vicinity* (1967), p. 84. W.S. MacNutt referred to Raymond's transcription briefly in *New Brunswick: A History, 1784-1867* (1963), pp. 168, 171.

356

Bates wrote the material on religious dissent printed below from 30 to 60 years after the events described. This and the fact that it was not his purpose to provide a history of dissent but merely an extended aside to his principal theme account for the numerous apparent errors. I would hesitate to attribute his mistakes to deliberate falsfication, but it is fair to say that his primary concern was not mere factual correctness. Where practical I have attempted in the text to draw attention to some of his lapses. In general his errors are as follows: Dr. Collens was at Sheffield in about 1784 (not prior to Henry Alline); Lunt and Hammond were gaoled before their trial and acquittal (not as a result of conviction); John James and Charles Milton arrived in New Brunswick and the Congregational meeting-house was removed to Sheffield in the late 1780s (not following the Lunt-Hammond affair); the Hale reformation on the Belleisle took place in the winter of 1809-10; Polly Davis' conversion occurred on 30 October 1809; there is no hard evidence that Henry Hale "fled" to the United States (but see *Mass Bapt Miss Mag*, March 1811, p. 35); Gilbert Harris' preaching at Sussex occurred about 1801 (Bates implies a decade later). In preparing these extracts for publication I have attempted to be faithful to Bates' spelling while sometimes necessarily standardizing punctuation. A few of the addenda in brackets are my own attempts to clarify the text, but most of the bracketed material represents passages that cannot now be read in the original but which are preserved in Raymond's transcription.

[Text]

[A]s my object has been the true history of the Church in this country, I have been induced to state the proceedings of the opposite parties — but verry Briefly. [Regar]ding their Inquiery — Why are not the numbers of the Church through all the Province Equal in number with the increse of population — as when the Church in Kingston was [fi]rst dedicated by the rev'd James Scovil [in] 1789 — Which seems to require my personal Experience — for more than half the Cent'ry past... .

[Thirty [*sic*] years ago there was not a single dissenting congregation in this whole County where there now is, as I have obtained, not less than eleven ministers of different denominations each having from two to four congregations. Espetialy those under the name of Anabaptists and New Lights who have crept in from the United States with such avertion to Kings and Bishops as might harm more than Episcopecy might remedy in an age.]

And here dear Brethren, that are yet alive, who with me first landed in the wilderness, let me call your attention to the mysterious and miraculous maner by which the Divine light and truth of the Apostolic Succession of Christ in His Church and Gospel, preserved through two hundred years persecution in the Wilderness of New England, in token and pleadge of future protection for His Church and Nation, which blessed token and protection we are happy to find rekindled in this wilderness of New Brunswick, and finally in this Church deposited at Kingston, with succession of priesthood in one same family [the Scovils] ordained untill the third generation. Wherefore I think the Church at Kingston at this time presents one singular and interesting Spectacle well worthy of the attention of all Churchmen; planted in the wilderness of a country and at a time when the people were hostile to her, and for many years the country allmost anihilated with Fannattic preachers into schisms and sects... .

My Kingston Friends I address this my History of the Church to you, because I wish the sentiments it contains to be more generally known, than in the ordinary way. When I consider that for the greater part of the last century past, since the the establishment of this Congregation ... who in 1783 at the close of the Rebellion removed from the Church on Eaton Neck ... Long Island, on board the good ship Union, and landed in the wilderness and established this Church in Kingston — this neighbourhood like every other has been subject to changes of familyes, yet verry few families who have worshiped with me have ever removed away. When I look over the Parish register, I find that during this period about [350] persons are or have been communicants in this church, and but one of that number I ever knew to revolt to any other Denomination, who by the by, was not one from on board the ship Union of the Church on Eton Neck... .

358

Not one of those preachers of new light have ever been permit[t]ed to preach within the limmits of the first Churchmen who came from Eatons Neck on board the ship Union and landed in the wilderness at Kingston in 1783. [Whatever this means, it certainly would not be true that no Dissenter had ever preached within the parish of Kingston.]

While Methodist, Baptists and all other denominations increase rapidly ... in abundance of wealth and riches, build expensive large meeting houses [and] support numerous traviling missionarys from their large funds raised in this country ... the Church of England if not otherways paid their missionaries [*ie,* by the SPG] in this country would soon be overrun... .

I have Observed, that in 1783 — there was no Church [of England] nor Church Minister in this Country the people mostly living in the townships of Maugerville, Sheffield and Waterbury. When first in Maugerville [in] 1783, I was informed of a preacher by the name of Collens — who had been some time with them — that on some jealousy among them, he soon after left them, but one other named [Henry] Allen remained, whose followers, were called Allenites. In Sheffield, and Waterbury, also the people were divided into three Sects, named after their own preachers, namely, Hartites, Brooksites and Hamonites. Each Sect principly preach[ed] their own Doctrine, But [were] annually Inspired, by two traveling preacher[s] from Nova Scotia — one of them [a Manning], on his fathers being hanged for murder, became Converted to a new light preacher — And it is too well known from Experience, that the preacher who comenceth with despising all lawfull ordaination or licence for man to preach the Gospel, vilifying the Church [of England] Service and deprecating all wise and good Churchmen, will never find himself long without an Audience, who like himself, are Gratified with feasting their appetites with callumny on murdered Church reputation[s] — and to hear wise and Good Churchmen doomed only to Exist in this world, like virtue and religion, by the struggles it makes.[T]o this purpose persons at this time, under disguise of more zealous protesta[ntism] set up extemporare praying, with greater purity than in the Church of England, fomented we doubt not by Satan, the great Enemy of mankind who [with intent to mislead] left his own habitation in that form which cherubim [had from God and appeared unto] Adam in the garden of his Church in Eden... .

[T]here soon appear'd among them an abandonate profligate character [John Lunt], a sort of necromanser and fortune teller, who by his slight of hand, and profligate Insinuations, very soon Imposed himself upon the ignorence of the good people of Sheffield and Waterbery to believe that he was truly a prophit and Inspired from heaven to preach. That he could perform Miricles, and if their faith was pure he could procure [any] Blessing for them he might ask from heaven. Consequently his night meetings [became] exceeding popular, which led to many acts too Simple and numerous for me to [mention]. I shall therefore be verry brief with what I say of the good people of Sheffield or Waterbury. [M]en and women, espetially young women, who became so infatuated by him as to believe, that what the Spirit dictated him to do, he might do, by himself, or by a cre[w] no matter who: whence once converted, it was no sin for lambs of God to play all together. [A]t one of his popular meetings held late of night, a young lady having more modesty, or not suffitiently converted as to comply with his spirit: one of his pure converts by the name of [Archelaus] Hammon attempted to assist him in his design. [O]n applycation to proper authorities, they were boath arrested, and brought to trial [in 1793] before Chief Justice Ludlow, in a Supreme Court at Gagetown, Queens County. [A]t this Court I was myself present the whole trial. Lunt was Indicted for an attempt to committ a Rape and Hamon for Accessory: who from Witnesses before an Impertial Jury, I heard them pronounced Guilty, and Sentenced by the Court to fine and twelve months impresenmen[t] in the common Gaol of the County. However for certain considerations, parts of Hamons imprisonment was respeted on Bail for Good. Lunt at the end of his punishment fled to the United States, leaving to Queens and Sunbury Counties their Hamonites, Hartites and Brooksites, with traveling preachers occationally.

When the two students [John] James and [Charles] Milton from the Colledge of Lady Huntington came out to Saint John, where Milton remained untill he fled to the State of Main[e] while James went on to Maugerville, where he

360

commenced [as an] extemporare prodestant preacher, without [respect to Bishop,] priest, deacon or form of Worship — which soon united the people [of Sheffield and Waterbury to remove] [in 1789] a large Meeting hous[e] began in Maugerville to a [Glebe lot in Sheffield and complete it] with Galleries and finish & furnish a [comfortable parsonage house with house keeper and] servants to attend him, with [every necessary provided for his comfort and Independence, with a crowded congregation] to attend all his preachings. Yet being Intimate with the [better class] of people belonging to the Church [of England], became acquainted with her Doctrines [which] caused a jealousy amongst his people and who employed their Deacons with power to Investigate his principles on the subject, with whom he decided that he was in favour with the Church, and did attend upon the Bishop at his Visitation in our Church at Kingston. But for certain causes he could not obtain ordination in this province. Consequently he soon fled to New York [in 1792 or 1793].

The Church at Springfiel[d] Kings County was well attended when a [popular] preacher from the United States by the name of [Henry] Hail came late in the month of November [1809] and took lodging [at the] house of Caleb Davis, near a small Church [Christ Church] built [by or in 1792] principly on the responsibility of Capt [Thomas] Spragg [Davis' father-in-law], a respectable old Churchman, and Capt [William] Grey from the part of [New] York where there never was any Churchmen. [B]eing a loyalist [he] fled to the Citty, where on a bed of sickness he was thought past recovery. In a vision of the Night with his Eyes open, he saw angels looking upon him and said [you] shall not now die but live untill he shall die spiritually. Which [the Church] the inhabitance of Springfield with some assistance from Kingston completely finished, where the Rev'd James Scovil performed public Worship every first Sunday in the month, where Capt Grey learned that to become a member of Christ['s] Church it was necessary to be Baptized, and was Baptised. When this Inspired preacher [Hale] proclaimed that he had come by a spetial commission of new light from heaven to reveal the true spirit of religion of God, in opposition to that carnal Church of England, in em[n]ity with God. And first, in order to convince

the old Churchman of his Divine Commission he called upon
him in his family, and seeing a Bible and prayer Book lying
upon his table, took the prayer Book and said, whoever put
their faith in what was contained in that Book would surely be
lost — which not haveing his desired effect upon the old man
and his family, he returned to the family of Caleb Davis, where
by his exhorting, praying, sighing and groaning [he] converted
his Eldest Daughter [Polly] which had his desired effect for
calling her young friends together by night, to hear her relate
the blessed effects of her Convertion, where he [Hale] soon
found himself the devoted leader of a large party of followers.
[B]y preaching, exhorting and using his frightfull expressions
and gestures by night to move their stony hearts. In which he
succeede[d] in bringing many of his converts to confess to him
[their crimes, and] some that made restitution. So vehement
was [his threatenings of the terrors of eternal] Death, and
severe Execution upon the sinner, [repesenting God so terrible
in his] Majesty and Justice, that all [hope of the favor of God
was lost, which distracted their] mind. Those fears Encreased
[by the suggestions of Satan, the thoughts of death and]
judgment sting them by fits and the flashes of contience
startled [them like moments of] lightening; then again relaps
into their former Stupidity of unbelief and by renouncing their
faith in the Church, juditiously give themselves to Satan never
to return. Amoung them Captain Grey was represented as an
oracal, that the same hour of the night in which the angels
foretold he should die spiritually, he had passed from Death
into a state of Grace by Convertion: and by his renouncing his
faith in the Church [actually Gray had become a Baptist by
1803, six years earlier] had a wonderfull effect upon the people
of Springfield.

   Driving in [parties upon] the ice by night along the
Shores of Bellile Bay, even into the main river, singing hymns
and spiritual songs, collecting Multitudes and Exorting every
house that opened their doors to them; [when a wealthy farmer
[Hezekiah Scribner] opened his doors which being convenient,
no one preacher passed; consequently frequent night meetings
collected. On notice of two preachers one a Methodist and the
other a noted New Light, the good Inhabitants assembled in a
Crowd. The New Light preacher resumed his gestures and

expressions, representing God so terrible in Majesty executing vengeance upon the unconverted Sinner that all hope of the favor of God was lost. Those fears began to distract the minds of his audience when one being a little more hardened on whom the preacher fixed his attention distinctly [remarking] Everyone that did not accept of his call this night he would appear in the day of Judgment a witness against him: to which he boldly replied, "Then you shall be certioraried to a higher power" [a legal witticism]. Soon after the wealthy Farmer was met going to Springfield Mill: who [presumably the legal wit] said, "I see you have become so religious you cannot go to Mill without a preacher, and you will never want for preachers as long as your old Ham lasts to feed them; and you may shake in your shoes yet or I am mistaken". From thence to Springfield, where as converts from Queens County they attended upon the noted preacher Hale in his numerous assembly of his own converts] which so raised his pride and vanity as to believe [all] the people were converted into the Spirit of his work of the Lord, and that no human power would be permitted to oppose them. With this faith he taught his converts that all the institutions in this country were carnal and of the Divil and that as children of God it was their duty to destroy. Upon which the attorney General [Thomas Wetmore] wrote the Sheriff [Bates] to obtain witness of the fact. When on enquiry being made, his followers publicly determined that they would defend [him] with their last drop of their Blood: but taking prudence with his Wisdom fled to the United States, leaving many of his converts to preach his doctrine to no further purpose than by the segeston of Satan Keeping them from returning to the Church.

[A]t this time a popular precher in the State of Main[e], fancying another mans wife, came off with her to this county, and finding preaching no[t] as profitable as other means perhaps not more criminal ... [he forged] the like of an order, on which he received money. Being convicted [he] was sentenced the fine of fifty pounds, and six months imprisonment in my custody in the preson of Kingston.

A certain person who had been accused of the like act being converted became a travelling preacher, who after a tower of three months in winter, returning to his family stopt at

Kingston for some refreshment, just at the time the prisoner was to be released. [S]eeing the Gaoler [the traveller] said unto [him] with a deep sigh, Ah poor creature what does he think to do with himself. I think, said the Gaoler, by what I hav[e] heard him say, he thinks of preaching again for his living.

The next traveling preacher that came unto my custody was James Ennice [Innis], who had been marvelously converted [from long habits of] intemperence [torn] his own throat which led him to exort others [with success until in the spirit of his pride] he believed that he was divinely inspired [to preach and and to baptise and from thence commenced] [a] new light preacher, [which he laboured in with success. At a large meeting a] respectable old Scotchman [hard of hearing] attentively sat near the preach[er] who proclaimed the Lord had [ordained that a] number present should be Baptised by him this day and that [that] old Gentleman should be one of them putting his hand upon his head. Well, well, you or the Lord must be mistaken [was the reply].

[H]owever there was a young couple of his own Converts who wished to be Married by none but spiritual ministers. Being his duty to marry in opposition to law which was carnal; consequently [in 1810] a warrant was sent to the sheriff of Kings in order to bring him to justice, upon which he was arrested and brought to prison, where bail was required: He refused to give any but God. Consequently [he] was put in prison with a debtor [ie, in the more comfortable part of Kingston Gaol], who after a long prayer sent for a bottle of Spirits, which inspired them to sing and pray all nigh[t] untill morning, when he consented to give [human] security to appear in court at Saint John. He was bailed there to take his trial [where] he was convicted and sentenced to thirty pounds [£50] fine and six months [one year] Imprisonment. The fine was paid by his friends, and his Conduct while in prison was truly so disgracefull and ridiculous that for the Credit of his family, being an old man, part of his imprisonment was respited, which put the final end to his preaching.

Next [about 1801] came a notorious preacher into the Parish of Sussex by the name of [Gilbert] Harris, who told the people, he had come to them by an irresistable call from heaven to offer Salvation in Sussex this night, which if he had not obeyed the call, the stones in the street would have rose up against him, for now was their accepted time, now only was their day of salvation offered in Sussex. To which many gave great heed and were Converted, espetially one respectable member of the Church and his son [Ozias & Thomas Ansley], who had been disappointed [by Bishop Inglis' refusal to ordain the younger Ansley], became enlightened to preach the same spirit to much greater perfection, in so much that many followed them in preference, dividing his congregation, untill he repented he had ever offered salvation in Sussex, and removed from thence to Norton, on a farm of M'r Baxter, where he commenced preaching with success, and continued untill a young couple of his own converts desired to be married by none but [a] spiritual minister, and for the Lord's sake only he marryed them [in 1811], in oposition to the law of man. Being informed of the fate of Ennice [Innis] in the like case, [he] became suspitious and finding it would be difficult to escape the Sheriff, in his wisdom fled to the States, which put an end to his preaching in this country.

[T]here are many others about the country who keep up the same spirit. As none ever entered the limits of our church in Kingston [I] think them not worthy my notice, and as it has been a subject too painfull for me to dwell upon; must beg leave to conclude with the words of [Simon?] Baxter [with two travelling] preachers that visited him in his sickness: [not so much on account of his authority] as the solid sense contained in them.

> [I am plagued, said he, with my friends & my] neighbours to boot,
> To know [which religion will my conscience best suit.]
> [As for all your professions] I speak as I think,
> [I wish mankind better, I take the good drink.]
> [There is the old] Church of Scotland, that I like very well:
> And I believe thee, good Quaker, [will ne'er] go to Hell.
> Yet the good Church of old England, is the church which I love;
> They trust in their Saviour, who now dwells above.
> Their Bibles and prayer Books they boath treat of Him,

They fear God, love mankind, and honor their King.
But all those night meetings, I do greately dis[ap]prove,
Night is the time to discharge fleshly love.
Night is a time in which adulter[er]s hunt,
I fear you will all prove like Hammon and Lunt.
For such vain lambs would greatly David Shock,
To see them sitting with the Dogs of his Flock.

SELECT BIBLIOGRAPHY

HENRY ALLINE

Armstrong, Maurice. *Great Awakening in Nova Scotia, 1776-1809*. Hartford, 1948.

_____ "Neutrality and Religion in Revolutionary Nova Scotia" (1946), in G.A. Rawlyk (ed), *Historical Essays on the Atlantic Provinces* (Toronto, 1967), pp. 33-43.

Bell, David G. "The death of Henry Alline: Some Contemporary Reactions," in (1984) 4 *Nova Scotia Historical Review* (#2), pp. 7-12.

Beverley, James and B.M. Moody, eds. *Life and Journal of the Rev. Mr. Henry Alline*. (1806) Hantsport, 1982.

Britton, W. David H. Henry Alline: Sounding the Awakening in Nova Scotia. BA thesis: Mount Allison, 1982.

Bumsted, John M. *Henry Alline, 1748-1784*. Toronto, 1971.

Burnett, Frederick C. "Henry Alline's 'Articles & Covenant of a Gospel Church'," in (1984) 4 *Nova Scotia Historical Review* (#2), pp. 13-24.

Filschie, Margaret A. "Redeeming Love Shall Be our Song": Hymns of the First Great Awakening in Nova Scotia. MA thesis: Queen's University, 1983.

Rawlyk, George A. *Ravished by the Spirit: Religious Revivals, Baptists and Henry Alline*. Montreal, 1984.

367

Scott, Henry E., ed. *Journal of the Reverend Jonathan Scott.* Boston, 1980.

Scott, Jamie S. " 'Travels of my Soul': Henry Alline's Autobiography," in (1983) 18 *Journal of Canadian Studies* pp. 70-90.

Stewart, Gordon T., ed. *Documents Relating to the Great Awakening in Nova Scotia, 1760-1791.* Toronto, 1982.

——————— & G.A. Rawlyk. *People Highly Favoured of God: The Nova Scotia Yankees and the American Revolution.* Toronto, 1972.

Vincent, Thomas B. "Alline and Bailey," in (1976) 69 *Canadian Literature* pp. 124-33.

POST-ALLINE GENERATION

Ahlin, John H., ed. *The Saint's Daily Assistant: James Lyon, his Life and Meditations.* Machias, 1983.

Bumsted, John M., ed. "Autobiography of Joseph Crandall," in (1973) 3 *Acadiensis* (#1), pp. 79-96.

Cuthbertson, Brian C. "Rev. John Payzant: Henry Alline's Successor," in (1980) 40 *Coll NS His Soc* pp. 57-80.

——————— ed. *Journal of the Reverend John Payzant (1749-1834).* Hantsport, 1981.

Knowlan, James. *Review of Edmund J. Reis's Short Account of Michael M'Comb, &c. and also, A Short Refutation of Some of the Errors of the Baptists.* Saint John, 1814.

Levy, George E., ed. *Diary and Related Writings of the Reverend Joseph Dimock (1768-1846).* Hantsport, 1979.

Rawlyk, George A. "From Newlight to Baptist: Harris Harding and the Second Great Awakening in Nova Scotia," in Barry Moody (ed), *Repent and Believe: The Baptist Experience in Maritime Canada.* Hantsport, 1980.

_____ ed. *New Light Letters and Spiritual Songs, 1778-1793*. Hantsport, 1983.

_____ "New Lights, Baptists and Religious Awakenings in Nova Scotia, 1776-1843: A Preliminary Probe," in (1983) 25 *Journal of the Canadian Church Historical Society* pp. 43-73.

Reis, Edmund J. *Short Account of the Life, Conversion and Death of Michael M'Comb* (1814) 2nd edn. Newburyport, 1815.

BROADER PERSPECTIVE

Bastarache, Michel. "Acadian Language and Cultural Rights," in Jean Daigle (ed), *Acadians of the Maritimes: Thematic Studies.* Moncton, 1982 pp. 347-61.

Bell, David G. *Early Loyalist Saint John: The Origin of New Brunswick Politics, 1783-1786.* Fredericton, 1983.

Brebner, John B. *Neutral Yankees of Nova Scotia: A Marginal Colony during the Revolutionary Years.* (1937) Toronto, 1969.

Buggey, Susan. Churchmen and Dissenters: Religious Toleration in Nova Scotia, 1758-1835. MA thesis: Dalhousie University, 1981.

Bumsted, John M. "Church and State in Maritime Canada, 1749-1807," in *CHA Report.* Toronto: 1967 pp. 41-58.

Condon, Ann G. *Envy of the American States: The Loyalist Dream for New Brunswick.* Fredericton, 1984.

Fingard, Judith. *Anglican Design in Loyalist Nova Scotia, 1783-1816.* London, 1972.

French, Goldwin S. "Papers of Daniel Fidler, Methodist Missionary in Nova Scotia and New Brunswick, 1792-1798," in (1959) 12 *Bulletin: Records and Proceedings of the Committee on Archives of the United Church of Canada* pp. 3-18; (1960) vol. 13, pp. 28-46.

Harrison, John F.C.   *The Second Coming: Popular Millenarianism, 1780-1850.* London, 1979.

Humbert, Stephen. *Rise and Progress of Methodism, in the Province of New Brunswick, From its Commencement until about the Year 1805.* Saint John, 1836.

Ivison, Stuart & Fred Rosser. *Baptists in Upper and Lower Canada before 1820.* Toronto, 1956.

[McColl, Duncan]. "Memoir of the Rev. Duncan M'Coll," in *BNA Wesleyan Methodist Magazine* (March 1841) pp. 251-58, *et seq.*

MacNutt, W. Stewart. *New Brunswick: A History, 1784-1867.* Toronto, 1963.

Marini, Stephen A. *Radical Sects of Revolutionary New England.* Cambridge MA, 1983.

Moir, John S., ed. *Church and State in Canada, 1627-1867: Basic Documents.* Toronto, 1967.

Murphy, Terrence. "Emergence of Maritime [*sic:* Nova Scotian] Catholicism, 1781-1830," in (1984) 13 *Acadiensis* (ƒ2) pp. 29-49.

Rawlyk, George A. *Nova Scotia's Massachusetts: A Study of Massachusetts-Nova Scotia Relations, 1630 to 1784.* Montreal, 1973.

Raymond, William O., ed. *Winslow Papers.* Saint John, 1901.

Richey, Matthew. *Memoir of the Late Rev. William Black, Wesleyan Minister.* Halifax, 1839.

Smith, Thomas W. *History of the Methodist Church . . . of Eastern British America* vol. 1. Halifax, 1877.

Watts, Michael. *The Dissenters: From the Reformation to the French Revolution.* Oxford, 1978.

BAPTIST DENOMINATIONAL HISTORIOGRAPHY

[Acadia University]. *Catalogue of the Maritime Baptist Historical Collection in the Library of Acadia University.* Kentville, 1955.

Bell, David G. "All Things New: The Transformation of Maritime Baptist Historiography," in (1984) 4 *Nova Scotia Historical Review* (#2), pp. 69-81.

Benedict, David. *General History of the Baptist Denomination in America* vol. 1. Boston, 1813.

Bill, Ingraham E. *Fifty Years with the Baptist Ministers and Churches of the Maritime Provinces.* Saint John, 1880.

Dunbar, Duncan. *Concise View of the Origin and Principles of the Several Religious Denominations Existing at Present in the Province of New Brunswick.* Eastport, 1819.

Greenleaf, Jonathan. *Sketches of the Ecclesiastical History of the State of Maine.* Portsmouth, 1821.

Levy, George E. *Baptists of the Maritime Provinces, 1753-1946.* Saint John, 1946.

Millet, Joshua. *History of the Baptists in Maine.* Portland, 1845.

Saunders, Edward M. *History of the Baptists of the Maritime Provinces.* Halifax, 1902.

Tupper, Charles. "History of the Baptist Churches in Nova-Scotia" (1828), in (1829) I *Bapt Miss Mag* pp. 287, *et seq.*

LOCAL HISTORIES

Aiton, Grace L. *Story of Sussex and Vicinity.* Sussex, 1967.

Drisco, George W. *Narrative of the Town of Machias.* Machias, 1904.

Graham, Ernest G.C. *History of the Anglican Church in the Parish of Springfield.* Springfield, 1983.

——————— *Mills, Hills and Early Settlers of Springfield Parish, Kings Co., N.B.* Belleisle Creek, 1983.

Hannay, James, ed. "Documents of the Congregational Church at Maugerville," in (1894) 1 *Coll NB His Soc* pp. 119-52.

Kilby, William H. *Eastport and Passamaquoddy.* Eastport, 1888.

Maxwell, Lilian M.B. *Outline of the History of Central New Brunswick to the Time of Confederation.* Fredericton, 1937.

Raymond, William O. *Progress of the Church of England in the Seven Rural Deaneries.* Saint John, 1897.

Wright, Esther C. *Loyalists of New Brunswick.* Moncton, 1955.

——————— *The Petitcodiac.* Sackville, 1945.

——————— *Planters and Pioneers.* Hantsport, 1978.

Trueman, Howard. *Chignecto Isthmus and its First Settlers.* Toronto, 1902.

ADDENDA

To p. 14 Jacob Bailey's allusion is to Geoffrey Wildgoose, a character in Richard Graves' anti-Methodist satire *Spiritual Quixote* (1772). Concerning John Cooper, see also T.B. Vincent, *Narrative Verse Satire in Maritime Canada, 1779-1814* (1978), p. 34.

To p. 63 On the interesting question why the Church of England was not "established" in New Brunswick under the *Act for Preserving the Church of England*, it is relevant to note that Edward Winslow apparently *assumed* that the Church was established: [Winslow], *Substance of the Debates, in the Young Robin Hood Society*/ Saint John, 1795/, p. 5.

To p. 82 Sheriff Bates' allegation that John Lunt fled to the United States in the wake of the rape trials is confirmed by the genealogical data in M.F. Barto, *Passamaquoddy: Genealogies of West Isles Families* (1975) supp. p. 90. Barto gives Lunt's wife as Hannah Garrison; hence the Sarah Garrison of the first rape charge was his sister-in-law. Hannah (Garrison) Lunt was aunt of the American anti-slavery controversialist William Lloyd Garrison. Further information on the varied religious travel of this remarkable connection will be found in M.H. Blom & T.E. Blom, *Canada Home: Juliana Horatia Ewing's Fredericton Letters, 1867-1869* (1983), p. 138.

To pp. 90, 151 On Edward Manning's early labours in St Andrews and St George, see the not very reliable recollection printed in David Benedict, *General History of the Baptist Denomination* (1848 edn), p. 534.

To p. 150 In support of Sheriff Bates' charge that Gilbert Harris fled to the United States to avoid the consequences of illegal solemnization of marriage, see *ibid*, p. 535.

To p. 177 In addition to the early Congregational ministers visiting Charlotte County that are noted in the text, Jonathan Fisher, Abijah Wines and, perhaps, Jothan Sewell, visited in 1801: M.E. Chase, *Jonathan Fisher: Maine Parson, 1768-1847* (1948), pp. 177-78. Fisher's journal of his St Andrews campaign is evidently very particular. The ordained Presbyterian James MacGregor visited Charlotte in 1805: George Patterson, *Memoir of the Rev. James MacGregor* (1859).

To p. 209 James Innis was the first and probably the only preacher successfully prosecuted under the *Marriage Act*, and Innis and Gilbert Harris are the only preachers known to have solemnized marriages in entire disregard of it. Yet two other proceedings for violation of the Act are known. They involved Presbyterian ministers, who claimed that they fell within the ambiguous "Kirk of Scotland" exception to the Act. Because these ministers claimed to have conformed to rather than violated the *Marriage Act* their actions were not a protest against it in the sense that those of the Baptists Innis and Harris obviously were.

In 1820 Attorney-General Thomas Wetmore laid an information in the Supreme Court against "James Wilson, late of the Parish of Saint Andrews . . . Gentleman", alleging that he had on 2 December 1819 unlawfully solemnized the marriage of Michael Dyer and Jesse Sutherland: MC288, ms2C, pp. 226-27, PANB. Jerome Alley, the obnoxious rector of St Andrews who prompted Wetmore's action, alleged that "M'r Wilson only attends here once in each fortnight", suggesting that Wilson acted in some religious capacity. In fact there is little doubt that Wilson was a Presbyterian minister from northern Ireland. He was moderator of the Presbytery of

New Brunswick when it was organized at Chatham in 1820. His 1820 prosecution was dropped when he met with the attorney-general and explained that "Kirk of Scotland" was a term broad enough to include all Presbyterian ministers, whether within the Church of Scotland or (like Wilson) without it. Wilson was then told that "I might go and do my duty": *St Andrews Herald*, 15 August 1820. See also D.R. Jack, *History of Saint Andrews Church*, Saint John (1913), pp. 32, 66.

In 1825 Alexander MacLean, Presbyterian minister at St Andrews, solemnized marriage between two Baptists, Edward Sealey and Jane McFarlane, both of St Patrick parish. The rector of St Andrews again complained to Attorney-General Wetmore and on 24 June 1826 Wetmore at length warned MacLean not to repeat the offence. MacLean denied that the ceremony had violated the *Marriage Act* and dared the attorney-general to proceed against him. Nothing more was done: M.N. Cockburn, *History of Greenock Church* (1906), pp. 17-20.

To p. 298 On New Brunswick marriage customs without benefit of either clergyman or magistrate, see Williamson to Williamson, June 1791: CB, NBM ("if they get a prayerbook they read the form and join hands and so the job is finished"); and Howard Temperley (ed), *Gubbins' New Brunswick Journals* (1980), p. 23 ("the mutual consent of the parties is often the only contract").

NOMINAL INDEX

Fay, Martin 246
Fenwick, Matthew 181, 188-89, 204, 245, 264, 293
Ferris, George 297
Fidler, Daniel 71, 85, 142, 163, 261
Finch, Titus 262, 296-97
Fisher, Jonathan 375
FitzRandolph, Robert 153
Fletcher, Mary 43
Forshay, Peter 143
Foster, 246
Foster, Ezekiel 264, 320, 323
Foster, Moses 300
Fountain, 243
Fowler, Aaron Sr. 330
Fowler, Aaron Jr. 330
Fowler, Aamon 329
Fowns, William 285
Fox, George 82, 297
Francis, John 274
Freeman, Elisha 42
Freeman, Philip 293
Freeman, Samuel 31, 293
Freeze, William 149, 188, 246, 293, 320
French, James 153
Frost, Jeremiah 297

GALLISHAM, Lydia 58
Gallishan, Stephen 308
Gallop, Nathaniel 300, 307
Gallop, Nathaniel Jr 307
Ganong, Thomas 330
Gardiner, Henry 153
Gardner, Robert 154
Garrettson, Freeborn 9, 10, 13, 41
Garrison, Abijah 82, 143
Garrison, Elizabeth 39, 143

Garrison, Hannah 373
Garrison, Joseph Sr. 80
Garrison, Joseph Jr. 82, 143
Garrison, Nathan 143
Garrison, Sarah 81, 82, 142-43, 373
Gates, Amos 99, 112, 164
Gates, Ezra 300, 308
Gates, Margaret (Larlee) 164
Geddes, T.O. 42
Gellison, Lydia 58
George, David 72, 84, 139-40, 278
Gerow, 123, 125
Gerow, James 167, 322
Gerrish, Enoch 300, 308
Gesner, Abraham 16, 45
Gilbert, Isaac 297
Gillies, Jesse 325, 329
Glasier, 117
Glasier, Beamsley 165
Glasier, Benjamin 165
Glasier, Rebecca 165
Glasier, Stephen 165
Glenie, James 291, 298
Goddard, Giles 323
Godfrey, Elisha 286
Godfrey, John 222, 286
Godfrey, Phebe (Payzant) 286
Godfrey, William 286
Godler, Mary 193
Good, David 307
Goodin, Daniel 342
Goodspeed, Thomas 297, 308
Goold, Arthur 59, 133
Graham, Ernest 267
Grandin, William 278
Grant, William O. 272
Graves, William 323
Gray, Abraham 325, 330

Gray, Charles 330
Gray, James 322
Gray, Justus 330
Gray William 325, 330, 361-62
Greeno, 246
Greer, Mary 283
Griffin, Thomas 200, 273
Gunter, Charles 120, 166
Gustin, John 262
Guthrie, Bridget 193

HAGERMAN, 142
Hale, Henry 26, 27, 49, 178-79, 181, 194-98, 203-04, 206, 209, 260-61, 270, 278, 288-89, 315, 357, 361-63
Hall, Mr & Mrs 97, 98
Hall, Abner 44
Hall, Mercy (Babcock) 182-86, 188, 336-41, 344-54
Hamilton, Elizabeth 283
Hammond, 109
Hammond, Archelaus Sr. 5, 16, 17, 72, 78, 80-82, 140, 143-44, 162, 302, 357, 360, 366
Hammond, Archelaus Jr. 82, 162
Hammond, Bathsheba (Joslin) 164
Hammond, Elizabeth 82
Hammond, Jerusha 82
Hammond, Lathrop 75, 82, 114, 143, 162, 164, 167, 187, 192, 196, 265
Hammond, Sarah 82
Hammond, Simon 162
Hanford, Thomas 329
Hanington, William Sr. 332-34, 336-37, 339-42, 344, 347-54

Hanington, William Jr. 257, 347
Hannay, James 131
Harding, George 104-05, 127-28, 162, 325
Harding, Harris 10, 12-14, 17, 18, 20-22, 25, 26, 30, 45, 47, 49, 50, 66, 93
Harding, Theodore 10, 24, 32, 50, 67, 87, 88, 94, 122-24, 144, 149, 180, 185, 192, 196-97, 203, 212-13, 231-34, 254, 268-69, 274, 286-87
Harding, William 162, 311, 314, 325
Hardy, Elias 309-10
Harrington, Andrew 297
Harrington, Lydia 282
Harris, David 150, 156-57
Harris, Gilbert 12, 69, 84, 88, 148-50, 184, 193-96, 203-04, 281-82, 288, 320, 357, 364-65, 374
Harris, Thaddeus 39
Harrison, William 153
Hartley, Abigail (Estey) 142, 163
Hartley, George 111, 142, 163
Hartt, 120
Hartt, George W. 167
Hartt, Henry A. 167
Hartt, John 308
Hartt, Jonathan 58
Hartt, Samuel Sr. 79, 86, 144, 166, 296
Hartt, Samuel Jr. 167
Hartt, Thomas 296-97
Harvey, James 225-26, 286
Hatheway, Ebenezer 119, 166, 307

Manning, Edward xii, 12, 13, 15-18, 20-26, 28, 30-33, 35, 44, 48, 50, 67, 72, 79, 80, 85-93, 95, 98, 142, 147-48, 150-52, 155, 157, 177, 180, 185-86, 190, 196-97, 205-06, 211-13, 235-36, 254, 260, 272, 275-76, 278, 280, 286, 345, 359, 374

Manning, Frances (Farnsworth) 91, 94, 95, 97, 98, 106, 112, 157

Manning, James xii, 12, 13, 17, 18, 20-23, 31, 32, 35, 36, 48, 72, 79, 80, 88-99, 150, 152, 155-157, 160, 177, 186-87, 189, 192, 194, 197, 212, 254, 359

Manning, James Edward 94, 97, 98

Manning, Nancy 89

Manning, Peter 89, 359

Manzer, John 87, 110, 163

Marsden, Joshua 134, 173-74, 182

Marsh, John 120, 166, 297, 308, 322

Marsters, Nathaniel 29

Martin, John 136

Martin, Peter 12, 46, 212, 234-35, 288

Masters, J. 286

Maybee, Jeremiah Sr. 330

Maybee, Jeremiah Jr. 330

Maybee, Oliver 262

Maybee, William 279, 330

Mead, 261

Medcalf, 274

Medley, John 136

Merrak, Elijah 269

Merrill, Daniel 181, 269-70

Merrill, Joseph 262

Merritt, 124

Miller, 255

Miller, George 297

Miller, Henry 297

Millikin, Charlotte 253

Millikin, Dominicus 253

Millikin, Nancy 253

Mills, Reuben 334

Milton, Charles 357, 360

Mitchell, John 177, 183, 248-49, 257

Mitchell, Lewis 142-43

Montgomery, Alexander 142

Montrose, Levi 262

Moore, Robert 279

Moore, Samuel 112

Moore, William 279

Moores, Samuel 164

Moran, Elizabeth (Hamilton) 219, 283

Moran, James 220, 283

Moran, Mary (Greer) 283-84

Moran, Mattias 283-84

Morris, David 308

Morris, Edward 139

Morrison, George 258

Morse, Alpheus 244, 292

Morse, Theodora (Crane)244, 292

Mosher, 286

Mosher, Elizabeth 220, 223, 283-84

Mosher, Philip 192, 220, 223, 284

Munro, Evan 118, 165

Munro, George 300, 307

Murphy, James 90-92, 97, 98, 103, 152, 154-56, 161, 177, 180, 189

388

GENERAL INDEX

393

394